WICKED CITY

NICHOLAS HEWITT

Wicked City

The Many Cultures of Marseille

HURST & COMPANY, LONDON

First published in the United Kingdom in 2019 by
C. Hurst & Co. (Publishers) Ltd.,
41 Great Russell Street, London, WC1B 3PL
© Nicholas Hewitt, 2019
Maps © Stephen Ramsay Cartography, 2019
All rights reserved.

A Cataloguing-in-Publication data record for this book
is available from the British Library.

ISBN: 9781787381995

This book is printed using paper from registered sustainable
and managed sources.

www.hurstpublishers.com

Printed in Great Britain by Bell and Bain Ltd, Glasgow

CONTENTS

Acknowledgements   vii
List of Illustrations   ix
Map 1: Marseille and the Mediterranean   xi
Map 2: Marseille and the Provence Region   xii
Map 3: Marseille   xiii

Introduction   1

PART ONE

1. *Le Comte de Monte-Cristo*: The Vieux-Port and the Hinterland   15
2. *Tartarin de Tarascon*: La Joliette, Algeria and the 'Mediterranean
   System'   37
3. *Ma Petite Tonkinoise*: The Exposition Coloniale and the Belle
   Epoque   65

PART TWO

4. *The Wicked City*: The Port in the Interwar Years   93
5. *Marius*: Marcel Pagnol and the 'Good City'   117
6. *Les Cahiers du Sud*: Marseille Modern   137
7. *Transit*: Occupation, Destruction and Liberation   161

PART THREE

8. *Le Docker Noir*: Immigration, Architecture and Housing   187
9. *Total Khéops*: Marseille Noir   213
Afterword   235

Notes   237
Index   259

ACKNOWLEDGEMENTS

This project has benefited from the collections of many museums, galleries and libraries, as well as from the helpful advice and suggestions of numerous friends and colleagues. I am grateful to the staff of the London Library, whose assistance has been of inestimable value, of the British Library, and to the library of the Musée d'Histoire and the Bibliothèque de l'Alcazar, whose staff were unfailingly helpful and courteous. The collections of the Musée de l'Immigration in Paris and the Musée des Beaux-Arts, the Musée d'Histoire, MuCEM, the Chambre de Commerce and the Musée Cantini in Marseille were also rich sources of visual and documentary material. I am also unfailingly grateful to those friends and colleagues who have helped me to formulate my ideas on Marseille over a long period, in particular Yves Doazan and Jean-Louis Fabiani, who selflessly gave up their time to help me organise a conference at the Vieux-Charité in Marseille in 2013 and who, along the way, shared their rich knowledge of the city with me; and Professor David Pomfret, of the University of Hong Kong, who made available to me his work in the Marseille Archives Municipales on the cultural life of the city during the Belle Epoque. I am also grateful to Emyr Tudwal Jones and Margaret-Anne Hutton, who more or less simultaneously introduced me to the work of Jean-Claude Izzo; to John Flower and Pascal Ory for their advice and comments on the progress of the book; to my colleagues on the Editorial Board of *French Cultural Studies*, who have shared their insights into Marseille, especially Sue Harris, Steven Ungar and Herman Lebovics; and to Tania Woloshyn, who co-edited a volume of essays on the Midi with me and introduced

ACKNOWLEDGEMENTS

me to aspects of Southern painting of which I was unaware. I am also deeply conscious of the debt I owe to Catherine Davies and Richard Fardon for their constant interest in this project and particularly for their efforts in helping secure a very happy publishing home at Hurst. In Marseille, my debt is also to François Thomazeau, the city's most gifted biographer and pioneer of the Marseille *polar*, who has shared his insights with me, and, especially, to Mary Fitzgerald, who has taken from the outset a caring interest in the progress of this book and has helped to steer it through the complexities of contemporary Marseille. Finally, I am grateful to Stephen Ramsay for the maps of Marseille, and to the production team at Hurst, in particular my editor, Lara Weisweiller-Wu. As always, the greatest debt goes to my wife, Helen Meller, for her constant concern and advice. It was with her that I explored Marseille in the late 1990s when she was researching her own book on European cities.

Nicholas Hewitt

LIST OF ILLUSTRATIONS

Fig. 1. Engraving by Franz Hogenberg of sixteenth century Marseille in *Atlas of Cities/Civitas Orbis Terrarum*, Vol II ed. Georg Braun (1575, Cologne). (Ullsteinbild/Topfoto).

Fig. 2. Alexandre Dumas, *The Count of Monte Cristo* (1844–5). (1996 Penguin Classics edition) (Front cover © Penguin Books Ltd).

Fig. 3. Zarafa the giraffe by Nicholas Hüet (1770–1828). (© The Morgan Library & Museum, NY. Purchased with Sunny Crawford Bülow Fund 1978).

Fig. 4. Le Palais Longchamps. (Photo courtesy of Musée d'Histoire de Marseille).

Fig. 5. Strike in Marseille 1901, watched by an Italian docker. Artist, Louis Sabattier for *L'Illustration*, 30 March 1901. (© David Nathan-Maister. SSPL/Getty Images).

Fig. 6. Marseille docks, early twentieth century. (Gallica: Bibliothèque Nationale de France, Département Estampes et Photographie).

Fig. 7. The Transporter Bridge. (Gallica: Bibliothèque Nationale de France, Département Estampes et Photographie).

Fig. 8. Vieux Port from Transporter Bridge. (Gallica: Bibliothèque Nationale de France, Département Estampes et Photographie).

Fig. 9. Poster: Marseille's First Exposition Coloniale 1906 [David Dellepiane]. (History Collection/Alamy).

Fig. 10. Poster: Marseille Exposition Coloniale 1922 [Leonetto Cappiello] (Gallica: Bibliothèque Nationale de France ENT DN-1).

Fig. 11. Marseille Exposition Coloniale 1922. West African Village. (Gallica: Bibliothèque Nationale de France, Département Estampes et Photographie).

LIST OF ILLUSTRATIONS

Fig. 12. Pavilion of Indo-China under construction for 1922 Exposition. (Gallica: Bibliothèque Nationale de France, Département Estampes et Photographie).

Fig. 13. *Viaduc à l'Estaque*, Georges Braque, 1908. (© ADAGP, Paris, licensed by DACS, London).

Fig. 14. *Le Vieux Port*, Paul Signac, 1905. (Metropolitan Museum of Art, NYC [public domain]).

Fig. 15. French journalist and writer, Albert Londres (1884–1932). (Roger-Viollet/Topfoto).

Fig. 16. Street scene in poor area: women washing at public tap 1938. Circa 1930. (Roger-Viollet/Topfoto).

Fig. 17. Street scene in poor area near the Vieux Port, 1930. (Roger-Viollet/Topfoto).

Fig. 18. La Canebière in the 1920s. (Gallica: Bibliothèque Nationale de France, Département Estampes et Photographie).

Fig. 19. Front cover of *Les Cahiers du Sud*, 1932. (Manuscripts and Special Collections, University of Nottingham).

Fig. 20. Jazz music venue in Marseille, advert in Les Cahiers du Sud,1931. (Manuscripts and Special Collections, University of Nottingham).

Fig. 21. Advertisement for Aéropostale. Les Cahiers du Sud,1933. (Manuscripts and Special Collections, University of Nottingham).

Fig. 22. Poster for *Topaze*, play by Marcel Pagnol. (Cci/Shutterstock).

Fig. 23. Poster for *Marius*, film of the play by Marcel Pagnol. (Alamy).

Fig. 24. The unemployed at the Vieux Port during the Great Depression. (IMAGNO/Topfoto).

Fig. 25. Jean-Claude Izzo (1945–2000) Marseillais poet, playwright and novelist of neo-noir crime novels, taken in Strasbourg, 1998. (Olivier Roller, photographer, www.olivierroller.com).

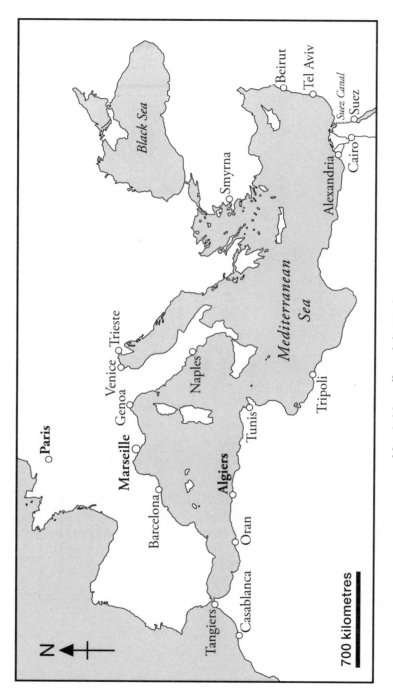

Map 1: Marseille and the Mediterranean

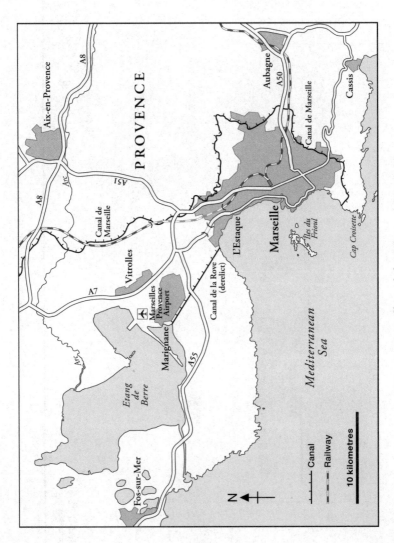

Map 2: Marseille and the Provence Region

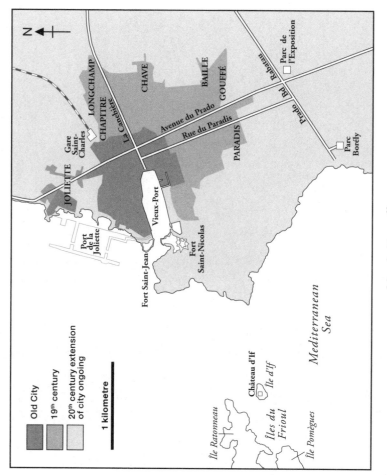

Map 3: Marseille

INTRODUCTION

Marseille Train

In 1939, the passengers on the eight o'clock train from Paris would have had their first glimpse of Marseille as they emerged from the Nerthe Tunnel north of L'Estaque at just after seven in the evening. After the eleven-hour journey from Paris, it would have seemed to many of the travellers that they had arrived in a country which was, to all intents and purposes, entirely foreign. Below them in the evening light was the magnificence of one of Europe's greatest ports, from which many of them were about to embark, and in the background, the hillside of Le Panier and the escarpment topped with the nineteenth-century basilica of Notre-Dame de la Garde. Out to sea, the roads were dotted both with moored ships awaiting entry to the port and the Iles Frioules, lying off the entrance to the Vieux-Port, including the Château d'If: it was, as the guidebooks agreed, one of the most spectacular deep-water ports of Europe, rivalling the panorama of the Bay of Naples. Around, but still mostly hidden by the intervening hillsides, was France's second city, with a population of over 900,000, and the undisputed gateway to its Empire: from North Africa, geographically as close as Paris, to Senegal and the African colonies and, through the Suez Canal (constructed by Marseille's adopted son Fernand de Lessops) to Annam, Tonkin and Cochin-China. Many of the passengers on the train would have been bound for the port, either going directly to their boats for embarkation or spending the night, as Richard Cobb suggests,[1] in one of the many hotels around the Gare Saint-Charles or along the city's major thor-

1

oughfare, the Canebière. Even as late as 1939, however, the city they encountered as they carried their baggage down the monumental 'Porte de l'Empire', would have been quite as mysterious as the exotic destinations to which they were heading.

Not only was Marseille the oldest city in France, founded by Phocean traders from Asia Minor in 600 BC—although the highly sophisticated Gaulish civilisation already there to greet them might have disputed this[2]—it had, over the intervening centuries, acquired an image as France's most cosmopolitan city through the assimilation of waves of migrants: rural French from the countryside to the north; immigrants, the Catalans and Spaniards; the Piedmontese and Neapolitans; refugees from the Southern and Eastern Mediterranean, including Jews from North Africa, Greeks, Corsicans; and, after the 1922 genocide, Armenians from Turkey;[3] followed by increasing numbers of migrants from North and West Africa—all with their own customs and cultures, but all relatively harmoniously integrated. In addition, Marseille, like all port cities, was a frontier town, with all the attendant lawlessness and disorientation. It lay at the extremity of a whole series of frontiers separating the Northern traveller from a familiar world, each crossed in turn as the Paris train progressed south: Lyon, at the southernmost extremity of northern and central France; Valence, where, according to the old proverb, 'le Midi commence', with the transition from grey slate to red tile roofing; and, most importantly, from the Northern *langue d'oïl* to the Southern *langue d'oc*, an older, distinct language with is own Occitan or Provençal civilisation and its distinctive, even outlandish, accent when applied to French; the arid, inhospitable landscape of Provence, culminating in the desert of the Crau which the train traversed just before entering the Nerthe Tunnel. This feat of engineering heralded arrival into Marseille, itself located, not on the reassuring domesticated coastline of the Côte d'Azur, but on a chain of industrial ports from Toulon and La Ciotat to Sète, and as alien as the North African Barbary Coast. Even though the first half of the journey, from Paris to Lyon, took place through a recognisably 'French' geography and civilisation, the long last stage, from Lyon to Marseille, took the Northern traveller through a bewilderingly disorientating series of cultural transitions to an ultimately unfamiliar city, a frontier outpost which was already partly in a foreign country

INTRODUCTION

and which owed more to its Mediterranean origins and position than to its official 'French' designation. After all, in spite of lending its name to the national anthem, the city had suffered the indignity of being bizarrely stripped of that name in 1795 for allegedly conspiring against the Convention in the name of its 'Provençal' allegiance.

In more recent memory, the newly disembarked traveller would be only too conscious that this frontier town was by no means entirely benign, overshadowed by its international reputation as a 'Wicked City'.[4] Just five years earlier, in 1934, King Alexander I of Yugoslavia had been assassinated along with the French Foreign Minister Louis Barthou as they progressed along the Canebière at the beginning of a state visit, which, while clearly a failure of national security, was also blamed on the inadequacies of the local police force. More recently, in November 1938, the fire which engulfed the Nouvelle Galeries departmental store on the Canebière, with the loss of seventy-seven lives and in the full view of the nation's press, in town to cover the governing Radical Party's annual congress, reinforced the perception of corruption and inefficiency at the heart of Marseille municipal government, shored up by organised crime (travellers on the train might have fancied that they had glimpsed in the first class compartments elite gangsters like Paul Carbone, famous from the pages of *Détective* magazine as the *voyageurs* because of their shuttling between their business interests in Marseille and Paris); clientelist politics; and the political dominance of the Communist Party and the CGT union confederation. In March 1939 local government was taken into central government administration—a sanction with uncomfortable reminiscences of the 1795 edict reducing the city to anonymity—although a durable and seemingly insurmountable legacy remained in the form of one of the most persistent images associated with Marseille from the First World War onwards, detritus and effluent dominating the Old Town and flowing down the Canebière to the Vieux-Port.

If Marseille could appear intimidating and often overshadowed by sinister images of crime and corruption, it also presented a much more positive aspect. If many of the train's passengers were ultimately heading for the port, it was because, one way or another, they were in thrall to what Marcel Roncayolo terms the 'imaginaire de Marseille',[5] centred on the city's role as a springboard to the colonies of the French

3

Empire and the wider world in which they were situated. In this sense, Marseille became more than a mere functional staging post for colonial journeys, but, rather, as Albert Londres suggests in his 1927 reportage, the repository of all the *invitations au voyage* directed at the nation's, and Northern Europe's, youth, and fuelling not merely *voyages imaginaires*, but also bona fide missions and journeys and making the city's shipping lines, with their travel posters, their flags and their livery, as iconographic of late nineteenth-century and early twentieth-century travel and adventure as any other medium.

Nor was the city's reputation universally daunting. Corrupt the Marseille administration might be, with its close links to organised crime and clientelist politics, while the accent was often impenetrable and the tall stories (*galéjade*) tedious, but still the population had a *bon enfant* (good natured) side to it which, though far from refined, was nevertheless reassuring. The Canebière might have been the site of the assassination of Alexander I and the Nouvelles Galeries fire, but it was also still one of the most exciting thoroughfares in the world, and the crowd which lent it its vibrancy also contributed to the unique experience of watching the Olympique de Marseille football team in their new Vélodrome stadium or the music-hall performances at the Alcazar. It was this rough, but good-natured side to the Marseille population which was both the result of generations of assimilation of different ethnic and cultural groups and the means by which this assimilation could be continued. Hence the city's reputation as not merely a *ville carrefour* (crossroads) but as a *ville d'accueil* (town of welcome) or even *ville d'asile* (town of asylum), which became ever more pertinent as the 1930s counted down to the beginning of war. By 1939, the travellers on the train would probably have included an advance party of the Eastern European and German refugees who began to flock to Marseille in increasing numbers as the certainty of war grew and would indeed find that their trust was not wholly misplaced. All in all, Marseille was, in the words of M.F.K. Fisher, 'a considerable town',[6] and exerted a unique influence on the French, and international, imagination.

More than sixty years later, in 2001, the passengers streaming off one of the first high-speed TGV trains from Paris, having made the journey in just three hours, would have had a very different perception

INTRODUCTION

of Marseille from their counterparts of 1939. Since the TGV line, unlike the old track, does not skirt the Etang de Berre, they would not have seen the oil refineries and tanker terminals of the Port of Fos. Nor would they have passed the industrial wasteland which was all that remained of the grandiose petro-chemical and steel-making projects of the early 1970s. Joining the old line at L'Estaque, however, they might have been struck by two things. Ahead of them and to the right, before the hillsides shielding the Vieux-Port, was the port itself; but a port, in contrast to 1939, uncannily empty, populated merely by a handful of roll-on roll-off ferries bound for Algeria, Tunisia and Corsica, and not yet supplemented by the cruise ships which would begin to arrive after 2010. The great port of the late nineteenth century and the first half of the twentieth century had vanished, along with its ships, its warehouses and its dockyard installations. In contrast, they might have noticed that on the hillside to their left and crowding against the railway line and the highways, there were buildings from the 1960s and 1970s, great twenty-floor slabs of concrete which constituted Marseille's response to its post-war housing crisis, the famous *cités* (housing estates) of the *quartiers nord*, whose reputation was, and had been for some time, indissolubly linked with the city's identity.

These passengers on the TGV would have been very different in composition and attitude from their pre-war counterparts. Few of them, unless they were tourists or from North African families, would have been heading for the port and the awaiting ferries. Instead, most would have engaged in what had become a routine and recurrent visit, part of the progressive *désenclavement* (opening-up) of the nation's peripheries in the last quarter of the twentieth century, in which the motorways, budget airlines, and TGV networks played a crucial role. The city of Marseille which, until the Second World War, had been ten or eleven hours distant from Paris, and, in the 1990s, still eight hours, as far away and as mysterious as Germany or London, had become, thanks to three hours of high-speed travel, little more than an extension of the capital's outer suburbs; had lost once and for all its aura of the unknown and the intriguing. Nor, with the disappearance of most of the activities of the port, could Marseille still claim purchase on the nation's yearning or nostalgia for travel: the Corsican ferries could not possibly exert the same stimulus on the imagination as the Paquet,

Fraissinet and Messageries Maritimes liners which had gone to the breakers' yards in the 1970s. In short, by the beginning of the twenty-first century, it was by no means clear that Marseille constituted either 'the considerable town' of the interwar years or that it still had purchase over the nation's imagination. Perhaps Marseille never quite lived up to its potential—the dream of its Mediterranean magnificence collapsing under post-war circumstance before it could ever be fully realised—yet, somehow, both the ideals and the negative stereotypes surrounding the city have lived on in its culture.

These elements of tension and contradiction run right through the modern history of Marseille, and its arts: the sense of cultural and sometimes political conflict pitting Marseille and its region against Paris and the consolidating French nation-state, especially after 1870; the contrast between the port in its heyday and the loss of local identity and national importance after World War One; the dual forces driving the city's post-war transformation, both central French and broadly European economic realities, and distinctly Mediterranean events of decolonisation and immigration; the conception of the 'wicked city' idea by outsiders, yet also its adoption and development by local cultural figures. Marseille's elusive, plural nature is what truly makes it a great city, and so there can be no strictly linear or reductively thematic path to understanding it, its art or its people.

'Marseille Imaginaire'

The aim of this book is to explore this unique hold exerted by Marseille on the nation's imagination, one aspect of what Jean-Louis Fabiani and Sophie Bias term the 'exception marseillaise',[7] by unpicking and supplementing the cultural baggage of the hypothetical passengers on their journey from the North and by dissecting the cultural self-perception of the Marseillais themselves. As such, it is not a conventional cultural history of Marseille, still less a political or social one: rather, it constitutes a series of snapshots, like the photographs from Nadar's studio on the Avenue de Noailles in the 1890s or from Assadour Keussayan's Studio Rex near the Porte d'Aix from the 1930s onwards. The travellers on the 08.00 Paris-Marseille express in 1939 would have had their impressions of Marseille formed by a variety of sources, whether they were Parisians or foreigners visiting for the first time, or citizens of the port returning home. All would have been owners of a certain 'imaginary' of Marseille, constructed from a plethora of formal and informal sources, ranging from anecdote, gossip and rumour, often conveyed by the press, to more tangible artefacts like the posters of railway companies and shipping lines, newspaper cartoons, like the popular 'Marius et Olive' series in the 1920s, Marseille music-hall stars like Raimu and Fernandel and popular songs by the city's greatest popular composer Vincent Scotto.

The richest source of documentation is to be found in literary texts, both fictional and non-fictional, ranging from the classic novels of Dumas, Daudet and Conrad to the international novels of the interwar years and the Occupation; the post-war fiction of Sembène, Le Clézio and Edmonde Charles-Roux; and the *polars* (detective novels) of the 1990s, alongside the memoirs of Joseph Méry and Victor Gelu, the journalism of Albert Londres, the interwar essays of Walter Benjamin and the theatre of Rostand and Pagnol. They are accompanied by extravaganzas like the 1899 six-hundredth centenary celebrations and the 1906 Exposition Coloniale, with their elaborate stage management and iconography, and accompanied by popular music like Scotto's *Ma P'tite Tonkinoise*; the high-cultural revolution in painting carried out by Cézanne and the Fauves in L'Estaque at the turn of the century; and by the wealth of popular imagery embodied in the railway companies' and shipping lines' promotional posters. Similarly, popular culture has been a powerful vehicle for the creation of a Marseillais identity for its own citizens, as well as an image for wider consumption across France and beyond, including music hall, cinema, popular music and sport, in which the city's football club, Olympique de Marseille, the UEFA Champions' League cup-winners in 1993, plays a crucial function. Finally, that image is sealed by landmarks of the urban fabric itself, from the *Bonne Mère*, Notre-Dame de la Garde, presiding over the city from its pinnacle on the south of the Vieux-Port, to the now-defunct transporter bridge across the mouth of the harbour, held up in the 1920s as the epitome of modern metal construction; from Le Corbusier's modernist temple, the post-war Unité d'Habitation on the Boulevard Michelet to the buildings which, like the MuCEM on the harbour mouth, mark the regeneration of the city in the second decade of the twenty-first century and serve as reminders of the importance of the cultural infrastructure, notably museums, theatres, the opera, discos and jazz clubs.

These snapshots can be laid out in more or less chronological order as they illustrate and follow a narrative of the city's progress over the nineteenth and twentieth centuries, from Marseille's ambiguous relationship with the French state during the Revolution and Empire to its ascent to a peak of maritime and economic power just before the First World War, reflected in its unparalleled purchase on the national imagination during the interwar years; to be followed by partial physical destruction during the Second World War and a seemingly irreversible decline in the post-war era, during which the city's image, a composite of immigration and crime, was unfailingly negative. At the same time, the snapshots can also be re-shuffled to bring into focus definable and interlinking strands. The most important of these is its role as a Mediterranean city-state at the centre of a pan-Mediterranean network which included its rivals Genoa and Barcelona and its 'twin city' Algiers, with which it had closer affinities than with the Northern capital, Paris, 750 kilometres away. Crucial to this perception was not merely the city's role as a major Mediterranean port, but also its vast rural hinterland, much of it within the municipal boundaries, which gave to Marseille a broader Occitan and, specifically, Provençal, identity, with the lingering distinctive accent and traces of a Southern language which were sufficient to designate it to the Northerner as a foreign country. Connected with this Mediterranean strand is another one, perhaps one of the most powerful and most durable, and embodied in reportages, travel novels, paintings and the iconography of the shipping lines, which consecrates Marseille as the repository of the nation's travel imagination, the source of all its *invitations au voyage*, with the lure of North Africa, the Eastern Mediterranean and the wider Empire, a role which it had gamely fulfilled since at least Napoleon's Egyptian Campaign and which lasted, with often increasingly devastating consequences, until decolonisation in the 1960s and France's more sinister neo-colonial presence in Africa in the last quarter of the twentieth century.

This Mediterranean identity, these days found in concrete terms mainly in the departure boards of Marseille-Provence airport, and especially the way in which the city came to embody an ideal of travel gave rise to two apparently contradictory images of Marseille in the public consciousness. The first, carefully marketed and packaged by Pagnol in his *Marius* trilogy, relies upon a stereotypical perception of the city as a Southern, Mediterranean, city whose inhabitants, in spite of an irritating tendency to lapse into *galéjade* and verbal violence, are essentially good-hearted, fundamentally decent and rightly responsible for Marseille's reputation as a *ville d'accueil* (welcoming city). According to this narrative, which runs from Dantès and Morrel in *Le Comte de Monte-Cristo*, via Marius in *Les Mystères de Marseille* to Robert Guédiguian's trade unionist protagonist in *Les Neiges de Kilimandjaro*, the overwhelmingly working-class population of the city demonstrated its reputation for acerbic criticism and internal solidarity in institutions like the Alzacar music hall and, more durably, in its support for Olympique de Marseille at the Vélodrome, whilst remaining faithful to certain moral code at odds with the ambient corruption of the city's establishment and governing classes. A counter-narrative, however, which is already present in the politically-motivated persecution of Dantès and his unjust imprisonment, points to a darker side which assumes increasing prominence in narratives and depictions after the First World War and which gives birth to the enduring notion of Marseille as the 'Wicked City', originally coined as the sub-title for the Franco-American production of Edouard Peisson's *Hans le marin*, and continued by John Frankenheimer's *French Connection 2* of 1970. Whilst the association with organised crime from the 1920s onwards is a convenient hook on which to hang a dystopian image of the city, it tends to be more intimately associated, as Jean-Claude Izzo suggests in *Solea*, with Marseille's status from the Belle Epoque onwards as a working-class city—a typical case of Louis Chevalier's conflation of *classes laborieuses* with *classes dangereuses*[8]—and as an immigrant city, especially after the early 1960s, in which working-class and immigrant were perceived as criminal by default and when the *cités* of the Quartiers Nord had achieved national prominence and the city and its hinterland were perceived as bastions of the Front National. In one sense, of course, this association is already present in Marseille's identity as a Mediterranean city and as a colonial frontier-port, with Mediterranean and former colonial populations now installed on

French soil. It also relates, however, to another recurrent trope in descriptions of the city, namely the role of refuse, waste, *ordures* or detritus, clogging the streets and reminiscent of a Third World community.[9] This image, which surfaces in the 1920s at the same time as the insistence on Marseille as a capital of crime, has proved remarkably durable, from Edouard Peisson's rag-pickers in *Hans le marin* to the almost pornographic lingering of the cameras of Germaine Krull or Lazslo Moholy-Nagy on the rubbish piled high in the alleyways of the Vieux-Port, the articles of Walter Benjamin, the infested streets of Le Clézio's *Désert* and culminating in the nightly *train des ordures* which makes its way round Marseille in Philippe Carrese's *Trois jours d'engatse*. The implications of this strand of imagery are fairly stark and have little to do with the efficiency or otherwise of the municipal authorities (although lucrative contracts for refuse collection have been perennial sources of allegations of corruption)[10] and reside more in the argument that all that stands between Marseille and its destiny as a clean and beautiful city is the physical detritus clogging its streets and, barely figuratively, the unemployed, especially immigrant, population, who are not merely blamed for causing it but constitute also the human flotsam and jetsam which must be contained or removed, just as the inhabitants of the Vieux-Port were uprooted from the city centre in 1943.

These four major strands—the Mediterranean, exotic travel, the 'Good City' and the 'Wicked City', all built up from various overlapping cultural communities—are ultimately profoundly influenced by a force which is often unstated, but always present: the ambiguous and contradictory relationship between Marseille and Paris, against which the city strained throughout the nineteenth and twentieth centuries but to which it remains uncontestably beholden. From the dictatorships of the Convention and Napoleon to the invasion of Algeria; the construction of the new port and the Empire to the flawed rebuilding of the city and port after the Liberation; the botched immigration policy of the post-war years in the wake of decolonisation to the modernisation programmes of the first decade of the twenty-first century, Marseille's trajectory has been more determined by decisions in Paris than by those in the Hôtel de Ville. Just as the advent of the TGV in 2001, accompanied by low-cost flights into Marseille-Provence Airport at Marignane, can be viewed as either a positive step in the désenclavement of the Midi or a further tightening of the strangle-hold of Paris over its 'second city', which, in the process, has become 'provincialised.'[11]

The importance of this unequal relationship with the capital is nowhere so starkly drawn as in the cultural sphere. In their *Sociologie de Marseille*, Michel Peraldi, Claire Duport and Michel Samson carefully unpick some of the most persistent misconceptions about the city—its levels of immigration, for example, or its crime statistics, both lower than either greater Lyon or the outer Parisian department of Seine-Saint-Denis, but stress that these myths have been remarkably durable in the construction of the nation's image of Marseille. In contrast, there is undoubtedly an indigenous Marseillais culture present in the Provençal poetry of Victor Gelu, the painters of the nineteenth-century Ecole de Marseille, the poets and literary journalists who founded *Les Cahiers du Sud*, the exponents of the Marseille *polar*, and hip-hop bands like IAM and Massilia Sound System, although this culture is never entirely isolated from the effects of the external image: witness Pagnol's recreation and packaging for a Parisian market of the Vieux-Port or the transformation of Marseille music-hall stars like Raimu or Fernandel into 'professional Marseillais.'[12] In both cases, the subtle and internally generated self-image of Marseille artists and writers themselves, as well as the cruder external picture as seen from Paris and beyond, Marseille is best seen, not merely, or perhaps predominantly, as an economic, political or sociological reality, but rather as a reflection of the shifting preoccupations of the observer, what Philippe Pujol describes as 'a sort of safety valve to release the dangerous pressure of the repressed problems of France as a whole.'[13] Or as Robert L. Cioffi observes regarding the Phoenicians: 'In the Greco-Roman literary imagination, the Phoenicians were a catch-all model of alterity for eastern sea-faring people, a canvas onto which to project fears and anxieties from the linguistic to the political.'[14] It was not necessary for the Phoenicians to exist in any particular form in order for them to incarnate the fears and anxieties of the Mediterranean world. As such, Marseille is not merely an integral part of France, it provides a privileged reflection of the problems, and aspirations, of the nation overall: 'The prettiest city in France doesn't hide its wounds. It is sincere. That's all. This city is merely the visible illustration of the defects of the French Republic.'[15] Those national defects, but also the local prettiness and sincerity, are at the heart of the different layers of Marseille's cultures.

PART ONE

1

LE COMTE DE MONTE-CRISTO

THE VIEUX-PORT AND THE HINTERLAND

Zarafa

On 31 October 1826 a ship arrived in Marseille's Vieux-Port from Alexandria, carrying a giraffe called Zarafa (Arabic for 'giraffe'). She was a gift from the Ottoman Khedive of Egypt to King Charles X designed to win French support in the Greek War of Independence.[1] The voyage from Alexandria had taken thirty-two days, and, after wintering in Marseille, Zarafa completed the journey to Paris on foot over forty-one days, with huge crowds greeting her at every stage, before finally arriving at the Château de Saint-Cloud on 9 July 1827. Yet this famous story tells us about more than France's fascination in the early nineteenth century with exotic animals. It also shows us that Marseille was the natural French port of arrival from the Middle East, that it was associated in the French imagination with the outlandish, that France itself was intimately involved in the geopolitics of the Mediterranean, and that a sea voyage from Alexandria was quicker than a journey to Paris by land: all elements which go to make up the complex picture of Marseille in the first half of the nineteenth century.

Central to this story is the Vieux-Port. A century after Zarafa's arrival, in his book on French ports in the 1920s, the American journalist Herbert Adams Gibbons recalled:

Old Marseilles, still in the heart of the city, is built around and inland from the Vieux-Port, which is the only landlocked part of the harbour. In the days of sailing-vessels and African corsairs... the Vieux-Port was sufficient. From the Greek period of Marseilles to the invention of the steamship and railway, the Vieux-Port answered every purpose. Vessels sailed in, moored at the quays, discharged their little cargoes, took on new loads, and weighed anchor again—all within a few hours. Except in certain specialities of comparatively small volume, no port served more than its immediate vicinity. At every break in the coast, where sailing-craft were sure of temporary refuge from the wind, there was a port.[2]

By 1826, when Zarafa arrived, this little port on the Lacydon, one of the many *calanques* (rocky inlets) on the Marseille coastline, had managed to survive the eclipse which had overtaken many of its rivals like Ragusa (now Dubrovnik) in the sixteenth century, and more recent threats like the 1720 plague, the Revolution and the Napoleonic blockade, to become one of the dominant ports on the Mediterranean. After a particularly harsh period under the Revolution and the Empire, the port began to grow again under the Restoration and, later, the July Monarchy, although its trade was predominantly Mediterranean. Pierre Guiral comments that 'in 1817 the port was visited by flags of all countries', though traffic was made up of 2,017 French ships, 667 Sardinian, and 506 Spanish ones, with a significant presence of Swedish (ninety-nine), English (ninety-four) and American (thirty-four) vessels.[3] In 1816, the population supported by this trade stood at just 107,000, after falling as low as 90,000 in 1811,[4] and would grow slowly throughout the first half of the century, reaching 183,186 in 1846, before accelerating under the Second Empire from 195,138 in 1951 to 260,310 in 1861 and 300,151 in 1866.[5]

This population was made up of three constituencies. The popular city was tightly packed in the area around the port, with more than 75,000 inhabitants per square kilometre, especially along the north side of the Quai du Port and in the area abutting it.[6] These districts, like the Quartier Saint-Jean, under the shadow of the fort, were traditionally the preserve of the fishing community and the *portefaix* (dockers), whilst the majority of builders and stone masons were concentrated in the Corsican, and later Italian, enclave of Le Panier, on the hillside rising from the port to the north. The aristocracy and bourgeoisie occupied the more sparsely populated districts in the Ville-Nouvelle, to the south and south-east of the Vieux-Port, in the classical grid-pattern of the streets constructed on the site of the former slave-galley arsenal, as well as areas further to the east on the Allée de Meilhan and Allée de Noailles. These crossed a north-south axis that ran from the Cours (de Belsunce) to the Rue de Rome, extended eventually to the Avenue du Prado. Mixed, often commercial or administrative, districts at the east end of the port, grew along and around what would become Marseille's most famous thoroughfare, the Canebière, which constituted the 'maritime axis' of the city, perpendicular to the north-south Cours de Belsunce-Rue de Rome axis.[7] Merchants and shopkeepers tended to be based to the north and north-east of the port as well as to its immediate south-east, along the Cours Julien and Cours Lieutaud. As Emile Thémime comments, in these two urban districts at the beginning of the nineteenth century, 'the sea governed everything.'[8]

In addition to this tight community around the port, however, was the *ville-campagne*, the 'third Marseillais space'[9] in Joseph Méry's words, and what Michel Vovelle describes as 'a vast rural territory, where the settlements of the peasants were mixed up with the "bastides" of the bourgeoisie'[10]—those country houses, some grand, some modest, where the city's well-to-do escaped to the country for relaxation and refuge in times of crisis. Not only were the *bastides*, along with their more humble equivalent the *cabanons*, a unique feature of Marseille domestic building,[11] but this rural population was also unusually large. This had considerable consequences for the city's development and cultural identity, as we shall see. Marseille's extensive network of villages beyond the inner city became prime targets for urban expansion as the population grew, an expansion which remained within the jurisdiction of the municipality, whereas similar developments in other agglomerations, most notably Paris, were transferred to other administrative bodies in the form of new *départements*. At the same time, this massive rural hinterland provided Marseille with a multiple identity, as Mediterranean sea port, manufacturing city, and Provençal rural region: all with very distinct characteristics, yet all too often amalgamated into one simple image. As one tourist later described the city: 'Marseille could no more be considered a typical town of Provence, than Paris could be considered a typical town of France, both having become metropolitan cities which happen to rest on French soil'.[12]

In other words, the port in which Zarafa arrived in 1826, when Dumas' hero Edmond Dantès was still imprisoned on the Château d'If, was complex in its social and political composition, dominated by the sea, perhaps, but with a significant Provençal hinterland and an urban population which was already in part orientated towards the country-side or nascent industrial development. At the same time, the politics of the city were often unpredictable, veering from revolutionary enthusiasm in 1792 to counter-revolution a year later, and marked by hostility to the Napoleonic Empire. These fluctuations were motivated in part by a long-standing distrust of the centralised power wielded from Paris, by a commitment to the financial well-being of the port, and by a very real sense of non-French, Mediterranean identity. To this must be added the growing power of the city's workforce and its will-ingness to resort, on occasion, to violence. As a guide to this complex three-dimensional model, involving the evolution of French politics from the Revolution to the end of the first half of the nineteenth cen-tury and the competing claims of the three different 'estates' which made up Marseille—*ville populaire*, *ville bourgeoise*, and rural hinter-land—it is useful to examine two novels which evoke the city at differ-ent moments in this time-span, Alexandre Dumas' *Le Comte de Monte Cristo*, set from 1815 to 1838, and Zola's early work *Les Mystères de Marseille*, written in 1867 but whose plot culminates in the 1848 Revolution and the 1849 cholera epidemic. Both, it could be argued, are dominated by the legacy of the *Marseillaise* and the epic of the Marseille battalion of 1792, a mythology still potent at the time of the Front Populaire in the form of Jean Renoir's film of 1938.

'Le Comte de Monte-Cristo'

In 1844 Marseille entered the popular imagination as smoothly as Edmond Dantès sailed *Le Pharaon* into the Vieux-Port. The first instal-ment of Dumas' novel *Le Comte de Monte-Cristo* appeared in the *Journal des Débats*, and its subsequent episodes and the publication of the entire novel in 1846 went on to make the city and the Château d'If at the mouth of its harbour internationally famous.[13] The tobacco workers in Havana named the Monte Cristo cigar after Dumas' hero and the novel became the most sought-after volume in socialist lending libraries in the Ruhr. It is important to emphasise that, before the railway and the construction of the new port, Marseille was, for the overwhelming majority of French people, not to say Europeans, a place which barely impinged on the imagination, coming after Paris, Fontainebleau, Versailles, Chantilly, Bordeaux and Lyon in Graham Robb's list of urban centres visited before the Revolution, and outshone by natural sites like the Mont Saint-Michel. In Provence, the rare tourists were more likely to visit the Fontaine de Vaucluse than Marseille.[14] As Claude Camous comments, before this, 'Marseille was only known by a small number of people, through travel-stories, a few works of history aimed at specialists and some very rare poems'[15] and 'Marseille owes a great deal to Alexandre Dumas who gave it a "literary existence" and a glowing and fascinating image.'[16] In other words, Dumas, who had already set an earlier novel, *Monsieur Coumbes*, in the South, single-handedly invented the modern image of Marseille.[17]

The Count of Monte Cristo was written with the intention of becoming a popular success, although it was impossible to predict the scale of the sensation which followed publication. Like Zola twenty-three years later, Dumas had been encouraged by his publishers to exploit the market created by Eugène Sue's *Les Mystères de Paris* and settled on the story after a visit to the island of Monte Cristo in 1842 with a party including the exiled Prince Louis Napoléon.[18] The following year, after exploring the Château d'If with his friend, the Marseillais poet and historian Joseph Méry, whose influential *Marseille et les Marseillais* was published in 1866,[19] he constructed the plot of Dantès' revenge with his collaborator Auguste Maquet, borrowing heavily on the memoirs of an ex-policeman, Jacques Pauchet, *Le Diamant et la vengeance*.[20] *Le Comte de Monte-Cristo*, however, contrary to Camous' assertion that 'Marseille is barely present',[21] is essentially a Marseillais novel. Although much of the action takes place in Rome and, especially, Paris, the plot is triggered and sustained by the city's political intrigue and it is altogether fitting that the novel should end, apart from the final scene on Monte Cristo itself, on the Vieux-Port where it began in 1815. Moreover, the early chapters, with their sense of place and detail, constitute realist *scènes de la vie de province*. As Robin Buss comments:

Dumas' novel reversed a prejudice, namely that Marseille was, in the words of Murray's *Handbook for Travellers in France* (1847), 'a busy and flourishing city… [but one that] has few fine public buildings or sights for strangers'. *The Count of Monte Cristo*, on the contrary, with its intimate topography of the area around the old port and its dramatisation of Marseille as the focus of mercantile activity, the meeting-place of Mediterranean cultures, and the gateway to the Arab Maghreb, is a good deal more flattering than Murray's *Handbook*. Dumas was allegedly thanked by a Marseillais cab-driver for promoting the city.[22]

Indeed, Dumas pays precise attention to the mid-nineteenth-century city's topography: the Vieux-Port itself; the modest villa of Dantès' father, just off the Canebière, the Rue de Noailles, and the Allées de Meilhan, 'under the shade of the fine avenue of lime trees, which forms one of the most frequent walks of the idlers of Marseilles' (p. 839); and the aristocratic Saint-Mérans' house on the Rue du Grand-Cours (now the Cours Belsunce), identified specifically as being built in the style of Marseille's greatest classical architect Puget; the prosecutor Villefort, Dantès' nemesis, lives near the Palais de Justice. Dantès' vessel, the *Pharaon*, 'built, rigged and laden in the old Phocée docks',[23] rounds into La Réserve basin in the Vieux-Port, before its acting captain, after meeting with the ship's owner, M. Morrel, disembarks at the Quai d'Orléans (now Quai des Belges) and heads up the Canebière to see his father in Dantès' father's modest villa, just off the Rue de Noailles and the Allées de Meilhan, 'under the shade of the fine avenue of lime trees, which forms one of the most frequent walks of the idlers of Marseilles' (p. 839). This very precise topography is complemented by the settlement of Les Catalans, to the south-west of the Vieux-Port, where Dantès' fiancée Mercédès and her cousin Fernand live, and still remembered in the present-day Plage des Catalans.

In fact, the use of Les Catalans is one of many reminders in the novel of the multi-cultural nature of Marseille in the early nineteenth century, essential to its status as a Mediterranean city and to its image as a *ville d'accueil*. Dumas recounts the origins of the Catalan village in ways which specifically echo the founding myth of Gyptis and Protis:

> Long ago this mysterious colony quitted Spain and settled on the tongue of land on which it is to this day. Whence it came no one knew, and it spoke an unknown tongue. One of its chiefs, who understood

Provençal, begged the commune of Marseilles to give them this bare and barren promontory, where, like the sailors of old, they had run their boats ashore. The request was granted; and three months afterwards, around the twelve or fifteen small vessels which had brought these gypsies of the sea, a small village sprang up. This village, constructed in a singular and picturesque manner, half Moorish, half Spanish, still remains and is inhabited by descendants of the first comers, who speak the language of their fathers. (pp. 14–15)

These elements of cultural and linguistic independence, existing within the wider community of the city and the even wider Mediterranean basin, become important elements in the subsequent cultural mixture of Marseille. In this, they are reinforced by the city's proximity to the Italian ports like Marseille's great rival Genoa, to the extent that Italian is readily understood and used amongst the population. Morrel, for example, cites an Italian proverb to Dantès—*Chi ha compagno ha padrone*—'he who has a partner has a master' (p. 8), in full expectation that he will be understood.

This multi-cultural community of French, Catalans and Italians is joined by another significant group which impinges more closely on its cultural identity: the Provençal population, represented particularly by the character of Caderousse and his wife, La Carconte. Caderousse is the neighbour of Dantès' father and the accomplice of Danglars, but his cultural significance only appears when the Count tracks him down to the country inn he runs between Bellegard and Beaucaire in the Gard. Gaspard Caderousse is described as a 'perfect specimen of the natives of those southern latitudes', with 'dark, sparkling, and deep-set eyes, hooked nose and teeth white as those of a carnivorous animal' and wearing 'no other protection for his head than a red handkerchief twisted around it, after the manner of Spanish muleteers' (p. 173). On festive occasions, we are told, 'he dressed in the picturesque costume worn... by the inhabitants of the South of France, bearing equal resemblance to the style adopted both by the Catalans and the Andalusians' (p. 174), whilst his wife, 'displayed the charming fashion prevalent among the women of Arles, a mode of attire borrowed equally from Greece and Arabia' (p. 174).[24] This appearance of Provençal culture is not merely a feature of the novel's Southern exotic: it also introduces an additional piece in the Mediterranean jigsaw, by which Provence joins Catalonia, Italy and the Middle East as an integral part of a cultural coalition. At the same time, however, it poses the ambiguous relationship between Marseille itself and its deeper cultural hinterland, by which the city strives to be at one and the same time a part of the Provençal heritage but also much more than that, indeed something quite distinct. This tension between Marseille's own identity and its role as a Provençal capital plays out from the beginning of the nineteenth century, illustrated in the career of Dumas' contemporary the poet Victor Gelu and his relationship with the Félibrige.

This self-consciously Mediterranean context for the novel is particularly clear in one of the concluding chapters, where it is described as 'the immense lake, extending from Gibraltar to the Dardanelles, from Tunis to Venice' (p. 866), easily recognisable in the interwar years to the writers of *Les Cahiers du Sud* or, in the 1990s, to Jean-Claude Izzo. As we have seen, *Le Comte de Monte-Cristo* opens with the arrival of the *Pharaon*, 'from Smyrna, Trieste and Naples' (p. 5), the well-trodden trade route between the Eastern Mediterranean, Adriatic and Italy which has lasted from the ancient world, through the sixteenth century documented by Braudel, until the last quarter of the twentieth century. The map is supplemented in the novel by the islands to the south and south-east of Marseille: Corsica, Elba, where Dantès makes his fateful detour to visit the exiled Napoleon, and Monte Cristo, 'twenty-five miles from Pianosa, between Corsica and the Isle of Elba' (p. 133); by the port's near-neighbour Genoa; and the two cities, Rome, where Dantès constructs his new identity after his discovery of the treasure of Monte Cristo, and Madrid, where the treacherous Danglars, fluent in Spanish, finds work in a finance house. Within this extended Mediterranean world, it is unsurprising that the novel's characters should be caught up in its political upheavals. Caderousse reports that, the 'war with Spain', Danglars served in the 'commissariat of the French army, and made a fortune' (p. 187), whilst Mercédès' cousin Fernand, having deserted Napoleon to go over to the English, served as a captain in the Spanish war in 1823 and then, promoted to colonel, fought in the Greek uprising, but, unlike the European Romantics, as the aide to the Turkish leader Ali Pasha (pp. 188–9). Marseille thus becomes closely involved with the conflicts of its neighbours to the east and west, just as Zola's *Les Mystères de Marseille* will reflect the impact of

Garibaldi's supporters on the Revolution of 1848, or the Carlist Wars of the 1870s will constitute the backdrop to Conrad's *The Arrow of Gold*.

In fact, one of the most unusual and distinctive aspects of the novel is its interest in the Middle East and Arabia. Not only do the references to Smyrna and Turkey establish the Eastern Mediterranean as a concrete presence in the novel, they point also to an important non-European cultural territory represented by the *Tales of the Arabian Nights*, which will become a recurring allusion in Marseillais literature. Thus, when the Count embarks on his rescue of the bankrupt house of Morrel, his former employer, he approaches Morrel's daughter Julie with the instructions: 'one day you will receive a letter signed "Sinbad the Sailor". Do exactly what the letter bids you...' (p. 204). This allusion is taken up and amplified in the episode when Franz d'Epiny, on a visit to Elba and Pianosa, is enticed to the island of Monte Cristo and led to the Count's sumptuous quarters. On being informed that his host is called 'Sinbad the Sailor', Franz's natural response is that 'decidedly... this is an *Arabian Nights* adventure' (p. 223) and that he is in the role of Aladdin (p. 225). The Count is 'dressed in a Tunisian costume— that is to say a red cap with a long blue tassel, a vest of black cloth embroidered with gold, pantaloons of deep red, large and full gaiters of the same colour, embroidered with gold like the vest, and yellow slippers' (p. 223), whilst his chamber is furnished with 'a kind of divan, surmounted with a stand of Arabian swords in silver scabbards, and the handles resplendent with gems; from the ceiling hung a lamp of Venetian glass, of beautiful shape and colour, while the feet rested on a Turkey carpet...' (p. 224). The scene is completed by the presence of the dumb servant Ali, punished for 'wandering nearer to the harem of the Bey of Tunis than etiquette permits' (p. 225), and by the presence of his mistress, Haidée, the daughter of Ali Pasha (p. 606). Whilst on one level this is blatant Orientalist kitsch, Dumas is not merely exploiting reminiscences of his own journey to North Africa in 1842[25] or the early nineteenth-century vogue for the exotic following Napoleon's Egyptian campaign, to which, incidentally, Dantès' vessel, the *Pharaon*, owes its name. Rather, he has also identified one of the major reference-points of Marseille culture, namely its awareness of the Eastern Mediterranean and North Africa, an awareness which goes further than mere trading partnerships. As Izzo argues in *Total Khéops*, Marseille culture is under the sway, not merely of the Greek epic of Odysseus, but also of the legends of his Arab counterpart, Sinbad, in a way that an important pan-Mediterranean mythology. In other words, whilst Dumas' novel catered for a contemporary taste in the exotic on two levels—the exoticism of the French South and that of the wider Mediterranean—it also succeeded in repositioning Marseille as a key component of a Southern and Eastern culture.

In fact, the political and cultural compass of *Le Comte de Monte-Cristo* points in several different, and opposing, directions. Marseille looks south, east and west to its neighbours in the Mediterranean, but also north to the French state, of which it is, sometimes reluctantly, a part, and to its capital Paris, with which it is often in conflict—a conflict explored obliquely by Dumas, but which begins with an expression of unparalleled solidarity in the form of the *Marseillaise*.

'La Marseillaise'

If there is one single thing which has embedded Marseille in the collective Western memory, it is the French national anthem, the 'Marseillaise'. One of the most popular tourist attractions in the present-day city is the Mémorial de la 'Marseillaise', just east of the Cours de Belsunce on the Rue Thubaneau, a few doors down from the site of the Marquis de Castellane's tennis court and the head-quarters of the revolutionary Société Patriotique des Amis de la Constitution. It was here, in July 1792, that Rouget de Lisle's *Chant de l'Armée du Rhin* was first heard in the city, and that the Marseille Battalion was formed of 517 carefully vetted volunteers, who marched north to Paris signing what was now their song.[26] 146 years later, ninety-six years after the publication of Dumas' novel, what is still one of the most moving evocations of the Marseille Battalion was presented in Jean Renoir's film *La Marseillaise*, celebrating the Front Populaire as the rightful heir of the spirit of 1792.

The film is deeply embedded in Marseille's culture of the interwar years, in which Marcel Pagnol played a crucial role. Renoir had first met Pagnol in April 1934 during the shooting of *Angèle* and had enlisted his collaboration on *Toni*, a film about migrant workers in Provence, for which he used Pagnol's locations, his actors and his laboratory facilities.[27] Two years later, when he came to work on a project on the French Revolution, he decided to recount the story from the Marseillais' perspective, using some of the same cast from *Toni* and the same Provençal locations. He had initially envisaged a much closer collaboration with Pagnol, involving him for the Marseille dialogues,[28] although eventually the script would be supplied by Renoir himself, based mainly on historical documents. According to Pascal Ory, what remained, nevertheless, was 'a good-humoured style, sometimes bordering on *galéjade* [tall tale]… which was the signature of the Studios Marcel Pagnol',[29] which permeated the film as a whole, contributing to its unificatory historical vision.

The film is essentially a series of brief tableaux or snapshots, which build up into a newsreel-like coverage of the Revolution. After an opening episode in Versailles on 14 July 1789, it moves to June 1790 and a village in Provence, where a poor peasant is caught killing his landlord's pigeon and is sentenced to ten years in the galleys. He manages to escape, however, and flees to the mountains, where he meets two Marseillais, Arnaud, a customs officer, and Bomier, a stone mason, talking with a dissident priest. When they see smoke in the distance from aristocrats' châteaux being burned, they know that the revolution has begun and they return to Marseille. The film moves to the port itself, with Arnaud, Bomier and their fellow revolutionaries capturing the Fort Saint-Jean at the mouth of the harbour[30]—not through any act of violence, but through the trick of concealing armed insurgents in a cask of wine—and sending the commander, the Marquis de Saint-Laurent, into exile, but not before being instructed by Arnaud as to the meaning of the words 'nation' and 'citoyen'.

Marseille re-emerges in 1792, after episodes amongst the émigrés in Germany, in a scene set in the Jacobin 'Club des Amis du Peuple', where a crowd is addressed by 'citoyenne' Louise Vauclair, who denounces the King and Queen and calls for the city to raise a battalion to defend Paris against the invading Prussians. Arnaud and Bomier, together with their comrades from the Fort Saint-Jean, volunteer as *fédérés* (National Guard troops) and prepare to march north, blessed by their families and even by a sympathetic priest. It is at this point that they hear for the first time Rouget de l'Isle's *Chant de l'Armée du Rhin*, which will become the *Marseillaise* and the battalion's marching song.

These patriotic scenes are followed by Arnaud and Bomier taking an idyllic fishing trip off the coast, which is the last that we see of Marseille itself in the film. Thereafter, the battalion marches north and the remainder of the film takes place in Paris, culminating in the capture of the Tuileries Palace on 10 August 1792, the fall of the monarchy. It ends on the eve of the Battle of Valmy, with Goethe's commentary: 'From this day and from this place dates a new stage in the history of the world.'

What is interesting about *La Marseillaise* is that it was, in all senses, a cooperative film, 'the first film to be commissioned by the People.'[31] More important, though, is the way in which the film, in line with the overall Front Populaire policy of the 'outstretched hand', avoids divisiveness and antagonism. As Pascal Ory points out, the only real enemies are foreign: the Duke of Brunswick and his Prussians, Marie-Antoinette and her Austrians, the Swiss Guards of the Tuileries. Even Louis XVI, played by Pierre Renoir, is personally sympathetic, and the émigré aristocrats in Coblenz are more pitiable mechanical anachronisms than threats.[32] In fact, as the Communist André Seigneur commented, the film was noteworthy for having showed 'peasants, workers, shopkeepers, soldiers, priests, young people, women and proletarians.' Similarly, the customs clerk Arnaud,

> an intellectual from the petite-bourgeoisie, becomes... the conscious mouthpiece of a group comprising a docker, a builder and an artist. Amongst the women the young generations unhesitatingly joined a movement which still frightened their mothers. In short, a sample of 'representative Frenchmen'.[33]

There are few direct echoes of this stirring epic in *Le Comte de Monte-Cristo*, but it is important to emphasise that the novel is profoundly political, with the Revolution and the Empire in the immediate past and the Bourbon Restoration threatened by Napoleon and the 100 Days. However, if the Revolution and Empire remain shadowy, they determine the fate of both Dantès and his enemies: his career begins to unravel from the moment he sets foot on the Isle of Elba and unconsciously enters a world of Napoleonic intrigue which will lead him inexorably to the Château d'If, that visible symbol of royal despotism. Not merely is Villefort's persecution of Dantès entirely due to his fear that his father's role as a Girondin in the Revolution (p. 39) and, under the Restoration, as a Bonapartist agent, will be discovered, shattering his career and marriage, but Morrel's failure to defend his captain adequately also stems from his family's Bonapartist allegiances. Even though Dumas remarks on the South's Federalist Revolutionary past, which makes it antipathetic to Napoleon (p. 69), the Restoration monarchy appears from the point of view of Marseille as very much the primary enemy, imprisoning the innocent and rewarding the corrupt. In this sense, it is entirely fitting that Monte Cristo's project of revenge is put into effect with the fall of the Bourbons and the beginning of the July Monarchy. In other words, *Le Comte de Monte-Cristo* presents a picture of Marseille beset by the same distant power in Paris which can, on occasions, reward as well as punish, which continues to the present day and questions its unswerving loyalty to the nation.

In fact, it was the disproportionate exercise of arbitrary power by the French state, governing from Paris, together with the fluctuations in the prosperity of the port, which largely determined the attitudes of the Marseillais from 1789 to 1815, from their initial revolutionary enthusiasm, captured by Renoir's film, to their lurch towards Federalism and counter-revolution in 1793, and continued antagonism to Napoleon and the Empire. As Thémime comments, in 1790 the symbolic targets of the Marseille revolutionaries, as depicted in Renoir's film, were the port's 'bastilles': the Forts Saint-Jean and Saint-Nicolas guarding the entry to the port and the Fort Notre-Dame overlooking the city, embodying that 'military control which had been wielded since Louis XIV over a city always suspected of insubordination.'[34] Initially, this anti-centralist revolutionary current served Marseille well and it enthusiastically joined the battle against counter-revolution emanating in late 1791 from the rival northern Provençal cities Arles and Avignon, which were to become centres of the Félibrige in the following century. The ascendancy of the Jacobins in 1793, however, put an end to the spirit of the Marseillais Battalion of the previous year and ushered in a return of centralised power. As a consequence, the city's Federalist revolutionaries not merely turned against their own Jacobin faction by closing the Club in the Rue Thubaneau, they also performed a volte-face by putting the grandly-named 'departmental army' under the command of the Royalist Marquis de Villeneuve-Tourettes and even attempting to negotiate an alliance with the English

27

Admiral Hood. As Marc-Antoine Julien, the 'commissaire' with the Revolutionary armies of the South commented: 'this city, which was once so ardent in its support for the Revolution, has become the tool of the counter-revolutionaries.'[35] Retribution swiftly followed: on 25 August 1793 General Carteaux's army entered the city and re-imposed revolutionary order, whilst the arrival in October of the two Parisian emissaries Paul Barras and Louis-Marie Stanislas Fréron effectively initiated the Terror in Marseille, with trials, executions, the destruction of religious buildings, and, most dramatically, the law of 6 January 1794 consigning the city to outlaw status and by literally removing its name by designating it as a *Ville Sans Nom*. Temporary as the punishment was, the indictment was by no means unfamiliar and remained one which Marseille would have difficulty shaking off in the following two centuries. As Fréron reported to the Committee of Public Safety:

> All Europe knows that when you ask a Marseillais if he is French, he replies: 'No, I am Provençal'. This naïve reply describes the spirit of Marseille. This is the belief which people here are born with; it is an original sin, an indelible idea... Even the best patriots from here see only Marseille; Marseille is their nation, France is nothing.[36]

This incident is a remarkable stage in the evolution of the French perception of Marseille as being irredeemably alien. From its preferred self-image during the Ancien Régime as either a Provençal capital or, even better, a Mediterranean city-state, the equal of Genoa, Naples, Venice, Ragusa and the 'Echelles du Levant' (the ports of the Levant), to its politically subversive reputation during the Commune of 1871, allegations of disloyalty on the Western Front during the First World War, and the subsequent image of the port dominated by crime, communism or immigration, Marseille's pariah status was reinforced in the French political and popular imagination, and the removal of its name altogether, looking forward to the abolition of its council's powers in 1939, was merely a logical, if extreme, component of the process of the construction of the 'Wicked City'.

The city's dissidence, however, under the Revolution and the Empire, was not solely motivated by its natural antagonism towards Paris and the North, but was grounded in very real economic concerns. Indeed, Marseille's disaffection with the Revolution coincides with the beginning of the war with England in 1793, lasting more or less uninterrupted until 1815, and the blockade of the trade routes on which the port depended for its survival: the lucrative West Indian market and, most important, the traditional ascendancy in trade with the Eastern Mediterranean, including the Ottoman Empire, the Black Sea and the Echelles du Levant, to which Marseille sent an accredited ambassador, as if, indeed, it were a city-state. All of this rapidly collapsed, with catastrophic effects on the city's economy, industry and merchant fleet, and was exacerbated under the Empire, in spite of Napoleon's personal interest in the Middle East and his founding of a chair of vernacular Arabic in Marseille in 1807.[37] In this context, the voyage of Dantès' ship the *Pharaon* takes on its full significance: arriving from Smyrna in 1815, just before the 100 Days, and with its proudly Egyptian name, it marks the resumption of Marseille's traditional trading partnerships with the Eastern Mediterranean and the Italian ports after more than twenty years of disruption. It was arguably this economic disaster, much more than the indignities of subjection to centralised power from Paris, which motivated the Marseillais during the Revolution and the Empire and which led them to welcome the return of the monarchy in 1814. It was also a mixture of economic factors and distrust of centralisation which lay at the origins of Marseille's belated support for the end of the July Monarchy thirty-four years later in 1848, but connected this time with a factor only alluded to at the beginning of Renoir's *La Marseillaise*, but developed in detail in Zola's novel of 1867, *Les Mystères de Marseille*: the roles of the rural hinterland and the urban crowd in the city's political history.

'Les Mystères de Marseille'

Zola's novel was an even more blatant attempt to exploit the success of *Les Mystères de Paris* and was written whilst Zola was working on his first serious novel, *Thérèse Raquin*. Approached by his friend, the journalist Marius Roux, and by Léopold Arnoux, the owner of the newspaper *Le Messager de Provence*, he was persuaded to provide a Provençal version of Sue's novel and was given access to the files on the most recent criminal cases. As Zola put it in a letter to his friend Antony Valabrègue, 'I'm buried under documents.... The work is not well paid; but I hope

29

to make an impact throughout the South',[38] an indication that he did not see this as a vehicle to Parisian or national success. Instalments of the novel appeared from March to October 1867, but, as Robert Abirached comments, *Les Mystères de Marseille* is hardly a success compared with the novels in *Les Rougon-Macquart*.[39] Yet in spite of the blatant sentimentality of the plot, the novel marks a breakthrough in the use of documentation, the creation of an urban landscape, the exploration of character through certain types, the beginnings of an understanding of the power of money and, finally, the ability to sustain the description of a major political event, the Revolution of 1848, with what will become one of Zola's most significant preoccupations, the role of the crowd.[40] All these elements are important in themselves, but they are reinforced by the light which *Les Mystères de Marseille* sheds on the popular view of the city, both from within and outside.

The novel was based on the newspaper's story from 1823 about the abduction of the daughter of a Marseille *député*. Zola's version is about two brothers, the good-looking, ambitious thirty-year-old Philippe Cayol and his more serious brother Marius, who supports the family through his work as a clerk for the ship-owner Martelly. Philippe elopes with Blanche, the niece of the reactionary Marseille *député* de Cazalis and is relentlessly pursued throughout the novel, whilst his younger brother, assisted by his future wife, the flower-seller Fine, works to help him escape. It is through the various attempts to raise the money which will enable Philippe to leave prison and flee Marseille that Marius encounters the various aspects of Marseille low-life which constitute the *Mystères* of the novel's title. These include the exploits and retribution of a crooked financier, Douglass; an embezzling clerk; a gambling den; and the world of prostitution, in which his guide is the self-important businessman and former *portefaix* Sauvaire. This shamelessly melodramatic plot ends in an extended description of the Revolution of 1848, in which the shifting political events are accompanied by the schemes of de Cazalis and his agent Mathéus to kill Philippe and kidnap Blanche's child, and by the 1849 cholera epidemic which sees off most of the characters apart from Marius and Fine.

Beyond its status as a literary curiosity, *Les Mystères de Marseille* is interesting for the picture it provides of the city in the 1840s from the perspective of a writer and reader in the 1860s. What is immediately striking in comparison with *Le Comte de Monte-Cristo* is that Zola, who was brought up in Aix and knew Marseille far better than Dumas, gives a very different picture of the city and places its centre of gravity away from the Vieux-Port towards both the port's and the city's hinterland. The novel opens outside de Cazalis' *bastide* in Saint-Joseph, 'near the Aygalades',[41] now a *cité* in Marseille's 15th Arrondissement, but, in the mid-nineteenth century, very much in the countryside.[42] Philippe's flight with Blanche takes him first to his mother's 'country-dwelling' (p. 230), in the Quartier Saint-Just, now in the 13th Arrondissement on the east of the city and then to her gardener's house in Saint-Barnabé, south of Saint-Just. In other words, the novel's initial geography is outside the urban development and far from the Vieux-Port, in the countryside surrounding it to the north and east, and it is only later that it moves to the centre, although even that is by no means synonymous with the port. Before then, however, the action moves further out of Marseille: to Aix, where Philippe is tried and imprisoned, and to Lambesc, even further north, near Salon-de-Provence, where the Saint-Simonian aristocrat M. de Girousse has his property. The *Mystères de Marseille*, therefore, are also Provençal mysteries and cater to that same taste for the Southern exotic as *Le Comte de Monte-Cristo*.

Similarly, when Zola moves his narrative into the centre of Marseille, the Vieux-Port assumes relatively little importance, a reminder that port and city are by no means synonymous, a point made by more recent commentators such as Jean-Claude Izzo and François Thomazeau. In Izzo's *Total Khéops*, Fabio Montale sits on the ferry-boat crossing the Vieux-Port and reflects that, contrary to popular mythology, 'the Marseillais don't like voyages… In bourgeois families, the sea was off-limits to children. The port facilitated business, but the sea was dirty. That was where vice came from. And the plague…',[43] whilst in 2013 the journalist and novelist François Thomazeau, brought up in Saint-Marcel, recalled that 'as a kid, I saw the sea no more than once a month. Except in Summer. There are thousands of us like that, Marseillais with our backs turned away from the Mediterranean.'[44] Zola's characters are part of that population and references to the port are few and far between: admittedly, Marius' employer, the Republican Martelly, who shares his good nature with his predecessor Morrel in *Le Comte de Monte-Cristo*, is a ship owner, whilst Marius himself takes the only visible boat journey in the novel, in 'one of those little pleasure-craft, covered with narrow awnings with yellow and red stripes' (p. 384), across the Vieux-Port to La Réserve, where his patron Sauvaire is lunching with two of his mistresses in one of the fashionable restaurants which 'resemble those in Asnières and Saint-Cloud' (p. 384). Philippe does indeed go to sea, along the coast to exile in Genoa, but the voyage is not narrated (p. 394).

Overwhelmingly, however, Zola's Marseille is an industrial and commercial centre. The exotic 'Lorette' Armande, another of Sauvaire's 'mistresses',

> ...had landed in Marseille one day, like one of those birds who from a long distance can sniff out a rich country at the mercy of all types of enemy. By settling in a rich industrial city, she had shown a rare intelligence. From the moment of her arrival, she targeted the businessmen, the young dealers who move cash around with a shovel. (pp. 315–6)

There is no mention here of the maritime commerce which dominates *Le Comte de Monte-Cristo*, nor, for that matter, the traditional port trade of fleecing transitory seamen. On the contrary, Zola is already broaching what will become an obsessive theme in *Les Rougon-Macquart*, the psychological, symbolic and real operation of money,[45] removed from the actual process of acquiring goods: the Vieux-Port (the new port of La Joliette, opened in 1844, is strangely absent, as it is from Pagnol's *Marius* trilogy) lacks the returning *Pharaon's* associations with the East and the Mediterranean.

Instead, the novel is firmly rooted in an urban environment, which, though close to the Vieux-Port, skirts round it, from the Rue Dastre south of the Rive-Neuve, to the Eglise Saint-Victor, where Blanche's confessor the Abbé Chastanier officiates, and Marius' and Fine's home in the Cours Bonaparte (now Cours Pierre-Puget). It then moves north along the Cours Belsunce from the Place Royale (currently Place Général de Gaulle) across the Canebière to the Place-aux-Oeufs behind the Bourse, which becomes the setting for the hardest fighting during the 1848 Revolution. And it is with his depiction of the Revolution in Marseille that Zola departs from the formulaic sequence of criminal episodes and melodramatic plot-lines which dominate the first half of the novel and moves into an area more recognisable in his later work.

P. Guiral comments that 'the Revolution of 1848 came as a surprise to Marseille as it did elsewhere',[46] that, initially, 'the Second Republic began favourably', with little violence, and that unlike other French cities and ports, like Rouen, Marseille saw no aggression against foreign workers.[47] For Zola, on the other hand, 1848 was the climax of a long process of social antagonism, the *duel social* which he used as the title for the 1873 edition of the novel.[48] Initially, the dominant concern amongst Marseille's businessmen was the same priority for laissez-faire trade which had guided them during the Revolution and Empire:

> The news of a revolution was met with consternation in the city. This people of businessmen, instinctively conservative, caring only about material interests, was entirely devoted to the Orleanist dynasty which, for eighteen years, had favoured the development of trade and industry. The dominant opinion at Marseille was that the best government is one which leaves the greatest freedom of action to the speculators. (p. 436)

With even Republicans like the poet and polemicist Victor Gelu favourable to Louis-Philippe's family,[49] the potential revolutionary base was small and split between 'a few salon republicans' (p. 436) and the 'people, lower down, without leaders and without clearly-defined political tendencies' (p. 436). Against them were pitted 'two powerful camps: the legitimists, who silently rejoiced in the fall of Louis-Philippe, hoping to profit from the struggle to take back power, and the conservatives, the crowd of businessmen who demanded peace at any price' (p. 436).

With these unspoken battle-lines drawn, in which the essential ingredient is money, and in which the Right's hand was immeasurably strengthened by the re-establishment of the Garde Nationale, 'designed to keep the people in check' (p. 437) and insulted by the workers as 'Carlists' (p. 464), Zola charts the hesitant establishment of the Republic on the Canebière (p. 442) on 29 February. All remains relatively peaceful, however, until problems arise from an unlikely source, the *Ateliers Nationaux* (National Workshops), the revolutionary public works projects established across the country. Initially, whilst the Ateliers Nationaux projects in Paris were seen to be a failure, in Marseille they were managed competently and used to accelerate work on the fresh-water canal from the Durance to the city.[50] By the summer, however, the municipal committee, which had maintained the local norm of ten hours work per day, instead of the national tariff of eleven hours, lowered the hourly rate of pay, whilst the employers deducted the wage for the hour which fell short of the national workload. Even then, the Marseille working class, which 'was one of the most peaceful and most conservative in France',[51] might not have budged had it not been for outside influences connected with Marseille's neighbour Italy. Guiral notes that from March there had been an Italian Committee in favour of Italian unification and that '5 to 600 Italians had enthusiastically marched' through the city before embarking,[52] followed in June by the arrival of Parisian workers hoping to join them. As de Cazalis' agent Mathéus, now an agent provocateur in the revolutionary clubs which had sprung up across the city, explains, 'The Marseillais would perhaps never have budged, but they have just received the visit of some Parisians who were present during the February days and that has fired them up' (p. 449). Hence, whilst the Parisians have now left for Italy, 'they have left behind a revolutionary spirit... Tomorrow, the workers, who are very discontented, are going to hold a big demonstration, which I hope will turn badly' (p. 449).

The description of the demonstration, which starts off at the 'railway station' (p. 354) and the subsequent scenes on the barricades, may well owe a debt to Victor Hugo's *Les Misérables*, published three years earlier and similarly featuring a hero called Marius, and looks forward to the mature Zola and the confrontation between miners and troops in *Germinal*, in which the mass psychology of the crowd becomes all important:

> A low indistinct sound, like that of the rough voice of the sea, ran through the ranks of that crowd. It was frighteningly quiet. It moved forward, without shouting, without causing any damage, brooding and silent. It fell upon, rolled upon Marseille, it seemed to have no consciousness of its actions, to be obeying physical laws of gravity and removal. An enormous rock, thrown on to the plain, would have rolled like this as far as the port. (p. 454)

Eventually, in the heat of the battle de Cazalis' plot unravels: his henchman Mathéus is killed and Philippe, Marius and Fine, with the help of M. de Girousse, rescue Blanche's baby and carry her to safety. The dénouement occurs a year later during the cholera epidemic of summer and autumn 1849 (which shows, incidentally, that the new aqueduct from the Durance was insufficient by itself to guarantee pure drinking water for the whole city), when M. de Cazalis mortally wounds Philippe in a duel (the physical embodiment of the 1873 title, *Le duel social*) and he is transported to the hospice. There he is laid next to the dying Abbé Chastanier and cared for by Blanche, now a nursing sister, who contracts cholera and dies in her turn. M. de Cazalis succumbs to the epidemic as well, shortly after witnessing a procession 'carrying the statue of Notre-Dame de la Garde to her church' (p. 502).

The contrast between the rural and urban preoccupations of Zola and Dumas' emphasis on the life of the port is highlighted by the fact that, whilst *Le Comte de Monte-Cristo* ends with Dantès and Haidée sailing out to the open sea, the final scene of *Les Mystères de Marseille* shows Blanche's son Joseph opening the hunt with M. de Girousse at Lambesc thirty kilometres to the north, in the Provençal heartland. Nor is this is the only difference between the two novels. *Le Comte de Monte-Cristo* opens in what is still essentially an eighteenth-century city, dominated by the Vieux-Port and comfortably re-engaged with its traditional network of Mediterranean trading relations. Between 1815, however, and the events which conclude *Les Mystères de Marseille* in 1848–9, the city underwent a rapid transformation, seeing its population increase, its economic base extending to local industry and finance operating in parallel with the port, and a revolution in its communications. The reference to the 'railway station' in Zola's novel is an allusion to a transformation in Marseille's connection to the cities of the North, including Paris, still reliant on roads and water-ways, which would dramatically reduce journey times in subsequent decades. Passed over in *Les Mystères de Marseille*, but an essential part of the economic development of France during the last years of the July Monarchy, the port was about to be transformed by the invention of maritime steam power, ushering in larger ships and necessitating the building of a new port to the north of the Lacydon. In this sense, both *Le Comte de Monte-Cristo* and *Les Mystères de Marseille* are backward looking and provide invaluable documentation on French perceptions of the port and the city before it became synonymous with modern passenger and cargo traffic.

Yet Dumas, in particular, is not wholly insensitive to Marseille's new role. At the end of his novel there is a final lyrical evocation of Marseille: 'Marseille, white, fervid, full of life and energy—Marseilles, the younger sister of Tyre and Carthage, the successor of them in the empire of the Mediterranean—Marseilles, old, yet always young' (p. 838). Dantès' last visit to Marseille, in 1838, is undertaken to accompany Mercédès' son, Albert de Morcerf, on his departure as a young lieutenant for newly conquered Algeria. This emergence of Marseille as a hub for global commerce, travel and empire became the focus of artistic production following Dumas, as we will see in the next chapter.

2

TARTARIN DE TARASCON

LA JOLIETTE, ALGERIA AND THE 'MEDITERRANEAN SYSTEM'

Visions of both Marseille and Algiers as 'white cities' like Casablanca, and notions of them as a pair of twin cities, dominated the French imagination for over a century. The growing links between Marseille and France's expanding empire positioned it as an integral partner in the 'Mediterranean Empire', rather than merely a 'second city' to Paris within the French nation. This role as the privileged bridgehead to the world of empire redefined Marseille's identity for the rest of the nineteenth century, bringing prosperity and modernity, but also indelibly marking it with the ambiguous colours of the frontier outpost.

Loubon and Daudet

Emile Loubon's large canvas, *Une Vue de Marseille prise des Aygalades un jour de marché* (A View of Marseille Taken from the Aygalades on a Market Day), was painted in 1853 and is the flagship of the mid-nineteenth-century Ecole de Marseille, which constituted the city's first tentative steps towards a separate artistic identity. The initial impression is of a pastoral, in the style of the Barbizon School which heavily influenced Loubon, and looks south towards the city and beyond from the countryside of the Aygalades, where Zola's villainous M. de Cazalis has his bastide. The perspective is dominated by an immense foreground depicting the barren Provençal landscape to the north of the city, with what is ostensibly the main subject, a herd of cattle being driven by the cowherd and his dogs to the slaughterhouse hidden in the distant city below the skyline. In the very far distance are the mountains of the Chaîne de l'Etoile, with the sea and the islands and, in the middle distance, but dwarfed by the surrounding landscape, Marseille itself, recognisable from the forts of Saint-Jean and Saint-Nicolas and the hill of la Bonne Mère, still devoid of Henri-Jacques Espérandieu's basilica of Notre-Dame de La Garde, which was built just afterwards. What is interesting in this apparently time-less depiction of Marseille amidst its dominant Provençal scenery, however, is the presence of factory chimneys belching out smoke between the herd of cattle and the city: an indication that, in the hidden ground between the Provençal plateau which dominates the foreground and the eternal Vieux-Port in the distance, an important new factor has appeared since Dumas' and Zola's portrayals, the transformation of the city's economy by the creation of a new port fit for steam power at La Joliette and the development of modern indus-try accompanying it. In this sense, Loubon's painting not merely cap-tures the competing claims of Marseille as a Mediterranean sea port and centre of a vast rural hinterland, it is also highly significant in locat-ing the early 1850s as a moment when the economic, social and cul-tural identity of the city changed. Not least in this transformation was, as we have seen, the colonisation of Algeria in 1830, which supple-mented Marseille's already intimate relations with its partners, and rivals, along the northern and eastern littorals of the Mediterranean with a powerful North African dimension, in which the unusually strong affinity with Algiers was paramount. If Loubon's picture serves as a useful signpost to the changes just over the horizon, liter-ally, for Marseille in the early 1850s, Alphonse Daudet's novel *Tartarin de Tarascon*, written nearly twenty years later in 1872, sketches in some of the indispensable detail.

A picaresque satire of small-town Provençal bombast, *Tartarin de Tarascon* follows the adventures of the middle-aged hero on a doomed expedition to Algeria. Having recklessly promised to go on a lion hunt in the new colony, he uproots himself for the first time in his life from his home town, taking the train to Marseille, and dressed, as he thinks befits his mission, in Arab hunting garb. This device enables Daudet not merely to indulge his Parisian readers' stereotypical image of the loquacious and vainglorious Provençal (which proved an astute move, making the work his first bestseller and prompting two successful sequels), but also to satirise the vogue for Orientalism deftly manipulated by Dumas. At the same time, Daudet is also able to present Marseille in the 1860s through the innocent eyes of a gullible traveller who has never seen the city before, as well as exploring and testing the mythologies surrounding the Algerian project.

Marseille is first characterised by its cosmopolitanism and exoticism. Tartarin appears on the Canebière at midday on the first of a December in the 1860s dressed as a *Teur*, his word for 'Turk'—although he probably merely means 'Arab'—but a *Teur* of the sort that the Marseillais had never seen before, 'and God knows that there's no lack of Turks in Marseille.'[1] Indeed, such is the exoticism of the port[2] that Tartarin, who is witnessing it for the first time, invokes the already by-now familiar myth of Sinbad: 'he seemed to be dreaming. He felt as if he was called Sinbad the Sailor and that he was wandering in one of those fantastic cities that are found in the *Thousand and One Nights*' (p. 88), a point made more strongly when Tartarin wanders through the port and sees the cargoes piled up: 'a prodigious mass of goods of all kinds: silks, minerals, planks of timber, lead ingots, linens, sugars, carobs, rapeseeds, liquorice, sugar canes. The Orient and the Occident jumbled together' (p. 91).

Tartarin, like many subsequent visitors to the port, including, as we shall see, Albert Londres in the 1920s, is overcome by its immensity: 'as far as the eye could see, there was a tangle of masts and yards, intermingled in all directions. There were the flags of all countries: Russian ones, Greek, Swedish, Tunisian, American…' (pp. 88–9). The dockside is lined with the effluent from the soap factories and crowded with dockworkers: 'customs officers, forwarding agents and "portefaix" with their *bogheys* drawn by little Corsican horses' (pp. 89–90). On the grain dock, 'the porters unloaded their sacks on the quayside from the top of high scaffoldings. The corn poured out in a golden torrent amidst a pale cloud' (p. 91), whilst the air is full of the sounds of the sailors' cries, 'the drums and bugles from the Fort Saint-Jean and the Fort

Saint-Nicolas, the bells of the Major, the Accoules and Saint-Victor' (p. 93), and

> Above them was the mistral which took all these sounds, all this clamour, rolled them, shook them, mixed them up with its own voice and created a mad, wild and heroic music, like the great fanfare of a journey, a fanfare which made you want to leave, to go far, to have wings. (p. 93)

La Joliette and the Golden Age

Daudet's description of the port of Marseille in the 1860s bears some resemblance to Dumas' evocation of the Restoration era in *Le Comte de Monte-Cristo*, but it is obvious that there has been a considerable change of scale. Rather than the sporadic arrival of long-haul ships like the *Pharaon*, the horizon is now dotted with 'ships speeding away under full sail', whilst 'others, far off, were approaching slowly' (p. 92). Moreover, and crucially, unlike the *Pharaon*, the *Zouave*, on which Tartarin embarks for Algiers (p. 98), is a steamship, an example of the new technology which was revolutionising maritime transport.[3] Nor is the introduction of the steamship the only change that has occurred between the two novels: Tartarin's port is no longer the Vieux-Port of Dumas' era, but the result of the dramatic expansion in the last years of the July Monarchy and the first half of the Second Empire which made Marseille the largest and most important port in France and ushered in the city's 'Golden Age'.[4]

There had been three major impediments to the realisation of Marseille's potential as it approached the mid-century: the inadequacy of the Vieux-Port to deal with both the increasing volume and size of shipping; the poor transport connections to the North, reliant on roads and river-traffic along the Rhone; and the lack of a sufficient freshwater supply, which affected both public health and industrial output. These obstacles did not, in themselves, prevent the city from expanding rapidly between 1830 and 1850, when its population rose from 116,000 in 1826 to 156,000 in 1841, fuelled by an influx of immigrant workers, but they did hinder Marseille's ability to assume its 'pivotal role between Europe and the Mediterranean.'[5]

The legislation siting the new port at La Joliette, to the north of the Cathedral of La Major, was passed on 5 August 1844;[6] the first ships docked in 1847, and the work was completed in 1853. The docks, built on the models of Liverpool and London, were protected by an immense pre-fabricated mole, first developed in the construction of the port of Algiers. In fact, La Joliette rapidly proved insufficient to the constantly increasing demand and the new port crept northwards, eventually reaching the fishing port of L'Estaque. It was La Joliette and the northern docks which were to typify Marseille in the popular imagination in the last half of the nineteenth century and the first half of the twentieth, but they by no means eclipsed the enduring attraction, and activity, of the Vieux-Port, which still remained the centre of the Marseille fishing fleet and played host to a variety of vessels, sail or steam. In fact, the new basins and the Vieux-Port were only separated by the outcrop guarded by the Fort Saint-Jean: the populous quarter of Le Panier was astride the new and old ports and it was a short walk for sailors disembarking at La Joliette to the red-light district at the north-eastern end of the Vieux-Port.

Whilst the Vieux-Port was still seen as the authentic expression of Marseille, the new port at La Joliette and beyond was viewed with increasing suspicion by the local population, not least because its initial financing came from Paris and because, under the operation's director, the engineer Paulin Talabot, it became increasingly independent of the city, especially after the development of large-scale steam navigation. Under Talabot, the Compagnie des Docks et Entrepôts acquired a monopoly over all dock operations for ninety-nine years, covering La Joliette and the more recent basins of Arenc and Lazaret, and, in 1860, constructed a vast complex of warehouses, known as the 'Grand Entrepôt', a city within a city from which the rest of the population was excluded.[7] The modern working practices imposed by the 'Compagnie' included the replacement of the independent *portefaix* by an army of *dockers*: stevedores hired on a daily basis without tenure. The decline was dramatic: whereas in 1864 there had been 3,000 *portefaix*, by 1898 there were only 300 and, in 1914, a mere 183.[8]

The success of the new port was spectacular, in spite of the periodic crises under the Second Empire, with traffic, both incoming and outgoing, nearly doubling from 8,672 ships of 2,026,678 tonnes in 1860 to 16,601 ships totalling 4,107,048 tonnes in 1868.[9] The scale of increase can also be seen by comparing imports and exports over a longer period, from 1828, under the Vieux-Port and the Restoration, to the new port in 1860, with imports rising from 1,243,000 tonnes in 1828 to 5,088,000 tonnes in 1860, whilst exports rose from 487,000 tonnes to 2,926,000 tonnes in the same period.[10] The figures also show important changes in the major commodities being shipped, with coal, sugar, flour, bricks, tiles, metal products, linseed cakes and lumber replacing traditional commodities like olive oil, wines and spirits, soap, wheat, coffee and salt. Nevertheless, despite this progress, Marseille was still limited by its role as a predominantly Mediterranean port: in 1833, the total Mediterranean trade accounted for 71 per cent of all Marseille's shipping, with the West Indies and long-haul Atlantic routes accounting for just 18 per cent and the Far East only 2 per cent; in 1860, these figures had hardly changed at all, with Mediterranean trade at 72 per cent, the West Indies and Atlantic accounting for 11 per cent and the Far East rising to only 3 per cent.[11] It was not until the Third Republic, after the opening of the Suez Canal, that Marseille was to become a truly global port.

This modernisation and expansion of the maritime industry went hand in hand with the birth of the shipping lines whose names became synonymous with Marseille. The Compagnie de Navigation Mixte, which owned Tartarin's *Zouave*, was founded in 1850 and dominated the North Africa trade.[12] The Messageries Maritimes was founded in 1852 and was mainly associated with the Levant before later becoming the principal conduit to the Empire in Indo-China.[13] The Compagnie Fraissinet similarly specialised in trade with the Levant, Constantinople and Egypt, and it was one its ships, the *Asie*, which was the first to sail through the Suez Canal, an expression of its ambitions to profit from the India trade.[14] The Compagnie Nationale Transatlantique was founded by the Péreires in 1861 and used Marseille as a base, in addition to Le Havre, whilst the Compagnie Paquet, founded in 1862, served Morocco and Senegal. Finally, Talabot set up the SGTM (Société Générale des Transports Maritimes à Vapeur) in 1865 to transport iron ore from Algeria to Marseille, but rapidly diversified into carrying Greek and Italian emigrants, not merely to Algeria, but much further: to Rio, Montevideo and Buenos Aires. This trade proved immensely lucrative[15] and paved the way for Marseille's pivotal role as a staging post for Southern European and Middle Eastern emigrants en route to the Americas in the 1920s, and, incidentally, as a key player in the 'white slave' trade. At the same time, Marseille consolidated its role in international networks of passenger travel, when the English shipping line P & O set up the 'Grand Trunk Mail' service, which took passengers and mail from London to Marseille by land on the 'Bombay Express' before travelling by sea to Alexandria and then to the Red Sea by rail before re-embarking on the ship that would take them to Bombay,[16] a route which would become even more popular with British passengers after the opening of the Suez Canal in 1869.

Because France lagged behind Britain and Germany in railway construction, the P & O service had initially relied on the stagecoach for the French leg of the journey, but work was already under way on the rail connection between Marseille and Paris which was as essential to its growth and prosperity as the new port at La Joliette. The same year as the establishment of the P & O route, 1843, Talabot was awarded the concession for the Avignon-Marseille stretch of the line from Lyon and Paris, including a spur to La Joliette,[17] adding to his line from Alès to Beaucaire on the west bank of the Rhône to ship coal down from the Cévennes coal-fields. Subsequently, the Avignon-Marseille line was important in providing direct access to coal for Marseille and establishing a rail link with the river port at Arles. The new line was an engineering feat, crossing the chalk plateau of the Crau and boring through the tunnel of La Nerthe, opening in early 1848,[18] although Marseille had to wait until the completion of a final section through Lyon in 1856 for a direct rail link to Paris and the North. Subsequently, the Paris-Lyon-Méditerranée company was established in 1857, under the control of Talabot, the Rothschilds and Marseille investors,[19] although it aroused regional opposition by sidelining Aix-en-Provence and Gardanne in favour of Arles and the Rhône corridor and appeared to be a further example of Parisian economic colonisation, rendering Marseille merely a 'bridgehead for Parisian speculators.'[20] The completed railway ran from the Gare de Lyon in Paris to the Gare Saint-Charles in Marseille, a distance of 862 kilometres, which, in 1873, took over nineteen hours, although in its early years the journey was by no means luxurious, as Edward Lear, one of the early travellers, records in his correspondence.[21] Obviously, the railway and the new port fuelled each other's growth: the railway transported the coal to fuel the steamships and its own engines (until demand outstripped supply and Marseille began importing coal from North-East England and South Wales) and, with its spur line to the *Grand Entrepôt*, was essential to the expanding freight trade. At the same time, it enabled the increasingly rapid transit of passengers between Northern cities and the Mediterranean ports and further afield and fed the flourishing shipping lines on which Marseille's economy and image were built.

Along with the new port and the railway, the third engineering achievement to ensure Marseille's passage into the modern era was the canal bringing the waters from the Durance to the centre of the city. Work began in 1838, under the direction of the Swiss engineer Franz Mayor de Montricher, who, like Talabot, had studied at the Ecole Polytechnique and Ecole des Ponts et Chaussées, and was completed in 1848: an extraordinary feat comprising forty-one tunnels and sixteen aqueducts, including the Roquefavour Aqueduct, compared by one contemporary observer to the Temple of Kheops.[22] In its turn, the end of the canal in Marseille was enshrined in an ornate grandiose building, the Palais Longchamp, the gift of the water company to the city in return for the municipality's financing of the project, and which now houses the Musée des Beaux-Arts and the Musée d'Histoire Naturelle. As Emile Thémime points out, however, the benefits of the canal were not immediately obvious. Because most of the system was open to the air, there were problems with the purity of the water supply and, in any case, there remained a great deal of work to be done to distribute the water across the whole city.[23] Hence, as Zola suggests, the canal by no means eradicated cholera. Where the impact was most felt was in the industrial sector, affecting both the traditional trades of soap manufacture, flour milling and sugar and cooking-oil refinery, which were all enhanced by the acquisition of constantly available steam-power, and new developments in chemicals, especially soda, and metallurgy, machine tools, ship-building and steel.[24] As Marcel Roncayolo argues, the first wave of the industrial revolution of the early nineteenth century, rooted in coal and textiles,[25] passed Marseille by, and such technological innovations as did take place were often accomplished by outsiders, in particular by English industrialists in iron and steel, the Spanish Luis Figueroa in the lead industry,[26] or the international financier, Jules Mirès, who came from outside the city, but had important mining interests in the Gard, as well as owning the monopoly for the city's gas lighting and owned Marseille's only steel plant.[27] Nevertheless, as its export tables show, Marseille was always more than a colonial entrepôt recycling goods from its client ports, and constituted an industrial centre in its own right, supported by an extensive local banking infrastructure.

Finally, this industrial development, alongside the construction of the railway, the canal and the new port, transformed a relatively small city into a modern metropolis, nearly tripling its size between 1821, when the population had fallen back to 109,482, and 1872, when it reached 312,868, larger than Hamburg and just behind Barcelona, with an astonishing growth of 186%, outstripping Paris and Lyon.[28] This population growth was due almost exclusively to immigration, either from the surrounding departments to the north and east, or from the same Mediterranean neighbours encountered in *Le Comte de Monte-Cristo*, including Corsica, Italy, Spain, Greece and the Levant. This first wave of immigrants, some of whom originally planned to travel further, towards South America, amounted to 19,857 in 1831–36, 25,361 in 1841–46, rising to 40,610 in 1851–56 and 35,443 in 1861–66, whilst foreign nationals rose from 18,000, or 9.6 per cent of the population, in 1851, to 32,765, or 12.7 per cent in 1866, before steadily increasing to 21 and 22 per cent in 1906 and 1911.[29] Within this multi-ethnic context, it is important to emphasise the significance of Marseille's Jewish population, a feature which it shared with many of its Mediterranean neighbours, including Algeria. As Guiral reminds us, 'in this golden age of capitalism, the Jews occupy a place which they had never had previously',[30] rising from 458 in the census of 1808 to 1,684 in 1846, 2,113 in 1861 and 2,680 in 1872. This relatively small Jewish group, which was highly influential in international trade and had a monopoly over municipal transport, was remarkably well integrated, to the extent that the city council stated in 1868 that the Jewish population 'had merged with our great municipal families',[31] and that a new synagogue was opened in the Rue de Breteuil in 1864, partly funded by Mirès. With this influx of foreign immigrants, the urban structure changed, with working-class districts being established between the new Gare Saint-Charles and the port, especially Le Panier and the Belle-de-Mai, which included the sugar refinery and tobacco factory. By 1870, therefore, Marseille had assembled the principal elements crucial to its subsequent development: a modern port and rail connections, an independent industrial base with a reliable water supply, and a large, increasingly multi-cultural population. There was, of course, one additional crucial ingredient to this mix, the reason for Tartarin's expedition, the new colony of Algeria, with which Marseille's destiny was to be intricately linked in the future.

Algeria, Marseille and the 'Mediterranean System'

There may have been a trellis of masts in the port where Tartarin joins the *Zouave* in the 1860s, but they now conceal funnels for steam engines and the port and its vessels have immeasurably changed since Dantès' *Pharaon*, as has the port of Algiers to which he is heading, even though the colony was already a longstanding part of Marseille's history. A trading rival in the sixteenth century, a constant threat and irritant as a pirate port until the nineteenth century, Algiers, was already unusually close to Marseille, both geographically—at 750 kilometres, it was nearer than Paris—and emotionally. Yet the comedy in *Tartarin de Tarascon* derives not merely from the satire of Orientalism brought down to the level of the common man, it also relies on the discrepancy between the image of Algeria as a savage frontier-land and the reality of the coastal cities, especially Algiers itself, as sophisticated Western urban centres. This is already apparent during the two-and-a-half day journey: whilst Tartarin, clad in his faux-Arab finery, lies in his bunk tormented with sea-sickness and tortured by every turn of the propeller (p. 99), the rest of the passengers, 'officers rejoining their units, ladies from the Alcazar in Marseille, ham-actors, a rich Muslim returning from Mecca, a rich Montenegrin...' (p. 101), spend their time drinking champagne in the saloon with the captain, Barbassou, who has homes in both Algiers and Marseille and shuttles between them. It is only when the *Zouave* has entered the bay that Tartarin can see, 'on a hillside, the white city of Algiers, with its little matt white houses coming down to the sea, bunched together' (p. 103)—one of the first literary references to the mythical 'Alger la Blanche'. When Tartarin disembarks, however, and begins his journey to the hotel, he becomes aware of his mistake:

With his first steps in Algiers, Tartarin de Tarascon opened his eyes wide. He had imagined a fairytale, mythological oriental city, something between Constantinople and Zanzibar... He had landed in the middle of Tarascon... (p. 112)

The only exotic element is Tartarin himself, still in his Arab garb. The subsequent comic narrative is based on the discrepancy between Tartarin's own perceptions of his adventures—an Arab mistress and house in the old town, a lion hunt in the desert—and the reality: Tartarin has been entrapped in a brothel, and the 'desert', constituted by the suburbs of the modern city, is entirely domesticated with 'a plantation of artichokes, sandwiched between plantations of cauliflowers and beetroot' (p. 127). In fact, the 'pretty verdant coastline of upper Mustapha, with its Algerian villas, all white, glistened in the dew of the rising sun: you could have believed you were in the surroundings of Marseille, amidst the *bastides* and the *bastidous*' (pp. 127–8).

Tartarin's experience was by no means isolated or contrived. In the same period, the US Congressman Samuel S. Cox, an experienced Mediterranean traveller, had the same impressions as Daudet's hero, initially experiencing a 'special feeling as we passed out of Europe with our prow turned towards Africa',[32] and not disappointed by his first view of Algiers:

At first the city was a little triangle of white specks; then it grew into a city whose surroundings from the Sahel hills to the Atlas snowy mountains on the left, were full of real interest. Then the long low line of the coast came into view and the white square houses loomed up before the vision... We could perceive to the right the dark rocky inlets and forts which the corsairs made their lair; and, finally, we round into the jetties of the bay and the harbour, and were at rest in the tranquil waters of Africa.[33]

Yet the Congressman's impression rapidly turns to anticlimax: 'the French are here, for we see the soldiers and cannon... Nor is the city wanting in European comfort. The new Hôtel d'Orient received us', and Algiers is little more than a conveniently-situated Berber theme park:

Who would come so far to see so little? This is all that remains on this coast to mark the power of the Barbary corsairs who held Europe in fear so long?... It was the Orient, at the door of Europe. Forty odd hours of sea-going, and here we are in the very home of Abd-el-Kader, and among the children of the desert![34]

By 1866, the population of Algiers stood at 60,000, a fifth of the size of Marseille in 1872, and was predominantly French (21,000) or Southern European (20,000), with 11,000 Muslims and 7,000 Jews[35] out of a total population of nearly three million for the country as a whole.[36] As both Daudet and Cox record, Algiers soon acquired the characteristics of a small capital city, complete with the wide boulevards and square, a prestigious lycée, to be followed in 1882 by the Université d'Alger, and, the jewel in the crown, the Théâtre Impériale d'Alger, built between 1850 and 1853, and which housed the Algiers Opera. This cultural and intellectual life, supplemented by a rich music-hall culture, was an important component in Marseille's own cultural development, which maintained exchanges and collaboration with its 'twin' across the Mediterranean until independence in 1962.

The immediate impetus for the military conquest of Algeria in 1830 originated in Marseille, the result of a dispute over long-standing debts owed by the French government to the Ottoman dey of Algiers over grain shipments to Southern France during the 1790s, in which Marseille merchants were prominently involved. When the dey raised the issue with the French consul in 1827, the 'consul allegedly answered in a high-handed way that the august French king could not condescend to enter into correspondence with a North African potentate on a subject such as debt' and 'the dey took offense, lost his temper, swatted the consul six times on the arm with his ceremonial fly-whisk and ordered him out.'[37] The conflict escalated, resulting in a French naval attack on the city and the retaliatory destruction by the dey of the trading posts in the *Bastion de France*, causing a 'serious blow to French Mediterranean commerce, the cost to be born by Marseille traders.'[38] Eventually, in 1830, with no resolution in sight, growing domestic unrest against his regime, and pressure from the Marseille merchants, Charles X decided to teach the Algerians a lesson: a fleet set sail from Toulon on 25 May and on 5 July 'the French raised their flag over the kasbah',[39] beginning 132 years of colonisation.

A long campaign of conquest and pacification ensued, culminating in the capture of the Algerian leader, the Emir Abdelkader, in 1847, but not completed until 1871 with the defeat of el-Mokhrani. The campaign was accompanied by a policy of settlement designed to make the territory into a southern extension of the French metropole, with further port cities established in Bône (Annaba) to the east and Oran (Wahran) to the west, both of which developed steamship routes with Marseille, and the inland cities of Constantine and Orléansville (Al-Asnam). The settlement process was fraught with difficulties, not least because it became confused with the political deportations, especially after 1848–1851, and attracted emigrants from France and Southern Europe with the wrong skills—urban artisans rather than the peasant farmers the original agricultural plans for the colony demanded.[40] However, the fertile coastal strip proved a rich source of grain, vegetable and fruit crops, whilst the interior yielded considerable deposits of minerals, transported to the ports by new railways, for onward shipment to Marseille. During this first phase of French colonisation, after an initial increase from an estimated 1.5 million in 1830 to 2,554,100 in 1851, the overall population of Algeria remained remarkably static until the beginnings of the 1880s, peaking at nearly 3 million in 1862 but falling back by 100,000 in 1872.[41] This stability masks a catastrophic decline in the indigenous population, with mortality rates in the large urban centres outstripping birth rates by some thirty per cent between 1856 and 1872. The number of indigenous inhabitants fell from 2,307,349 to 2,125, 052, whilst the French population rose from 92,738 to 129,601 and that of other Europeans from 66,544 to 115,516.[42] In other words, as Robert Aldrich concludes, by the end of the Second Empire, 'with farms and vineyards, French-style cities and European settlers, Algeria was well on the way to becoming *Algérie française*',[43] and firmly anchored in the French, and Marseillais, identity.

In the case of Marseille this was the logical consequence of the dominant philosophy of the new port's founders. A significant number of the 'captains of industry and entrepreneurs' who contributed to the construction of the nineteenth-century city—the Talabots, the Péreires, de Lesseps—were Saint-Simonians,[44] for the most part engineers who were graduates of the Ecole Polytechnique and had espoused the quasi-mystical utopian belief in a society built upon reason and the collective mastery of natural resources. This movement wielded considerable influence in France under the July Monarchy and the Second Empire, and its members oversaw some of the major industrial and infrastructural developments in the country in the mid-nineteenth century. Saint-Simonianism, however, also had global aspirations, centred on the relationship between East and West, in which the Mediterranean was a natural fulcrum. These were founded on the nine-volume scientific record of Napoleon's Egyptian expedition, *Description de l'Egypte*, the reciprocal technological collaboration between Paris, London and the Egyptian Viceroy Mehemet-Ali, who had dispatched the giraffe Zarafa to Charles X. They were also part of the ensuing vogue for Orientalism, which often portrayed East and West in sexual terms and in 1831 led the Saint-Simonian Barthelémy-Prosper Enfantin, to 'liken the Orient to the flesh, the West to the Spirit: "The LAW is the PROGRESSIVE harmonisation of *flesh* and *spirit*, of *industry* and science, of the *Orient* and the *West*, of *woman* and *man*."'[45] The following year, his colleague Michel Chevalier expanded this sexualised metaphor, arguing that the Mediterranean, previously the zone of conflict between East and West, could become its 'nuptial bed', the birthplace of a new 'Mediterranean system', an 'economic and spiritual entity' rooted in material developments such as railways, steam boats, canals in Suez and Panama, the telegraph and international banking, and leading to vague aspirations for universal peace.[46] This 'Mediterranean System', the meeting point between Europe, Africa, Asia and the Americas, not merely enshrined some of the most significant strategic economic and political thinking of the mid-nineteenth century, but foreshadowed the pan-Mediterranean geo-political projects centred on Marseille in the interwar years, including those of *Les Cahiers du Sud* and Le Corbusier.[47] Moreover, it also built upon Marseille's natural long-term alliances with its Northern Mediterranean neighbours. Ferdinand de Lesseps, for example, was by no means unknown to the Marseillais. He was French Consul-General in Barcelona when, in 1842, 'Don Baldomero Espartero, Regent of Spain [...] pitilessly bombarded the city of Barcelona, the great commercial centre of the Western Mediterranean'.

Méry records that:

Marseille and Barcelona are sisters. They have numerous interests in common and whatever affects one inevitably affects the other. The news of the bombarding of Barcelona inevitably produced a profound sensation and soon from the Canebière to Saint-Jean, from the heights of the Rue Paradis to the heights of the Rue d'Aix, from the calm *quartiers* of

La Plaine to the Rue du Tapis-Vert, there swelled a massive cry of outrage. (pp. 204–5)

When de Lesseps returned to France, he received a hero's welcome from Marseille, with a splendid reception laid on by the Chamber of Commerce (p. 205), although this was not enough to get him elected as deputy for Marseille in the 1869 legislative elections.[48]

For the Saint-Simonians, it was Marseille which was to become the principal beneficiary of this Mediterranean System. As Chevalier continued:

> It is Marseille which holds the keys to the Rhône and the Mediterranean... Marseille can hold in its hands the Mediterranean trade with England, Belgium, Central Germany and Switzerland. Marseille is a necessary staging post on the route from England to India. Marseille as a business centre is called upon to attract the trade of a maritime entrepôt which has always flourished in the Mediterranean... Once we have completed the rapid and economical communications by steamboat and by railway, from Paris to Marseille, who knows what the Marseillais can make of their city?[49]

Marseille was poised to become 'the capital of the Mediterranean world' and 'the capital of Southern France just as Paris is the capital of the North',[50] an ambition which endured for 150 years.

This 'new Eldorado' delivered mightily in practical terms: the Saint-Simonians were the inspiration behind the Suez Canal, opened by Empress Eugénie in 1869, even though de Lesseps never acknowledged their influence,[51] and the canal was essential in establishing Marseille's links to India and the Far East. Similarly, even though the initial colonial and settlement project was a failure, Algeria reaped rich rewards for the Saint-Simonians who invested in it, particularly the Talabots and the Péreires, through their railway and mining constructions. It was also the Saint-Simonian, and, like Dumas, mixed-race Ismail Urbain who was the most influential policy-maker on the colony in the mid-century, fusing Napoleon III's vision of Algeria as an 'Arab kingdom' in the French Empire with a commitment to maintaining it as a French country.[52]

The importance of Algeria in the development and subsequent career of Marseille cannot be overestimated. It was one thing for the Marseillais to see their city and the Canebière as the centre of the world, or for this to be enshrined on the *table d'orientation* on the *Pont*

Transbordeur, but quite another for this same vision to be elevated to a geopolitical pseudo-philosophy which influenced colonial and post-colonial planning. As such, the relationship between Algiers and Marseille as the nexus of the new world order endowed the latter with considerable self-ambition and at the same time compounded its repu-tation in the French, and especially Parisian, psychology as a literally outlandish frontier town, on the very rim of France and Frenchness, and now with a quasi-official status as the gateway to France's 'far-west'. As with the American drive west, it did not matter that the result was the spread of an all-too recognisable European urban domes-tication, because Algeria still yielded a continuing frisson of the unknown, as the wars of pacification continued, whilst the coastal strip, with its cities of Bône, Oran and Algiers, held out the delights of a French California. At the same time, Marseille became a frontier city, which owed its new-found wealth and status to *l'Afrique du Nord* in general and Algiers in particular and forged an enduring economic, political and cultural attachment to its twin city 750 kilometres away, an attachment commemorated and mourned by César's monument to the Algerian *rapatriés* on the Corniche at Roucas Blanc.

Joseph Méry and Victor Gelu

The period which saw the conquest of Algeria, the construction of the new port, the coming of the railways and an efficient water supply saw a new self-confidence reflected in the development of Marseille's urban fabric and cultural life, chronicled by the city's most famous mid-nineteenth century writers, Joseph Méry and Victor Gelu.

Méry was not merely a native of the Quartier Saint-Jean,[53] where he was born in 1797, but also an important national literary figure, extremely well-connected in Parisian cultural circles; the author of a number of adventure novels, some of which were set in Provence; a distinguished librettist, best-known for Verdi's *Don Carlos*; and a promi-nent journalist. Towards the end of his life, in 1860, he published a collection of reminiscences and reflections, *Marseille et les Marseillais*, which constitutes an important document on the mid-nineteenth-century city, including an indispensable guide to the culture of *bastides* and *cabanons* in the surrounding countryside. Méry's first target is the tired joke about the Canebière which Dumas himself recycles in his introduction to *Le Comte de Monte-Cristo*:

> One day, a commercial traveller invented this phrase: 'If Paris had the Canebière, it would be a little Marseille'. He adopted a phoney Provençal accent, like all mimics, and provoked hearty laughter amongst his simple audience. (p. 50)

For Méry, this is part of a general caricatural perception of the city in the capital, akin to the mockery of the Irish in London (p. 51), by which a Marseille accent has become obligatory for portraying simple-minded servants on stage—a comic tradition which would persist in the twentieth-century Parisian music hall, through stars like Raimu and Fernandel and become an essential ingredient in the enduring success of Marcel Pagnol. This caricatural perception is easily explained. For the Parisian,

> Marseille is two hundred leagues from Paris; our common language is Provençal; we all learnt French as a foreign language. In Marseille we have no Collège Charlemagne, no Collège Bonaparte, no Sorbonne, no public education. (p. 51)

In fact, as Olivier Bourra points out, Méry was playing a complex double game in fashioning and marketing a stereotypical image of Marseille for his Parisian readers—including Dumas himself, who uses the jibe about the Canebière at the beginning of *Le Comte de Monte-Cristo*—whilst at the same time denouncing it.[54] He also does much to create a myth of Marseille criminality, built on the '*nervi*, a sort of Parisian street-urchin, but writ large' (p. 71), with all the allure and unreality of the Parisian *apache*. In response to this self-created image of a primitive, philistine, Marseille, which has proved remarkably durable up to the present day, Méry counter-attacks by displaying the city's urban and cultural developments. Marseille in the 1860s is not the frontier town of caricature, although it does have all the characteristics of a great port. To those passengers arriving by train or by steam boat it can offer elegant hotels, restaurants and cafés, like the Hôtel du Louvre on the Canebière, where Joseph Conrad's aristocratic Mr Mills stays in his novel *The Arrow of Gold*, or the Maison Dorée café on the corner of the Canebière and the Rue des Feuillots, where we are first introduced to the young narrator

Monsieur Georges.[55] The urban landscape had changed dramatically under the July Monarchy and, especially, the Second Empire, with the construction of the new cathedral of La Major between the Vieux-Port and La Joliette, the piercing of the Haussmann-inspired Rue Impériale (now Rue de la République) from the Quai des Belges to La Joliette, and the water company's Palais Longchamp. At the same time, whilst the Canebière itself, begun by the city's great classical architect Puget, is an impressive thoroughfare, unjustly mocked by the Parisians—'on a holiday, nothing is more beautiful than these great lines of architecture, ending in thousands of sails and flags.... a street bounded by the infinite' (p. 53)—the really impressive nineteenth-century Marseille avenue is the Prado, 'the most beautiful promenade in the world' (p. 53), outclassing even the Champs-Elysées, a broad and elegant thoroughfare prolonging the Cours Belsunce and the Rue de Rome to the south, and later extended still further by bending west and reaching the sea at what became the Plage du Prado. It is on the Prado that Conrad's heroine, Doña Rita, lives, in the faded grandeur of the painter Henri Allègre's mansion. It would become the grand avenue leading to the Exposition Coloniale of 1906.

At the same time, if architecturally Marseille is no longer the crude Southern port of Parisian myth, it is also by no means as culturally or intellectually deprived as it is often depicted from outside. Indeed, Méry compiles an impressive list of thinkers and writers, musicians and artists which would be the envy of any capital: 'If Paris, with its colleges and its million inhabitants, had a Canebière like that, it would be a great Marseille' (p. 52). This argument is supported to some extent by Pierre Guiral's reference to the founding of the medical school in 1818; a free music school in 1821; the 'Athénée', a forerunner of the university; the bookshop, the Librairie Laffitte, which opened in 1846; a thriving theatrical and operatic life; and a considerable interest in the plastic arts.

Marseille had two established theatres, the legal maximum for provincial cities at the time: the Grand Théâtre, founded in 1787 on the Place Beauveau, and the Théâtre du Gymnase, on the Canebière, founded in 1804. One chronic problem besetting both theatres, but especially the Grand Théâtre, was funding. The Gymnase was privately owned (Méry disparagingly refers to its proprietor as a 'sau-

sage manufacturer'), but the Grand Théâtre was the responsibility of
the city and struggled throughout its existence until the fire of 1919,
which ultimately destroyed it. These financial difficulties were a crucial factor in the uncommonly high turnover of directors: fourteen
between the Restoration and the Second Empire, and nine under the
Second Empire itself, a phenomenon attributed by the theatre's historian, Victor Combarnous, almost exclusively to financial deficits.[56]
Indeed, the first director under the Restoration, Armand Verteuil,
making the first of many requests for a subsidy from the municipality
for the 1816–17 season, highlighted the difficulties of running an
expensive opera purely on ticket sales and in the face of a variety of
competing entertainments:

> Since November I have been the victim of the lotto games in the cafés,
> which deprived me of my young audience in the stalls, of a dancehall
> which has depopulated the sailors and prostitutes in the gods. The bour-
> geois comedies and private balls have destroyed my Sunday revenue.[57]

As Combarnous records, this plea fell on deaf ears, and, whilst
Verteuil continued with a repertoire of drama and comedy, including
prestigious visitors from Paris, he cannily adapted to popular taste by
establishing a 'first-class lyric troupe', because 'opera, more than comedy or drama, had become the favourite entertainment for the regular
audience.'[58] This fashion proved durable, and was a passion which mid-
nineteenth-century Marseille shared with its Mediterranean neighbours. As Méry commented, 'never has a people better understood and
loved great music and great artists. Everyone sings, well or badly, in the
old town; all the workers know by heart *Moïse*, *La Favorite*, *Norma* and
William Tell' (p. 41). Not that the vogue for opera completely eclipsed
the success of big-name actors from Paris, like Méry's friend the trage-
dian Rachel, whose visit to Marseille in 1843 attracted such a crowd
after her performance at the Gymnase that her carriage was blocked
and she had to be ushered to her hotel by a phalanx of *portefaix*
(pp. 76–8). In other words, as Marseille's wealth and importance
expanded, so it could maintain, if sometimes precariously, two major
theatres and attract high-profile actors and singers.

The same tentative steps towards independent cultural growth took
place in the plastic arts. Marseille's Ecole des Beaux Arts was established in 1752, thirty-five years before the Grand Théâtre, and moved

in 1796 under the directorship of Joachim Guenin from its original location on the site of the arsenal to the Cours Julien, which it shared after 1806 with the Lycée Impérial (subsequently the Lycée de Marseille and then Lycée Thiers). As the Ecole de Dessin de Marseille, under Augustin Aubert from 1810 to 1845 and Emile Loubon from 1845 to 1863, it was a powerful force for training locally born artists, and particularly for developing a distinctive Marseille style, based upon certain concepts of landscape, which became known as the Ecole de Marseille.

The profoundly urbane Joseph Méry, equally at home in Paris and his native Marseille, was, like his protégé Dumas, an unashamed publicist for the city. In this respect, he contrasts markedly with his younger colleague Victor Gelu, now commemorated by a square just north of the Vieux-Port. Born in 1806 in the traditional working-class, Provençal-speaking district of La Bourgade, near the Porte d'Aix,[59] he became the most famous author from the city to write and perform in Provençal, collected in *Chansons Provençales*, of 1840, which shed light on the relationship between Marseille and the wider world of Occitan culture. At the same time, he was, like Méry, the author of a volume of memoirs in French, which remained unpublished until 1971, when they were edited as *Marseille au XIXe siècle*. They are, like Méry's commentary, a precious record of life in the city in the first half of the nineteenth century.

In spite of being born in La Bourgade, Gelu was not as much a *fils du peuple* as his supporters often implied. His father, a Spanish migrant, had become a prosperous baker, and Gelu was brought up in a relatively comfortable petit bourgeois setting, with a Catholic education which gave him both a solid grounding in classical French literature and a life-long anti-clericalism. The family's fortunes went into decline, however, with the death of Gelu's father in 1822 and he was forced to abandon his studies before the baccalaureate and instead take over the family business, although his efforts were rapidly undermined by his mother's improvidence and his own lack of dedication. His early career was marked by a nomadic existence, visiting Bordeaux and Paris; Toulon in 1830, at the time of the Algiers Expedition; and Lyon, where he witnessed the silk weavers' rebellion. He returned to work for his brother Noël, running flour mills, first in Aubagne and then in

Roquevaire, where he married and eventually retired. Gelu therefore experienced two key aspects of Marseille life in the first half of the nineteenth century: brought up in the inner artisanal city, he also knew the Marseille hinterland intimately, the countryside of the cabanons and bastides prominent in Zola, and later in Pagnol, and already threatened by the city's encroachment.

Emile Ripert concludes his study of the Provençal Renaissance by noting that:

> The most interesting—in fact, the only—poet produced by old Marseille was Victor Gelu, but he can really be considered a great poet, if not by the extent, at least by the intensity of his work. He immediately resembles a sort of Provençal Rousseau....[60]

Gelu owes his reputation as the great nineteenth-century poet of Marseille popular life to his immersion in the city and its outlying districts and, especially, to the popular cultural life which provided him with an apprenticeship and constituted his major audience. As an adolescent, Gelu had become fascinated by the theatre and was a regular member of the audience at the Théâtre-Français, later the Gymnase, and the Grand-Théâtre.[61] At the same time, as Lucien Gaillard records, he also 'frequented the little local theatres'[62] and became absorbed in amateur dramatics, especially in the Confrérie de la Tasse near the Porte d'Aix.[63] After his brief, semi-professional career with the Théâtre de la Colonne, which ended in 1829,[64] theatricality remained an indispensable quality in his writing, which, like most Provençal poetry of the time, was essentially declamatory and performance-based.

What Gelu's career illuminates is the extent and importance of the plethora of popular social organisations in the development of cultural activity in Marseille during the first half of the nineteenth century, including the *Athénée Ouvrier*, founded in 1845 and bringing together an exceptionally large number of working-class poets, to the extent that, in 1847, it played host to the left-wing hero Lamartine.[65] The *Athénée* was an early version of the *université populaire*, but, unlike the later models, designed and managed by the liberal bourgeoisie, it was a profoundly grass-roots organisation, run by its members as a 'literary society' and a 'proletarian Academy'.[66] Essentially, it was a forum for working-class poets and artists to display their work, and a typical meeting would include recitations, choral work and a display of paintings.[67] More importantly, like Gelu himself, it gradually gave primacy to Occitan as the privileged language of the Marseille and rural poor, going so far as to re-name itself as the *Athénée de Provence* in 1855.[68]

The meetings of the *Athénée* were supplemented by dinners at the Café de l'Europe and meetings of the Société des Purs, where Gelu first became known for his renditions of songs by Béranger, an experience which made him determined to become a *chansonnier*. He reserved the first performance of his own works, however, for another drinking and dining society, the Société des Frères Endormis, made up of 'mature men, many of whom were former soldiers... drinking, eating, laughing, playing piquet and singing every evening at the top of their voices and in great merriment.'[69] It was before this body, on 16 October 1838, that he performed his first, and most famous Provençal song, *Fenian e grouman* ('Idle and Greedy'), the first of fourteen songs in Provençal that he wrote between 1838 and 1840 and which constituted the first volume of the *Chansons Provençales*. As Gelu noted to his satisfaction, he was now 'sought after, invited, welcomed in all the well-off country dwellings and in all the smallholders' *cabanons* around Marseille'[70]—an interesting insight into the persistence of the itinerant troubadour into the mid-nineteenth century, serenading social gatherings and banquets and touring the villages of the hinterland.

Performance was integral to Gelu's poetry and the key to his phenomenal popularity. As Ripert comments, 'from time immemorial Marseille has held gatherings where people sing. It was its greatest pleasure... It was under the Restoration that these gatherings were the most in fashion...',[71] and we can judge the dramatic impact of Gelu's performances from the reaction of the high priest of the Occitan Renaissance, who described the performance of *Fenian e grouman* at the meeting of Provençal poets in Arles in 1852:

> Suddenly, at the corner of a table a man stood up. He must have been about fifty, a solid brown-haired man with broad shoulders. Without ado, he took off his jacket, bared his chest, turned up his sleeves to the elbow and, raising his naked athletic arms to impose silence, he began to sing.
>
> Was he hamming it up? I don't think so. He had to become a member of the populace again, with his bare chest and arms to express with emotion, with truth, the popular soul, and that day he was to sing the song of the lazzarone.

He sang us 'Fainéant et Gourmand', but with a force, an emotion and a rage which are impossible to copy. With his voice of bronze, bursting sometimes like thunder, with his proud appearance, his rough gestures, his natural comportment of a man of the people, he was beautiful, he was superb, and we applauded as if our hands would crack.

Thematically, Gelu's songs constitute an extraordinarily vivid evocation of the lives of the Marseille dispossessed:

He is the meticulous and passionate painter of the Marseille population... In his short poems, there is all the dishevelled poverty, all the hateful or placid vulgarity, all the salty language of the port workers, of the vagabonds stretched out in the sun, of the cobblers, of the lock-pickers, of the carters, and also the cynicism of those on the make, who, thanks to revolutions, can rise from the gutter to the banking houses.[72]

It is not easy, however, to extrapolate a coherent political position from what is essentially a poetical and theatrical rhetoric, and Gelu, whose second volume of the *Chansons Provençales* was censored in 1855, though for reasons of impropriety rather than politics, later rejected accusations of socialism.[73] In fact, in spite of his antipathy to the Napoleonic dynasty, he was closer to his idol Béranger in his beliefs in nineteenth-century liberalism, whilst at the same time giving voice to the frustration of the dispossessed, a voice which 'has the accent of 1793 and ... will be that of the Commune' and lends 'a terrible revolutionary accent to all his songs',[74] like those of Richepin and Jehan Rictus.

Whatever the exact political nature of Gelu's political project in his *Chansons*, it is clear that it is integrally bound up with the language he uses. Nonetheless, he distinguishes between the high cultural mission of Mistral's Félibrige and his own primary purpose, which is to communicate with the Marseillais urban population in their own vernacular. Ripert comments:

[T]here is an exact relationship, impossible to break, between the people and its language, or, rather, its patois. In order to paint the people, you have to use patois, just as using patois limits you to painting the people. It is not through national pride that he uses Provençal, but for artistic reasons, because the heroes he has chosen cannot express themselves other than in that way.

'My heroes', he will say, 'are Marseillais first and foremost. They do not think in French in order to express themselves in Provençal. They speak the patois of Marseille, and not the language, if there is a written language. Their dialect is the dialect of the streets, of the quays and the markets. It has nothing to do with the Dictionary of the Academy or with Provençal grammar.'[75]

And he concludes, 'if Mistral represents the people from the countryside around Arles, whose nobility had in its day something of the antique, Victor Gelu remained the violent, impassioned and proud poet of the Marseille plebeians.'[76] This geographical and social antipathy towards the northern Provençal writers was mutual and translated into the Félibriges' distaste for the apparent vulgarity of some of Gelu's poems, like the erotic fantasy in *S'eri Tur* ('If I were a Turk'), not assisted by his sense of superiority over writers he considered minor figures, including the Gascon poet Jasmin, with whom he lumped the Félibrige leaders, Mistral, Aubanel and Roumanille. For Gelu, the 'Troubadours' of Arles or Avignon were no match for the plebeian strength and authenticity of the Marseillais.

Undoubtedly, much of the mutual distrust between Gelu and the Troubadours was personal and rooted in class: the incompatibility of the cultivated bourgeois poets of northern Provence and the self-styled proletarian entertainer from the Southern city. Yet this personal antagonism masks a much more important divergence as to the nature and ambitions of Occitan culture and language. Whilst Mistral, Aubanel and Romainville were dedicated to a wholesale renaissance of Provençal culture, in which the preservation, codification and revival of the Occitan language was central, Gelu was not merely more pragmatic and modest in his use of the local language as a 'patois' which his readers and listeners spoke, he was also more realistic as to its future prospects, suggesting as early as 1840

> ...the Provençal idiom is dying... At the rate that this century is evolving, carrying off customs, habits, character, costumes and the old language... in thirty years this language will be as difficult to explain as the language of hieroglyphics for ninety-nine out of a hundred of our Marseille population.[77]

Thus, whereas the Félibrige was embarked upon a grandiose cultural project which would restore independence to Southern France and

reinstate Provence as a legitimate member of the Mediterranean community (a project which often, but not invariably, manifested itself in
explicitly right-wing politics), Gelu's frame of reference remains more
modest both geographically—limited to Marseille and its hinterland—
and temporally. For the next century, the two currents coexisted,
albeit with fluctuating fortunes on both sides. Under the direction of
Jules Charles-Roux, the Colonial Exhibition of 1906 was a celebration,
not merely of Marseille as an imperial port, but of its place as a capital
of Provençal culture. Meanwhile, as the twentieth century progressed,
whilst there was a general erosion across France of regional, and linguistic, distinctiveness, *Les Cahiers du Sud* was at pains to recognise
Occitanie as a vital component in the Mediterranean coalition, and, as
Izzo reminds us, in the last decades of the century, bands like Massilia
Sound Sysem used Provençal lyrics to assert their Marseillais identity
against the authority of the state.

Finally, Gelu is important, not merely for his Provençal-language
poetry, but also for the unique importance of his memoirs as a record
of Marseille at the time of *Le Comte de Monte-Cristo*, *Les Mystères de
Marseille* (*Marseille au XIXe siècle* contains an account of the de Roux
abduction case on which Zola based his novel),[78] and *Tartarin*, but dis-
appearing by the mid-century as rapidly as the city's popular dialect.
His earliest memories include the White Terror during the 100 Days,
when his own quartier was the scene of bloody persecution of
Bonapartist soldiers or Republicans (though he is careful to note that
most of the mob of thirty or forty brigands 'had a very pronounced
Avignon or Arles accent')[79] and the desecrations of the old city, like the
construction of the Arc de Triomphe at the Porte d'Aix.[80] He is also an
invaluable chronicler of the *crime* and *plaisir*[81] of nineteenth-century
Marseille: the apprentice *nervis* (the Marseille equivalent of the Parisian
apaches) who make up some of his youthful acquaintances,[82] and the
geography of pleasure of the city, which often followed, as it did in
Paris, the line of the customs wall, with taverns and cabarets springing
up beyond the reach of the city's taxes:

> All the *guinguettes* [were] established beyond and within the line of the
> *octroi*, but all the restaurants, cabarets and bars in all the hamlets of the
> area. The municipal tax zone was much more restricted than at present.
> It followed the old city walls from Saint-Victor to Castellane via the

Cours Bonaparte, the Quartier des Princes and the Quartier Breteuil…
[All around the city] we were known and welcomed like old friends by
all the hoteliers, even though we normally spent very little.[83]

Yet this idyllic city of the first half of the nineteenth century was no
more, and Gelu's memoirs essentially finish in 1851 with a gloomy
recognition that Marseille has fallen victim to the march of industrial
and financial progress, or, rather, greed:

The sight of this countryside once so cheerful, now needlessly disem-
bowelled by the vandals of property speculation in order to make space
more often for foul-smelling foundries, unhealthy factories, sordid
alleyways, miserable shacks for criminals, has always pained me… Oh,
the Marseille of my youth, where are you? What have you done with
your modest demeanour, your patriarchal customs, your colourful
language, your simple but picturesque costumes, your honest senti-
ments, the rough sincerity of your citizens, my contemporaries? You
have even lost your old landscape!… Where are the beaches on whose
sands I used to frolic in the summer sun?[84]

This elegiac tone is in stark contrast to the conclusion of Méry's memoirs, which are much more positive and optimistic, precisely because
they embrace the integration of Marseille and Provence into the French
nation. At the end of a promenade with some friends and his brother,
the city's archivist, along the coast north of the city to Carry, where the
Duchesse de Berry launched her doomed counter-revolution in 1832,
he looks back south to Marseille, from very much the same view as that
adopted by Loubon in his *Jour de marché*:

In becoming essentially French, Provence is inaugurating a new era.
Before long, Marseille will show the Mediterranean the mercantile and
industrial might of Liverpool and New York. The railways will complete
the work of the steamships; it will become one of the three or four
great centres from where the vitality of the world will fan out. And
what Liverpool or New York will never show is that nature has given to
this most fortunate city a benevolent sun which does not give rise to
any of the terrible plagues of the tropical world.[85]

Méry, the Parisian boulevardier and native of Saint-Jean, has no
problem in reconciling Marseille's exceptional status as a great port
with its French nationality, nor its expanding trade across the world
with its immunity from the risks of contagion. As such, he looks

forward, much more than Gelu, to the ebullient self-confidence of Marseille at the turn of the century, which we will explore in the next chapter.

3

MA PETITE TONKINOISE

THE EXPOSITION COLONIALE AND THE BELLE EPOQUE

In 1906, the young Marseille composer Vincent Scotto teamed up with
the lyricist Henri Christiné to produce *La Petite Tonkinoise*, the lament
of a French colonial soldier finishing his tour of duty in Indochina and
about to leave his Annamite lover:

> Ne pleur' pas si je te quitte
> Petite Anna, petite Anna, p'tite Anamite
> Tu m'as donné ta jeunesse
> Ton amour et tes caresses
> T'étais ma p'tite bourgeoise
> Ma Tonkiki, ma Tonkiki, ma Tonkinoise
> Dans mon cœur j'garderai toujours
> Le souv'nir de nos amours.[1]

The song became one of the classics of the French music hall and made
Scotto's name, leading to his later collaboration with Marcel Pagnol in
the 1930s as both as a composer and actor. It is testimony to a vigorous
popular culture in Marseille from the beginning of the twentieth
century.

The composition of *Ma Petite Tonkinoise* coincided with the Exposition
Coloniale of 1906, the first to be devoted entirely to the French colonies. Coming only seven years after the twenty-fifth centennial celebra-

tions of the foundation of Marseille, the exhibition was an important opportunity for the city to explore and publicise its identity, both nationally and internationally, at the beginning of the twentieth century. If the commemoration of the founding of the city celebrated the 'arrival in the West, 600 years before the birth of Christ, of civilisation',[2] the Exposition was designed to mark the city's role as the indispensable point of transit between France and Northern Europe and the French Empire. At the same time, Scotto's *Ma Petite Tonkinoise* is a reminder that the 1906 Exhibition was as much a cultural event as it was a celebration of the city's economy or imperial mission and that, as it entered the twentieth century, Marseille was beginning to develop its own cultural activity at all levels: from music hall, café-concert and cabaret to theatre and opera; from Cézanne and the painters of L'Estaque to the first generation of nationally-recognised writers, including Edmond Rostand, André Suarès and Edmond Jaloux.

Whilst the celebration of Marseille's foundation myth and its renewed role as *Porte de l'Empire* was generally welcomed by most sectors of Marseille society, it came at a complex time in the history of the city and did not entirely succeed in papering over all of the fissures which had become apparent in the last decades of the nineteenth century. Imperial expansion, facilitated by the opening of the Suez Canal in 1869, did not automatically entail an expansion in the port's prosperity, even though it was accompanied by a continuing rapid growth in the population. This population growth, in itself, was by no means unproblematic and placed severe strains on the city's housing and services, accompanied by moments of heightened tension between different ethnic groups: in particular, the Italian community at the time of the Franco-Italian rivalry for Tunisia and the beginnings of a policy by employers to break the power of the French unions by importing non-unionised labour from Algeria. Whilst these inter-ethnic rivalries were either nascent or, in the case of the Italians, relatively momentary, the labour disputes from which they often sprung are a reminder that, from the fall of the Second Empire to the First World War, politics in Marseille was highly polarised. A revolutionary tradition, marked by the Commune of 1871 and continuing with anarchist and socialist militancy throughout the first period of the Third Republic, contrasted with a vigorous Royalist presence, an echo of the 'White Terror' of the

Restoration, championed by Action Française and certain elements in the Félibrige.

The Twenty-Fifth Centennial and the Exposition Coloniale

In the third week of October 1899, Marseille organised a week-long celebration of the twenty-fifth centenary of the founding of the city in 600 BC, centred on re-enactments of the founding myth of the betrothal of the Gaul princess Gyptis and the Phocean seafarer Protis, who received the land around the Lacydon as a dowry, reflected in the settlement of Catalans including Mercédès in *Le Comte de Monte-Cristo*. As such, the anniversary was conceived as a celebration of Marseille's origins—in Greek civilisation and Middle Eastern skill in trade and intrepid travel—as a truly Mediterranean city, and positioned it as an exception in relation to both the French nation and its capital.

The event was an exclusively municipal affair, the brainchild of the Socialist mayor Siméon Flaissières, supported by the Chamber of Commerce, celebrating its three hundredth anniversary the same year, the Conseil Général, and the Syndicat de la Presse Marseillaise. Designed for local consumption, with little outreach to a regional or national audience, its activities were confined to a restricted area encompassing the Canebière and the Vieux-Port, especially the spot where the Phoceans first landed. This area was well suited to the activities planned for the celebration listed in the poster designed by the Genoan artist David Dellepiane, who had emigrated with his parents to the Quartier Saint-Jean in 1875 and became one of the city's most important graphic artists of the Belle Epoque:[3] a 'grand historical parade', 'nautical celebrations, games, a grand Venetian gala', culminating in the 'decoration and illumination of the major districts of the city'.[4]

If this was a genuine celebration of the port's history, with none of the commercial ambitions of most nineteenth-century exhibitions, it was by no means devoid of political connotations. As Emile Thémime notes, at this point in his career, Flaissières was 'a man of progress, whose first mayoralty was marked by a socialist commitment (single-priced public transport, free school canteens…)', who used the twenty-fifth centennial as a 'means of associating the population with this collective celebration. But also, in this period of nationalism and xenophobia, to re-kindle local patriotism by breathing life into a mythical past.'[5] In other words, his project was to tap into the regional and municipal tradition of Victor Gelu's radical populism and to demarcate it from the right-wing Provençalism of elements of the Félibrige and Maurras' Action Française. In the context of the creation of genuinely popular civic pride, it is by no means coincidental that the twenty-fifth centennial coincided with the foundation of the Football Club de Marseille, which, as L'Olympique de Marseille, was to become one of the major sources of municipal pride and cohesion.[6]

The 1906 Exposition Coloniale was a quite different affair, with much wider ambitions and a larger target audience. It was also sponsored by the state, the first national exhibition to be held outside Paris. The driving forces behind it were the veteran Marseille politician Jules Charles-Roux, one of the dynastic leaders of the Marseille bourgeoisie and local *député*, and his associate Edouard Heckel, who had arrived in Marseille in 1877, the date of the foundation of the influential Société de Géographie de Marseille. Heckel almost single-handedly transformed the city's colonial strategy, creating the Musée Coloniale in 1893 and the Medical School in the Palais du Pharo, in 1899, both of which specialised in research and documentation vital to the colonial enterprise; and, finally, the Institut Colonial, established in 1906 by the Chamber of Commerce, which became 'the real centre of colonial studies and documentation' in France.[7] As head of the Union Coloniale, Charles-Roux was the very public voice of Marseille's colonial interests on the national stage and a staunch defender of free trade against protectionism. A proponent of the French annexation of Dahomey in 1892,[8] he had served as an energetic director of the colonial section of the 1900 Paris Exhibition. When, in 1901, Heckel launched the idea of the first French exhibition to be entirely devoted to the colonies and to be held in Marseille,[9] Charles-Roux won over a reluctant municipal council, secured the endorsement of the state, and, in 1902, was appointed as the exhibition's director, with Heckel as his deputy.

Underneath Charles-Roux's pragmatic colonial objectives, namely 'to attract capital (to the colonies), to set up a mechanism and to retain and settle the colonists', his real motivation was unashamedly Marseille-centred: 'the Exposition Coloniale was a useful tool for a long-term political strategy which extended beyond Marseille but where Marseille could once again play a "capital" role, that of a genuine imperial metropolis.'[10] This long-term strategy was not immediately welcomed by the city council. Supporters of the project pointed to the continuing expansion of the French Empire, with the protectorate of Tunisia established in 1881, that of Madagascar in 1885, the Tientsin Treaty of 1885, recognising French Indochina, and the Congress of Berlin of 1884–5 preparing the division of Africa between the European powers,[11] making it second only to Britain in the colonial pecking order, with a near-domination of the Levant and North Africa, to be extended in 1912 with the Moroccan Protectorate. But opponents argued that this imperial expansion was taking place in the face of the domestic economic depression of the 1880s, heightened labour unrest in the port itself and, above all, the ambiguous consequences of the Suez Canal, which had by no means delivered the unassailable benefits heralded at the end of Méry's *Marseille et les Marseillais*. It was undoubtedly true that the canal, in making the long journey round the Cape redundant, had opened up India, China and South-East Asia to the Mediterranean ports, but by no means to the exclusive benefit to Marseille, which now found itself in renewed rivalry with Genoa and Trieste, connected since 1880 by rail links through the new Saint-Gothard Tunnel with the lucrative German and East European markets.[12] Also, as Thémime explains, 'the opening of the Suez Canal coincided with the accelerated development of mass steam navigation, with a consequential sharp fall in freight charges, causing a veritable "neutralisation" of the effects of maritime distance'.[13] In other words, freight transport costs were no longer the single determining factor in shipping goods to and from Europe, and Marseille lost one of its major trump cards to Northern ports like London, Hamburg, Amsterdam and Antwerp, which benefited from proximity to the industrial centres of Britain, Northern Germany and the Rhineland.[14]

Neither Charles-Roux nor the municipal council were unaware of the dangers posed by this transformation in the economics of the merchant marine or by old and new competitors in the Mediterranean and the North Sea. With the construction of the Bassin National north of La Joliette in 1888, and the beginning of the Bassin de la Pinède in 1890, local industrialists successfully broke the monopoly of Talabot's

Compagnie des Docks and laid the basis for local industrial development along the dockside. This was more than a taking-back of control
of ship-repairs and other port works, and embraced a new concept of
the role of Marseille itself: no longer a mere entrepôt, like a 'railway
station which a train passes through without stopping',[15] but a port
'where cargo, especially raw materials, can be retained for the greater
profit of local industry, whose products can then be redistributed to
the rest of France and abroad'.[16] This radical departure from the
Talabot plan, which used Marseille as a mere conduit of imported
goods, envisaged the city as an industrial and manufacturing centre, in
which the port would be a key component, but not the sole source of
activity. Clearly, however, colonial trade became a major factor in this
strategy and Charles-Roux could proclaim in 1906 that '[w]e have had
the wisdom and intelligence to convert ourselves into an industrial
city and to transform in situ the major share of the products which we
receive from the colonies and from abroad.'[17] In the long term, at the
very least, the colonies represented a valuable insurance policy, a
'storehouse for the future, the supreme hope for our industry and
commerce who see foreign markets progressively closing to
them...',[18] an optimism borne out by the fact that, whereas in 1903
colonial trade represented fourteen per cent of imports and thirty-
seven per cent of exports, in 1938 those figures had risen to thirty-
two per cent and sixty-three per cent respectively.[19] In addition, the
colonies represented a solution to the problems caused by the fractious Marseille labour market: the first Algerian workers were
recruited by the cooking oil manufacturer Maurel et Prom in 1907
and, three years later, more were hired in the sugar industry 'in order
to put an end to a strike without succumbing to the workers' demands
for a rise in salary';[20] by the outbreak of war in 1914, the Algerian
population had risen to 2,000, the beginning of a new phase in
Marseille's immigrant population.[21]

The 1906 Exhibition, which ran from 14 April to November, was a
success, confounding the initial scepticism of some of its critics. In
spite of a slow start, 1,800,000 visits were recorded, mostly from local
inhabitants, although an intensive publicity campaign, including
another striking poster by David Dellepiane, at major railway stations
and shipping offices, brought in people from further afield, especially

travellers transiting through the city:[22] the Gare Saint-Charles noted an increase of nearly a million passengers for 1906. In fact, because of the nature of the attractions, which combined fun-fair rides like the giant water flume, performers like the American dancer Loïc Fuller, the star of the 1900 Paris Exhibition, the popular *danseuses cambogiennes* and the *Cinématographe Indo-Chinois*, with recreations of Arab 'souks' and colonial sites, many of these 1,800,000 entries were multiple, with Marseillais coming back for more throughout the summer, facilitated by easy access from the city centre—a five-centime tram fare from the Place Castellane or a fifteen-centime trip along the Corniche, with a view of the sea—and a whole range of catering options, from exotic restaurants and cafés, where the Marseillais could have their first taste of colonial cuisine, to picnic areas.[23]

The decisive factor leading to the exhibition's success was its generous layout, in contrast with the cramped terrain allocated in the Trocadéro for the colonial section of the 1900 Paris Exposition.[24] A site of over thirty-six hectares, which was planted with a thousand new trees, allowed for a spacious layout and subsequently became an important item in the city's portfolio of open spaces, when it was bought by the maire, Amable Chanot, on behalf of Marseille, as a *parc populaire* matching the more aristocratic Parc Borély.[25] Now named the Parc Chanot, it is now the site of the annual *Foire de Marseille* (Marseille Fair).

The site of this *spectacle perpétuel*[26] included a long central avenue linking the Rond-Point du Prado to the major building, the Grand Palais, lined with fifty palaces or pavilions devoted to representative trades or the different colonies themselves,[27] and it 'was visibly designed to the glory of Marseille and Marseille trade.'[28] What the crowds came to see, however, were not these celebrations of Marseille's economic power, but what Eliane Richard calls the 'ville imaginaire',[29] built in light, easily disposable materials, and which created a fairy-tale collection of exotic buildings from all corners of the French Empire: the 'old' colonies, the Antilles, Réunion, India; followed by the North African territories of Algeria and Tunisia; Madagascar and the West African colonies; and, finally, Indochina[30]— all housed in ornate palaces and pavilions (the Cambodian pavilion contained a replica of one of the ruined towers of Angkor Wat)[31] and offering cultural displays, hitherto unknown gastronomies, and, above all, the semblance of being transported to an exotic country. It was this, above all, which associated Marseille in the collective imagination with the adventure, travel and exoticism which became the major selling-point of its shipping companies.

The Exhibition and Marseille Painting

Given the single-mindedness of Charles-Roux and Heckel in their use of the exhibition to promote the interests of Marseille as an imperial metropolis, and bearing in mind the frequent criticisms levelled at the city for its supposed philistinism, it is illuminating to discover just how important art and culture were to the project. From Dellepiane's *Art Nouveau* posters and prize certificates to the spectacles offered by Loïe Fuller and the Cambodian dancers, the concerts of Western and non-Western music, and displays of colonial sculpture and art, to say nothing of the possibilities of becoming immersed in colonial street life and food, the Exposition was a rich cultural experience. Nor was the celebration of Marseille confined to its own culture: the Pavillon de Provence, also called the Mas de la Santo Estello, from the name of the seven-pointed Félibrige star,[32] was accompanied by a wing of the Grand Palais devoted to an exhibition of Provençal art, reflecting the personal artistic taste of Charles-Roux and the Exhibition's artistic director Frédéric Mistral, and showing 1,252 works of art, produced by fifty-four artists, including members of the *Ecole provençale*—Barry, Cellony, Fragonard, Guigou, Van Loo, Monticelli, Puget, Stanislas Torrents, Seyssaud and Ziem.[33] The Exhibition, therefore, as a multi-media work of art in its own right, asserted not merely Marseille as an economic power at the fulcrum of the imperial project, but also as the centre of a regional, Southern, cultural entity completely separate from the suspect North, long the target of the Marseille free-traders, who saw the struggle between protectionism and free trade as one between Paris and Northern privilege and the South.[34]

The 1906 Exhibition coincided with a growth in cultural activity and production which outstripped anything seen before and which, for perhaps the first time, made it possible to talk of a coherent 'Marseille culture' in painting, literature and popular entertainment. Crucial to this cultural development was the fraught relationship with Paris, as Marseille explored paths between a proud, but sometimes sterile, parochialism and a subordinate role as a Parisian cultural outpost.

Nowhere was this tension more visible than in the development of painting in Marseille in the years between the Franco-Prussian War and the First World War. As Jean-Roger Soubiran notes:

> [I]f the major critics of the Second Empire were in agreement in recognising the existence of an Ecole de Marseille, under the direction of Loubon, things were very different twenty years later: the Parisian press rarely used the term, to the extent of making the Marseillais doubt it themselves.[35]

Earlier, the first modern painting of Marseille coincided with the founding of the Ecole des Beaux-Arts in the eighteenth century. Joseph Vernet's *Intérieur du port de Marseille*, of 1754, part of a series of paintings of French ports commissioned the previous year by Louis XV, established the template for subsequent depictions of Marseille, adopting a perspective from the present Quai des Belges looking out to the port mouth, bounded by the merchants' warehouses and the Mairie on the Quai du Port, with the Arsenal des Galères dominating the foreground on the Quai de Rive Neuve. On both quays the port is full of merchant ships, one outward-bound. The foreground shows a vessel unloading grain and the variety of workers associated with the port, from the fishermen and *portefaix* to the weights and measures inspectors. Significantly, the foreground shows a large number of figures in Turkish, or more generally, Arab, costume, reflecting the port's oriental trade links, later highlighted by both Dumas and Daudet.

Orientalism had been an important element in Marseille painting in the first half of the nineteenth century: Loubon himself went to Palestine in 1849, bringing back paintings on biblical subjects like *Jésus et la Samaritaine* and *Vue de Nazareth*, but also painted a *Razzia par les Chasseurs d'Afrique*, inspired by the campaigns in Algeria, in the tradition begun by Delacroix. With his encouragement, his pupil Fabius Brest went to Turkey in 1855–1859 and became a major Orientalist painter in the second half of the century, known for landscapes like *Un Caravansérail à Trébizonde* or *Les Bords du Bosphore à Bebeck*, in addition to Algerian scenes like the *Café Maure à Alger, café des platanes*. Similarly, Marius Engalière, who had studied under Aubert, produced numerous paintings of provincial Spain in the 1850s, before moving to landscapes of Italy, the Middle East and Algeria. Like its trading network, the painterly hinterland of Marseille includes the eastern and southern shores of the Mediterranean.

Overwhelmingly, however, the Marseille painters of the first half of the nineteenth century had chosen as their subjects the landscape and populations of the Provençal hinterland and coastline, and their work was primarily influenced by the naturalism of the Barbizon School, represented by Corot and Millet. Like Loubon himself, most of the Marseille painters of this period, who constituted the first 'Ecole de Marseille', worked within this framework. Auguste Aiguier (1814–1865), who was a student of both Aubier and Loubon, specialised in the effects of sunsets on the Mediterranean from various points on the coastline around Marseille, whilst specific adherents of the Barbizon School included Prosper Grésy (1804–1874), known for rural scenes from the Provençal interior, but most famous for his *Les Baigneuses*, which later influenced Cézanne, and Paul Camille Guignou (1834–1871). The two most important Marseille adherents of the Barbizon School, however, were Adolphe Monticelli (1824–1886), who influenced both Cézanne and Van Gogh, and Félix Ziem (1821–1911), whose own studio was also influential in training local artists. Ziem was helped early on in his career by Monticelli, and then went on to paint scenes from Venice and Constantinople, as well as Marseille and Martigues, and latterly became associated with Montmartre, where he moved in 1860. What is interesting about the first Marseille School is that, at the very time that the city and port were expanding and modernising, its painters, like Loubon in *Vue de Marseille*, in spite of hints at factory development, emphasise Marseille's pre-industrial past and celebrate its timeless rural context, much as Constable records a vanishing English countryside. It was only in the last quarter of the nineteenth century that Marseille painting began to recognise the potential of the industry and modern port as subjects. Before then, it remained stretched between its Provençal cultural heritage and the lure of the Mediterranean exotic.

The problem was that what had constituted the particularity of the Marseille School, its distinct Provençal realism, had, with exceptions like Ziem, already begun to exhibit a highly parochial character, which became accentuated during the Belle Epoque. Artists continued to focus on Marseille and its Provençal hinterland and often rejected contact with the national, or international, community. An exhibition of painting organised by the watercolourist Paul Martin in 1882 revealed the scope of the problem: 'out of 476 works displayed, 210–220 were produced by Provençal artists, with most of the rest being contributed by local collectors.'[36] In contrast, 'direct contributions from Parisian artists, the only ones really capable of stimulating local creation, were in the minority. Hence, the artistic inferiority of Marseille, the second city of France, overtaken by Bordeaux, Lille or Amiens.'[37] Similarly, Alfred Lombard, in *Une Renaissance provençale*, of 1966–7, 'described Provence as a desert and Marseille as a city in a state of complete lethargy.'[38] The 'Ecole de Marseille' appears as 'completely disconnected from the Parisian avant-gardes and recent progress' and 'in Provence, even the names of Cézanne and Van Gogh are completely unknown.'[39]

In the years leading up to the First World War, two remedies presented themselves, the one organisational and the other based on personal contact and cross-fertilisation. With the Exposition of 1906 at its centre and Jules Charles-Roux as its impresario, the pre-war years saw a succession of structural changes to Marseille artistic activity, involving societies, salons and exhibitions, the Ecole des Beaux-Arts, and contacts with other art-forms, notably literature, which opened the city's painting to a wealth of influences from Paris and beyond. During the same period, Marseille was 'discovered' and painted by a number of subsequently influential painters from the Parisian avant-garde, most notably Cézanne himself, who attracted the Impressionists, the Fauves and, especially, Braque, to the Marseille coast and, in particular, to L'Estaque.

Jules Charles-Roux was the patron and friend of many Provençal artists and became President of the Cercle Artistique in 1874, which he transformed into a powerhouse of contemporary art.[40] He was a champion of Mistral, who planned to make Marseille the 'centre of his dream of a Latin federation'[41] and had organised, with Philippe Auquier, the Provençal art section at the 'Exposition.'[42] Although Mistral's 'Southern separatism' coincided with his own antagonism to the dominance of the North, Charles-Roux was by no means confined in his artistic tastes to Provence and was open to all contemporary influences and contacts. Hence the massive importance artistically of the Exposition Coloniale, which constituted a revolution in Marseille artistic taste: 'a sort of awakening of artistic activity took place in Marseille in 1906, triggered by the revelations brought by the first Colonial Exhibition',[43] including 'non-western art forms, which permitted a renewal of the aesthetic vision analogous to the effect produced by primitive or Japanese art.'[44]

At the same time, the Exhibition crystallised the growing close relations in Marseille between painters and writers. Alfred Lombard notes that 'at that period links were forged between young artists, both painters and writers... who met at the Exposition Coloniale' and that he himself started to work closely with the poets Edmond Jaloux and Emile Sicard, editors of the review *Le Feu*, published in Aix and Marseille, 'who subsequently became key players in the establishment of publications and celebrations around Provençal art.'[45] At the Exhibition, he also met Mario Meunier, who also wrote for *Le Feu* and was Rodin's secretary, and later came into contact with Joachim Gasquet, the poet Xavier de Magallon, and the art historian Elie Faure.[46] What is interesting about this self-styled Provençal 'renaissance' is that it was conceived as neither isolationist, as its predecessors had tended to be, nor as a rejection of either regional cultural traditions or Parisian and international styles. Instead, it attempted to maintain a Provençal distinctiveness and identity whilst becoming open to wider influences, especially from Paris. In this respect, *Le Feu*, which was one of the forerunners of *Les Cahiers du Sud*, was able to combine a fiercely Provençal with a broader French perspective, just as Jean Ballard's editorship of *Les Cahiers*, whilst rejecting a regionalist label, saw Occitan culture as an important component in the humanist culture of the Mediterranean and its contemporary activity as an integral part of the European avant-garde.

In the years between the Exhibition and the War, Lombard's influence was again crucial through the organisation of the three Salons de Provence, which took place in 1907, 1912 and 1913. After the closure of Charles-Roux's Cercle Artistique in 1904, painters and writers had continued to meet in Lombard's own studio or in those of the artists Carrera and Cauvet, and decided to organise an exhibition which, contrary to the 'rubbish assembled by the Salon of the so-called Marseille artists', would introduce the work of young painters.[47] The Salon opened in the former premises of the Caisse d'Epargne on the Rue Nicolas in February 1907 and ran until April and was noticeable for showcasing, not merely Lombard himself and Chabaud, but Cézanne, shown for the first time to a Marseille public. In spite of what the critic for *Le Feu*, Henri Bérengier, called a background of 'monotonous and uninteresting' work, the 1907 Salon broke new ground in bringing to Marseille 'painters with modern tendencies who have the merit of novelty.'[48] In the two subsequent Salons, in 1912 and 1913, the aim was 'to show their compatriots a collection of canvasses which will enable them to be aware of the realities and promises of contemporary art.'[49] In particular, the two Salons revolutionised artistic consciousness and practice in Marseille, at a time when even the keenest Marseille artists had not yet seen an original canvas by Cézanne. 'In the exhibition (of 1912), Cézanne, Rodin, Renoir, Bonnard, Denis, Van Dongen, Friesz, Lebasque, Luce, Maillol, Marquet, Puy, Rouault, Roussel, Signac, Vallotton were displayed alongside works from the Provençal avant-garde.'[50]

This was doubly ironic, since, from the 1870s, there had been a stream of avant-garde artists visiting Marseille and, especially, L'Estaque, including Cézanne himself, Renoir, Monet, Signac and the Fauves, notably Derain, culminating in Braque's visit in 1908 and his extended stay in 1910, which marked his transition to Cubism. This raises an important distinction between the development of a locality as a creative artistic community and its use by visiting artists as a mere location, prized for its light and its landscape, but with little communal interaction and minimal contact with local practitioners, like Pont-Aven, Auvers-sur-Oise or Collioure. In the case of Marseille, this problem is by no means confined to painting in the late nineteenth century and it runs, from Dumas onwards, through its depiction in literature and film, but it is neatly summed up in the ambiguity of the English translation of the title of Marielle Latour's *Marseille et les peintres* as *The Painters of Marseille*, which encompasses both painters originating in the city and those who used it as a subject.

The most instructive example is Cézanne himself, who first visited L'Estaque in 1870 and stayed for ten months, producing one painting, the pre-Fauvist *La Neige fondue à l'Estaque* ('Melted Snow at l'Estaque').[51] He came back on many occasions during the next sixteen years, especially for an extended period in 1882–3, not least in order to hide his liaison (eventually marriage) with Hortense Fiquet, as well as their child, from his father, and produced a considerable number of canvasses using L'Estaque as a subject. As Marielle Latour points out, at that time the port was:

> reached by rail or by horse and carriage along the stony coastal road. A suburb more or less, centred on a large fishing village, already urbanised, with a few simple hotels—Hôtel Mistral, Hôtel des Bains—frequented by the lower middle classes on holiday. Anchored to the coast by its ramrod chimney, with the brick kiln spreading a large red patchwork cover from the cobalt of the sea up to the hillside pitted with the ochres of the quarries. On the flanks of the white cliffs rose the first factories, one above the other, like espaliers or staircases. On the triple-vaulted viaduct, a plume of grey smoke from a train would appear out of a clump of pines.[52]

As Cézanne himself described it, 'I have rented a little house with a garden in L'Estaque just above the station and at the foot of the hill where the rocks start behind me with the pines. I'm still busy with painting. I have some excellent views here, without being exactly motif-like…'[53] Now in the 16th Arrondissement of Marseille, L'Estaque in the early years of the Third Republic was that mixture of the modern and industrial and the old-fashioned and bucolic which had so captivated the Impressionists on the Seine between Auteuil and Argenteuil. Moreover, as Latour hints, the architectural and geological features of the village coincided with Cézanne's experimentation with geometrical shape, taken to its ultimate conclusion by Braque.

Although Cézanne welcomed his friends to L'Estaque in the early 1880s, notably Monet and Renoir, whose *L'Estaque* dates from 1882, he had little contact with any Marseille artists, with the exception of the aging Monticelli, whom he admired, and the younger Charles Camoin, who was introduced to him by Signac, who became, in his turn, a devoted painter of the Vieux-Port. He met Monticelli, twenty years his senior, in 1883, and they sometimes painted together, although Monticelli worked mainly in his studio and there is no overlap in their styles—if anything, the use of colour in Monticelli's *Avant-port de*

L'Estaque, of 1871–83, has more affinities with Fauvism than with Cézanne. Working essentially on his own, Cézanne used L'Estaque in the period 1880–86 to pursue his experimentation with colour and form, culminating in the *Maisons à L'Estaque*, of 1880–1885, which 'more than anticipates the arrival of Cubism.'[54] However, he abruptly abandoned the village as a subject in 1886, citing its over-population and increasing urbanisation as reasons for his departure. In fact, as Marielle Latour suspects, the motivation was technical:

> … more a question of principle than of boredom. There was nothing more to be learned from L'Estaque… The growing importance of the jagged outlines of the Marseilleveyre hills; the prisms representing the town; all these foreshadowed the need for subjects like the Sainte-Victoire or Bibémus.[55]

In working with a few chosen visitors with similar interests and remaining largely aloof from the wider local artistic community, Cézanne was by no means unusual in his relationship with L'Estaque and Marseille as a whole. The same primacy of technique over allegiance to a particular locality was at the root of the relationship between the Fauves and L'Estaque, and Marseille in general, although it was mitigated by their relations with Marseillais Fauvists like Camoin and the Provençal artists Seyssaut and Chabaud. The problem becomes clearer with attempts to define Fauvism itself and its adherents. For Judi Freeman, it was 'not a movement, but made up above all of elective affinities amongst artists… the powerful expression of a double ambition to break with academic painting and the later, fading variations of Impressionism.'[56] As such, its membership was notoriously fluid:

> A principal nucleus around Matisse, Derain and Vlaminck, with whom were associated, for diverse reasons…, Braque, Dufy, Friesz, Manguin, Marquet and Puy. There was also an inner periphery comprising Camoin, Valtat and Van Dongen, and an outer one composed of Czobel, Girieud and Rouault, and, finally, painters who were stylistically close, including the Provençal artists Seyssaud and Chabaud.

Apart from their few Provençal associates, the vast majority of the Fauvists were from the North—Paris, Le Havre, Chatou—and were attracted to the South in general because of its light, its geological features and its landscape. In this respect, however, Marseille and L'Estaque, although often important as subjects for some of the Fauvist painters, were no more important, and sometimes less so, than other Southern locations. Matisse's adoption of Collioure, on the Spanish border, where he stayed over long periods between 1905 to 1907 and where he played host to Derain, Vlaminck and Braque,[57] was far more important to the development of Fauvism than L'Estaque, as, indeed, was his discovery of Algeria in the same period. It is true that Derain, Braque and Friesz were in L'Estaque in 1906[58] and that they painted scenes from the coastline around Marseille—Martigues, Cassis, La Ciotat—but, with the exception of Braque, there is little evidence that the region was of any special significance for them, nor that they had any contact with local painters. Indeed, even local Fauves took care not to stray from their fellow avant-gardists: as Camoin wrote to Matisse, 'in Martigues, I will mainly come across regional painters, and they have the advantage that they all paint ad infinitum the same motif. Outside of a certain corner, covered with shavings that you would find in a studio, you are guaranteed to be left alone.'[59]

If L'Estaque and the Marseille coastline merely offered to the Northern Fauves the opportunity to continue the experimentation already begun elsewhere, the case of Braque is more compelling, not least because his work on L'Estaque coincides with a transition from his brief Fauvist period to the beginnings of Cubism and because, as with the case of Cézanne, the geometry and geology of the landscape are crucial. This revolution can be seen clearly in the movement from the Fauvist *L'Estaque*, of 1906, to the paintings of 1908, such as *La Route de L'Estaque* and, especially, the *Maisons à L'Estaque*, which are early examples of Cubism.[60] However, as Marielle Latour poins out, 'it is the "Viaducts" which open the story of Cubism',[61] with the transition from the first *Viaduc*, of 1907, still recognisably Fauvist, to the second one, *Viaduc à L'Estaque*, rejected by the Salon d'Automne the following year, marking at least one of the births of Cubism. Although L'Estaque may not have played a defining role in the development or elaboration of French Fauvism, it was undoubtedly important in the progression of Cézanne's style and the Cubist revolution.

Finally, it is important to recognise the relative prominence of avant-garde painters from Marseille and Provence during the Belle Epoque, who often had more than a foot in Paris, but who retained links with their origins. On the 'periphery' of the Fauves, the oldest was René

Seyssaut, born in Marseille in 1867, who had trained at the Ecole des Beaux-Arts and was recognised by Matisse himself as a precursor of Fauvism.[62] Charles Camoin, born in 1879, was, like Seyssaut, trained at the Ecole des Beaux-Arts before moving to Paris in 1897 and studying in Gustave Moreau's studio, 'the crucible of Fauvism', where he met Marquet and Jean Puy.[63] Assimilated into the Fauves, as a 'junior member', he became based in Paris, but visited Marseille, especially in 1904, when he produced two major canvasses, *La Rue Bouterie* and *Le Vieux-Port et Notre-Dame de la Garde*.[64] In addition to Chabaud, born in Nîmes in 1882, and Verdilhan, who, although born in the Gard in 1875, moved to Marseille two years later, a more significant figure was Pierre Girieud, born in Paris but brought up in Marseille and who had a studio in the city. In Paris, through his meeting with the Montmartre ceramicist Paco Durio, he met Gauguin and exhibited successfully with dealers like Berthe Weil.[65] It is not surprising, therefore, that, as a Marseillais, he was present in the summer of 1906 in L'Estaque, along with Braque, Friesz and Derain. In addition, he rapidly acquired an international reputation, especially in Germany, where he was taken up by the Expessionists and the Blaue Reiter group. Finally, the story of Fauvism and Marseille concludes with Albert Lombard, and his vision of a *Renaissance Provençale*. He was born in 1884, the youngest of the Provençal Fauves and studied, like many of his compatriots, at the Ecole des Beaux-Arts before moving to Paris, where his work was shown at the Salons d'Automne and the Salons des Indépendents. As Sophie Biass-Fabiani comments, however, it is paradoxical that Lombard, whose work 'corresponded the most exactly to the definition of Fauvism',[66] was slightly cut off from the group because of his age and 'did not reach artistic maturity at the same time as they did.' Moreover, he had few personal links with other Fauves, except Derain, whom he met in Paris and not in Provence. In other words, it would appear that a genuinely Marseillais Fauvist School was difficult to sustain without the life-support system provided from Paris.

The Literature of the Belle Epoque

The same is largely true of literature in Marseille during the period between 1870 and 1914. Most authors who wrote about Marseille in the nineteenth century, were, like Dumas, Daudet and Zola, by no means native to the city, and those who were born Marseillais either, like Méry, became half-Parisian or, like Gelu, remained anchored in the vernacular culture. In the same way that talented provincial artists gravitated naturally to the capital, young Marseillais writers were tempted to follow the same path. Whilst during the Belle Epoque there was no recognisable 'school' of young Marseille writers, for the first time, in the 1860s and 1870s, there were born members of a generation which would go on to make a considerable national impact, represented principally by Edmond Rostand, André Suarès and Edmond Jaloux. All three had been students at the Lycée de Marseille (now Lycée Thiers), which had been founded in 1802 and was as important for Marseille writers as the Ecole des Beaux-Arts was for painters: the literary, and specifically dramatic, ambitions of Marcel Pagnol, himself a student at the Lycée de Marseille, were nourished by the example of his predecessor Rostand.

Unlike Pagnol, however, Rostand, born in 1868, came from Marseille's bourgeois elite. His father, an economist and member, along with Jules Charles-Roux, of the Académie de Marseille, was a powerful figure in the city's business world and part of a local mercantile dynasty. With his family's wealth, Rostand, after his studies at the Lycée de Marseille, went on to Paris, where he began his literary career, with a volume of poetry, *Les Musardises*, and two early plays, *Le Gant rouge*, of 1888, and *Les Romanesques*, of 1894. The following year, *La Princesse Lointaine*, was performed at the Théâtre de la Renaissance, and transferred to London, starring Sarah Bernhardt. In 1897, a biblical drama, *La Samaritaine*, opened at the Théâtre de la Renaissance. Whilst none of this early work was particularly distinguished, it demonstrated the young Rostand's versatility. Above all, to break into the most prestigious theatres in Paris at an implausibly early age indicated a promise subsequently confirmed by the overwhelming success of the verse drama *Cyrano de Bergerac*, which opened at the Théâtre de la Porte Saint-Martin on 28 December 1897, when Rostand was just twenty-nine, and ran for over three hundred performances, making Rostand the most famous French contemporary playwright. *Cyrano* was followed by another verse play, *L'Aiglon*, of 1900, produced by and starring Sarah Bernhardt, and depicting the life of Bonaparte's son, which was another major success—so much so that Rostand was elected to the Académie Française in 1902, at the age of thirty-four, the youngest writer ever to be so honoured.

What is significant about Rostand's writing is that, apart from the Troubadour hero of *La Princesse Lointaine*, there is no debt to his Provençal, let alone Marseillais, background, even though he spent the period from 1903 to 1910 working in Provence on his final, unsuccessful, drama, *Chantecler*. Instead, his rapport with the public came from a canny cultivation of Neo-Romanticism, packaged in an archaic verse structure and set in a past which, in the case of *La Princess Lointaine*, is allied to the idealised fantasy worlds of Maeterlinck and Wagner, and which constituted a challenge to the materialism of the late nineteenth century and its literary and dramatic expression in Naturalism.

Rostand died, in 1918 during the Spanish Influenza epidemic at the age of fifty, and never wrote about his city of birth, although his final work, the long poem *Le Vol de la Marseillaise* ('The Flight of the Marseillaise'), originally published in the *Revue des Deux Mondes* in 1917, contains a stanza on the adoption of Rouget de L'Isle's hymn in the Rue Thubaneau in Marseille.[67]

In contrast, both Suarès and Jaloux, in spite of spending long periods in Paris, never entirely lost sight of Marseille. Suarès followed a trajectory which was as different from that of Rostand as is possible to imagine. Born in 1868 into a wealthy Marseille Jewish family, he lost his mother when he was seven and then his father, originally from Genoa, after a long illness which wiped out the family fortune. A star student at the Lycée de Marseille, he went to the Ecole Normale Supérieure, but failed the *agrégation* in history and, bankrupt, returned to the South in 1895, living in poverty as a recluse in Roucas-Blanc for almost three years before setting out again for Paris at the age of thirty in 1897.[68] His experience in the capital, however, was far removed from the instant success of Rostand, and required painstaking efforts in literary journalism, essays and poetry before he became established. However, it is a measure of the status he had achieved that, in 1912, he became one of the key figures, along with Gide, Valéry and Claudel, in the management of the *Nouvelle Revue Française*, then France's most distinguished progressive literary journal. Despite falling out with its editor Jacques Rivière after 1914, Suarès returned to the *NRF* in 1926 under Jean Paulhan and remained until the Occupation in 1940.

Unlike Rostand, Suarès' cultural homeland was very much the Mediterranean, with an adolescent passion for Greece which persisted throughout his life, although he never actually visited, and a later fascination with Italy, which he tramped to on foot in 1895, and which was the subject of the *Voyage du Condottière*, of 1910. Despite his highly ambiguous feelings for Marseille, which had bored and stifled him during his adolescence and rejected him on his return from Paris, he retained a natural affinity with Provence, which he considered a 'Greek colony', epitomised by the village of Les Baux which he visited every year and where he was buried. In contrast, perhaps influenced by Gauguin's paintings from Pont-Aven and Wagner's and Maeterlinck's medievalism, he was also fascinated by Brittany and Celtic culture, fantasising about his possible Breton origins.

In 1931, Suarès published *Marsiho*, a collection of what almost amount to prose poems on Marseille and which constitute a final reconciliation of his fraught relations with the city of his birth. *Marsiho* moves across the topography of the city, from the Vieux-Port to the Cours Belsunce and the Grand-Rue, from the Sainte Victoire to the Bonne Mère, and from the Château Borély to Roucas-Blanc, before concluding with the Grand Lupanar, an acknowledgement to Marseille's Latin poet Petronius and a reference to the red-light district which became the focus for depictions of the city in the interwar years and the object of retribution in 1943.

Despite everything, Marseille's heart and soul manage to survive:

> The anarchy of Marseille is its tide: the flood of races rises and, wave after wave, seems about to submerge it. In vain: the antique and ever-young Marseille, the female lair of joy and energy, re-establishes its order: the instinct for living is an ebb-tide more powerful than anarchy. The Greek and Provençal essence of this people resists the swell of chaos.[69]

What is interesting is that Suarès' perspective, and style, belong to the 1900s, rather than to either the journalism of Albert Londres or contributors in the 1920s to *Les Cahiers du Sud*, like Louis Brauquier or Gabriel Audisio. There are more references to the masts of sailing ships than there are to ocean liners, and the text Suarès provided for Germaine Krull's *Marseille* in 1935 seems strangely mismatched to her modernist photography and celebration of steel architecture. The book begins with a description of the view of a distant Marseille from the Château Fallet, described by Méry, and Suarès approaches the city from L'Estaque, much as the Fauves and Braque would have done—through the industrial nightmare of the industrial quarters of Arenc.[70] Suarès ends his collection with a chapter entitled 'Sur le môle', which depicts the departure of a steamship carrying away travellers who will never return:

> As the ship reaches the open sea, Marseille reveals itself. All grime disappears, with the noise. There is no more ugliness or vulgarity… Everything is a mirage, everything is pure. Marseille is, at present, the oasis of pink and lilac… Marsiho, adieu! Adieu, Marseille![71]

Not only does this conclusion reflect both the emotions of the passengers leaving the port for ever and Suarès' own departure, it finally resolves Suarès' tensions with Marseille and re-seals the city's oneness with Provence and Mediterranean culture as a whole, all couched in a style borrowed from Impressionism and post-Impressionism.

The same retrospective vision governs the late work of the third member of Marseille's literary generation of 1870, Edmond Jaloux. Born in 1878, he was the youngest, but also studied at the Lycée de Marseille, where, like Pagnol a generation later, he founded a small journal, the *Revue Méditerranéenne*, the first of his many associations with literary journalism. His collaboration with Emile Sicard on the journal *Le Feu*, based in Aix, was instrumental in opening the dialogue between progressive writers and painters at the time of the 1906 Exhibition. Unlike Sicard, who remained in Provence, continuing to edit *Le Feu* and direct its publishing house, and becoming a respected poet and member of the Félibrige, Jaloux moved to a French government post in Lausanne, before becoming a distinguished literary critic, producing books on both French and German literature and writing for the magazines *Candide* and *Les Nouvelles Littéraires*. As a successful psychological novelist, often setting his work in Provence, he was elected to the Académie Française in 1936.

Towards the end of his career, in 1941, he published a novel, *Le Pouvoir des choses*, which is a remarkable depiction of the claustrophobic world of the decaying Marseille aristocracy in a period 'long before the War'.[72] Narrated by the aged Horace Badetty, who lives in a remote *bastide* in Les Caillols, now part of Marseille's 12th Arrondissement, just east of Saint-Barnabé, the novel depicts the increasing and contagious obsession of his cousin, Louis de Brignolles, with indiscriminate antique-collecting: 'the power of things' in the title. The novel's importance, however, lies in its evocation of a society and a topography which had vanished by 1943, and, indeed, by the First World War itself. Jaloux's Marseille is not the familiar territory defined by Joseph Méry's Canebière, the Grand-Cours where the royalists of *Le Comte de Monte-Cristo* live, or the Second Empire villas on the Avenue du Prado in *The Arrow of Gold*, and still less the working-class quartiers of Le Panier and the Belle-de-Mai. Instead, it is to be found in the dark, gloomy streets near the Cours Lieutaud, centred on the Rue Fongate, where Louis de Brignolles lives: 'A little three-storeyed house with three windows at the front. A house without character, of sad appearance, as they all are in this street inhabited by modest folk.'[73] This is a Marseille resembling the claustrophobic, oppressive towns of Balzac's Loire, and the only brief moments of escape are to be found in the countryside and coast: the narrator's own home in the still rural Les Caillols, the walks he takes with his future wife, Janine de Casteyrie, along the valley of the Huveaune, on the Plage du Prado or to the property they plan to buy in Saint-Menet. Set during the Combes administration at the time of the 'Affaire des Fiches', when the War Minister was accused of keeping records on Catholic and Royalist officers,[74] *Le Pouvoir des choses* provides an invaluable insight into a rarely-seen aspect of Marseille at the time of the Exhibition, the dying days of the Legitimists of *Le Comte de Monte-Cristo*. At the same time, much as the gloomy Rue Fongate may resemble Balzac's Saumur in *Eugénie Grandet* or Mauriac's Bordeaux, Jaloux is insistent, as the former Editor of *La Revue Méditerranéenne*, on the Southern culture by which his characters are defined. When Louis' aunt, the old Ursule de Brignolles, dies, even though 'she had lived as a complete recluse for years',[75] all the relatives take part in a very public formal outpouring of grief. As the narrator concludes, 'her death left everyone indifferent, but it was a matter, I think, of a Mediterranean rite, almost an Oriental one, of a sort of *vocero* for several voices, a meeting of public mourners, as seen in Greek and Roman antiquity at funerals'.[76] At the end of his career, during which long periods were spent away from the South, Jaloux, like Suarès, retained a powerful sense of the Mediterranean cultural identity of which Marseille, even at its least exuberant, is a part.

Popular Culture

Finally, if the Exhibition was a celebration of Marseille's pre-eminent role in the forging of the French Empire and proved a powerful impetus for the city's artistic development in both painting and literature, it was also, and perhaps above all, a popular entertainment, visited by a cross-section of the population on several occasions, and, as such, the pinnacle of a vibrant popular culture which had developed from the Restoration onwards.

In theatre and opera, the Gymnase and the Grand-Théâtre continued to welcome audiences, although the latter still lurched from crisis to crisis due to insufficient funding. This culminated in the decision in 1897 of the Flaissières administration to remove the municipal subsidy in favour of public health, education, housing and social care provision, and the Grand-Théâtre was closed, with performances being transferred to the Alhambra music hall and the Gymnase. This aroused such opposition that the municipality was forced to reverse its decision the following year, although this time Flaissières stipulated a reduction in the price of seats occupied by the working classes.[77]

In contrast to the constant precariousness of the Grand-Théâtre, the music halls, café-concerts and cabarets went from strength to strength. The most famous music hall was the Alcazar, opened on the Cours Belsunce in 1857, initially as a café-concert, where the clientele could sit at tables drinking and smoking whilst watching the entertainment. Gutted by fire in 1873, it reopened in 1889, the same year as the inauguration of the Moulin Rouge in Paris, with a mixture of local performers and celebrities from the capital. The Alcazar was a truly inclusive venue, with the stalls occupied by the city's bourgeoisie, many of whom were shareholders, and cheaper seats taken by the petit bourgeois shopkeepers and artisans. Like the Funambules in Carné's *Les Enfants du Paradis*, the upper galleries, the 'gods', were the preserve of the working class, who were the true 'connoisseurs' and whose vociferous approval or scorn could make or break a performer's career.[78] The Alcazar was not the only music hall in Marseille, and it was followed by the Alhambra and the Palais de Cristal, which opened on the Allées de Meilhan in 1880.[79] The inner city music halls were joined in the late 1880s by the growth of the Plage du Prado as an entertainment centre, linked to the city by the tramway in 1879, which made the Parc Borély and the beach an attractive excursion in the heat of summer. The most successful venture in this new centre of leisure was the Casino de la Plage, which opened in 1888 as a café-concert, with an outdoor music hall running from June to August. After some initial hiccoughs, including the banning of gambling in the Bouches-du-Rhône department in 1894 and the rival attractions of the beach itself, the Casino re-opened in 1900, with a successful mixture of a popular orchestra and well-known performers in the café-concert, together with vaudeville performances, including an irreverent pastiche of Rostand, *Cyrunez de Blaigerac*.[80] In addition, by the outbreak of war in 1914, popular theatres and music halls also included the Variétés and the Châtelet-Théâtre, together with new cinemas like the Modern, the Régent, the Trianon and the Eldorado.[81]

These forms of modern entertainment were accompanied by a passion in the 1890s for sports, often in the form of associations or clubs which practised several sports under one umbrella, of which the most prominent were the Sporting Club de Marseille in 1893, and the Football Club de Marseille, founded in 1897, becoming L'Olympique de Marseille in 1899.[82] The club's first football match, played on its home ground in the Parc Borély, was in 1902 and thereafter the OM went on to become a dominant force in regional and national football, with an increasing number of supporters and members, including the actor Harry Baur. This expanding popular culture, especially in the city centre, which reflected the growth of the population in general and the increasing numbers of passengers in transit through the port, was made possible by improved street lighting and, especially, expanding public transport, notably in the form of the tramway system, introduced with horse-drawn trams in 1876 running over eight lines, and growing to over 100 lines by the First World War, after the electrification of the network from 1892 onwards.

In addition to the music halls, café-concerts and cinemas, which played to a broad social mixture and a whole range of popular tastes, one phenomenon stands out, which testifies to a more sophisticated and bohemian clientele. The growth of Montmartre-style cabarets in Marseille, in imitation of the Chat Noir, which opened in Paris in 1881, began in 1889 and 1890. In 1889, Horace Bertin, the President of the Marseille press and Méry's successor as major publicist for the city, established the Confrérie du Dahlia Bleu at 20 Rue Paradis, which every Wednesday became the Taverne de la Cigogne, in which young bohemians recited their work, 'just like in the Chat Noir.'[83] The following year, the owner of the premises in the Rue Paradis, Théodore Sirdey, put on a shadow-theatre (*théâtre d'ombres*), which had become one of the major attractions of the Chat Noir's programme, and, in August 1892 the Montmartre company itself was invited to perform at the Alcazar. This popularity of Montmartre cabaret mushroomed, with J. Mestré's 'Very Provisional Marseille Chat Noir' on the first floor of the Café de la Bourse and the Café Méridan, which then re-appeared in May–June 1893 at the Café Martino, the Taverne de l'Epoque and the Concert des Courses. By the end of 1893, the Compagnie de la Lune Rousse[84] met regularly at the Café Martino, followed by the opening of new dedicated cabarets, like the Café de la Souris, at 8 Rue Haxo, the Cabaret des Truands, at the Café de l'Univers, and the Cabaret de Trèfle, at the Boîte à Musique, at 5 Rue Pisançon. After 1914, new cabarets opened, like Ouistiti, Tabaris, Pupu's, Le Cabaret Poupon, Le Merle Blanc, Le Chat Rieur and La Pie qui Chante—all on or around the Canebière, which became 'like a corner of Paris'.[85] This bohemian, though rapidly gentrifying, culture, made up of young journalists, writers and artists, provided that fruitful cross-fertilisation between Parisian and Marseille culture which never quite took off in the literary generation of 1870 or the Provençal development of Fauvism, and laid the ground for the growth and reception of Modernism in Marseille after the War, as the city and its regions embarked on a new cultural chapter.

PART TWO

4

THE WICKED CITY

THE PORT IN THE INTERWAR YEARS

The original Montmartre model served as the bridgehead to the early
twentieth-century avant-garde in literature and painting, but its
Marseillais imitators were less successful. Cultural renewal and innovation after the end of the First World War came instead from a combination of the Parisian avant-garde and the cultivation of Marseille's
Mediterranean roots in ventures like *Les Cahiers du Sud*. Simultaneous
with these new intellectual and artistic trends came the rise of a new,
dark mythology surrounding Marseille, which underwent major demographic and topographical changes in the early 1920s. Travellers' tales
in the interwar years rehearse and compound this mythology of the
'wicked city'. The British travel writer Basil Woon, for example, in
From Deauville to Monte Carlo: A Guide to the Gay World of France, warned
his readers off Marseille:

> Thieves, cut-throats and other undesirables throng the narrow alleys
> and sisters of scarlet sit in the doorways of their places of business,
> catching you by the sleeve as you pass by. The dregs of the world are
> here unsifted... Marseille is the world's wickedest port.[1]

In the end, though, the criminal reputation of interwar Marseille
comes down to something as banal as hats. Evelyn Waugh's novel of
1927, *Decline and Fall*, has a brief episode in which the hapless Paul

Pennyfeather visits the Quartier Réservé on the Vieux-Port, whose reputation had clearly, by this time, become international. Tasked by his fiancée Margot Beste-Chatwyn to secure the safe transit of two of her 'girls' to a waiting boat for South America, the former theology student flies from Paris to Marseille, dines at Basso's on 'bouillabaisse and Meursault' before taking a cab to Chez Alice in the Rue de Reynarde. The 'scene could scarcely have been more sinister had it been built at Hollywood itself for some orgiastic incident of the Reign of Terror',[2] and, before losing his hat to a young prostitute who attempts to lure him into retrieving it, he is accosted by 'a negro sailor, hideously drunk, (who) addressed Paul in no language known to man, and invited him to have a drink.'[3] Pennyfeather flees, conducts his dubious business the following morning when the quarter is calm, and returns to London. The episode is clearly built on Marseille's by now established reputation as a major Southern European point of transit disproportionately notorious as an international centre of vice and corruption.

Most accounts of the city in the interwar years make persistent reference to this habit of prostitutes in the Quartier Réservé stealing the hats of foreign tourists passing underneath their windows. The practice can be portrayed as merely playful, but also as downright sinister when it comes to cases where the victim attempts to retrieve his property and is lured inside to be mugged or even murdered. Whilst there is no doubting that this image was rooted in fact, the important question is why and how Marseille achieved, in the years after the First World War, this exceptional image of wickedness.[4] It is certainly true that Marseille had a *quartier réservé*, a red-light district established in 1863 for transitory seafarers on the north-eastern corner of the Vieux-Port and centred on the Rue de la Bouterie, 'between the Rue de la Raynarde to the East and the Rue du Radeau to the West, the Rue de la Caisserie to the North and the Rue de la Loge and the Rue de Lancerie to the South', in which the prostitutes occupied the old town houses of the aristocracy.[5] This is hardly sufficient, however, to distinguish Marseille from other large European sea ports with their world-famous red-light districts, like Le Havre's Rue des Gallions, Rouen's Rue des Charettes or Hamburg's Reeperbahn, all chronicled by the great pathologist of the interwar underworld, Pierre Mac Orlan.[6]

It is true that, before the First World War, voices had been raised, not least by Jules Charles-Roux, against the increasing militancy of the

Marseille workforce, especially the dockers, which had elected France's first Socialist mayor, Siméon Flaissières, in 1892. His election had 'a serious effect on our reputation in France and abroad' and 'diverted our commercial traffic to rival ports',[7] but this was part of the campaign in favour of the Colonial Exhibition and the stock-in-trade of conservative politicians across France at the turn of the century. It is also true that the war itself, which firmly established Marseille as the principal French colonial port, with massive troop movements inwards from the Empire to the Western Front and outwards to the Middle East and the Balkans as part of the *Armée de l'Orient*, helped forge the image of the city as a base camp for a constantly fluctuating, often foreign, military population. Yet the same could also be said of Le Havre in the North, which, although not quite on the same scale, also played host to troops from Britain and its Empire and, after 1917, from the United States, without incurring the same inordinate criminal opprobrium. Perhaps more serious for the city's reputation was the recurrence, in 1914, of the old suspicion about the depth of Marseille's loyalty to France as a whole. After the retreat of the French army in Lorraine, Senator Auguste Gervais placed the blame firmly on the shoulders of the XVth Corps, made up of a majority of Provençal, and especially, Marseillais, troops,[8] in spite of the fact that the 141st Infantry Regiment, recruited directly from Marseille, had sustained appalling losses in August 1914, with the loss of twenty out of fifty-four officers and 1,400 out of 3,000 men, including a famous athlete and a *député*.[9] The myth of the population's allegiance to Marseille itself and to the South, rather than to the French Republic, which went back to the bizarre *ville sans nom* (nameless city) sanction of 1794, still had considerable traction. It is perhaps the perception of Marseille as a Southern port city, not quite part of France, as a frontier town between the familiar North and the exotic South, as a border city between the hygienic and the filthy, between order and disorder, between tidiness and rubbish, that accounts for its 'bad reputation'. Most commentators from the interwar years and after insist on the defining role of the city's *ordures* in their evocations of Marseille; these take on extensive social and political, as well as aesthetic and symbolic implications.[10]

Marseille, Ville-refuge

Despite its relative isolation from the various fronts, Marseille was by no means immune from the effects of the conflict. Not only did it suffer the same loss of its young male population as other cities closer to the fighting, its trading status, despite a boost during the war itself, was seriously damaged. The major problem was that, with the collapse of the Ottoman Empire, and the Russian Revolution and Civil War, Marseille's traditional trade with the Eastern Mediterranean and the Black Sea was seriously disrupted and its freight traffic suffered in consequence, falling to its 1895 level whilst passenger numbers did not reach pre-war levels until 1924.[11]

Nevertheless, by the mid-1920s the port had largely regained its pre-war status, at least until the Depression of the 1930s. With improved rail journey times from Paris, now down to ten and a half hours, the port was not merely the obvious point of departure for North Africa and the French colonies in West Africa and Indo-China, it also benefited from the temporary collapse of the German shipping industry and the temporary eclipse of Trieste; it was a powerful rival to the Italian ports of Genoa and Brindisi for the lucrative passenger trade to India and the Far East. Indeed, just as before the war, many British travellers found it quicker and more convenient to join a ship at Marseille for the journey to India or China than to take the longer route from London through the Bay of Biscay and the Straits of Gibraltar. One of the early signs of Marseille's recovery was the resumption, in 1919, of the Indian Trunk Mail service (the *Malle des Indes*), which connected London with the P & O ship waiting at Marseille via the Bombay Express train.[12]

From 1927, these passengers in transit would be funnelled down the new monumental staircase of the Gare Saint-Charles, with statues representing France's colonies, towards the Canebière, now extended to include the newly-broadened Avenue de Noailles, with its luxury hotels and grand cafés, the Riche, the Glacier, the Commerce or the Noailles, the haunt of local businessmen and travellers,[13] or, for the more modest, down the Rue des Petite Maries to the Cours Belsunce. Whilst writers and journalists, like Waugh or Albert Londres, or businessmen and grand British imperial functionaries made their way through the Porte de l'Empire to the city and port below, staying at the luxury hotels on the Canebière, most of these transient travellers were the foot-soldiers of the colonial enterprise and the trading networks which predated it, and, as Richard Cobb reminds us, their experience was far from glamorous:

> Perhaps, in an interval between hustling from the Gare Saint-Charles to the port of la Joliette, the transient, on his outward journey, might spend the night in a noisy, carpetless, stone-floored hotel room in the cours Belsunce or in the quartier de la Bourse. But, in his flickering sleep, he would be drifting in a sort of geographical limbo or already ahead of himself physically, in a gently throbbing ship.
>
> He might take a meal, or several meals, in a large restaurant facing the Vieux Port... He, the transient, is rather like a drowning sailor who clings on to a piece of floating wood... Actually, he is removed by thousands of mental kilometres from those sitting opposite... and something of his apartness would be communicated to them too.[14]

Hence:

> Such literature as concerns Marseille has been written by strangers and by travellers on their way somewhere or other, whose only reason to be in the city would be to get out of it, and so only aware of the place as a point of resting or waiting, preferably brief, but always uncertain or unwelcome duration.[15]

Although this judgment is something of an exaggeration, in post-war Marseille the isolation of the traveller in transit was briefly matched by the alienation of the existing population in the face of massive demographic changes resulting from the war, exceeding even the immigration into the city during the Belle Epoque.

Thémime notes that 'the new immigrations... give to the city, or at least to its centre, a more remarkable cosmopolitanism than before',[16] quoting Joseph Roth's comment, 'Marseille is the crossroads of the nations', and Londres' remark on the second Colonial Exhibition, in 1922, that 'if you want to see Algeria, Morocco, Tunisia... give me your hand. I'll take you to the rue des Chapeliers'. This new diverse population resulted from the huge loss of life during the war, compounded by massive levels of war injuries, which led Marseille, like the nation as a whole, to have recourse to immigrant labour in order to replenish the workforce. Thus the population of the city rapidly accelerated to 652,000 in 1926,[17] of which approximately one quarter were foreign, as opposed to thirteen per cent in 1870.[18] The vast majority of this immigrant population were from the Mediterranean, and the largest share was contributed by Marseille's immediate neighbours in Italy, and Spain, especially Catalonia, Valencia and Murcia, places already solidly implanted in the city's life. The new Italian population settled in the narrow streets of Le Panier, between la Joliette and the Vieux-Port (home also to a new wave of Corsican immigrants who arrived in 'exceptional numbers' in the 1920s)[19] and came mostly from Piedmont and Liguria, although there was a significant representation from Naples. In the case of Spain, many immigrants who had come to Marseille to replace Italian workers conscripted into the Italian army during the war remained in the city, with a population of some 15,000 in 1930, a figure which undoubtedly rose during the Civil War.[20] Finally, this post-war surge in immigration from Marseille's traditional sources was supplemented by new influxes from Greece and Algeria, especially Kabylie—the Algerian population rose from 2,000 in 1914 to 8 to 10,000 in 1939—whose communities, although smaller, were well-established; and also by immigrants from West Africa.[21]

The new factor in the composition of Marseille's post-war population was the upheaval in the Ottoman and Russian Empires, which had not merely disrupted traditional trade links—they were the port's second most important suppliers and clients[22]—but had also caused a large-scale refugee crisis. These migrants, who, as both Thémime and Londres point out, did not necessarily intend Marseille to be their final stopping-point, were made up mainly of inhabitants of the Eastern Mediterranean coast, Syria and Lebanon, 'White Russians' (a notoriously nebulous term), and, most important, Armenians, who had 'survived the deportations and massacres of 1915' and 'scattered to diverse cities of the Eastern Mediterranean, before leaving, in a second wave, for more distant destinations when the Lausanne Treaty, in July 1923, put an end to their hopes of an independent Armenia.'[23] In Marseille, this new Armenian population, which numbered 16,000 in 1923, rising to 20,000 in 1936,[24] was the object of fierce racist opposition, unexpectedly led by the mayor, Siméon Flaissière, who, in a famous letter to the prefect in October 1923, warned against 'a redoubtable current of immigration of people from the East, notably Armenians', bringing with them 'smallpox, typhus and the plague', and 'deprived of everything, opposed to our Western customs, rebelling against all measures of hygiene, immobilised in their resigned, passive, ancestral passivity...'.[25] This denunciation by an erstwhile liberal and socialist provides an important corrective to the cosy image of Marseille as an automatic place of welcome.

What this influx of immigration of the early 1920s, welcome or not, did, however, was create, or at least reinforce, the image of Marseille as both a predominantly Mediterranean and working-class city.[26] In a revealing phrase, Thémime comments on 'the durable settlement and survival of an Italian colony which ended up by feeling, if not French, then certainly Marseillais'[27]—an important distinction which lends weight to accusations of Marseillais separatism and looks forward to Michel Samson's analysis of the 2005 French urban riots,[28] stressing the allegiance of Marseille's immigrant communities to the city rather than to the nation. At the same time, the demographic map of the city was changed, with different populations occupying different quartiers: the Corsicans and new Italian immigrants in Le Panier, for example, with more established Italian communities in the Belle de Mai or La Petite Sicile, and the Armenians in the outlying districts, like Saint-Antoine, Saint-Jérôme, Beaumont, Saint-Loup or Saint-Julien.[29] However, and by no means for the last time, the city's infrastructure was totally inadequate to deal with the massive surge in its immigrant population, and the newcomers found temporary accommodation in the Cours Belsunce, before being housed in former army camps on the periphery, like the Camp Mirabeau or the Camp Oddo, whilst several hundred Russian exiles were herded into the Camp Victor Hugo, a 'veritable bidonville' near the Gare Saint-Charles.[30] When Marseille encountered a similar wave of immigration after the Second World War, from North Africa and Indo-China, it was no better prepared and had recourse, not merely to a similar system of camps, but, in many cases, to the very same camps.

In the early 1920s, this newly arrived immigrant population not merely reinforced Marseille's position as a Mediterranean and working-class city, it also led to a realignment of status within the working class. The rapid decline over the previous sixty years of the rural population within the city's boundaries, reduced to a community of small-holders and market-gardeners, was balanced by a rise in the *gens de mer*, sailors and fishermen, who, with industrial workers, accounted for over half the population in 1935.[31] Moreover, the new immigrant population permitted social mobility amongst the more established communities, especially the Italians, who made up the majority of dockers in 1900, but who in 1938 accounted for only 1,500 out of 7,000, replaced by a thousand Spaniards, a thousand Armenians, and 1,400 North Africans and West Africans, together with 3,000 recently-naturalised French citizens.[32] As Olivesi concludes, 'in two generations, social mobility proved possible for many Italians, for example into the building and food trades.'[33]

The visitor to Marseille in the 1920s, therefore, would have encountered a strongly working-class city which was highly cosmopolitan, politically to the left and geographically divided along the west-east axis marked by the Vieux-Port, the Canebière and the Palais Longchamp, to the north of which lay the industrial quarters, the new port and the workers' *quartiers*, leaving the south as the preserve of the bourgeoisie. Just to the north of this frontier, on the Vieux-Port, the Quartier Réservé, the object of Paul Pennyfeather's fleeting visit, became the focus of attention, by virtue of its exoticism, vibrant delinquency and sheer squalor: a combination of factors which contributed disproportionately to the city's reputation and sealed the quartier's fate in 1943. In addition to the episode recounted by in *Decline and Fall*, the late 1920s provided two important fictional guides to Marseille's most notorious area, Claude McKay's *Banjo* and Edouard Peisson's *Hans le marin*, both of 1929; they were preceded by an important reportage on the city as a whole in Albert Londres' *Marseille, porte du Sud*, of 1927.

Albert Londres, 'Marseille, porte du Sud'

In the 1920s, Albert Londres was the most famous living French journalist. The doyen of French foreign correspondents, and to a large extent the genre's founder, he had a spectacular career as a war correspondent during the First World War, before becoming an investigative reporter in Russia, the Balkans, North and West Africa and, especially, the Far East. Indeed, it was on his return journey in 1932 from China to Marseille that he died in a mysterious fire on the liner *George-Philipar* as it crossed the Red Sea, prompting rumours of a conspiracy to silence him. What distinguished his work was not merely his highly critical reports on the effects of Western colonialism, but his pioneering use of the book-length grand-reportage, which allowed him to collect and pursue his investigations in depth. One example was *Marseille, porte du Sud* ('Marseille, Gateway to the South'), of 1927. In this book, Londres reflects that, although he has travelled through Marseille on countless assignments to the wider world, he has never actually stopped in the city itself. As he notes in his introductory chapter, the coat of arms of Marseille should include a gate, for the simple reason that, apart from the indigenous population, it is essentially a city of transit, which the visitor is expected to 'pass through' rather than dallying: '"To pass through!" The term suits the city. You go to Lyon or Nice. But you "pass through" Marseille.'[34] Londres, who had previously only 'passed through' the city on the way to cover stories across the world, decided that, for once, he would go no further and would unearth the stories of Marseille itself, subjecting it to the same scrutiny as he devoted to his foreign correspondent's stories.

Part of Londres' narrative is the staple diet of the professional journalist, the exotic elements of Marseille as they feature in the national imagination, the crime and drugs which already dominated the popular press in the 1920s. In one chapter, 'The Mysterious Opium "War"', Londres even dons his old war correspondent's uniform to follow the police in their investigation of drug-trafficking through the nocturnal city (pp. 103–115), while in another, 'Le Maquis', he explores the rich world of Marseille criminality, through its back-street bars and the *caïds* who operate through them:

> The underworld is in its element here. As it is anywhere, there is no lack of scum, for the terrain is rich. They do everything here: preparations for 'multiple crimes' or 'one-off crimes' (a 'multiple crime' is one which is preceded or followed by a murder), receiving of stolen goods, false passports, false papers.

> White slave trade. Transformation of jewels. Money laundering. Forging of identity papers. Sale of tools of the trade: knives, revolvers, knuckledusters.... This is the city of crime (pp. 118–9).

By the 1920s, the criminal reputation of Marseille had changed dramatically from the pre-war mythology of the petty-criminal *nervis* to that of powerful organised crime, the preserve of the new waves of Corsican and Italian immigrants and built upon prostitution, including white slavery, protection and, especially, the import, refining and distribution of Far Eastern opium through the port in what became the heroin boom of the 1920s.[35] The development of organised crime in Marseille in the 1920s was important, not merely because it compounded the growing myth of the city as a criminal capital akin to Chicago, but also because the Marseille gangsters were largely responsible for the growth of the underworld in Paris, especially in Montmartre, the Faubourg Montmartre and the Champs-Elysées.[36] In this way, the Marseille Milieu, represented by the Corsican Paul Carbone and the Italian François Spirito, supported by the Corsican politician Simon Sabiani, became nationally famous and featured frequently in burgeoning crime magazines like Gallimard's *Détective*. With a prominent underworld organisation, readily identified through its charismatic leaders, with alleged access, through figures like Sabiani, to real political power, and supported by corrupt municipal officials and police, the Marseille Milieu, with its tentacles reaching out as far as Paris, assumed the role of Chicago in the French popular imagination.[37]

Yet what particularly interests Londres is the transitory nature of the city: the all-too short shore leaves of the long-distance sailors (pp. 98–102) and the strange and shifting population of France's second city. Indeed, his first impression is that Marseille is not a French city, but a foreign one: in his hotel, his chamber-maid is Italian; the valet is Italian; the sommelier is Italian; the lift-porter is Italian; and so on. When he meets the mayor, Siméon Flaissières, the once-great reforming politician of the pre-war era, now tarnished by the xenophobic outburst against the Armenian immigrants (an issue which Londres prefers to avoid), he asks:

'Actually, what city are you the mayor of?'
M. Flaissières asked me to have a walk with him for ten minutes.
'Listen', he said, as we walked.
'I can only hear people speaking in Italian'.
'Right! Do you get it now?'
'That doesn't tell me what city you're the legal head of'.
'Look, you're being very dim this morning. You must see that I'm the mayor of Naples!'.[38]

What Londres is getting at is the ambiguous nature of Marseille's identity and its allegiance, already cause for concern in the era of the Convention and, more recently, of Senator Gervais. Writing at the same time as Londres, the American journalist Herbert Adams Gibbons, who worked for James Gordon Bennett's *New York Herald*, commented: 'Keen observers of French life... have declared that Marseilles is too cosmopolitan and the Marseillais too mixed in their blood to represent France or even the Provence... A great port, and an interesting port, yes... but not a French port',[39] before concluding that cosmopolitanism and Frenchness are not incompatible: 'to one who looks beneath the surface, Marseille is unmistakably French, not less French than other great cities, not less meridional than other sections of the Midi.' For:

> Catalans and Spaniards, Corsicans and Sicilians and Italians, Greeks and Armenians, Algerians and Kabyles and Tunisians one meets everywhere among the landsmen; and the mariners are as polygenetic and polyglot as in any other world mart. The Marseillais, however, have the French national consciousness fully developed.[40]

This, however, for the moment, remains in the realm of assertion and Londres' next discovery points still further in the direction of a non-French contribution to the Marseille economic powerhouse. For, if the Italians numerically and culturally are the dominant group in the Marseille population, it is the Greeks who really exercise commercial power:

> The Greeks are the overlords of Marseille. Some of them will sell you grilled almonds, but that does not prevent them from being high financiers. The Greek from Piraeus, who tries to sell you, every day between eleven and midday, peanuts at the ice-cream parlour, is also a major figure on the stock exchange! In the morning, he works for thirty centimes for a cornet; in the afternoon, he supports the olive oil market to the tune of two hundred thousand francs. It's odd, but that's how it goes.... (p. 25).

It is in the docks that the real gradations of the Marseillais social mixture really emerge. Visiting the Place de la Joliette at six-thirty in the morning, Londres is struck by his vision of what he calls the 'foreign legion of employment' (p. 67): 'white Europeans: Spanish deserters, Greeks, from everywhere. I didn't see any French' (p. 67). They live in the *quartier* of the Belle-de-Mai: 'French nomads, Arabs, Syrians, Spanish, Belgians, Italians' (p. 65), and, as for all dockers, their work is strictly hierarchised, with general cargo being reserved for the Europeans, the elite of the profession. Beneath them are those who work as colliers: 'a coal-loader on the docks is lower even than a docker. He is the detritus of the port, a piece of life's debris' (p. 66). Yet even below them, there are the Arabs and the Blacks: 'they fall below the lowest level of the social scale, in other words at zero' (p. 66), a description corroborated by contemporary fictional accounts by Peisson and McKay, and still echoed in later works like Sembène's *Le Docker noir*, of 1956, reflecting the growing political and financial ascendancy of Southern Mediterranean immigrant communities, especially as they enjoy increased social mobility in comparison with their North and Black African counterparts.

What distinguishes Londres' reportage, however, is his positive view of the city. As the foreign dockers, covered with the grime of their various cargos, stagger off duty, they are nevertheless 'richer by twenty-six francs [and] they all go off as free men in the ever-welcoming Marseille' (p. 68). It is this optimism which also informs his key chapter, devoted to emigrants. Recalling a scene he had witnessed at the Damascus railway station just before the departure of the train for Beirut, he was struck by the apparently disproportionate grief being displayed at someone undertaking a journey of only 134 kilometres, only to be told that, on the contrary, this is merely the first stage in a much longer journey of emigration, which inevitably passes through Marseille. In the aptly-named Hôtel des Emigrants, in the Rue Fauchier, he encounters the full extent of a wide European, but essentially Mediterranean, diaspora: Poles and Spaniards; Mesopotamian Christians fleeing persecution en route to New York or Argentina; Syrians or Lebanese on their way to Brazil; Serbs waiting for a boat to Australia (pp. 71–3). What distinguishes them, however, is that their journey is by no means a serendipitous gamble:

> 'Emigrant' does not mean 'gypsy'. On the contrary, an emigrant is cold and calculating. Some calculate better than others, and they are the ones who return as millionaires. But they all calculate their own little project. In the first place, the individual is prudent. You do not become an emigrant on a whim. Nor is it a vocation. It is a decision which was

taken a long while back. They had to save up the money for the journey. It's a strange impression! The poorest of those living in this improbable hostel has at least two thousand francs in his money-belt. (pp. 72–3)

The talisman of this calculated emigration is the orange-box, the *panier*, which each of the Mediterranean emigrants carries with him. Initially packed with oranges, it serves as a source of food on the journey from Spain, Greece or the Levant to Marseille. Once empty, it becomes an improvised suitcase for the longer journey to South America:

> Once he has paid for his hotel and his journey, when the *Valdivia* docks in Rio, he will still have 200 francs… and the orange-box.
>
> Then, for him, will begin the cycle of the emigrant from the Levant. For twenty francs he will buy non-perishable products. Then, with the products in the orange-box and the orange-box under his arm, he will go amongst these new crowds and turn those twenty francs into forty. His sobriety will never betray him. He is therefore totally confident. From the orange-box he will graduate to a stall, and will then move to a real shop with his name painted on the glass door. At that point, some relative in his home country will receive a cheque from Rio, in order to buy a plot of land. A year later, another cheque reaches the relative, for the ground floor of the house. Three years later, he will send the first floor, and another three years later, the second floor. Finally, one day, preferably a holy Thursday, because of the bells which go to Rome, he, from America, will send the roof!
>
> 'So, you will return to your country as an important person?'
>
> 'Oh yes!', says the butcher's assistant, already smiling at his fine future. (pp. 74–5)

And, as if to prove the point, whilst Londres is at the hotel, it receives a distinguished visitor and his young daughter. Once an emigrant in the hotel, 'today, he is an Argentinian, with fifteen thousand head of sheep and a thousand head of cattle' (p. 79). Before departing, he leaves two thousand francs at the desk, 'for the poorest', and, when asked his name, he replies: 'Auguste Bardec… you can even write it up on the wall as an example and an encouragement' (p. 79).

What Londres illuminates remarkably clearly in this piece is the predominantly Mediterranean nature of this diaspora, with Marseille at its centre, epitomised by the inhabitants of the Hôtel des Emigrants.

It is this which, for Londres, renders Marseille so complex and so ambiguous. On the one hand, as the gathering-place of the dispossessed of the Mediterranean, like the dock-workers or the emigrants, it is a locus of deprivation and degradation. Yet, at the same time, it is the self-styled *ville-accueil*, the smiling city with arms outstretched, which welcomes even the rag-pickers at the end of their gruelling day (p. 68).

The same applies to both the reality and symbolism of the port itself. In his introductory chapter, Londres poetically celebrates the crucial role of Marseille in the national, and international, imagination, personifying the *invitation au voyage*:

> Climb the gangplanks of my boats. I will lead you to all the wonders of man and nature. I am the way to Fez, to the Bosphorus, to the Acropolis, to the walls of Jerusalem. I am the way to the Hindu temples of the South, to the Taj Mahal, to Angkor, to the Bay of Along and even as far as Enoshima! I will show you birds which dive and fish which fly. Come aboard! Come aboard! (pp. 14–15)

Yet, if, in Emile Thémime's words, the 'Phocean port is predestined for the adventurers of the impossible',[41] the 'dreams of adventure' are the exclusive property of the white European, until, after the Second World War, the dreams are reversed and it is the colonised, like Diaw Falla in Sembène's *Le Docker noir* or Lalla in Le Clézio's *Désert*, who focus their imagination on Marseille from Senegal or Morocco. In this respect, Londres, in spite of the radical perspective of his journalism, is still locked in the colonial vision of the 'white man's burden'. The ships in the port are testimony to:

> The unbelievable creation of the men of the white race ('les hommes de la race blanche'). The English, French, Italians, Germans, Dutch, Belgians, Spanish: come and see how they have worked! They have gone as far as attacking the body of the Earth itself. They have cut right through it in three places: Suez, Corinth and Panama. Five days away from here I can show you in the middle of the sea the statue of a Frenchman who dared to do that: Lesseps.[42]

Jean-Claude Izzo will point out over sixty years later that these grandiose projects come at a price and that Marseille's colonial past will return to haunt it, but, for the time being, if Marseille is there to lure the dreamer like Pagnol's Marius, as well as the calculating emigrant, away over the horizon, it is also there to bring them back. If, as Londres suggests, the coat of arms of the city should be a gateway, it is, like the iconic transporter bridge at the entrance to the Vieux-Port, a gate through which one exits, but also enters: a point of departure and a point of homecoming. The book is dedicated to

> my great unknown friend, towards whom I was ungrateful for a long time: the keeper of the Planier Lighthouse, who, on each of my departures and each of my homecomings, seemed to have hung a lamp at his window to bid me God-speed or welcome! (pp. 16–17)

The ramifications of this process of departure and arrival are multi-layered, however, and the image of Marseille as uniformly welcoming to its visitors is undoubtedly focused on the privileged outsider—witness the chamber-maid and the sommelier in his luxury hotel. An important corrective was provided two years later, however, by two novels, which appear both to support and contradict this comforting image and which look at Marseille from beneath, from the point of view of its transient underclass: Claude McKay's *Banjo* and Edouard Peisson's *Hans le marin*.

Claude McKay, 'Banjo'

Banjo has undergone something of a re-discovery in recent years, by historians of both Marseille and the Harlem Renaissance. McKay was born in Jamaica in 1889 and received a good literary education, which enabled him to publish two books of poetry in 1912 at the age of twenty-three,[43] after which he left Jamaica definitively. After spells at Booker T. Washington's Tuskeegee Institute in Alabama and Kansas State University, he moved to New York City and then London, where he became involved in radical journalism, writing for *The Liberator* and Sylvia Pankhurst's *Workers' Dreadnought*, before making the pilgrimage to Moscow in 1922, where he was feted by the Soviet leadership. He spent the next twelve years travelling round Europe and North Africa, during which he published *Banjo* and two other novels, *Home to Harlem*, in 1928, and *Banana Bottom*, in 1933, before returning to America, where he died, largely unremembered, in 1948.

It was at the beginning of these European wanderings, in the early 1920s, that McKay found casual work as a docker in Marseille, an experience which resulted in *Banjo*. The novel's sub-title is 'A Story without a Plot', but, aside from its modernist elements, the book consists of a series of interconnected episodes about the life of a group of Black Americans living hand to mouth in the Quartier Réservé, often through casual work at the docks of La Joliette. Dominated by the exuberant character of Lincoln Agrippa Daily, known as 'Banjo' because of his favourite instrument, the novel follows the fortunes of other musicians, Malty, Ginger, Goosey and Bugsy, and their efforts to form a jazz band, both for reasons of artistic expression and to make some money. Their efforts are observed by Ray, the author's representative, an intellectual who has travelled widely in Europe, is fluent in French, familiar with contemporary French culture (he cites Paul Morand, Action Française and Léon Daudet) and who provides the radical cultural and political perspective from which to understand the position of Marseille's Black communities in 'this white man's big city'[44] through his reading of Francophone Black writers like René Maran (p. 207),[45] the Paris-based West African review *La Race Nègre* and Senghor (pp. 76, 215, 277).

The novel takes place within a precise and confined topography, between the Môle protecting the modern port and the Canebière, with the Rue de la République as its eastern frontier, and concentrated on the port facilities of L'Arenc and La Joliette and the Quartier Réservé itself, principally the Rue de la Bouterie and the Rue de la Reynarde, familiar from *Decline and Fall*. To move out of this space is dangerous and on one occasion Banjo and his friends, travelling back from La Joliette to the Quartier Réservé, prefer to take the Boulevard de la Major, by the cathedral, rather than the Rue de la République, where they are likely to have their papers inspected (p. 24). Beyond this area, there are references only to the suburban *cabanon* owned by Ray's chauffeur friend (p. 296), and the bistro near the Gare Saint-Charles where Banjo meets up with 'the many Arabs and Negros and white touts' who inhabit the district (p. 236), which will become the locus of *Le Docker noir* in the 1950s.

What McKay excels at is the evocation of the squalor, crude glamour and constant threat of the Quartier Réservé itself, with the 'sombre, rubbish-strewn alleys' (p. 58), which became an important stereotypical representation of the city in the interwar years. The population of the Quartier Réservé was made up of the transient inhabitants of 'a rough town, like any other port town, where you'll see rough stuff if you stick around long enough' (p. 218), together with the predators who feed off them: the prostitutes, bar-owners and Corsican *voyous* (rogues) (p. 184). Unsurprisingly, this unstable community is made up of the lowest strata of society: first, Mediterraneans, 'Provençales, Greeks, Arabs, Italians, Maltese, Spaniards and Corsicans' (p. 90); then the black Americans, like Banjo and his friends; and finally the West Africans, known collectively as 'Senegalese', who keep aloof from the North Africans. As McKay suggests, 'there is a great gulf, of biological profundity, between the ochre-skinned North Africans and the black dwellers below the desert. The Negro's sensual dream of life is poles apart from the Arab's hard realism' (p. 174). These different communities produce a further set of frontiers which the visitor is called upon to negotiate, signalled by the differing characteristics of bars and cafés.

The raison d'être of this violent, shifting and enticing district is, of course, the port itself, and on this subject McKay is torn between the same enthusiasm and recoil as Londres. On the one hand, he is quite explicit about the rigours of the docker's life, as opposed to his positive portrayal of the career of the seaman. He recognises the gradations of work in the docks and the naked exercise of patronage along ethnic lines, as when austerity begins to bite at the end of the 1920s and there is a shortage of dock work, with a new law being introduced to make a permit obligatory. However:

> The new law did not in any way affect those dock workers who were strangers. The majority of the little bosses were Italians and when men were wanted to load and unload ships, they took the men who were at hand. When work was scarce the strangers yielded place to the favourite sons, of course. And the favourite sons were naturally Italians, who were strangers in the unnaturalized sense, but not foreigners in the generally accepted sense. (pp. 238–9)

McKay depicts the antagonism between the Italians and the 'Senegalese', culminating in a pitched battle, due to 'much jealousy between the rival groups', with the Senegalese aggressively reminding 'the Italians that they were French and possessed the rights of citizens' (p. 75). As both Londres and Thémime record, the lowest level of worker on the docks was the collier, a task reserved almost exclusively for the Black immigrant, although McKay acknowledges that it can encompass the down-at-heel of all origins:

> It was high, hot, golden noon. Blackened from head to foot, clothes, hands, neck, face, a stream of men from the coal dock filed along the Quai des Anglais, across the suspension bridge, and into the Place de la Joliette. There was no telling blond from dark, yellow or brown from black.

> The men were half-day workers. They circled round the fountain in the square stripped to the waist, and splashed water over their bodies. (p. 235)

It is a mark of Banjo's fall from grace after the loss of his instrument that he is reduced to membership of this group in all its degradation.

At the same time, McKay shares Daudet's and Londres' wonder at the riches of the port, expressed in a highly sexualised metaphor for the city his characters call 'the bitch':

> The eternal harvest of the world on the docks. African hard wood, African rubber, African ivory, African skins, Asia's gifts of crisp fragrant leaves and the fabled old spices with grain and oil and iron. All floated through the oceans into this warm Western harbour where, waiting to be floated back again, were the Occident's gifts. Immense crates, barrels, cases of automobiles, pianos, player-pianos, furniture; sandpapered, spliced, and varnished wood; calico print, artificial silk; pretty shoes and boots; French wines, British whiskeys, and a thousand little salesmen-made goods. Composite essence of the soil of all lands.

> Commerce! Of all the words most magical. The timbre, color, form, the strength and grandeur of it. Triumphant over all human and natural obstacles, sublime, yet forever going hand in hand with the bitch. Bawdy. In all relationships, between all individuals, between little peoples and big peoples, progressive and primitive, the two lovers spread and flourish together as if one were the inevitable complement of the other. (p. 317)

Marseille is doubly privileged. Not only does it capture the 'magic of the Mediterranean', for Ray the finest sea in the world—'Of all the seas he had ever crossed there was none like it' (p. 69)—it is also infinitely consoling: 'the Vieux Port had offered him a haven in its frowsy, thickly-peopled heart where he could exist *en pension* proletarian of a sort' (p. 69). For this very reason, 'of all the great ports there was none so appealing to seamen as Marseille in its cruel beauty' (p. 70). McKay's portrait of the city does not stint on the squalor, violence, racial tension and social labour inequalities which ooze from the port and its surrounding streets, but, like Londres, he remains ultimately optimistic about the city's charm and the welcome it extends to its visitors, and the exuberant syncopated transposition of the band's jam session represents both a distillation of the joy of the city and a triumph over its constraints:

> Dance down the Death of these days. The Death of these ways in shaking that thing. Jungle jazzing, Orient wriggling, civilised stepping. Shake that thing! Sweet dancing thing of primitive joy, perverse pleasure, prostitute ways, many-coloured variations of the rhythm, savage, barbaric, refined—eternal rhythm of the mysterious, magical, magnificent—the dance divine of life... Oh, Shake that Thing! (p. 60)

Edouard Peisson, 'Hans le marin'

Whereas McKay is now seen as an important representative of the Harlem Renaissance, recognised early in his career by Langston Hughes, Edouard Peisson's reputation, despite his considerable fictional output and being taken up by later writers like Izzo, has always been minor. He was born in Marseille in 1896, the son of a journalist for the Catholic *Petit Marseillais*, and joined the merchant marine in 1914, rising to the rank of radio officer and then captain with the Compagnie Paquet and the Compagnie Générale Transatlantique. Made redundant in 1924 as the result of the government's reduction of the size of the French merchant navy, he worked for a while as a civil servant in the Préfecture before becoming a full-time writer in a career which spanned thirty-five years and produced thirty-seven novels, most of which derived from his experiences at sea. His third novel, *Hans le marin* ('Hans the Sailor'), however is entirely shore-based and proposes a highly cynical view of his home city from the point of view of the marooned white American sailor Hans Muller. Made into a Franco-American feature film after the Second World War, in 1949, called *Wicked City*, directed by François Villiers and starring Jean-Pierre Aumont and Maria Montez, it helped to seal Marseille's bad reputation.

111

Like Eugène Dabit and Henri Poulaille, Peisson was a member of the *littérature prolétarienne* movement and this political perspective and formal simplicity, contrasting with McKay's stylistic innovation, determine his portrayal of Marseille in the late 1920s. Hans Muller arrives in the port on the steamship *Alabama* and goes ashore in the evening to enjoy the delights of the city. On the Cours Saint-Louis he meets up with a girl, Marcelle, who takes him to a hotel room where he is robbed, assaulted and left for dead. After a spell in the Hôtel-Dieu hospital in Le Panier, he is released, but, with no papers and no money, he is destitute and ineligible for repatriation. Sleeping in a dormitory one night, he encounters a mysterious figure called La Bête, who promises to make his fortune by employing him as a *chiffonnier*, a rag-picker, and introduces him to the rag-pickers' camp under the transporter bridge, next to the Fort Saint-Nicolas. As a chiffonnier he discovers the hidden topography of the underside of the city, and earns enough money to graduate to the position of tout, guiding tourists around the Quartier Réservé. On one such tour he spots Marcelle, lures her to a hotel room and murders her, before fleeing to Paris scot-free with a brand-new identity, his revenge accomplished.

The plot, with its cynical ending, is far removed from the exuberance of *Banjo*, even though the description of the riches of the port appear to match those of Londres or McKay in their appeal to the imagination:

> Here is silk. Here is porcelain. China, Indochina, Japan.
> Here is coal. England. United States.
> Here is wood. Norway. Russia.
> Here is corn. The Black Sea.

> As the belly of the ship empties, there are revealed all countries, all cities, all civilisations. New York, the city of skyscrapers. Rio de Janeiro, the city of flowers. Dakar, a hundred houses, the brush and the sharks which are thrown by the waves on to the beach. Cardiff, coal, rain, cottages lost in the arid hinterland. Algiers, a bazaar of trinkets. Oran, the proud city. Tunis, the Tales of a Thousand and One Nights.[46]

Similarly, the passenger ships appeal to the same dreams of travel:

> The Corsica mail boats, the larger Algerian mail boats and the bigger, more slender boats for China.

Further on there are the foreign cargo boats.
Two metal cranes frame the boat leaving for Morocco.
Every quarter of an hour the siren sounds… (p. 122)

The tone has become more bitter, however, especially when Hans spots the big liners, with 'only a few cabins' for the rich, but 'open decks for emigrants':

Emigrate. Easy work, well-paid. America, the land of millionaires. You leave poor and you come back rich. Come to me all of you who are dying of hunger.

The queue is long for the disinherited, the naive, the defeated…[47]

The radical in Peisson can see more clearly than Londres or McKay the trickery behind the façades of the grand passenger boats, all offering 'Comfort. Fine dining. Cruising', when in reality they are troop ships bound for Morocco or emigrant ships sailing for the New World. There is a subversive current inherent in this description, transmitted in the snatches of *L'Internationale* echoing through the fermenting *bouillon de culture* which is this city of 'six hundred thousand human beings thrown out on to the streets' (pp. 109–10).

Small wonder, therefore, that, even at the very beginning, the Planier lighthouse and the approach to Marseille do not have the same connotations of welcome as in Londres. Rather the bay is associated sexually with the calculating and commercial ploys of the prostitute: 'the bay is a woman who gives herself without resistance and without joy' (p. 9). Much more than McKay's Marseille, this is a city in which everything has a price: hence the utterly appropriate solution to Hans' poverty lies in him becoming a rag-picker. As La Bête says, for a man without papers, who effectively has no identity, all legitimate trades— docker, news-vendor, station porter, are outlawed, but:

if they throw you out like their refuse, well, live off their refuse! I'll give you a hook and a sack, and you'll make a collection. Everything is useful: rags, paper, tin cans. Bring them back here and I'll pay you and feed you. Only one person is more cunning that us. It's La Bête ['the Beast']. He has a secret. He takes a cobble-stone, spits on it and the cobble-stone turns into a hundred *sous* note. If you walk for a long time around the city you'll perhaps understand its secret. (p. 60)

Peisson, as an inhabitant and a sailor, has understood, not merely that Marseille, especially the Vieux-Port, is characterised by its waste and filth, but that there is an equation to be made between the physical waste of the big city and its rejected inhabitants. Moreover, that recognition can lead to an alternative geography, the 'secret' of the city, in which the rag-picker comes to see, as if in a silent film like Dziga Vertov's *Man with a Movie Camera*, of 1929, or John Dos Passos' 'camera eye' sequences in his novel *USA*, snapshots of mundane daily life, piercingly illuminated by 'a powerful spot-light which he shines on one side and then on the other in order to isolate each scene' (p. 106): a café, a tea-dance, an office, a gentleman's club, a bookshop, a tobacconist, a florist, more offices, a couple dancing, a woman in her nightgown, postmen, a shy young man posting a letter, a tram with two lovers surprised in the indiscreet light, a sumptuous limousine, an old crock, a man picking up cigarette ends, a horse-drawn omnibus, a prostitute enticing a client (p. 106).

Whilst Peisson is clearly on one level writing about the same city as Londres and McKay, his emphasis on a Marseille characterised by its physical and human detritus, and his exploration of an alternative topography, touch a more sensitive spot. Underneath the tempting vision of a vibrant, cosmopolitan port, the bringer of exotic abundance and the conveyor of Orientalist dreams from beyond the horizon, Peisson also transmits intense warning signals of the city's dangers, which converge in the years after the First World War and continue to amplify: crime, intimately connected to the port and its trade, and the overwhelming presence of detritus, of *ordures*, a product of municipal corruption, but also somehow symbolic of the perceived rottenness at the core of Marseille itself. In one sense, this was neither a new phenomenon, nor specific to the 1920s. André Donzel, for example, in a brief study of Marseille for the MuCEM exhibition *Ordures* in 2017, notes that refuse is a current issue in the city's history, while 'at the end of the Ancien Régime Marseille was frequently designated in travel memoirs as the filthiest city in Europe.'[48] Yet the issue does not surface significantly in nineteenth-century literary or visual accounts. Instead, it moves to the forefront after the First World War, when it becomes a town-planning, public-health and political issue. It is significant, for example, that Sabiani, as *premier maire-adjoint* (first deputy mayor), employed a huge number of extra municipal staff as refuse-collectors, a measure designed to swell the numbers of voters on the public payroll as well as to provide auxiliary shock-troops for his extreme right-wing political movement.[49] At the same time, the squalid living conditions in much of the inner city to the north and east of the Vieux-Port and the accumulation of refuse in the streets offended technocratic planners and architects, including Modernists like Le Corbusier and the editorialists of *Les Cahiers du Sud*, who looked for a new urban model and saw the old districts as ripe for redevelopment. Crucially, however, Marseille, whose major industry, ironically, was the manufacture of soap, came to be perceived as incarnating that nexus of poverty, squalor, insalubriousness, crime, vermin, foreign infiltration and political subversion which became associated with the South and the Mediterranean basin, and which stood in contrast to the equation of cleanliness and Godliness which supposedly characterised Northern European societies. It was this image which lay at the core of Marseille's 'wickedness' and accounted for the demolition of the Quartier Réservé in 1943. It did not go unchallenged, however, as we shall see in the next chapter.

5

MARIUS

MARCEL PAGNOL AND THE 'GOOD CITY'

A kinder, more positive picture of the city coexisted with its demonic counterpart. This was the almost single-handed achievement of Marcel Pagnol and his recreation of an idealised community on the Quai de Rive Neuve. Perhaps the first work of art to defend Marseille against its bad reputation, though, was Maurice Tourneur's 1935 film, *Justin de Marseille*, which opens with a Parisian journalist arriving in the city to investigate its familiar nickname of 'the Wicked City', only to be advised by a local lorry driver that the myths are not to be believed and that there is an entirely different, and more positive, story underneath the lurid tales of violence. With music by Vincent Scotto, now at the height of his fame, and the voice of the Corsican star Tino Rossi, Tourneur defuses both the genre of the film noir and the criminal image of Marseille by creating a light comedy in which the Marseillais gangster Justin easily turns the tables on his Neapolitan rival Esposito, who is trying to take over the local opium racket. The victory of the French and Marseille-born Justin over his Italian competitor culminates in a joyful celebration in which the *bon enfant* aspect of the populace comes to the fore and confirms the lorry driver's initial diagnosis of the city's rude health. Similar conclusions could be drawn from the public of the Alcazar, superficially threatening to those acts which fell short of their high standards, but essentially socially cohesive and fair-minded, or, indeed, the supporters of Olympique de Marseille, now about to move into their new ground in the Vélodrome on the Boulevard Michelet, and who, like the city itself, embraced a significant number of foreign players, including North Africans like the famous Moroccan Larbi Ben Barek, known as *la Perle Noire* (the Black Pearl), who first played for the club in 1938, and (a less well-known fact), Ahmed Ben Bella, the future leader of the FLN and Prime Minister of independent Algeria from 1963–1965, who played centre-half in the 1939–40 season whilst he was on military service.[1] As François Thomazeau points out, at this time the relationship between the crowd and these players differed remarkably from that of the Neapolitan fans, whose racist jeering marred the France-Italy international in 1938; whatever their views about France might have been, the North African players saw themselves as indelibly from Marseille.[2] In other words, if there is an image of Marseille as a 'wicked city', built upon crime, neglect and poverty, it is possible to locate a counter-image which portrays a fundamentally working-class population, rough at the edges and prone to exaggeration and excess, but essentially decent, even-handed and good-hearted, united in their liking for the iconic comic duo of the interwar years, famous in cartoons and, later, film, 'Marius et Olive'.[3] That this counter-image might be as carefully manufactured and packaged as its dystopian rival is, of course, always more than a possibility, and it is for this reason that the career, and success, of Marseille's best-known twentieth-century writer, Marcel Pagnol, is so instructive, in its manipulation of both the self-identity and the outside perception of the city.

Following Rostand: From Aubagne to Paris

Marcel Pagnol was born in Aubagne in 1895, the son of the local primary school teacher. Aubagne is some 17 kilometres east of Marseille. In the years before the First World War it was an isolated rural community belonging to the Provençal hinterland Pagnol would lovingly evoke in his later novels and memoirs, as well as in his screen adaptations of texts by Jean Giono. In fact, Pagnol's rural childhood was short: in 1897 his ambitious father was appointed to a post in the village of Saint-Loup, half-way between Aubagne and Marseille and now totally absorbed into the city as its 10th Arrondissement; in 1900 he was appointed to the biggest primary school in the city itself, the Ecole des Chartreux,[4] in the 4th Arrondissement, near the Palais Longchamp. The family initially lived in a staff apartment at 54 Avenue des Chartreux, before moving to the Rue Terrusse on 'La Plaine'—the Plaine Saint-Michel, now the Place Jean-Jaurès. The family remained in this area, at various different addresses, for the rest of Pagnol's childhood and adolescence, in what was a tight and interesting community, containing one of the city's major markets on the Cours Lieutaud, later policed by Jean Ballard in his role as weights and measures inspector, and a major theatre, the Théâtre Chave, on the Boulevard Chave, where Simone Signoret began her career and where Fernandel's parents, who lived on the Rue des Minimes, performed in amateur productions.[5] If Pagnol's early years were coloured by this urban society, he retained his close links with the Provençal countryside, since in 1904, his father, Joseph, together with other members of the family, rented a bastide in the hills between Aubagne and Aix, outside the village of La Treille, for the summer. The memories of these idyllic annual holidays in what was still very wild countryside remained with Pagnol and became the subject of his best-known prose works, *La Gloire de mon père* and *Le Château de ma mère*, both of 1957, as well as having a profound effect on his film-making in terms of location, subject-matter and production. What is highly significant, especially in the light of the phenomenal success of the *Marius-Fanny-César* trilogy, set on the Vieux-Port and driven in part by Marius' yearning to go to sea, is that Pagnol represents a continuation of that preponderant tradition amongst the Marseille population who were not particularly drawn to the ocean, were not intimately involved in the affairs of the port, and considered themselves, rather, as Southern big-city dwellers with intimate links to the Provençal countryside to the east, in the tradition of Méry or Zola. In this respect, the trilogy is something of an anomaly in Pagnol's work, which became, in film and prose writing, dominated by memoirs and tales of rural Provence.

Pagnol was admitted to the Grand Lycée de Marseille in 1905, despite having narrowly failed the scholarship examination. By no means an outstanding student, he did excel in French, along with his close friends Albert Cohen, brought up like him in the Quartier de la Plaine and who became an international civil servant and distinguished novelist, Yves Bourde and Fernand Avierinos.[6] It was with these friends that he spent long periods in the countryside around La Treille, whilst also immersing himself in Marseille's theatre culture, from the Opera, where he heard the 'greatest singers from the Paris Opera, La Scala, Covent Garden',[7] to the Gymnase, which, like the Opera, hosted celebrities from Paris; and also including the large number of variety theatres, such as the nearby Théâtre Chave, the Variétés-Casino, the Palais de Cristal, the Grand Casino, the Odéon, the Châtelet and the Capitole, 'where all the Parisian stars, Polin, Mayol, Dranem, Esther Lekain, Fragson, etc. performed.'[8] Pagnol's biographer Raymond Castans also notes that 'all these theatres performed local revues "with garlic and oil", in which you found characters from working-class quartiers: the fish-wife, the *boules* players, the Italian, the North African, the Neapolitan.'[9] This immersion in theatre at all levels, from grand opera to vaudeville, provided Pagnol with an indispensable education in dramatic sensibility and technique, whilst the local revues provided a bank of stock Marseillais characters which he would exploit to the full in the *Marius* trilogy.

Indeed, Pagnol's most pressing ambition, particularly in his final years at lycée, was the development of a literary career, a trait by no means unusual in intelligent adolescents, but, in his case, pursued with exceptional determination. Encouraged by his French literature teacher Emile Ripert, he contributed a poem to a school literature magazine, *La Bohème*, and, in 1910, when he was fifteen, he began to contribute regularly to an independent fortnightly 'literary, poetic and artistic revue' called *Massilia*.[10] Four years later, just before the outbreak of war, Pagnol, Yves Bourde and new friends like Gaston Mouren, established a revue of their own, called *Fortunio*, named after Musset's adolescent hero, which, after many interruptions, would become *Les Cahiers du Sud*. The source of this literary inspiration was, of course, one of the most famous alumni of the lycée, Edmond Rostand, whose success with *Cyrano de Bergerac* when he was only twenty-nine was an irresistible temptation to any budding adolescent writer. Despite the obvious social privileges from which Rostand had benefited, the message was clear to any ambitious provincial writer:

not only was the royal way to rapid success through the theatre, but it led inevitably to Paris, and Pagnol saw his future career and, indeed, that of his review, as lying in the capital.

In this respect, he benefited from an extraordinary stroke of luck. After passing the baccalaureate with the unremarkable grade of *assez bien* in 1912, he returned to the lycée to prepare for the entrance examination for the Ecole Normale Supérieure in Paris. When the war came, he was invalided out of the army for 'constitutional weakness'[11] and occupied a number of temporary teaching posts, mainly in English, in Digne, Tarascon, Pamiers in the department of the Ariège, Aix-en-Provence and, finally, back at the Lycée de Marseille. It was here that his lesson on *Hamlet* was observed by a schools inspector, who was so impressed that he advised Pagnol to enter the prestigious *agrégation* examination leading to a post in the lycée or university sector and promised to help him to move to Paris, a promise which came true in 1922, when he received a posting to the Lycée Condorcet, one of the most famous lycées in the capital. What is remarkable about Pagnol's early years in Paris is the single-mindedness with which, on top of the complexities of starting a new job and finding somewhere to live for himself and his young wife, he set to building a literary reputation, a task in which he showed an extraordinary talent for networking. Even before leaving Marseille, he had been taken under the wing of Marius Richard, the powerful owner of *Le Petit Provençal*, whose son, Jean Marius, he had tutored for the baccalaureate, and who had important contacts in the Parisian theatre, including at the Comédie Française and the actors Mounet-Sully, de Max, Albert Lambert and Sylvain. The last of these needed Marius Richard's support for his open-air theatre project in Marseille, the Théâtre Sylvain in the Vallon de la Fausse-Monnaie in Endoume.[12] In addition, a friend from Marseille, Paul Nivoix, who worked for the daily theatre newspaper *Comoedia*, had mentioned Pagnol to the veteran theatre-director Lugné-Poe, and, within weeks of his arrival in Paris, Pagnol was visited by both the great naturalist director Antoine, who, by this time, incidentally, was moving into cinema, and Sylvain, who invited him to dinner and introduced him to the Symbolist poet Paul Fort.[13] At the same time, through Nivoix, he met the team behind *Comoedia*'s rival, *Bonsoir*, comprised mainly of young figures from Lyon, like the journalist Henri Béraud, the playwright Marcel Achard and the actor-director Charles Dullin.[14]

The initial reason for this interest on the part of major Parisian theatrical celebrities was the play Pagnol had brought with him from Marseille, a verse drama in the mould of *Cyrano*, called *Catulle*, depicting the tragic love of the poet Catullus for his mistress Clodia. In the end, the play was never performed, but it was the strategic circulation of a few copies of the manuscript which brought Pagnol to the attention of the Parisian theatre world. In addition, he already had a number of other projects, some of which were considerably more commercial, including the first of his plays to be performed, *Tonton, ou Joseph veut rester pur*, which had its première at the Théâtre des Variétés in Marseille on 30 August 1923. The performance was a disaster and Pagnol congratulated himself on having adopted the pseudonym 'Castro' as co-author with Paul Nivoix, but he still nevertheless received 700 francs in royalties, four times his monthly salary at the Lycée Condorcet, which convinced him that a career as a dramatist was a viable proposition. More successful were subsequent projects with Nivoix: a war-drama, *Les Marchands de gloire*, performed in 1925 at the Théâtre de la Madeleine, with Pierre Renoir, and, in 1926, the boxing epic *Un Direct au Coeur*, for the Théâtre de l'Alhambra in Lille. Finally, Pagnol, who had taken indefinite leave from his teaching post in 1926, went solo with *Jazz*, which opened in Monte Carlo in 1926 and then immediately transferred to the Théâtre des Arts in Paris, with Harry Baur in the main role. This was followed by his first major hit, the comedy *Topaze*, which opened at the Théâtre des Variétés in Paris on 9 October 1928. Drawn from Pagnol's experiences in secondary teaching, *Topaze* narrates the cynical tale of a modest schoolteacher who is sacked for being too honest and finds success instead as an unscrupulous businessman. It was an immediate critical and commercial success, with a long run and a film adaptation by Louis Gasnier, starring Louis Jouvet and Edwige Feuillère,[15] and it established Pagnol once and for all as a popular boulevard dramatist. Whilst this may have been different from his original ambition to follow in Rostand's footsteps as a classical writer, it made him immensely, and precociously, wealthy, a factor which was to play an important role in the funding of his subsequent film career. In fact, alongside *Topaze*, he had been writing another play aimed at the boulevards and based upon his memories of Marseille popular theatre: *Marius*, accepted by Simonne and Léon Volterra for the Théâtre de Paris and launched six months after *Topaze* on 9 March 1929.

The 'Marius' Trilogy

It is difficult to overestimate the importance of Pagnol's trilogy for the creation of the image of Marseille in the twentieth century. Not only did it imprint a certain vision of the city on the imagination of its spectators, both nationally and internationally, it also constitutes an indispensable record of how the French themselves wished to view Marseille from the 1930s onwards. The Bar de la Marine, on the Quai Rive Neuve, despite never having existed in reality, is now as much a *lieu de mémoire* as the Château d'If, the Bonne Mère, the Canebière and the Porte de l'Empire. Moreover, it is an image which has continued to replicate itself through the original theatre productions of *Marius* and *Fanny*, the films of *Marius*, *Fanny* and *César* made by Pagnol himself in the 1930s, the published written texts, and successive new theatre productions, film remakes or television productions.

The original history of *Marius*, *Fanny* and *César* is complicated, due to the fact that the first two were stage plays, rapidly turned into feature films, and followed by the third film of the trilogy, *César*, made in 1936, which was only later, in 1946, performed on stage. The trilogy thus reflects not merely Pagnol's precocious accomplishment as a popular dramatist, but also his pioneering recognition of the possibilities offered by the recently invented talking cinema. The action of all three dramas takes place in the Bar de la Marine on the Quai de Rive-Neuve on the southern quayside of the Vieux-Port and its immediate neighbourhood, the Paroisse Saint-Victor. It deploys a restricted core cast of seven characters: the bar owner César and his son Marius; the fishwife Honorine and her daughter, Fanny, who runs the shellfish stand outside the bar; the prosperous ships' chandler Panisse, whose business is next door; Escartefigue, the captain of the ferry boat which crosses the Vieux-Port twenty-four times a day from the Mairie to the Place aux Huiles; and the customs officer M. Brun, who is from Lyon and, for no other reason, the object of good-humoured mockery. *Marius* follows the unspoken love-affair between César's son and Fanny, who is also being courted by the recently widowed Panisse, thirty years her senior. The barrier to the affair between Marius and Fanny is the former's obsession with the sea and travel, and the play depends on the tension between Fanny's love for Marius and his desire to leave on the schooner the *Malaisie*, bound for a five-year voyage to Australia. Eventually, after one night spent together, Fanny lies to Marius about her intention to marry Panisse and allows him to follow his dream. The play ends with the departure of the *Malaisie* and Fanny collapsing in a faint.

Fanny takes up the story, with the heroine's discovery that she is pregnant with Marius' child, followed by Panisse's renewed courtship and willingness to accept the child as his own. Panisse, who gains stature in the course of the play, moving from stock figure of fun to a more rounded and humane character, cares for Fanny during the birth of her son and proves a loving and caring husband and father. The idyll is interrupted, however, in the final act by the return of Marius, who discovers the existence of his son and tries to take him and Fanny away from Panisse; Marius is dissuaded for the time being by César, who takes him home. The final episode, *César*, takes place twenty years after Panisse's wedding, when the chandler is dying. Around his death-bed gather his old friends, the curé of Saint-Victor and the doctor, Fanny and their son Césariot, now in his final year of the Ecole Polytechnique and more a Parisian than a Marseillais. After Panisse's funeral, Fanny confesses to Césariot that he is really the son of Marius and the young man sets off to track down his father, who is now the co-owner of a garage in Toulon. Arriving incognito, he befriends Marius, who appears to be involved in shady dealings with his partner, and eventually brings him back to the Vieux-Port, where he is reunited with César and Fanny. Both Fanny and Marius remain intent on remaining honourably separate until, after a final meeting in the countryside outside the city, César persuades them to marry and have more children, continuing the family name.

Both of the plays and the three films were phenomenally popular and it is easy to see why. They were well-constructed popular comedies, with a strong ensemble cast drawn mainly from Marseille music hall and vaudeville: Raimu played *César* in all three films and in the stage version of *César*, only replaced by Harry Baur in the theatrical version of *Fanny* because of conflicting contractual obligations; similarly, Pierre Fresnay played Marius in all three films and took the lead role in the play *Marius*, leaving the much smaller role in *Fanny* to Berval; Pagnol's partner in the early 1930s, Orane Demazis, played

Fanny throughout with considerable success; Alida Rouffe played Honorine, with, once again, the exception of *Fanny*; Charpin played Panisse throughout, as did Dullac Escartefigue and Vattier M. Brun. This was a strong cast by any standards: it made the reputation of Raimu as a serious actor, albeit at the risk of type-casting him, and helped launch Fresnay as one of the great male stars of the 1930s. At the same time, the films and plays constructed a powerful sense of place and community in an idealised Vieux-Port, through a strong and clearly defined cast of characters. In this, the crucial factor is the relationship between the older generation, all aged around fifty in *Marius* and *Fanny*, and in their seventies in *César*, typified by the famous game of cards in *Marius*, nearly omitted from the original stage version until restored at Raimu's insistence.[16] The bonds between César, Panisse, Escartefigue and Honorine, which generate all the comedy in the trilogy, constitute the ballast which keeps the love-affair between Marius and Fanny afloat, as do the bonds between César and Marius. This allows a most effective coexistence between farce and comedy, on the one hand, and genuine emotion and passion on the other, and is the result of a very high level of technical dramatic construction.

The problem, however, is that this efficient construction is effectively the staple of the commercial boulevard theatre from which it derives: the well-made play, finely attuned to a middlebrow audience's sensibilities and expectations. In this respect, not only does Pagnol ground his trilogy in well-tested dramatic plot-lines from theatre and opera history: young lovers threatened by the ambitions of an older suitor, with stock characters from Molière or Beaumarchais;[17] he is also heavily reliant on the Marseille tradition of local vaudeville with recognisable local types—the 'theatre of oil and garlic' on which he was brought up. This makes it difficult to reconcile the plays and films themselves with Pagnol's alleged ambition to provide a 'slice of life' in the naturalist tradition of his patron Antoine and create a 'Théâtre Libre de Marseille.'[18] Moreover, this cosy reliance on stereotype is not easily compensated by the theme of Marius' dreams of sailing to the Windward Islands, which owe more to Pagnol's own longing to leave Marseille for Paris than to an exploration, as Castans suggests, of the vogue for travel at the heart of the 1920s 'nouveau mal du siècle.'[19] In fact, Marius' yearning for the exotic appears to derive from no more

125

than a *lycéen*'s reading of Baudelaire and Rimbaud, and does not begin to approach the dithyrambic exhortation to travel in Londres' reportage. It is perhaps for this reason that it becomes so quickly quenched in the third act of *Fanny* and that, in *César*, Marius can be found prosaically working in his Toulon garage.

It is this which is so problematic in the trilogy's depiction of Marseille itself, because it coincides so perfectly with a certain self-image of the city which outsiders were only too willing to accept, and which Pagnol was only too willing to package and sell. In this respect, he is the direct descendant, not of the self-styled plebeian Gelu, but of Daudet and, especially, Méry, who, for all his caveats about stereotyping, exploited an exaggerated comic image of the *Méridional* for the Parisian market: all extravagant gestures, nasal accent and flagrant *galéjade*; lazy, fun-loving and devious, yet with hearts of pure gold and a deeply engrained moral code: as César confides to Marius at the end of *César*, the man who had abandoned Zoé was not 'a Real Man'. In this respect, the Lyonnais customs official, Monsieur Brun, whom, incidentally, the *habitués* of the Bar de la Marine progressively corrupt, is a recurrence of the stock character of the Northern outsider in the local vaudeville productions, designed to highlight the human qualities of the Marseillais and create comedy through clashes of culture in which the odds are stacked firmly in favour of the home team. This process of theatrical caricature rises to a crescendo in set-piece comic scenes like the card-game in *Marius*, the game of *boules* in *César*, where the players hold up the tram-car so that they can measure their shots, or, in the same play, the Chaplin-inspired silent sequence in which a rock is placed under a bowler hat on the pavement in order to entice a passer-by to kick it—in the end, someone walks up to it, removes the hat from the rock, places the hat on his head, and walks on.

In fact, the trilogy owes as much to the tradition of village comedy, with loveable, type-cast, rural characters, as it does to the port setting itself, in spite of the schooner *Malaisie* as the object of Marius' wander-lust and the running gags about Escartefigue's modest ferry-boat, described by César as a 'buoy with a propeller'. The plays are situated in the parish of Saint-Victor, on the south side of the Vieux-Port, while the studio sets in the films, often facing away from the port towards the land-locked community, have nothing particularly nautical about them at all. This is simply small-town Southern France, easily recognisable from Daudet's Tarascon, with the same rivalries, friendly in this case, between the local doctor and the parish priest familiar from many accounts of rural France under the Third Republic. It is for this reason that the rare appearances of multi-cultural characters—the Malayan woman and Arab carpet seller in *Marius*, for example—are fleeting daubs of would-be local colour. Pagnol has no intention of joining Londres, Peisson or McKay in a realistic portrayal of the variegated shifting population of the Vieux-Port. When the lunch-time siren sounds, it is not dockers, but all-purpose workers who stroll across the sound-stage and, whilst there are recurrent dark allusions to the fate of Fanny's aunt Zoé, who falls into prostitution in the Quartier Réservé when she is abandoned by her lover, the action remains safely on the Quai de Rive-Neuve, a world away from the Rue de Reynarde and the Rue de la Bouerie just across the port. Indeed, the only time that the Quai de l'Hôtel de Ville is shown is during the sequence in *Fanny* when the heroine marries Panisse. Escartefigue's ferry-boat may be a risible, if strangely touching, vessel, but its journey is vast, from the modern, conflicted, multi-cultural, violent worlds of La Joliette and the red-light district, to the timeless, enduring and idealised community on the opposite side. In other words, there is a clear frontier stretching from west to east through the middle of the Lacydon, which also divides the corrupt modern world to the north from the healthy, timeless, peasant-like Southerness of the Quai la Rive Neuve. It is hardly surprising, then, that the plays and the films should have had such success in the year of the Wall Street crash and during the Depression which followed, nor that the films should have been re-released to renewed acclaim during the Occupation, in spite of the theme of the *fille-mère* being in conflict with Vichy orthodoxy.[20]

Pagnol and Cinema

Pagnol occupies a curiously ambiguous place in the history of French film. His discovery of the possibilities of sound cinema dates from a visit he made to London in May 1930, when he saw *Broadway Melody* at the Palladium.[21] He later spelled out his thoughts about what he saw as a new genre in an article for *Le Journal*, in which he correctly prophesied the demise of silent cinema and, more questionably, raised the threat posed to the traditional theatre.[22] In fact, what appealed to Pagnol was the possibility of replicating, and preserving, the best possible experience of the most privileged theatre audience, in the front row of the stalls, for a cinema audience of 1,500 people, multiplied by an unlimited number of cinemas across France and the world, a vision which looked forward, not so much to the infinitely broader possibilities of sound cinema as to the sophisticated live-streaming of theatre and opera performances which became available in the third millennium.[23] Predictably, the article enraged both dramatists, who saw it as a reckless attack on theatre itself, and film-makers, who pointed out, with some reason, that Pagnol had failed to understand the specific aesthetics of cinema, inherent in its silent form, and that what he was proposing amounted to no more than *théâtre filmé* or *théâtre en conserve* (filmed theatre or preserved theatre).[24] Both sets of critics were right: despite being touted as the end of legitimate theatre, film never replaced it and, indeed, continued to coexist symbiotically with it; moreover, Pagnol's understanding of film was, and arguably continued to be, remarkably narrow and focused merely on the necessity of adding dialogue to silent film, now that the technology was available.

In this respect, his limitations became immediately apparent in the film adaptations of the trilogy, which, with few deviations, follow the text and structure of *Marius* and *Fanny* and, in the case of *César*, adopts a theatrical progression. All three are composed of recognisably autonomous scenes, filmed in theatrical sets on sound-stages, interspaced with brief location shots, which, admittedly, grow longer and more sophisticated as the trilogy progresses. Nevertheless, the films are undoubtedly, and unashamedly, *théâtre filmé*.

In November 1930 Pagnol sold the film rights to *Marius* to Paramount, who had just set up their European studios in Saint-Maurice, six kilometres east of Paris, near the Pathé studios in Joinville.[25] To direct *Marius*, Paramount brought in Alexander Korda, who up until then had only worked on silent films and was happy to defer to Pagnol in matters of dialogue, a division of labour which Pagnol was to adopt in all the films he worked on or even directed, choosing significantly to work from the sound booth rather than from behind the camera. *Marius* was released in October 1931, with the original cast from the play, to immense popular acclaim, not merely in Paris but throughout the francophone world, especially Belgium and North Africa, although film critics still remained unconvinced that it constituted real cinema.[26] Paramount had also acquired an option on *Topaze* and *Fanny*, but Pagnol was so outraged by being sidelined by *Topaze*'s director Louis Gasnier, who even brought in another writer, Léopold Marchand, to write the dialogues, that he withdrew from the project on *Fanny*. Instead, he joined forces with a twenty-eight-year-old fellow Marseillais, Roger Richebé, already a successful film producer who had made three films with Raimu and two with Jean Renoir (*On purge bébé* and *La Chienne*), and had extensive studios in Billancourt. Together, they set up a production company to make *Fanny*, Les Films Marcel Pagnol, which was to become a major presence on the French film landscape for the next ten years.[27] *Fanny* went into production on 6 June 1932 and was directed by Marc Allégret, who had made four feature length films and four shorts, with the same cast as for *Marius*. The music was by Vincent Scotto, famous for *Ma P'tite Tonkinoise* in 1906, and now one of France's best-known music-hall composers, who was to reveal a considerable unexpected talent as an actor in Pagnol's later films.[28] The film was released at the beginning of October 1932, with the same success as *Marius*. The final film of the trilogy, *César*, written primarily for the cinema, did not appear until four years later, in mid-November 1936, this time produced and directed by Pagnol himself.

The three films, with their repertory cast, some of whom—Raimu, Fresnay and Charpin—had become stars as a result, constitute, like the plays, a serial with the compelling and addictive qualities of the soap-opera, following the characters in their well-defined locality from the doomed love-affair of Marius and Fanny at the beginning to its final resolution at the end of *César*. As Georges Sadoul comments, with faint praise:

> Despising technical refinements and putting film at the service of his temperament as a theatrical author, Pagnol has the merit of maintaining, from 1930–1940, a realist current relying on the traditions of his little homeland, Provence, and describing accurately and picturesquely the petit bourgeois milieu, especially the shop-keepers.[29]

Referring specifically to *Marius* and *Fanny*, he writes:

> The technique, which was flat and mediocre, did not entirely serve the talent of the actors... But it was Pagnol who was responsible for the

décors, which were scrupulously accurate and true, whilst the fairly extensive use of open-air shots gave to the audience the presence of a true and picturesque Marseille.[30]

In fact, as one might expect and in spite of the cohesion brought by the overarching vision of the author, each of the individual directors' contributions is very different. Surprisingly, it was Korda's version of *Marius* which is the least successful in cinematic terms, since it is almost totally constrained by the straitjacket of Pagnol's concept of 'filmed theatre' and slavishly follows the scene-sequences of the original play on the studio sets. Nor are Korda's open-air shots by any means as extensive as Sadoul suggests, instead reduced to a small number of random views of the Vieux-Port, including the transporter bridge and the Bonne-Mère, and only coming to life with the recurrent quayside scenes around the increasingly ominous shape of the *Malaisie* and its eventual departure from the Vieux-Port to the open sea, shot from the air. These barely compensate, however, for the recurrent shots of the Planier lighthouse, so dear to Albert Londres, which is plainly filmed from a crude miniature mock-up. In comparison, Allégret's *Fanny* is altogether more accomplished, perhaps in part due to the absence throughout most of the action of Pierre Fresnay as Marius, which allows uninterrupted focus on the three figures of Panisse, Fanny and César. This concentration on the three main characters, whilst still adopting the pattern of a linked series of dramatic scenes played out on set, nevertheless makes fluid use of exteriors, with wider and more systematic use of the landscape of the Vieux-Port, including the wedding-scene at the Hôtel de Ville. In particular, the transporter bridge, which in Korda's *Marius* figures mainly as mere wallpaper, now regains its true significance as the gateway to the Vieux-Port, a threshold for departure and arrival. Allégret's version of *Fanny* also benefits from a significant change from the theatrical script. Whilst the play ends with Marius and César leaving Panisse and Fanny to fuss over their son, in the film Marius and Fanny, in the absence of Panisse, come close to embracing, until interrupted by César, who takes Marius off to his Paris-bound train. This effectively paves the way for the final reconciliation, twenty years after the events of *Fanny*, in *César*, which is the most adventurous cinematographically of the three films, but structurally the most flawed. Under Pagnol's direction, there are considerably more outdoor locations, which extend beyond the confines of the Vieux-Port: César's walk to Saint-Victor which opens the film, for example, or the extended *pétanque* scene on the tram tracks; the extended boat trip of Césariot to Toulon, where he tracks down Marius and hires him to take him out fishing; or the long final sequence in the countryside around La Treille, where Marius and Fanny are finally on the path to being united. Although the set-piece interior scenes dominate, the overall effect of the film is considerably more expansive. This is marred, however, by a highly contrived plot-line which sets up Marius as having been involved in criminal activity, and, indeed, imprisoned, only to enable him to easily exonerate himself. What is interesting, however, is that Fanny's son Césariot, now a student, and later graduate, of Polytechnique, has become completely alienated from Marseille and a true Parisian, with all the stereotypical qualities associated with the capital: superciliousness, superiority and coldness. In the end, he is effectively bundled out of the city to await his first posting, leaving the field clear for Fanny and Marius, who, as César hints, will have their own children, under their own name. In other words, order is restored and the Vieux-Port, or at least its southern quayside, can continue as it always has—the antithesis of Northern aloofness, and a powerful, if ultimately questionable, rebuttal of the realist portrayal in McKay and Peisson of Marseille as the 'wicked city'.

The Société des Films Marcel Pagnol

By the time Pagnol produced and directed *César* in 1936, he had moved a long way from the company he had set up with Roger Richebé to make *Fanny* four years earlier and was able to pour the considerable income from his plays, films and film-rights into full-blown independent film production. As Colin Crisp records:

> Pagnol created his own production company specifically to produce his own films, as had many of his predecessors in the twenties; but what distinguished his enterprise was the scale on which he was able to undertake it, as a result of the immense success of his theatrical works and the even more remarkable success of his first film, *Marius*.... With almost limitless funds at his disposal, Pagnol was able to build his own film studio in the suburbs of Marseilles, hire his own technicians to staff

it, hire artistic personnel on year-long contracts, purchase areas of Provence which served for location shooting, buy an advanced sound van to do his location recording, buy a laboratory to process and print his films, and buy a chain of cinemas in which to screen them.[31]

In fact, this ambitious project went through several stages, including the break with Paramount and the partnership with Richebé. In September 1933 he formed Les Auteurs Associés with his dramatist friends Marcel Achard, Stève Passeur, Roger Ferdinand and Arno-Charles Brun, a company modelled on Hollywood's United Artists, founded by Chaplin, D.W. Griffith, Mary Pickford and Douglas Fairbanks, and with the same ambition to secure independence from the big studio companies.[32] However, whereas Chaplin and his colleagues were actors and directors, Pagnol's team was composed exclusively of dramatists, an indication of his view of the primacy of the dramatic text in the film-making process. At the same time, for the production and distribution of all his films, Pagnol set up and retained exclusive control over the Société des Films Marcel Pagnol.

Pagnol's film-making took on an almost exclusively Provençal character, which distinguished it from the majority of French production in the 1930s and was anchored, not merely in the Marseille trilogy, but in his purchase of the film rights to a number of prose works by Jean Giono,[33] resulting in the medium-length *Jofroi*, of 1933; *Angèle*, of 1934; *Regain*, in 1937; and *La Femme du boulanger* ('The Baker's Wife'), of 1938, all extensively shot on location in the countryside around La Treille, which Pagnol had purchased for this purpose, and making progressive use of the production facilities he was acquiring in Marseille. In these films, Pagnol relied not merely on the repertory company of Provençal actors he had assembled for *Marius*, but also on newcomers to acting like Vincent Scotto and the music-hall performer from La Plaine Saint-Michel in Marseille, Fernandel.

The Pagnol empire in Marseille included, not merely the property near La Treille for location-shoots, but also, from 1934, processing laboratories, under the direction of a former lycée friend Albert Assouad, in the Impasse des Peupliers, off the Rond-Point du Prado.[34] These were supplemented in 1938 by the construction of the purpose-built Studios Marcel Pagnol in the Rue Jean-Mermoz, again just off the Avenue du Prado, with the following facilities:

Three sound stages of 35 metres by 15 and 15 metres high, three Debrie cameras, two Philips sound recording lorries, 80 spotlights, a hundred metres of tracking, development and printing laboratories, 3 editing suites, an auditorium, a workshop for building sets, administrative offices, a bar and a canteen-restaurant. Not to mention, ten kilometres away, hundreds of hectares of hills bought by Pagnol for *Angèle*, where directors could shoot all their exterior scenes.[35]

These were accompanied, as Colin Crisp indicates, by the acquisition of cinemas in Marseille, starting with the Châtelet on the Avenue Cantini and progressing to a new construction, the César, on the Place Castellane, with the express purpose of using them for preview screenings to test the audience's reactions before films went on general release.[36] In fact, Pagnol's venture in Marseille was the culmination, and, ultimately, swan-song, of a long process which had sought to establish the South of France, with its climate and unparalleled quality of light, as the French equivalent of Hollywood and the natural home of the French film industry. In this, it followed the Victorine Studios in Nice, constructed in 1921, and which had considerable success during the Occupation due to their location, like Marseille, in the Free Zone. As far as Pagnol was concerned, the final phase in this establishment of the film industry in the South was his project in 1941 to build a French *cinecittá* to the east of Marseille, around his Château de la Buzine, near La Treille.[37] However, the plans came to nothing, not least because film production had already begun to relocate to Paris after the initial scare of the 1940 *Exode* and because Pagnol became increasingly unhappy about filming under German patronage and sold his studios to Gaumont in 1942.

Nevertheless, for a period of nearly eight years, from 1934 to 1942, the Studios produced, not merely Pagnol's own considerable output of films, but also, to make the studios cost-effective, films by other directors, notably Jean Renoir, who shot *Toni* almost entirely on location at La Treille as well as parts of *La Marseillaise*. Pagnol's own films in this period were dominated by the rights to Giono's works which he had bought earlier, which, in spite of popular success, encountered a mixed critical reception. The Communist critic Georges Sadoul, for example, praised the 'almost perfect success of *Angèle*', but was reticent about the more ambitious and proto-Vichy-ite *Regain*:

[This film] depicted an abandoned village in Upper Provence and prescribed a 'return to the land' as a universal remedy to war, unemployment, moral corruption, mechanisation and all the ills of humanity. This
ideology, aggravated by one or two casting errors, spoiled a subject
which could have been full of poetry and truth, as long as it had really
studied the causes of the abandonment of the Provençal villages.[38]

In fact, it is ironic that Pagnol, whose direct experience of Provence
was limited to the Marseillais hinterland around La Treille and did not
fully understand or share Giono's feeling for the wildness and poetry
of Haute Provence, became best known as a film-maker for his dramas
and comedies of this landscape, rather than his films of the mid- to late
1930s. What is certain, however, is that, after the trilogy, he never
returned to Marseille itself as a subject in his films, although the continuing popularity of *Marius*, *Fanny* and *César* as plays, books and films,
reinforced by re-makes like the 2013 version by Daniel Auteuil, have
been enough to guarantee the persistence of a positive mythology of
the city and the port to counter the pervasive image of the 'wicked
city'. In this, they become merged into the more general vogue for
Pagnol's evocation of Provence in the late 1980s and 1990s: Claude
Berri's *Jean de Florette* and *Manon des Sources*, of 1986, and Yves Robert's
films of *La Gloire de mon père* and *Le Château de ma mère*, of 1990, look
back to an idealised picture of the Belle Epoque, in which human
endeavour is celebrated and human pettiness and cruelty subsumed in
the overwhelming natural Provençal scenery: in a sense, the triumph
of the camera operator over the director. If the first wave of the success
of Pagnol's films coincides with the rise and fall of the Front Populaire
and the approach of war, it is significant that his renewed popularity
should come about at the end of the *Trente Glorieuses* of French post-war
prosperity, when Marseille itself was perceived to be in freefall and
France as a whole was losing direction. If *Marius*, *Fanny* and *César* can
be seen as a riposte to the image of the city conveyed by novelists like
Mackay or Peisson, it is no coincidence that the phenomenal national
and international success of the Claude Berri and Yves Robert films
came about at the same time as the impact of Jean-Claude Izzo's dystopian vision of the city.

This is in part due, of course, to formal considerations as well as to
thematic ones and Pagnol's success was built, not merely on a comfort-

ing vision of inherent Southern decency underneath the exaggeration and the bluster, and, in the case of *Jean de Florette*, sheer peasant greed; but especially on the professional skill with which the message was packaged and Marseille sold: the consummate practice of the master boulevard dramatist, able to transfer his skills effortlessly to the cinema. From *Topaze* onwards, there remains little trace of the adolescent Symbolist poet or the founder of the avant-garde review *Fantasio*, but Marseille's Modernist project went on without him, most importantly in *Les Cahiers du Sud*. It is to this seminal journal that we turn in the next chapter.

6

LES CAHIERS DU SUD

MARSEILLE MODERN

In the interwar years, Marseille became, not merely an important focal point for European-wide artistic experimentation, especially in photography and film, it also saw the Mediterranean reappear at the forefront of the Modernist project. Above all, and combining the two, it was also the location of one of the most influential Modernist literary and intellectual journals of the interwar years and after, *Les Cahiers du Sud*.

This renewed energy in Marseille modernism was apparent in 1925, when Marseille's Galerie Bokanowski hosted the sixth Salon de l'Araignée, the annual exhibition of independent French cartoonists first organised in 1919 by the distinguished illustrator Gus Bofa. From its original aims as a showcase of the best of French caricature, Bofa had progressively expanded its remit to include foreign artists like George Grosz and painters and sculptors from the avant-garde including Van Dongen, Chagall and Alexander Calder. Its presence in 1925 in Marseille, only its second excursion outside the capital (the first was to French-occupied Mainz) and its first to the French provinces, built on Marseille's adoption of the avant-garde in 1880s in the form of the Parisian cabaret culture, the connections between local artists and the Post-Impressionists, Fauves and Cubists of L'Estaque and, contrary to its reputation, an openness to Modernist art from France and beyond, including, in popular culture, a thriving jazz scene.

The period covering the late 1920s and early 1930s saw an extraordinary growth of creative coverage of Marseille, from Londres' reportage, novels by Waugh, McKay and Peisson, and plays and films by Pagnol and his studios. The reasons for this unprecedented attention, coming from both external observers and figures native to Marseille, are multiple, involving the city's steady acquisition of prominence in the last half of the nineteenth century, especially through the importance of North Africa, and enhanced by the Colonial Exhibitions of 1906 and 1922, the role of Marseille as France's largest transit port during the First World War, and, crucially, the explosion of international passenger travel in the interwar years. Amongst these travellers were figures from outside France who observed the city, its people and its structures as a work of art in itself and who described it, in writing, in film and in photography, in ways which stressed the formal as well as the thematic. They included the German Marxist philosopher and *flâneur* Walter Benjamin, the Hungarian photographer and film-maker Lásló Moholy-Nagy, and the German photographer Germaine Krull. All three were concerned with the strange cosmopolitan properties which went to make up Marseille as a modern city. Their observations were joined, and sometimes channelled, by what became a powerhouse of indigenous cultural production, the monthly review *Les Cahiers du Sud*, which championed and showcased the vast range of Southern culture, including Occitanie and the wider Mediterranean, whilst remaining unusually open to an eclectic mixture of avant-garde and pan-European works, from the Surrealist poets to German Romanticism. What ultimately brought these two strands together, however, was their mutual interest in shifting patterns of geopolitics, which gave renewed primacy to the Mediterranean and placed Marseille at the centre of a web of crucial axes from north to south and from east to west.

The View from Germany: Walter Benjamin, Lásló Moholy-Nagy and Germaine Krull

Walter Benjamin visited Marseille and Naples on a number of occasions in the late 1920s and was strongly attracted by the social openness of the dirty Mediterranean port cities. His essay 'Marseille' was published in 1929 in the Zurich-based *Neue Schweitzer Rundschau*, and runs to a mere six pages. With a rubric derived from André Breton, 'The street... the only valid field of experience', Benjamin's essay consists of a series of ten paragraphs—impressions, snapshots or sound-bites—evoking locations ('Les Bricks', 'Notre-Dame de la Garde', the 'Cathedral', and 'Suburbs'); sensations ('Noises' or 'The Light'); and urban features ('Shellfish and oyster stalls', 'Walls' and 'Down and outs'). These nine features are linked in the introductory paragraph, 'Marseille', which depicts the city as:

> The yellow-studded maw of a seal with salt water running out between its teeth. When this gullet opens to catch the black and brown proletarian bodies thrown to it by ship's companies according to their timetables, it exhales a stink of oil, urine, and printers' ink. This comes from the tartar baking hard on the massive jaws: newspaper kiosks, lavatories and oyster stalls. The harbour people are a bacillus culture, the porters and whores products of decomposition with a resemblance to human beings. But the palate itself is pink, which is the colour of shame here, of poverty. Hunchbacks wear it, and beggarwomen. And the discoloured women of rue Bouterie are given their only tint by the sole pieces of clothing they wear: pink shifts.[1]

What is striking about such a description is its remoteness from the boosterism of Méry, Pagnol and Londres; the bleakness of Benjamin's 'rue Bouterie' compared with 'Booty Street' in *Banjo*; and the power of the images of detritus and bacilli, which connect the major motifs of *Hans le marin* and Moholy-Nagy's *Marseille Vieux-Port*. This is especially true of the section on Les Bricks, the red-light district, 'named after the barges moored a hundred paces away at the jetty' (p. 131) and divided by 'invisible lines' into 'sharp, angular territories like African colonies' (p. 131)—a reminder of the complex network of frontiers twisting through the city. Like Waugh and Peisson, Benjamin singles out the practice of stealing the hat from the unwary tourists: 'if he forfeits nothing else in this game, it is his hat', destined to join the collection of 'trophies of manhood—boaters, bowlers, hunting hats, trilbies, jockey caps' (pp. 131–2).

Alongside his impressions of the Bonne Mère, gaudily personified, with 'streamers and sails' as 'her earrings' and 'jewels of ruby-red and golden spheres' decorating her shady lips' (p. 133), or the Cathedral of La Major, seen as 'a gigantic railway station that could never be opened to traffic... the Marseille religion station' (p. 133), Benjamin focuses on the sounds and intermittent silence of the streets of Le Panier, or upon 'the light from greengroceries that is in the paintings of Monticelli' (p. 133). This, in its turn, takes him back to the city's streets: the 'grey houses of the Boulevard de Longchamp, the barred windows of the Cours Puget and the trees of the Allée de Meilhan', leading to the secret shade of the Passage de Lorette (p. 134), and, later, to the highly politicised struggle between Marseille's increasing urban encroachment towards the workers' quartiers in the north and the remaining territory of the Provençal countryside. The bastides and cabanons of Zola and Méry are being replaced by 'the long Rue de Lyon', which is 'the powder conduit that Marseilles has dug in the landscape in order, in Saint-Lazare, Saint-Antoine, Arenc, Septèmes, to blow it up, burying it in the shell-splinters of every national and commercial language'(p. 136)—a prophesy fulfilled in the second half of the twentieth century.

Benjamin's later essay, 'Hashish in Marseille', which was published in the *Frankfurter Zeitung* in December 1932, is slightly longer and explores both the clinical effects of hashish and the Vieux-Port area, adding a hallucinatory, distorting lens to the already impressionistic sketches of the city in 'Marseille'. The effects of the drug, as Benjamin is already forewarned by Baudelaire, entail a combination of 'totally different worlds of consciousness',[2] oscillating between extreme clarity and wild distortion: hence the precision of the recall of his dose, at seven o'clock in the evening on 29 July (p. 138), and of the meticulous detailing of his itinerary, from the 'café on the corner of the Canebière and the Cours Belsunce', the Restaurant Basso on the Quai des Belges, preceded by a visit to the 'little bar on the harbour', another frontier post, 'still sufficiently far from the rue Bouterie, yet no bourgeois was there', back to the Restaurant Basso past the little boats moored by the quay, with 'all the Christian names of France', and, after dinner, his return via a 'square off the Canebière where Rue Paradis opens onto a park', where he listens to music from a jazz club, and back to where he began, for 'a final ice cream at the little Café des Cours Belsunce [sic]... not far away from the first café of the evening' (pp. 138–44).

The journey really begins, however, in the little harbour bar where the hashish kicks in, leaving Benjamin with 'a primitive sharpness that I had scarcely felt until then. For it made me into a physiognomist, or at least a contemplator of physiognomies', who positively stares at the faces of those around him in a way he would not dare when lucid (p. 139). In the same way, the drug, combined with the jazz music from the nightclub, allows him to call up distant friends: 'G. rode past me in a cab. It happened suddenly, exactly as, earlier, from the shadow of the boat, U. had suddenly detached himself in the form of a harbour loafer and pimp' (p. 143). Moreover, the city now becomes a place of stories:

> 'Barnabé' read the sign on a streetcar that stopped briefly at the square where I was sitting. And the sad confused story of Barnabas seemed to me no bad destination for a streetcar going into the outskirts of Marseille. Something very beautiful was going on around the door of the dance hall …. (p. 143)

Finally, recalling the cacophony of voices in the little bar by the harbour, Benjamin notes that 'everything was suddenly submerged in the noise of voices, not of streets' and that 'what was most peculiar about this din of voices was that it sounded entirely like dialect. The people of Marseille suddenly did not speak good enough French for me. They were stuck at the level of dialect' (p. 144). The hashish-induced trance brings back the centuries-old prejudice against the city's accent.

As Benjamin lies on his hotel bed waiting for the hashish to take effect, he looks out of the window at 'this view of the belly of Marseille. The street I have so often seen is like a knife cut' (p. 138). Moholy-Nagy's film of the same year, *Impressions of Marseille's Old Harbour* (*Impressionen vom alten Marseiller Hafen*) begins with a similar image: a scissor-blade pierces a map of the centre of Marseille and then cuts across the mouth of the harbour, from the Fort Saint-Jean to the Fort Saint-Nicolas, turns to the east along the line of the Rue Neuve before turning north up the Rue des Capucines as far as the Porte d'Aix, and then in a diagonal back towards the west at La Major. The resulting shape is discarded, like so much of the waste in the film, to reveal a shot of a Marseille street scene, which then becomes full-frame and leads on to the rest of the 10-minute silent film. In other words, the film-maker displays the parameters of the film's location, whilst emphasising its main tool, the cutting-room's scissors as the major narrative instrument. The film itself was shot in 1929 and, in its sequence of apparently unconnected shots of the landscape around the Vieux-Port, creates the same 'impressions' as Benjamin's 'Marseille' article, which could easily serve as a story board for the film itself.

As Sheila Crane observes, the film falls into the same category of other silent Modernist city documentaries, like Ruttmann's *Berlin. Symphony of a City*, of 1927 and Vertov's *The Man with a Movie Camera*, of 1929, to which could be added Jean Vigo's *A propos de Nice*, of the same year.[3] It opens with a series of street scenes on the Canebière and the Quai des Belges, including some from upper floors. One sequence, on the Quai de Rive-Neuve, involves a fairground wagon with a performing bear sitting on the back, before moving to the Canebière, with shots of an amputee on crutches, a cheap shop front, a beggar-woman and a man in a white suit looking down at a scene below. An additional sequence involves views from a restaurant looking out towards the terrace and a busy street corner, before moving along the quay to the looming transporter bridge. There then follows a series of shots of the bridge itself, including patterns and detailing of the cast-iron structure (much praised by Siegfried Giedion in his *Bauen in Frankreich. Bauen in Eisen. Bauen in Eisenbeton*, of 1928), which look forward to Germaine Krull's photographs from the same location. After this celebration of modern design and engineering, the film moves to its real subject, the squalid neighbourhoods to the immediate north of the Vieux-Port. The narrow streets rising from the port are characterised by the timber buttresses shoring up the collapsing walls and scenes of back-street poverty, hints of knife-crime, begging and prostitution. Above all, as in Benjamin and Peisson the Vieux-Port is overwhelmed by detritus of all sorts, sometimes blocking the narrow passageways, in which the stray dogs and cats are equated with the human population, engaged in the same task of eking a living from the inhospitable landscape. As the rain begins to fall and the rich are able to take shelter in cafés, the camera lingers almost pornographically on the misery of the Vieux-Port before panning away to distant, but alluring, shots of the transporter bridge, intercut on one disturbing occasion with a close-up of a mooring rope which looks like a noose. A final sequence focuses on rubbish floating in the harbour before the camera looks back on the rapidly vanishing city from the stern of a fast motor-launch. Like Benjamin and Peisson, Moholy-Nagy reinforces the identity of Marseille as 'the Wicked City', where wickedness is associated with squalor—Marseille as 'the Dirty City'—and, from a professional artistic and architectural perspective implicitly engages in the debate about urban renewal, which dominated the 1930s and the Occupation years and continued into the post-war era. From this perspective, dirt and *ordures* were incompatible with Modernism.

Germaine Krull's album *Marseille* appeared in 1935, with its text by André Suarès, whose *Marsiho* had been published four years earlier. During the First World War, she had studied photography in Munich, where she married the Russian anarchist Towla Axelrod, and was influenced by Moholy-Nagy, whom she met after the war at the Bauhaus. Her breakthrough as a photographer came in 1927, with the album *Métal*, which, like Moholy-Nagy's shots of the transporter bridge, stressed the abstract geometrical shapes of industrial machinery, and became 'the manifesto of the resolutely modernist and unconventional new wave.'[4] This volume was followed by two others, *100 x Paris*, of 1929, on the Eiffel Tower, and *Marseille*, of 1935.

Apart from a section on La Joliette, Krull mostly restricts her portrait of Marseille to the Vieux-Port area and the looming transporter bridge. The album is made up of forty-four monochrome plates, which essentially fall into four sections: the first (pp. 6–27) contains multiple shots of the port activity, often alternating between the Vieux-Port and La Joliette, with the former characterised by a sailing ship and fishing vessels and La Joliette by cargo boats, liners and the docks. The second section (pp. 29–45) concentrates on the transporter bridge, incorporating views of it from a distance, close-ups of its iron work, and shots from the bridge looking down on La Joliette, the Vieux-Port and the city itself, including the Canebière and Notre-Dame de la Garde, and, finally the slums north of the Quai de l'Hôtel de Ville, seen through the cabling and superstructure of the bridge itself. This leads naturally to the third section (pp. 45–59), devoted to realist shots of unidealised street scenes in the old quarter, not devoid of the same pornography which characterises Moholy-Nagy's film, including two squares at the bottom of the Canebière, peopled with tramps and sailors between voyages, before finishing (pp. 61–9) with views of the slums and the steep streets of Le Panier.

What is striking about the volume is its muted, even sombre, mono-chrome which consciously and counter-intuitively works against the brilliance of the Mediterranean sun, even when there are glimpses of it in the reflections in the water and the shadows. Effectively, the sun is neutralised, removing the port's Southernness and emphasising its affinity with the great Northern ports of Amsterdam, Hamburg or London. This is not the vibrant vision of Londres' account, but a more understated, clinical record of the hard underbelly of a hard city. This is signalled by one of the strangest aspects of *Marseille*, which is the total and nearly systematic disjunction between the dispassionate, often cruel, images, and Suarès' over-flowery, almost saccharine, captions, mostly taken from *Marsiho*, with a literary tone and vision which had become dated by the interwar years. Whilst the use of his captions and introduction may have made good commercial sense for the publisher, the effect of their juxtaposition with Krull's images is both to empha-sise the bleak Modernism of the illustrations and to subvert the text's roseate image of Marseille as Mediterranean Eden. A grainy full-page print showing rows of cargo boats moored at a quayside lined with barrels and diminutive dockers, for example, is captioned: 'Commerce is a big word: it connects men through work, and promises them reward.' On the facing page is a half-print showing a steam boat moored in the distance, next to sheds and overshadowed by tall chim-neys, dominated by a foreground of mountains of coal, which three dockers are loading into sacks. It is juxtaposed with a bizarre caption:

> The old Marseillais Pytheas, visiting the King of Thule, probably to share a drink, twenty-three times one hundred years ago, had never seen these ships.
>
> But how we would like to see his! And hear him speak Greek from the Accoules to the Chamber of Commerce![5]

One of the final pictures, in the sequence on the slum streets of the old quarter and Le Panier, shows a sharply sloping narrow cobbled street falling away to the right, with its buildings precariously held up by timber props, and all the inhabitants washing, cooking and playing in the flood of sewage trickling down to the port, captioned incongru-

ously: 'In these streets which smell of seaweed, what a wonderful mari-
nated tuna is being prepared with new olive oil!'[6] The message is not
just in the photograph, and highlights the textual disconnect.

These three Modernist artists from Germany take the evocation of
Marseille in the interwar years to a different level from Londres,
Peisson and McKay. Working from a left-wing perspective and fascinated by the urban environment, they produced deliberately fragmen-
tary works, in which the formal qualities of both the landscape and
their own production is paramount, along with the social fissures they
are trying to explore. As such, this Modernist style, with its clinical
portrayal and dissection of, for example, the disadvantaged community
of the Quartier Réservé and Le Panier, departs from the humanist
approach present in the traditional theatre and film of Pagnol, the
documentary realism of Londres and, cynical as the former may be, the
fiction of Peisson and McKay.

In fact, these two currents merge, with an emphasis on technical
formalism and a recognition of the European, especially Mediterranean,
cultural tradition, in the city's, and arguably the nation's, most important cultural review.

'Les Cahiers du Sud'

Les Cahiers du Sud (both 'Notebooks of the South' and 'Southern
Journal') constitutes one of the great success stories of French literary
review production in the twentieth century. With a span of over forty
years, the journal was one of the longest lived publications in what is a
notoriously ephemeral field, surviving and outstripping French contemporaries like the *Nouvelle Revue Française* and *Europe*. Under its editor, Jean Ballard, it was also one of the most influential literary and
cultural periodicals of twentieth century France, not merely in the area
of contemporary poetry, which remained its mainstay throughout its
career, but also in broader literary and intellectual concerns. It was not
merely 'the test-bench of French literature',[7] in André Malraux's
words, but a genuinely international review in its subject-matter and
wide range of contributors. Above all, it constitutes a unique case in
French periodical publishing as 'the only provincial long-running
review which could be listed amongst the great French reviews.'[8] As

Paul Chaulot wrote in *Esprit* when *Les Cahiers* finally closed in 1967, 'thus disappears at the end of a half-century of activity, a collective enterprise which is unparalleled in the literary annals of our era.'[9]

The history of *Les Cahiers du Sud* comprises three stages of development.[10] Beginning its life as *Fortunio*, founded by the young Marcel Pagnol and his friends from the Lycée de Marseille, the first number appeared in 1914, followed by three more until the outbreak of war. It was essentially a student poetry magazine, but possessed of a sense of ambition and an embryonic organisation which was to serve it well in the future. After the war, Pagnol and the original team launched a second series in 1920, which ran for only five issues, before a third series came on the scene in 1921. It was this third series which evolved into *Les Cahiers du Sud* with its virtually unbroken run from 1921 until the final number of the journal, in 1966. The new *Fortunio* was underpinned both by a firmer financial base and by a more elaborate organisation, due in part to Pagnol's ambition to transform it into a journal of national importance and, fortuitously, to his absence from Marseille from 1922 onwards. With Pagnol in Paris, *Fortunio* fell under the effective control of Jean Ballard, who had joined the team for the fourth number of the original series and who was to run the journal virtually single-handed until the end. After two years, from 1922 to 1924, when it appeared every two months, the review settled down into what was to become until the Liberation its established monthly format, although, crucially, its title changed, reflecting the new editorial power structure. From 1924 to 1925, the main title was still *Fortunio*, with a sub-heading *Les Cahiers du Sud*; in 1925, the main title became *Les Cahiers du Sud*, with the sub-title as *Fortunio*; and in 1926 *Fortunio* vanished altogether, leaving only *Les Cahiers du Sud*. Although the staple product of the journal remained contemporary poetry, a new sub-title, adopted in 1930 and which lasted until 1942, *Poésie, Philosophie, Critique*, testified to its wider ambitions, although during the Occupation, in 1942, the sub-heading changed again to *Revue Mensuelle de la Littérature*. From the Liberation until 1966 it appeared only six times a year, an indication, not merely of post-war austerity, but of the decline of the fortunes of both the journal and the city itself.

The history of the journal illuminates a number of key elements. Firstly, in the original *Fortunio*, *Les Cahiers du Sud* had the familiar and

Fig. 1. Engraving by Franz Hogenberg of sixteenth century Marseille in Vol. II of early publication on world cities, *Atlas of Cities/Civitas Orbis Terrarum* edited by Georg Braun (1575, Köln).

Fig. 2. Front cover of the Penguin Classics 1996 edition of *The Count of Monte Cristo* by Alexandre Dumas, first published 1844–5.

Fig. 3. Zarafa the giraffe (Nicolas Hüet, 1827), who docked in Marseille on her way to Paris (she then walked there with her keeper). She was a gift from the ruler of Egypt to Charles X.

Marseille — Le Palais Longchamp

Fig. 4. Le Palais Longchamp built to commemorate the arrival of a new water supply for the city in 1869. Its two wings held Marseille's first municipal Musée des Beaux-Arts and Musée d'Histoire Naturelle.

Fig. 5. Strike at the Docks watched by a '*nervi*' [Marseillais slang for an Italian docker]. Drawing by Louis Sabattier for March 30th 1901 edition of *L'Illustration*, a Paris based journal.

Fig. 6. One of the Marseille docks, early twentieth century.

Fig. 7. The Transporter Bridge, built in 1905, destroyed by enemy action, 1944.

Fig. 8. View of the Vieux Port from the Transporter Bridge, early twentieth century.

Fig. 9. Poster advertising Marseille Exposition Coloniale 1906 [David Dellepiane] with exhibits to offer 'experiences' of the exotic cultures of its colonies and reaffirm French Imperial power.

Fig. 10. Poster advertising the second Marseille Exposition Coloniale 1922 [Leonetto Cappiello] in heyday of French Imperialism.

Fig. 11. 1922 Exposition. Representation of African village with villagers.

Fig. 12. 1922 Exposition. Exhibit for Indo-China under construction.

Fig. 13. *LeVieux Port*, Paul Signac 1905, Marseillais painter of national significance using the technique of post-Impressionism.

Fig. 14. *Viaduc à l'Estaque*, Georges Braque, 1908. Seminal work marking beginning of his transition towards Cubism.

Fig. 15. Albert Londres (1884–1932), leading French investigative journalist who wrote important report on Marseille in 1927.

Fig. 16. Street scene in poor area: women washing at a public tap, 1938.

Fig. 17. Street scene in poor area near the Vieux Port.

Fig. 18. La Canebière, a main road built in the 1920s as slum areas were pulled down.

19me Année   Juin 1932

Cahiers du Sud

POESIE ■ CRITIQUE
■ PHILOSOPHIE ■

D. H. LAWRENCE .... *Le Roman* (the Novel)
ALDOUS HUXLEY .... *Tour du Monde d'un Sceptique*
JEAN WAHL .... *Rêves*
FERNAND MENDEZ PINTO .... *Voyages adventureux*
MARCEL ABRAHAM .... *Poèmes*
JEAN PALLU .... *Poèmes Cinématographiques*

BENJAMIN FONDANE .... *Martin Heidegger*

CHRONIQUES

VICTOR CRASTRE .... *Le Greco, premier peintre moderne*
GABRIEL BERTIN .... *Avec Banjo et les « Frères du Port »*

NOTES, COMPTES RENDUS

LES LIVRES, par Jean Audard, Joë Bousquet, Léon Derey, Léon-Gabriel Gros,
  Marcel Brion, Roger Brielle, Georges Petit, Emile Dermenghem.
LETTRES ETRANGÈRES, par Marcel Brion.
LA PEINTURE: *Jacques Thévenet*, par Roger Brielle; *Dora Bianka, Louis
  Botinelly, le Salon de l'Opéra*, par G. B.
LETTRES DE PARIS: I *La Musique; La crise des Théâtres Lyriques*, par
  Claude Laforêt.
  II. *Le Théâtre*, par Pierre Missac.
  III. *Bibliophilie*: Vente Arman de Caillavet, par Odette Lieutier.
URBANISME.: *Marseille et l'Urbanisme* (Gaston Castel), par Gaston Mouren.
MACHINES PARLANTES, par Gaston Mouren. *Ted Lewis*, par H. Thomas
  Cadilhat.
CONFÉRENCES, LA VIE MARITIME, SPECTACLES, ECHOS.

RÉDACTION - ADMINISTRATION : 10, Cours du Vieux Port, MARSEILLE
AGENCE GÉNÉRALE : Librairie JOSÉ CORTI, 6, rue de Clichy, PARIS
France : No 5 fr.   Étranger : Le 6 fr. 50 Le No

Fig. 19. Front cover of *Les Cahiers du Sud*, 1932, literary magazine founded in 1925
and edited by Jean Ballard.

Fig. 20. Advertisement for jazz music venue in Marseille, in *Les Cahiers du Sud*, indicating the vibrant modern and popular music scene.

Fig. 21. Advertisement for the pioneering aviation company Aéropostale in *Les Cahiers du Sud*, 1933, looking for new revenue as advertisements from shipping lines declined.

Fig. 22. Poster for Marcel Pagnol's play *Topaze*, which premiered on 9 October 1928 at the Théâtre des Variétés.

Fig. 23. Poster for *Marius*, a film by Marcel Pagnol using a story from his famous trilogy set in Marseille, the others being *Fanny* and *César*.

Fig. 24. The unemployed at the Vieux Port during the Great Depression, c. 1930.

Fig. 25. Jean-Claude Izzo (1945–2000). Marseillais poet, playwright and novelist of neo-noir crime novels, photographed in 1998.

conventional origins of most literary reviews, profiting from the amateur enthusiasm of young writers and students and specialising in poetry, a product which is both easy to come by and simple and cheap to process. Where it differed, however, was in its unusual 'will to last', tied closely to Pagnol's personal, and national, ambition, and which led to no fewer than three successive launches when less determined figures would have given up. It was this ambition on the part of Pagnol which resulted in the journal's second peculiarity: two diametrically-opposed conceptions of both its role and future. For Pagnol, it was essential for the journal to gain a national reputation and, in order to achieve this, it was axiomatic that it should become a Parisian publication as soon as possible. In this, he was not merely following the well-trodden path of all provincial Rastignacs, but specifically paying homage to the model, prestige and challenge of the *NRF*, which he wished to emulate and, indeed, replace. Thus, from his teaching-post in the Lycée Condorcet, he harangued his colleagues: 'Will you never understand that in Marseille you are in a cul-de-sac? Write and come to Paris... We need readers, we need a public...'[11] Jean Ballard, however, in spite of his admiration for the *NRF*,[12] was by no means prepared to turn the journal into a Parisian publication, preferring instead to exploit the Parisian review's format to his own ends in a resolutely Marseillais setting. It was this profound difference of opinion which led to Pagnol's resignation and to *Les Cahiers du Sud* coming under the sole control of Ballard. It is in this context that the title of the review, consciously chosen and carefully introduced by stealth over a number of years, takes on its full significance. Whilst 'Cahiers' positioned the journal in the tradition of Péguy's *Cahiers de la Quinzaine*, by opting for 'Sud', Ballard intended to lay claim to a specific, and vast, pan-Mediterranean cultural space, quite distinct from Paris, of which Marseille could be seen as the capital and intellectual hub. In short, *Les Cahiers du Sud* is the story of two characters: a city, Marseille; and the editor for over forty years, Jean Ballard, the most gifted literary periodical manager of twentieth-century France, Jean Paulhan and the *NRF* not excepted.

Paul Chaulot's obituary for the journal in *Esprit* underlines its debt to the city in which it was born, making it both an international cultural journal and 'a publication solidly anchored in its Phocaean base, if not in its accent',[13] a distinction which would have appealed to the hallucinating Benjamin. Unlike Paris, Marseille was at the centre of the French geopolitical project, and the term 'Sud' in the review's title was by no means, until the 1950s, a merely geographical or metaphorical entity, but a potent political reality: the incarnation of the nineteenth-century Saint-Simonian dream of the meeting point between Asia, Africa and Europe.

If *Les Cahiers du Sud* was the expression of a unique Southern and Mediterranean French identity, it was also part of a specific urban culture. In 1923, the review moved into offices at 10 Quai du Canal (subsequently Cours du Vieux-Port and now the Cours d'Estienne-d'Orves)[14] in the old Quartier de l'Arsenal, where 'the intellectuals and artists had been attracted by the picturesque climate; the painters had established their studios in the attics since the beginning of the century'[15]—what Ballard termed 'our Rive Gauche'[16] and a continuation of the bohemianism of the cabaret-culture of the Belle Epoque. On the Quai du Canal *Les Cahiers du Sud* found itself part of an unusually rich cultural environment: a large cosmopolitan popular regional centre, a major international port, an 'imperial' capital able to turn its back on Paris and look towards its Southern and Mediterranean homeland, and an exciting local bohemian culture, including fellow-journals such as *Le Feu* and *La Criée*. This implantation into the life of the city was vital to the development and survival of *Les Cahiers du Sud*, which maintained until the end an apparently curious coexistence between national, indeed universal, preoccupations, and powerfully civic concerns, as evidenced by Ballard's regular features on Marseille town planning issues. For the review there was no contradiction in such a juxtaposition, by which, in the June 1934 number for example, Stephen Spender's poems, René Daumal's 'Le Livre des Morts Tibétain' and Roger Secrétain's essay on 'Gabriel Marcel et le Mystère Ontologique' rubbed shoulders with an article by Ballard and Gaston Castel on 'La Future Gare Saint-Charles'.

On the contrary, this apparent incongruity was at the heart of the review's identity and essential to its intellectual and financial survival. It was also a profound expression of Ballard's own personality. Unlike Pagnol, Ballard was a lifelong Marseillais from Le Panier. Like his father, he was employed as a *peseur-juré* (weights and measures inspector) in the major food market on the Cours Julien, a post he held until his retirement after the Liberation. Whilst it obliged him to start work at four in the morning, he finished at ten and was able to devote the rest of the day to the review, a work rhythm which prompted François Mauriac, on a visit to Marseille, to ask a friend, 'who is that little man who weighs fruit and vegetables in the morning? During his afternoons he weighs words and ideas'.[17] In fact, although Ballard developed into a formidable literary entrepreneur, he also excelled as a manager, often delegating choices in issues of taste, at least before the Second World War, to figures such as André Gaillard or Joë Bousquet. Right from the period of the first *Fortunio*, he showed a remarkable talent for organisation and, particularly, finance, a gift to which, on numerous occasions, *Les Cahiers du Sud* owed its survival. In particular, in addition to the creation of the money-making *numéros spéciaux*, which provided a much-needed supplementary income, especially with the onset of the Depression in the 1930s, he showed himself to be highly adept at gaining sponsorship through a canny exploitation of 'the economic fabric of his city.'[18] This took the form of subsidies from the municipality or the Chambre de Commerce et d'Industrie, but also, particularly, of advertising, especially from the shipping companies, such as the review's most faithful advertiser, the Compagnie Paquet, and the cities to which they travelled:

> The economic space of *Les Cahiers* was commercial: Africa, the Maghreb, the Near and Far East, America and Europe... Its literary space was France and the francophone world, the world of cultural exchanges with Europe and the New World.[19]

At the same time, under the Front Populaire government, Ballard was able to exploit the national prestige of *Les Cahiers du Sud* to obtain official subsidies from powerful patrons like Jean Zay's advisors at the Ministère de l'Education Nationale et des Beaux-Arts, Jean Cassou and Marcel Abraham.[20] Ballard, who was himself a Front Populaire sympathiser, was shortly able to repay Abraham's generosity by sheltering him, like so many others, in Marseille during the Occupation. Indeed, such was the prestige of *Les Cahiers* that Ballard was even able to cadge a subsidy out of Marseille's arch-rivals Edouard Herriot and the Lyon Municipality.

The paradox in the career of *Les Cahiers du Sud* is that this unashamedly Marseillais journal was able to exploit its civic identity in order to create a national and international prestige denied in some ways to its Parisian counterparts. As a review based in Marseille, but emphatically not a provincial, even Provençal, journal, it was able to establish and manipulate a unique and complex set of national and international cultural resources, of which three were the most important: the poetic avant-garde, the Mediterranean, and a broad international, non-French, culture in which Germany played a crucial role.

The literary focus of the review was dramatically set by the collaboration, in 1924, of André Gaillard, a poet with extensive contacts amongst the Surrealists. In 1925, which Michèle Coulet counts as the real date of birth of *Les Cahiers du Sud*, Gaillard persuaded Ballard to begin publishing Surrealist authors, such as Antoine Artaud, himself a native of Marseille, Benjamin Peret, Roger Vitrac, René Crevel and Paul Eluard.[21] This new direction for the review, which 'scandalised Marseille',[22] was the beginning of *Les Cahiers du Sud*'s long commitment to Surrealism, to the extent that 'during the second half of the 1920s the Surrealists were published and discussed more in *Les Cahiers du Sud* than in the *NRF*.'[23] In addition, in 1928–1929, Gaillard secured the entry into *Les Cahiers du Sud* of the Surrealist 'dissidents' of *Le Grand Jeu*, based in Rheims, including René Daumal, Léon-Pierre Quint and Georges Ribemont-Dessaignes.[24]

This sponsorship of Surrealism, which gained the journal a prominent place in the history of literary Modernism, brought *Les Cahiers du Sud* into contact with Parisian journals like *La Revue Européenne*, and also with the publisher Simon Kra and Le Sagittaire.[25] In particular, it reinforced and extended a policy which was to last until the end of the journal, which was to publish young avant-garde poets: the post-war *Cahiers* was the natural home for the early poetry of Philippe Jaccottet and Jacques Réda. In the case of Surrealism, the object of fierce controversy in the capital, the fact of being a non-Parisian outlet weighed in the journal's favour and allowed it to implant itself in Paris in a way that, paradoxically, a Parisian journal would have found difficult. In this, it benefited chiefly from the influence of Georgette Camille, who brokered a distribution arrangement for the journal itself and its ancillary publications with the Surrealists' publisher, José Corti,[26] who,

seeing *Les Cahiers* as merely a lucrative rival to the *NRF*, underesti-
mated, like Pagnol, Ballard's commitment to Marseille and the logic
which underpinned it.

As its title already indicated, *Les Cahiers du Sud* was committed to a
certain broad conception of Southern culture, but that vision took
some time to coalesce. In the first place, Ballard was very insistent
from the outset on a crucial distinction between Marseille as a global
city and the region in which it found itself. He wrote in 1927, '*Les
Cahiers* is not the regional review of Provence. It is the review of
Marseille and it lives at the same rhythm as the city.'[27] However, if he
was categorical in his rejection of Provençal folklore, he was more
sympathetic to the broader concept and cultural reality of Occitanie.
As in the case of Gaillard and Surrealism, a personal contact was crucial: this time, with Joë Bousquet, the poet and war-invalid from
Carcassonne, who exerted a considerable influence on *Les Cahiers du
Sud* and, in particular, on the very concept of 'Sud'. Bousquet and his
group, who published the review *Chantiers*, became a major force in the
development of the Southern identity of *Les Cahiers du Sud* from 1927
onwards, but also, more generally, in its literary orientation.[28] In fact,
with the collapse of *Chantiers* in 1930, the Carcassonne group looked
increasingly to *Les Cahiers du Sud* as an outlet and Bousquet came to
replace Gaillard, who had died in 1929, as a powerful adviser, claiming
in 1936 that 'the editorial offices of *Les Cahiers du Sud* go through my
bedroom.'[29] Yet if Bousquet and his circle provided a powerful new
definition of Occitan culture for *Les Cahiers du Sud*, Ballard, like Gelu
earlier, remained extremely circumspect regarding Occitanie's more
reactionary manifestations, particularly the Félibrige, which, with the
exception of some left-wing adherents, like Mistral himself, was on the
Maurrassian Right.[30] This was to characterise the attitude of *Les Cahiers*
towards Southern, and particularly Mediterranean, culture in general,
what Paul Chaulot defines as its 'defence of Mediterranean humanism
in all forms.'[31]

The commitment to Marseille was already there, as was an embryonic and tentative concept of the 'South', but they came together,
reinforced by the influence of Bousquet and his entourage, in an almost
systematic and prolonged meditation on the wider notion of the
Mediterranean, its culture and its societies. If Gaillard had made the

review open to Surrealism and if Bousquet had reinforced its links with modern poetry and the culture of Occitanie, a third figure came to influence the *Cahiers*: Paul Valéry, appointed in 1933 as *administrateur* of the Centre Universitaire Méditerranéen in Nice, and whose first report sounded a clarion-call for Mediterranean culture: 'Europe and the Mediterranean would become, through the self-same elements which had developed there, the elements of a second age of greatness of the human universe.'[32] The activities of the Centre were regularly reported in *Les Cahiers du Sud*, which also extended its coverage to cultural news from cities along the littoral, such as Nice itself, and, later, Menton and Cannes, and, crucially, including North African cities like Tunis and Algiers, where the review had permanent correspondents.

From the early 1930s, therefore, *Les Cahiers du Sud* saw Marseille as being at the centre, both geographically and spiritually, of a culture which was at once age-old and profoundly new, what the poet Gabriel Audisio called the *'jeunesse de la Méditerranée'* ('the youth of the Mediterranean').[33] This mission had been implicit at the outset and owed much to two of its major stalwarts, Audisio himself, and Louis Brauquier. Brauquier had been associated with *Le Feu*, which published his first two collections of poetry, *Et l'au-delà de Suez*, of 1922, and *Le Bar d'Escale*, of 1926, and was one of the original contributors to *Fortunio*. Allegedly a model for Pagnol's Marius because of his ambition to go to sea, he became a purser for the Messageries Maritimes, sailing throughout the Mediterranean before working in the line's shore offices in ports across the world, including Shanghai and Sydney, which he evoked in his writing and painting. His literary work, mainly poetry, reflects both his fascination with the sea and travel and his emphasis on a Mediterranean world, including Provence: his first poems, dating back to 1920, and collected in the volume *L'auciprès couronna de nerto* (*Le Cyprès couronné de myrte*), were written in Provençal.[34]

Gabriel Audisio was the son of Victor Audisio, who had been director of the Algiers Opera House before taking over as director of the Marseille Opera. Another graduate of the Lycée de Marseille, he subsequently worked in Algiers in the Governor-General's Office and later as the Head of the Algerian Economic and Tourist Board. In fact, his own and his father's career trajectories, like that of Brauquier, serve as yet a further powerful reminder of the closeness of North Africa, especially Algiers, to Marseille, and the professional and cultural links which bound the two together. In Audisio's case, not merely did his work in Algiers, reflected in his novels and poetry, bring him into contact with North African French writers and intellectuals like Max-Pol Fouchet, Camus[35] and Jean Grenier, it also reinforced still further a pan-Mediterranean cultural perspective encompassing Islamic and Classical influences. Two of his later works, the historical study *La Vie de Haroun el Rachid*, of 1938 and the essay *Ulysse ou l'intelligence*, of 1946, trace a broad cultural territory in which Marseille, with its Phocean origins, finds its rightful place amongst the legends and literature of the Middle East and the Greek world, a theme already familiar from Dumas and explored in the 1990s by Izzo.

This exploration of a broad Mediterranean cultural territory was pursued in some of the most important of the review's many special numbers. In 1935, it published a number on *L'Islam et l'Occident*, including articles by Albert Gleizes and Jean Hytier, followed in 1939 by *Retour aux myths grecs*. A major event in 1942, *Le Génie d'Oc et l'Homme Méditerranéen*, edited by Bousquet and René Nelli, was followed by *Permanence de la Grèce*, in 1948, and *Aspects du Génie d'Israël*, in 1950. With the Greek world as its centre, *Les Cahiers* undertook a quasi-systematic exploration of the Mediterranean cultures which surrounded it, in which Occitanie figured as an equal partner alongside Islamic and Jewish culture. From this sustained reflection, there rapidly emerged a solid concept of Mediterranean humanism and a corresponding devotion to writers of Mediterranean origin or with Mediterranean themes: *Les Cahiers* celebrated Gide's writings on North Africa, whilst one of Ballard's lasting regrets was at having rejected Camus' 'Noces à Tipasa'.

It was because of this enduring commitment to Mediterranean humanism that *Les Cahiers du Sud*, as in the case of Occitanie, was outraged at the expropriation of the concept by the political Right, attracted by Mussolini's reinvention of 'Mare Nostrum'. In *Jeunesse de la Méditerranée*, of 1935, and a series of articles in 1936, under the general rubric 'Vers une synthèse méditerranéenne', Gabriel Audisio launched a sustained attack on this right-wing expropriation, exemplified by the reactionary Académie Méditerranéenne in Monaco, commenting that 'the cover of humanism always shelters the same worrying shadows',[36] those of anti-Semitism and racism. Nevertheless, like its model, the *NRF*, it tried to be politically non-partisan, going so far as to publish, in June 1936, for example, an article by the extreme right-wing Robert Brasillach on *Le Cid*.

It was its commitment to humanism which, it derived from a broad concept of Mediterranean culture, which gave the review its internationalist liberal stance. From as early as 1928, *Les Cahiers du Sud* had published texts by British and American authors: T.S. Eliot, through the influence of the Anglicist Henri Fluchère, and Faulkner, Saroyan and Henry Miller due to the efforts of Gabriel Bertin.[37] The review's passion for English literature was reinforced, not merely by numerous articles on and extracts from T.F. Powys (a French obsession throughout the first half of the century), but, more importantly, by the decision to devote the first *numéro spécial* to the theme of *Le Théâtre élizabéthain*, edited by Georgette Camille. In particular, however, *Les Cahiers du Sud* was always attracted to Germany, initially because of long-term German interest in the Mediterranean and Classicism, but also because of the Enlightenment tradition, Romanticism and Liberalism. Undoubtedly, one of the longest and most important of the *numéros spéciaux* was that devoted to *Le Romantisme allemande*, originally published in 1937 and reprinted under Albert Béguin's direction in 1949. All the great German authors appeared in the journal in one form or another, and it was natural that, after 1933, *Les Cahiers du Sud* became an automatic haven for exiled German writers and intellectuals, like Ernst Erich Noth, who was a regular member of the editorial team from 1935 onwards, and after the declaration of war, refugees such as Ernst Toller and Walter Benjamin. This in itself was the result of an evolution towards explicit anti-fascism, culminating in 1935, when Léon-Pierre Quint represented the review at the Congrès International pour la Défense de la Culture contre le Fascisme in Paris—a commitment which continued throughout the Occupation when its offices sheltered refugees from the German and Vichy authorities.

Planning the Mediterranean

Marseille had become a favourite subject for reflections on the development of modern architecture. It was no coincidence, for example that in 1933 Marseille was the point of departure for the fourth

Congrès International de l'Architecture Moderne (CIAM), at which Moholy-Nagy's film was shown, nor that Le Corbusier, who was gradually fusing his concept of Modernism with a Mediterranean tradition of *latinité*, should work on the redevelopment of Algiers, should be fascinated by Marseille and would construct his *Unité d'Habitation* in the city after the Second World War. It was natural, therefore, that the development and planning of Marseille soon became a regular feature of *Les Cahiers du Sud* and one which was by no means distinct from its literary or intellectual goals. Indeed, the physical appearance and the layout of the city were intimately linked to issues concerning the journal's identity within a broad geographical and cultural context, and especially its role as a standard-bearer for the Modern. Ballard established a close working relationship with the Marseille architect, Gaston Castel, who had designed the new Opéra after the fire of 1919 and the Baumettes Prison south of the city in 1931, and contributed a series of articles on Marseille and regional planning, published as a collection in 1932, with a map, *Schéma de la Ville de Marseille*, subtitled *Capitale de la Méditerranée*.[38] Together Ballard and Castel promoted an openly modernist conception of the city's future layout in the context of fierce interwar debates on planning policy, which essentially coalesced around two issues: the role of the heart of the city and the geo-political significance of Marseille in the Mediterranean region. As regards the city centre, the key document was the new urban plan for the city by the Parisian town planner Jacques Greber, *Ville de Marseille*.[39] Greber, a professor at the Institut d'Urbanisme in Paris, with considerable experience of working in the United States, was appointed by the municipality, then run by the conservative mayor Georges Ribot and his all-powerful *premier adjoint* Simon Sabiani, to devise the city's 'extension and redevelopment plan', which was published in 1932. Clearly, his experience of working as a planner in America influenced his decision to prioritise the development of garden cities in the suburbs, connected by new roads, along with separate industrial and port areas and the expansion of tourism, not least in the *calanques* towards Cassis. It was his proposals for the centre of the city, however, which became the most controversial, including the 'demolition of the whole quartier round the Hôtel de Ville,... roads through the old town,... Le Panier, Les Carmes, the quartier du Cours and down to the Vieux-Port',[40] with the area behind the Bourse to contain 'ten ten-storey tower blocks around a vast central square' and the Quai de l'Hôtel de Ville to be lined with new apartment buildings, although no higher than their predecessors. Nevertheless, Greber stopped short of recommending wholesale demolition of the old quarters. As Sheila Crane explains, in spite of the squalor and criminality of the Quartier Réservé, which at least had the virtue of being geographically contained, the Vieux-Port was generally viewed positively,[41] with the municipal council making a formal request to the national government in 1931 'to classify the Vieux-Port as an official "picturesque site"',[42] thus rendering it an official 'place of memory'. Greber's plan fully endorsed this decision, recognising the important contribution to tourism of the Vieux-Port and influenced by the early prophets of town-planning Marcel Poëte and Camillo Sitte, who both prescribed an organic approach to city development. He 'described the Old Port as Marseille's structural core'[43] and 'symbolic heart and singular urban image',[44] though unlike Moholy-Nagy and Germaine Krull, he was no fan of the transporter bridge, joining the campaign for its demolition on the grounds that it obscured, rather than enhanced, the entrance to the Vieux-Port.

In fact, Greber's proposals were considerably more modest than those of *Les Cahiers du Sud*, where Ballard and Castel argued for the total destruction of the old town. '[T]his is the golden opportunity to clean out the city and its bad habits, to cast down the old citadel of cockroaches and infamy',[45] they wrote, and:

> the only solution which we consider equitable would be to pull every-thing down and reconstruct new quarters on the site… Let us act quickly and get rid of this rubble, so that the shame of Marseille can come to an end…. We can see only one way: raze everything quickly so that on the ruins of these old hovels a new city can be built.[46]

Predictably, the ensuing public outcry,[47] allied to a shift to the left at the Hôtel de Ville in 1934, meant that the *Plan Greber* was never imple-mented, but both Greber and Ballard and Castel were merely articulat-ing the distaste for Marseille's *ordures* that was already implicit in Londres, Mackay and Peisson, and, more strongly, in the accounts by Benjamin, Moholy-Nagy and Krull. In so doing they highlighted the inherently non-humanist functionalist nature of Modernism. It is no coincidence that Le Corbusier should have shown such a persistent interest in Marseille, as he did for the similarly 'disorganised' Algiers, and that the Vieux-Port's dual nemesis took the form of the *Plan Beaudoin*, commissioned by Vichy, and its enactment by the German occupation troops in 1943, who also destroyed the transporter bridge before retreating the following year.

If the debate about the Vieux-Port concerned the heart of the city, a parallel debate, though by no means unconnected, was conducted about the place and significance of the city itself within its wider geographical and cultural context. Ballard, in his regular column on Marseille town-planning, wrote of Castel's *Marseille Métropole*, 'you dare to believe that Marseille will be more central than Paris the day when North Africa and France will be one country',[48] and, as Crane reminds us, the transporter bridge had on its upper platform a *table d'orientation* donated by the Touring Club de France which displayed, not merely prominent sites on the Marseille skyline and surroundings, but also

> located the city within a much more abstract topography, as its outer register pointed in the direction of select destinations within and beyond France, including St. Petersburg, Vienna, Genoa, Rome, Malta, Bizerte, Algiers, Oran, Gibraltar, Madrid, Bordeaux, Le Havre, London, Paris and Marseille.[49]

Marseille's sense of itself in relation to the outside world was orientated on a grand international scale and developments in the interwar years would strive to give both conceptual and physical shape to that international identity, by which travel connections became paramount. One example was the modernising planner Henri Prost, who had worked with Marshall Lyautey on urban projects in Morocco before the war, and who, in the 1920s, proposed a 'new coastal highway that was to extend from Marseille to Genoa', thus connecting the two Northern Mediterranean sea ports.[50] In their turn, other planners were prompted to construct their own projects on a series of similar linear axes from north to south and east to west, which would place Marseille at their crossroads. Thus, Prost's embryonic east-west transversal, capable of extension eastwards to Istanbul, Odessa and beyond, or, to the west, to Toulouse, Bordeaux and even across the Atlantic to New York, would meet its vertical axis from Paris and Northern Europe to the Maghreb and sub-Saharan Africa in the grand

Mediterranean hub of Marseille itself: the fulfilment of the Saint-Simonian dream. Herbert Adams Gibbons' report in 1927, that

> from Batum at the end of the Black Sea to Dakar in French West Africa, Marseille expects to be the middleman for France—and part of central Europe—to be one tenth of the world's population. Thanks to a trans-Saharan railway, she expects to provide the shortest route from Europe to South America,[51]

was accompanied by more speculative and theoretical geopolitical schemes, often with imperial or right-wing connotations. Le Corbusier's Modernism went hand-in-hand with the contemporary esoteric notion of the 'Parisian meridian', linking Paris, Marseille, Algiers, Ghardaïa and the estuary of the Niger, and based on existing flight paths and projects like the trans-Saharan railway,[52] or Count Richard Coudenhove-Kalergi's and Herman Sörgel's notion of 'EurAfrica' as a means to the 'coordinated expansion of control over African resources and territory.'[53]

These grand modernist imperialist designs had already partly become fact, however, and in 1930 the PLM railway was already advertising Marseille as the essential conduit between Northern European cities, like London (merely twenty-one hours distant), Brussels (eighteen hours), Amsterdam (twenty-one hours), Strasbourg (fourteen hours), and Paris (twelve hours), and the French North African ports of Bizerte, Algiers, Oran, Tangiers and Casablanca, under the slogan: 'The Best Links with North Africa are through Marseille: Speed. Convenience. Comfort.'[54] The sea-times were not given in the poster, but in 1939 it would have taken twenty hours to Algiers, thirty hours to Tunis and twice that to Casablanca.[55] The 'Marseille Meridian' and the redevelopment of Marseille, including the clearance of the Vieux-Port, were both essentially modernist and imperialist projects,[56] which saw the city as a chess-piece, of considerable importance, in a global strategy and hence gained considerable interest amongst the politicians and technocrats in Vichy after 1940. In this context, the increasingly important phenomenon of commercial aviation, which, as Paul Morand had suggested in *Méditerranée mer de surprises*, of 1938, challenged established thinking on the geopolitics of the area, could easily be incorporated into the Saint-Simonian vision, which had no problem with Marseille as a global aeronautical hub, in addition to its role as a land

and sea crossroads and building upon existing air links between Paris and Northern Europe, North Africa, West Africa and South America.[57] A far greater challenge, however, to this grand global strategy would appear one year after Morand's book, with the Second World War, which would eventually transform both Marseille itself and the world in which it operated.

7

TRANSIT

OCCUPATION, DESTRUCTION AND LIBERATION

In Edmonde Charles-Roux's 1971 novel, *Elle, Adrienne*, the protagonist Serge, fleeing the German advance in June 1940, arrives in Marseille and is immediately struck by the city's air of normality, far removed from the war-zones which he has crossed on his way south:

> There, it was the eternal Summer, with its empty days which smelled of the sea. Girls walked in the streets, their bathing costumes rolled under their arms. They were the real youth of France, the youth which had never seen death, never approached misfortune, really beautiful as well, unconsciously so.[1]

Marseille was relatively untouched by the hostilities themselves, but played host to the influx of French and foreign refugees who made up the *Exode* of 1940. In fact, it benefited, as it had done between 1914–1918, from the Government's requisitioning of the merchant marine at full market rates, a situation which persisted until the post-war years, and from the increased traffic of troops and supplies inwards from North Africa and outwards to Syria.[2] Moreover, the removal of the mayor Henri Tasso and the replacement of the city council in March 1939 by direct rule from Paris provided the city with a foretaste of Vichy Government control from June 1940 onwards, under the administration of the lawyer Henri Ripert.[3] Thus, the experience of Marseille

161

during the Occupation falls into two distinct periods, the relative freedom of the *Zone Libre* from June 1940 to November 1942, and the
much harsher regime of the direct Occupation following the Allied
landings in North Africa, which ran from 12 November 1942 until the
liberation of the city on 28 August 1944. These periods open and conclude with devastating air-raids: the attacks by German and Italian
squadrons on 1 and 21 June 1940, and on 27 May 1944 the bombing
of the city centre by the US Air Force, causing the destruction of 1,200
buildings and the loss of 2,000 lives.[4]

Throughout this period from the *Drôle de guerre* (Phoney War) to the
Liberation and subsequent *Epuration* (purge), Marseille was dominated
by four crucial factors: the presence in the city of an unusually large
number of French and international refugees, making it the major port
of transit during the first period of the Occupation; the competing
forces of Collaboration and Resistance, often fuelled by international
militants and, in the case of Marseille, by rivalries between organised
crime factions; the level and nature of the physical destruction of
Marseille's infrastructure, which, in terms of aerial bombardment, for
example, was less serious than that suffered by Rouen or Le Havre, but
which was more than counterbalanced by the deliberate, and symbolic,
demolition of the north of the Vieux-Port and the final sabotage by the
Germans of most of the port facilities, including the iconic transporter
bridge; and, finally, the extraordinary cultural continuity, especially at
the level of popular entertainment, from the late 1930s to the post-
Liberation period.

One inevitable consequence of Marseille's status as a Mediterranean
port during the Second World War was the narrowing of the city's
relationship with the outside world due to the decline in its port traffic
from which, in spite of momentarily comforting statistics, it never
recovered. After the increased activity during the Drôle de guerre,
shipping to and from Marseille remained at healthy levels during the
first period of the Occupation, from June 1940 to December 1941,
when neither Germany and its Allies, nor the État Français at Vichy
were at war with the United States. During this period, not only did
Marseille maintain its sea links across the Mediterranean—insofar as
was possible under the British blockade—in particular with the North
African ports in Algeria and Tunisia, it also continued to operate long-

haul routes to West Africa and Indochina, as well as to North and South America, albeit, with crucial consequences for refugees, via the Atlantic ports of Casablanca and neutral Lisbon. The shipping news in the veteran daily *Le Sémaphore* of 1 March 1941, for example, lists arrivals from Valencia, Philippeville, Oran and Casablanca, with more local traffic from Bastia, Sète and the Rhône delta port of Saint-Louis, whilst the edition for 6 March 1941 carries advertisements for all the major shipping companies for services to Dakar, Rio, Montevideo and Buenos-Aires (Société Générale des Transports Maritimes), Indochina, via Casablanca and Dakar (Chargeurs Réunis), West Africa and the Caribbean (Fabre), Senegal (Paquet), with the important proviso 'se renseigner à la Compagnie' ('consult the Company'), which normally meant transit through an Atlantic port.

Pearl Harbour and the declaration of war by the Axis powers in December 1941 severed both the Atlantic links and the service to the Far East, following the Japanese invasion and occupation of Indochina. Nevertheless, services to Algeria and Morocco continued until the summer of 1942, whilst services to Corsica continued for some months after the German occupation of November 1942, but then came to a halt.[5] This gradual strangulation of the port, which had disastrous economic effects on the city, was of enormous symbolic value, in that it went to the heart of Marseille's identity as an international, pan-Mediterranean hub and, in spite of the efforts made to re-establish its role after the Liberation, it was a wound from which it never recovered. More immediately, however, the tightening of the noose around the port had profound implications for the sizeable population of refugees who found themselves in transit in 1940 and 1941.

Anna Seghers, 'Transit'

The events of May and June 1940 broke the illusion of the Drôle de guerre:

> The rout of the French army and the huge exodus which accompanied it were to push to the banks of the Mediterranean a panic-stricken population, a mass of refugees who crammed into the hotels and improvised shelters… An immense wave, in which scattered soldiers were mixed up with civilians, and which came from the interior to die

on an impermeable frontier all along the sea-coast. In a few months, this exodus had washed up on Marseille thousands of pieces of human wreckage.[6]

This human wreckage, French and foreign, military and civilian, and by no means as privileged as Charles-Roux's Serge, discovered that it was not alone in seeking refuge in Marseille. These arrivals joined a large number of foreign nationals who had been there before the outbreak of war and been interned at the outbreak of hostilities. These included not merely 'suspect foreigners, but also refugees from central Europe (sometimes anti-Nazis), who had not joined the Foreign Legion or the companies of volunteers who served as auxiliaries to the French army.'[7] They were imprisoned in the former Le Brébant theatre, on the Avenue des Chartreux, which was opened in 1939 as an immigrants' screening centre, before being turned into a 'centre de séjour surveillé' (internment camp) for foreigners, communists and criminals in 1940, and which would continue to operate as an immigration camp until long after the war. Women were housed in the Présentines prison, the Hôtel Bompard and the Hôtel Terminus in the city centre, and more refugees, especially Jews, were transferred to the old tile-works at Les Milles, outside of Aix, which was used as a concentration camp.[8] The *Exode* of May–June 1940 brought not merely vast numbers of French citizens fleeing the fighting in the North, but also new waves of foreign refugees, most of whom were Jews or political opponents of Nazism, who would turn the city into a vast transit camp and seriously test its long-standing, if ambiguous, reputation as a *ville d'accueil*.

The fate of these refugees 'in transit' is encapsulated in the 1942 Warner Brothers film, *Casablanca*, directed by Michael Curtiz, in which the American Rick Blaine takes the train for Marseille from Paris before ending up in Casablanca, whilst the European Resistance leader Viktor Laszlo and his wife Ilsa are waiting in the Moroccan port for the documents which will enable them to fly to Lisbon and freedom in the United States.[9] The key to this experience, as the film's sonorous prologue reminds us, is that this refugee community is simply 'waiting, waiting, waiting' for the documents and the transport which will liberate them from this limbo, and, whilst this was undoubtedly true for those groups in Casablanca and other ports of transit, it summed up even more so the experience of the far larger number of refugees who found themselves trapped at the first hurdle in Marseille itself. The drama of escape from occupied Europe was played out in the consulates of Marseille, where the refugees queued endlessly for the visas which would enable them to reach Casablanca over the Mediterranean and through Algeria or Lisbon across the Pyrenees and through Spain.

The definitive guide to this experience is Anna Seghers' novel of 1942, *Transit*, written in Mexico and published in English after her own escape from Marseille in 1940.[10] The novel is the first-person account of an unnamed German dissident who has escaped from a concentration camp in 1937 by swimming across the Rhine and has been interned in France in 1939 as a conscripted labourer, working on the Rouen docks. With the *Débâcle*, he moves south, ending up in Marseille, though looking for warmth and work rather than a means to escape. On his way south, however, he has passed through Paris, where he meets up with an old German acquaintance, Paul, from the Rouen camp, who asks him to deliver two letters to an exiled German writer, Weidel, in a hotel in the Latin Quarter. Here he discovers that Weidel has committed suicide, leaving a suitcase with an unfinished manuscript, and he opens the two letters. The first is from Weidel's estranged wife urging him to join her in Marseille, whilst the second, from the Mexican consulate in the same city, informs him that 'a visa and travel funds were waiting for him there.'[11] The subsequent plot involves the narrator being gradually drawn closer to the dead author, having an affair with his widow, and being presented with the unhoped-for opportunity to assume Weidel's identity and profit from his visas and travel funds to escape to Mexico, an opportunity which eventually, and with some bravado, he turns down in order to stay and fight. Alongside this plot, however, the real importance of *Transit* lies in the narrator's observations of Marseille in 1940 and the fate of the foreign refugees attempting to escape.

The narrator's first impression of Marseille, seen from the hills above it, is the familiar one, 'it seemed as bare and white as an African city.'[12] Later, he reaches the Canebière and realises that

the blue gleam at the end... was the Old Harbour and the Mediterranean... The last few months I'd been wondering where all this was going to end up—the trickles, the streams of people from the camps, the dispersed soldiers, the army mercenaries, the defilers of all races, the deserters from all nations. This, then, was where the detritus was flowing, along this channel, this gutter, the Canebière, and via this gutter into the sea, where there would at last be room for all, and peace.[13]

Here, Seghers takes up the persistent image of Marseille in 1930s fiction as the repository of refuse, both real and figurative, and gives it a new political twist, which, with hindsight, makes the destruction of the Quartier Réservé in 1943 inevitable. Initially, the would-be emigrants are confined to shabby hotels, like the narrator's in the Rue de la Providence, off the Cours Belsunce, and the cafés and bars around the Vieux-Port, the Rue de la République and the Canebière. In the Café Vertoux they swap stories, advice, and rumours of departing ships, and, especially, plot how to amass the tickets and the bewildering numbers of visas which will enable them to leave Marseille and arrive eventually at their destination. For it is the visas which constitute the almost impenetrable series of puzzles which must be solved before the refugees can leave. The narrator's lugubrious guide through this labyrinth is an old orchestral conductor from Prague who has been promised a post in Caracas and who patiently explains the fragile three-dimensional game of assembling all the necessary visas—exit, transit, entry—all of which are liable to expire before the refugee can depart, and of which the transit visas are by far the most difficult to juggle. It is a game which can collapse at any moment and, as he lectures the narrator:

> Now, son, imagine that you've managed to do it. Good, let's both dream that you've done it. You have them all—your visa, your transit visa, your exit visa. You're ready to start your journey. You've said goodbye to your loved ones and tossed your life over your shoulder. You're thinking only of your goal, your destination. You finally want to board the ship.—For example: Yesterday, I was talking with a young man your age. He had everything. But when he was ready to board his ship, the harbour authorities refused to give him the last stamp he needed.

> Why?

> He had escaped from a camp when the Germans were coming.... The fellow didn't have a certificate of release from the camp—so it was all for nothing.[14]

It is for this reason that the centre of the drama is the Mexican Consulate in the Boulevard de la Madeleine. Under its own Popular

Front, Mexico had been a staunch supporter of the Spanish Republicans during the Civil War and was emphatically anti-fascist, which, along with its border with the US, made it both a sympathetic and attractive target for those fleeing Nazism. This did not imply, however, that the granting of an entry visa was in any way automatic. Moreover, access was indirect, through Portugal, which, as we have seen, meant transit through Morocco or Spain, or through Martinique and thence to Cuba before the final leg to Mexico.

Unsurprisingly, few succeeded in making this journey, beset by bureaucrats of all nationalities, German agents and French profiteers: the manager of the narrator's Hôtel de la Providence, whom he suspects of sharing the spoils of unregistered aliens with the police, is far removed from the benign presence who oversees the emigrants' hotel in Londres' *Marseille, porte du Sud.*

Seghers had suffered just this frustration and indignity herself, although she was ultimately successful in escaping in 1941 on a ship also carrying Victor Serge, André Breton and Claude Lévi-Strauss. Indeed, many of the characters in *Transit* are drawn from the literary and intellectual community of German refugees who found themselves in Marseille in 1940 and who included Hannah Arendt, Ernst Erich Noth and Walter Benjamin, whose case was particularly tragic. As we have seen, he knew Marseille well in the 1920s and 1930s and had written perceptively about it. After the assumption of power by the Nazis in 1933, he had lived a hand-to-mouth existence, 'condemned to a way of life', as Peter Demetz puts it, 'closely resembling that of the émigré extras in Rick's Café in Casablanca.'[15] His luck ran out in late September 1940, when, having 'picked up his US visa in Marseille', he set off on the overland route to Portugal via Spain:

> [He] crossed the French-Spanish border with a small band of fellow exiles, but was told on the Spanish side by a local functionary (who wanted to blackmail the refugees) that Spain was closed to them and that they would be returning in the morning to the French authorities, who were just waiting to hand them over to the Gestapo. Benjamin—totally exhausted and possibly sick—took an overdose of morphine, refused medical help and died in the morning, while his fellow refugees were promptly permitted to proceed through Spanish territory to Lisbon.[16]

Benjamin, like many of the other German refugees, had forged close links during the 1930s both with Jean Ballard personally and with *Les Cahiers du Sud*. Ernst Erich Noth, for example, had settled in Marseille in the 1930s, where he wrote for the journal before being interned between 1939 and 1940, joining the Resistance and eventually escaping to the US in 1941. Undoubtedly, *Les Cahiers du Sud* looked after its own: committed under Ballard's leadership to a pan-European and pan-Mediterranean liberal humanism, a staunch supporter of the French Front Populaire, the Spanish Republicans, Italian anti-fascists and the opponents of Nazism, it had given space to dissident writers throughout the 1930s and, in 1940, became a crucial source of help for intellectual refugees from the German invasion and the Vichy regime. Not only did it act as an important *centre d'accueil* (welcome centre), helping with tickets and the numerous visas, it also offered a physical place of asylum by accommodating as many people as it could in its offices on the Quai du Canal:

> The 'eyrie' of *Les Cahiers*, in the first phase of the Occupation, was to serve as a place of safety and to provide a valuable service for numerous refugees who could not envisage returning to a country directly under the control of Hitlerian Germany, or, more simply, did not feel any more secure in the 'occupied' zone. Simone Weil, amongst others, visited it assiduously from 1940 to 1942.[17]

This precious contribution more than justified the agonising decision to continue publishing the review under Vichy and then German censorship,[18] although the continued publication of the review was not unanimously welcomed in Marseille. The Vichy Commissioner, Emile Ripert, who had vigorously defended Victor Gelu in *La Renaissance Provençale*, was particularly acerbic:

> This review… had, for twenty years, exercised on a section of the young people of Marseille an influence which I found extremely damaging, an influence which is more regrettable than ever because this review, which persists with its old errors, is doing nothing to support the actions of the government…[19]

Les Cahiers du Sud was merely one of a number of institutions and committees operating in Marseille from 1940 to 1942 which aided refugees of all sorts and which confirmed the city's reputation as a *ville d'accueil*. As the shifty exile Paul explains to Seghers' narrator, who is in search of funds:

— My dear fellow, just stand in line for a couple of hours at some committee.

— Which committee?

— Good heavens! There are the Quakers, or the Jews of Marseille, HICEM, Hayas (sic), the Catholics, the Salvation Army, or the Freemasons.[20]

Amongst this plethora of aid committees, mostly with religious affiliations, the best-known is undoubtedly the American Emergency Rescue Committee, established in 1938 by Thomas Mann, supported by Eleanor Roosevelt, and directed from 1940 onwards by the journalist Varian Fry, who arrived in Marseille in August. Although Fry's committee is credited with saving between 2,000 and 4,000 anti-Nazi and Jewish refugees, unlike other aid organisations its target was predominantly artists and intellectuals. As Fry wrote to his wife in February 1941: 'Among the people who have come into my office, or with whom I am in constant correspondence, are… some of the greatest living authors, painters, sculptors of Europe.'[21] Assisted by Albert O. Hirschman, Miriam Davenport and the heiress Mary Jane Gold,[22] Fry discovered that shipping these artistic celebrities out of the country was by no means easy, even for a quasi-official American organisation. Not only, as Seghers mercilessly emphasises, were the travel opportunities few in number and the bureaucratic hurdles immense, Fry's committee was looked at askance by both the Vichy authorities, who finally closed it down because it had 'saved too many Jews'[23] and, in spite of Eleanor Roosevelt's support, by the US State Department, which was anti-Semitic and resistant to Jewish immigration.

One significant and highly publicised part of Fry's activity concerned the Villa Air-Bel in the village of La Pomme, in what is now the 11th Arrondissement of Marseille.[24] This vast, run-down, but furnished *bastide* was found by Fry's secretary, Daniel Bénédicte, who was looking for furnished accommodation for the Committee's staff as an alternative to the cramped conditions of the Hôtel Splendide near the Gare Saint-Charles. With eighteen rooms, the space outstripped their needs, and they were able to accommodate Victor Serge and his wife and son and André Breton and his wife and daughter. Subsequently, the villa, baptised 'Espervisa', welcomed visitors like Arthur Adamov, René Char, Marcel Duchamp, Max Ernst, Peggy Guggenheim, André Masson, Pierre Péret and Tristan Tzara—mostly Surrealists whose work had been publicised by *Les Cahiers du Sud* since the 1920s. As we know, Serge, Breton, Duchamp and Ernst sailed on the same boat as Anna Seghers; Tzara was not so lucky: unable to gain visas for America, he remained in France and fought, like Char, with the Resistance.[25]

If Marseille seemed to confirm its reputation as a *ville d'accueil* through the activities of *Les Cahiers du Sud* and the international aid committees, it is important to remember that the refugees were also highly vulnerable to the Marseillais themselves, through bureaucratic obstruction, police zeal, racial and political prejudice or sheer financial greed, especially if, unlike Fry's clients, they were merely anonymous Jews who had no celebrity to trade. The reaction to the Italian air raids of June 1940 were already an indication of the fragility of the ethnic harmony in Marseille: in spite of causing particularly harsh damage to those 'old quartiers where the transalpine population was particularly large', it gave rise to 'a renewal of that anti-Italian xenophobia which had been in abatement for a long time.'[26] At the same time, Marseille's Jewish population, the largest in France and which had appeared successfully assimilated, fell victim to the Vichy anti-Jewish laws of October 1940, barring Jews from posts in the civil service, including teaching, and the law, and enforced the Aryanisation of Jewish businesses, along with the confiscation of Jewish property,[27] with little protest from the non-Jewish community. This discrimination culminated in the massive round-ups and deportations of French Jews in January and February 1943.

The crackdown on foreign refugees in Marseille in the summer of 1940, which swelled the number of Jews to 14,000,[28] was immediate and brutal. Not only was this immigrant population subject to internment, they faced the threat of deportation which would grow as the Occupation progressed. On 26 August 1940, nearly 2,000 prisoners were transported from the Camp des Milles to Compiègne for onward transport to Germany, including 2–300 from Marseille alone.[29] In other words, as Thémime puts it, Marseille was not merely a *ville d'accueil*, but also a *ville piège* (city of entrapment), a label which became literally true with the destruction of the Vieux-Port in 1943.

'Seven Thunders'

The most visible effects of the war and occupation were in the changed physical landscape of the city. In addition to the destruction caused by the two air raids of 1940 and 1944, the German demolition, during the last days of the Occupation, of the transporter bridge deprived Marseille of an essential feature of its skyline. This loss, however, was overshadowed by the events of January and February 1943, which saw the destruction of the old quarters to the north of the Vieux-Port, together with the internment and, in many cases, subsequent deportation, of its inhabitants.

The demolition and the events leading up to it were recalled in a curious British film of 1957, *Seven Thunders*, directed by Hugo Fregonese and starring James Robertson Justice. Conflating the case of the notorious Parisian Dr Petiot, who murdered the Jewish refugees he was supposedly helping to escape, and an improbable storyline about escaped British prisoners-of-war hiding out in the Quartier Réservé, the film nevertheless culminates in a highly evocative recreation of the 1943 round-ups and the cataclysmic destruction of the district. Whilst there is no dispute over the factual details of this destruction, the reasons and responsibility for the operation are more complex. On 22 January 1943, French police launched a massive security check in the city centre, in which 40,000 people were stopped and questioned. Of these, 5,956 were arrested, although 3,977 were almost immediately released, and only 30 were remanded on criminal charges. However, the remaining 2,000, 'mostly Jews and refugees from the East' were 'turned over to the Nazis and sent directly to the camp at Compiègne, and then to the death camps.'[30] At five in the afternoon on 23 January, an SS regiment surrounded the quartier of the Vieux-Port, cutting off all access, and at six the following morning, the inhabitants were forcibly evacuated, taken by tram to the Gare d'Arenc, loaded into goods wagons and transported to three camps in Fréjus, in the Var, previously used by colonial troops.[31] Of the 20,000 interned in freezing conditions in Fréjus, 1,500, mainly old or very young men, were more or less arbitrarily designated as 'criminals' and sent to Compiègne, where, on 28 April, they were deported to Germany.[32] The rest returned to their homes on 26 January, only to find that their property had been pillaged and most of their belongings stolen, and

171

were forced to remove what remained of their belongings to other districts, often, like the parents of Izzo's Fabio Montale, driven out of Le Panier to the working-class Italian district of Belle-de-Mai. They had to move fast, because on 1 February German sappers began the systematic destruction of the area to the north of the Vieux-Port, beginning with the Quartier Saint-Jean, and continued for seventeen days, wiping out 1,924 tenement buildings over 14 hectares of the old city, although leaving the Hôtel de Ville intact.[33] The gaping holes and ruins were all that was left of what had once been the city's heart and, for good or bad, one of the keys to its identity.

The reasons for the Vieux-Port's destruction are interesting, not merely for the conjecture and innuendo which surrounds them, but especially because they relate to the reputation the district had acquired as the nucleus of the 'Wicked City' and of the recurrent images of 'detritus' and 'vermin' which infested it. There is no dispute as to the initial decision-making, although accounts differ as to whether the order came initially from Hitler or from SS General Karl Oberg, the Head of German police in France, who was in command of operations on the ground.[34] In any case, it was at a meeting of 14 January 1943 in Marseille that Oberg addressed representatives of the Vichy regime, including 'René Bousquet, the Head of the Vichy Police, Lemoine, the Regional Préfet, Barraud, the Préfet in charge of the administration of the city, Chopin, Préfet of the Bouches-du-Rhône and de Rodelle-du-Porzic, the police quartermaster', and stated:

> Marseille is a hideout for international bandits. This city is the canker of Europe and Europe cannot live as long as Marseille remains unpurged. The terrorist attacks of 3 January, when soldiers from the Greater Reich were killed, are proof of that. That is why the German authorities want to cleanse the old quarters of all the undesirables and destroy them by mines and fire.[35]

The French managed to secure some concessions, including a brief delay, a scaling-down of the area to be covered, the delegation of the round-ups to French police and the assurance that the internees would be sent to Fréjus and not Compiègne. This was the most that could be gained, however, and the remainder of the operation was carried out, as we have seen, by SS troops and German engineers.

More intriguing is Oberg's assertion that the main goal of the operation was to combat Resistance terrorism. It is certainly true that on the
date referred to by Oberg, 3 January 1943, there had been a bomb
attack at the Hôtel Splendide, formerly Varian Fry's headquarters,
which killed two Germans. This attack was preceded by two bombs in
the city centre in December 1942, one in front of the Hôtel Astoria
and another at the Hôtel Rome et Saint-Pierre, in which one German
soldier was killed,[36] and followed by other attacks on cinemas and
brothels frequented by German soldiers.[37] A bomb also exploded on
22 January on a tram car crowded with Germans. These attacks were
the work of the Communist-Jewish FTP-MOI, which had been active
since the beginning of the Occupation, but there is little evidence that
Resistance activity was concentrated disproportionately in the Vieux-
Port, even though much of the movement's initial organisation was
directed by exiled Italian and Spanish communists, some of whom lived
in Le Panier.[38] Jean-Pierre Melville's film of 1969, for example, *L'Armée
des ombres*, based on Joseph Kessel's novel and set in 1942, opens in
Marseille, but this initial portrayal of the Resistance network takes
place in the square outside the Palais de Justice, on the Rue Emile
Pollak, and in a safe house on the Corniche,[39] and the Vieux-Port does
not figure at all. Whilst Provence as a whole acquired a reputation for
Resistance activity and whilst Marseille in particular was the setting for
a complex war between rival criminal factions, in which Paul Carbone
and François Spirito played a major role in Simon Sabiani's collaborationist politics, and where the Guérini brothers eventually sided with
De Gaulle, the city's Resistance activity was, like its organised crime,
by no means concentrated in the petty criminal district around the Rue
de la Bouterie. The artistic, intellectual and white-collar Resistance,
which was powerful in Marseille,[40] was clearly not made up of residents of Le Panier and its surrounding districts on the Vieux-Port.
More plausible, in fact, is the argument that the Quartier Réservé
represented a danger because it was the natural refuge of German military deserters.

As Edmonde Charles-Roux records in *Elle, Adrienne*, the results of
the round-up were disappointing. Instead of the expected terrorists and
German deserters, the victims were primarily 'trade unionists, Jews
and people from Central Europe',[41] whilst the bulk of those emerging
from the slums were:

Old men and women, retired people moving frighteningly slowly, laden down with derisory bundles, baskets and grocery bags. They looked like peasants going to the fair: a procession which you would never have expected to see coming out of this bolt-hole. Where were the masses of criminals?[42]

In Charles-Roux's fictional account, but one based on personal experience of the Marseille Resistance, the only voice to be heard against this crime and indignity comes from an unexpected source: the prostitutes of the Quartier Réservé, who let rip with a flood of 'swearing which seemed to come from their stomachs. Unimaginable obscenities',[43] against which the authorities are powerless:

The dark flood spared no-one. From the mud there rose in dark words the vengeance of the city… And the people from the alleyways felt avenged as well… All knew that they were avenged. And the women continued to shout obscenities as only they could invent them.[44]

Whilst the destruction of the Vieux-Port seems explicable in the light of German reprisals for terrorist activity in other occupied countries, it is more likely that, in this case, Marseille was the victim of both the adverse international image of the 'Wicked City' that the Quartier Réservé had attracted since the First World War, and of the allied stigma of the 'dirty city' which offended hygienists and urban technocrats. In this respect, January 1943 was the moment that Paris, via its Vichy proxy, and Nazi Germany, as the self-styled embodiment of Nordic principles of order, took on the cockily independent Mediterranean city on France's, and Europe's, southern border. From this Northern European perspective, Marseille was no different from Algiers: hence the importance of *Pépé-le-Moko* in creating an external assimilation of the two ports in the public mind. As Commissaire Hélène Pessayre reminds Montale in *Solea*, 'the repeated myth of "les classes dangereuses" ricochets towards the South and towards the migrants from the South to the North',[45] and Marseille, no less than Algiers, had its own Kasbah, a no-go area ruled by its own *caïds*, and which was a boil waiting to be lanced—an operation which occurred in 1943 in the Vieux-Port and thirteen years later in Algiers.

In addition to the international reputation of the Quartier Réservé, described by the Nazi theoretician Alfred Rosenberg as the source of 'new germs of bastardisation',[46] its alleged role as a base for Resistance activity, and conspiracy theories imputing collusion between the SS and the Marseille *Milieu* in order to pillage the quartier, there was a more compelling, if initially more mundane, reason for the destruction of the Vieux-Port, which concerned municipal administration, town planning and public health. Already in 1929, when 'the Marseille municipality finally put in hand a survey of housing need... the shocking extent of overcrowding and poor conditions was revealed.'[47] Greber's development plan of 1933, the PAEE, prescribed the immediate construction of 27,000 new dwellings linked with the centre by new roads, but, with the recession of the 1930s, there were neither the political will nor the resources to implement it and the issue remained a permanent social problem well into the post-war era. Instead, the situation got worse, and the area to the north of the Vieux-Port, which had already figured dramatically in the visual records of Krull and Moholy-Nagy, had become a dangerous slum, shored up with timber supports, with buildings about to collapse at any moment and with a high incidence of disease. As it was, the destruction of the area took place in the context of the plan drawn up by Greber's successor, Eugène Beaudouin, in 1942, and agreed without consultation by Vichy. Like Greber's plan, it concentrated on road layout, incorporating road-widening schemes for streets leading to and around the Lacydon, especially on the north in the area between the Vieux-Port and La Joliette. In other words, beneath the political and ideological antipathy in Vichy towards the Vieux-Port, the quartier was also the victim of long-term town-planning concerns, reinforced by Vichy technocracy, and the appalling state of the area's fabric and public health. Although the contemporary report in the municipal newsletter *Marseille* is clearly politically motivated, it also touches on undeniable evidence and conclusions already reached by Ballard and *Les Cahiers du Sud*:

> This slum should have been dead long ago, but there are dying people who have to be finished off. It is this beneficial crime which our administration wishes to perpetrate by profiting from the possibilities of the Law of 30 May 1941 on the major projects in Marseille undertaken by the government of Marshal Pétain....[48]

Unsurprisingly, this slum-clearance scheme in the very heart of the city immediately aroused suspicions of financial speculation,[49] not least because the area was gentrified in the building projects of the 1950s, especially along the waterfront of the Vieux-Port itself. As Anne Spartiello concludes: 'Gradually, the Vieux-Port had shut itself off in bourgeois comfort. Only a minority could come back to live in the new quartier.'[50]

Culture under the Occupation

Alongside the influx of refugees in 1940, the aerial bombings of 1940 and 1944, the destruction of the Vieux-Port and the creeping deprivation which took hold of the city as the Occupation progressed, the cultural life of Marseille continued, throughout most of the Occupied and Free Zones, remarkably uninterrupted at all levels. Indeed, as Jean Michel Guiraud records, in the sphere of high culture some critics, including those of *Les Cahiers du Sud*, went so far as to claim the advent of a 'Renaissance', although Ballard himself remained sceptical: 'This present activity is illusory... It gravitates around the same kernel of Marseillais writers...'[51] Ballard was undoubtedly right in that this enthusiasm for a Marseille cultural Renaissance in 1940 was predicated on two assumptions which were rapidly proved to be false. In the first case, Marseille commentators were dazzled, like Varian Fry, by the presence of so many famous names from the French and European artistic world in their city, and, used to the absorption of waves of foreign migrants, all too readily assumed that this new influx of Parisian and foreign artists would stay and enrich the community. The queues at the shipping-offices, the Prefecture and the foreign consulates, however, demonstrated, as Fry himself was only too well aware, the exact opposite and that, for them, Marseille, was merely a staging post, the best hope of escape from Occupied Europe. As it was, by the end of 1940, this foreign artistic and intellectual population had largely shipped out, and those French celebrities who had decided to stay in France, like Gide, Malraux or Martin du Gard, settled in Nice instead, which they found more congenial.

At the same time, the temporary relocation to Marseille of some Parisian radio stations and newspapers, along with the continuing operation of Pagnol's film studios, convinced the city that, free from the German military rule of the Occupied Zone, it would serve as the free cultural and media capital of France. Whilst this may have been a plausible conclusion in the weeks and months following the French defeat of June 1940, it was rapidly contradicted by German policy, promoted by the Ambassador Otto Abetz and his literary censor Gerhard Heller, of the re-establishment of cultural normality within fairly relaxed constraints: censorship, for example, applied mainly to Jewish and politically dissident authors, enshrined in the 'Liste Otto' signed by most Paris publishers, who also profited from the acquisition of Jewish imprints like Nathan and Calmann-Lévy. The result was that the devolution of the Parisian media to Lyon and Marseille, apart from the permanent location of the National Radio in the Grand Théâtre, was short-lived and that, across the entire cultural spectrum, the German policy of 'normalisation' and the resumption of activity in Paris proved remarkably successful: in publishing, controlled by the judicious use of paper rationing; the theatre, which underwent a golden age between 1940 and 1944; and the cinema, in which the attractiveness of the Parisian studios, close to the theatres where many of their stars performed in the evening, and shored up by German subsidies, proved unassailable, whereas the Southern studios in Nice or Marseille were unable to compete, in spite of the odd flourish like the Fernandel vehicle *Médor* at the Studios Marcel Pagnol.[52] If there was a cultural 'renaissance' in France in the period 1940–45, it occurred in Paris rather than in Marseille.

Rather, the cultural history of Marseille during the Occupation is dominated by continuity, symbolised by the Opéra reprising in February 1942 its 1939 production of *Faust*. Throughout the Occupation, both the Opéra and the Gymnase continued to host touring companies organised for the Free Zone, so that the Marseille public could see Harry Baur in Pagnol's *Jazz*, Suzy Prim and Géard Landry in *Le Vrai visage de la Dame aux Camélias* and Geroges Flamant in *Les Amants terribles*,[53] although, for the most part, major Parisian actors never performed in them, depriving Marseille theatre-goers of Marie Bell's *Esther*, Madeleine Renaud and Pierre Bertin in *Musset*, and the entire work of Anouilh, of whom they remained ignorant until after the war.[54] However, whilst Marseille, like the whole Free Zone, was subject to the 'death of provincial theatre', for lack of a real policy of decentralisation,[55] there were signs of an often ephemeral regeneration in the number of small independent theatre companies which came into being during the Occupation and which, in some cases, received either Vichy or municipal subsidy. The most important, Le Rideau Gris, founded by Louis Ducreux, opened with *Musique Légère* at the Pathé-Palace cinema on 19 September 1940 and achieved a distinguished reputation, not merely in Marseille, but also in Lyon and Paris, especially with reconstructions of Elizabethan theatre in collaboration with Henri Fluchère, who had edited the special number of *Les Cahiers du Sud*, and through the plays of André Roussin.[56] This company was joined by Les Jaloux, an amateur troupe directed by Marius Marseille and a vehicle for Vichy ideology, with a subsidy from the Conseil Administratif. Its first production was *Travail, Famille, Patrie*, which opened in the Salle Mazenod on 24 November 1940.[57] Another pro-Vichy troupe which came into being just after the Armistice was La Comédie Phocéenne, an off-shoot of the Centre Culturel Méditerranéen founded on 8 November 1940 by the Director of the Ecole des Beaux-Arts, Henri Brémond, and the former champion of Victor Gelu and fierce critic of *Les Cahiers du Sud*, Emile Ripert.[58] They were accompanied by the Centre Intellectuel Méditerranéen, which hoped to use the open-air Théâtre Sylvain as its base, the Compagnie des Quatre-Vents, founded by a former collaborator of *Les Cahiers du Sud*, Gaston Mouren, and which had the same aim as Ballard's review in encouraging young authors;[59] the Théâtre du Temps; and, significantly, Pierre Feuillière's Théâtre du Marais, which was provisionally installed in Marseille: a rare example of theatrical devolution from Paris to the provinces.[60]

More immediately imposing was the city's classical musical activity during the Occupation, in which the presence of the Radiodiffusion Nationale played an important role, both in enhancing the activities of the Opéra where it was based and in promoting open-air concerts across the city.[61] Its problem was that, as a national organisation, it was subject to political pressure from both the Vichy Government and the collaborationist press, especially in eliminating Jewish musicians,[62] who, along with unemployed refugees, received financial help and sometimes lodging from three grand bourgeois benefactors, Cécile de Valmalète, Marguerite Fournier and, most famously, the Comtesse Lily Pastré, in her 'Villa Provençal' in Montredon, south of the city.[63] Lily Pastré, who at the beginning of the Occupation liaised closely with

Varian Fry, used her considerable wealth and the unusual historical circumstances to not merely protect gifted Jewish performers in danger of starvation or arrest, but to establish an association, Pour que l'Esprit Vive ('So that the Spirit Might Live') which created an extraordinary series of concerts, with works by Mihalovici, Honegger and Martinu, and performers like the pianist Monique Haas, the violinist Lucien Schwartz and the cellist Pablo Casals. One concert was devoted to Negro spirituals, with Germaine Montero and Georges Jongegeans singing and Joseph Kosma and Jean-Armand Petit on the piano,[64] and the highlight of the series was *A Midsummer Night's Dream*, directed by Boris Kochno, Diaghilev's assistant in the Ballets Russes. It was a blow to post-war Marseille culture that when Lily Pastré came to endow a music festival after the war, she should do so in Aix-en-Provence and not in Marseille.

Finally, one of the beneficiaries of the Vichy regime was the Félibrige and the wider movement for Occitan culture. The representatives of an agrarian, non-industrial culture with its roots in the land, defiantly anti-Parisian and claiming a Mediterranean identity, and with the powerful support of Maurras, Léon Daudet and Action Française, the pro-Occitanie supporters were a powerful force in the southern half of the Zone Libre, as long as they did not actually threaten the cohesion of the 'Etat Français' itself. Whilst the Félibrige was not powerful in Marseille itself, it was a logical step in the *Les Cahiers du Sud*'s pan-Mediterranean cultural policy to tap into the Occitan ascendency during the Occupation by publishing the special number *Le Génie d'Oc et l'Homme Méditerranéen*, which appeared in 1943, edited by Joë Bousquet. An exemplary cultural journal during the interwar years, *Les Cahiers du Sud* maintained a delicate balance between political probity and pragmatism throughout the *années noires*.

The same continuity applied to popular culture, in which both attachment to the Vichy regime and subtle strategies of resistance are visible. Olympique de Marseille, now comfortably in its new stadium at the Vélodrome in the Boulevard Michelet, played in the new South-East League, along with Saint-Etienne, Nice, Cannes and Antibes, and continued to draw large crowds, finishing second in 1940 behind Nice and boosted by its two top goal-scorers during the Occupation, Emmanuel Aznar and Louis de Sainte de Maréville.[65] Similarly, the music hall continued to flourish, unimpeded, unlike in Paris, by any restrictions in terms of curfew, which meant that public transport continued to circulate until relatively late: tickets to the Comtesse Pastré's *Midsummer Night's Dream* extravaganza, for example, which did not start until 9.30 pm, informed spectators that special trams would be running to take them home afterwards. Moreover, unlike the theatre, where, as we have seen, Parisian actors were unwilling to perform in the provinces, music-hall stars remained wedded to their familiar tours across the country. Thus the Marseille public could still watch their favourite performers, Fernandel, Agnès Capri, Charles Trenet, Edith Piaf and Mistinguett, in music halls like the Alcazar, supplemented by the major cinemas, the open-air music halls like the Colisée-Plage and even a new establishment, the 'Cabaret Music-hall', La Mascotte.

The weekly magazine *La Revue de l'Ecran*, together with the copious cinema sections of the Marseille daily press, testify to the continued popularity of film, although what is noticeable is the reluctance of cinemas in Marseille to abandon the interwar vogue for American cinema until absolutely necessary. American films continued to compete with French ones until the autumn of 1942, in spite of Germany's declaration of war against the United States following Pearl Harbour in December 1941 and warnings from the highly collaborationist daily owned by Simon Sabiani,[66] *Midi-Libre*, whose motto was 'Pour la Révolution dans la justice et la Collaboration dans l'honneur' ('For the Revolution in justice and Collaboration in honour'), that 'American film, which is one of the first enemies of dramatic theatre will be banned. This will hopefully result in a return to the sort of theatre that we so desire for the renown of French art.'[67] Ironically, on the same page as this condemnation, the cinema listings advertised Humphrey Bogart and Bette Davis in *Marked Woman*, Dick Foran and Gloria Dickson in *Heart of the North*, Bette Davis and Georges Brent in *Dark Victory*, Claude Rains and Ann Sheridan in *They Made Me a Criminal*, Carole Lombard and Fernand Gravey in *Fools for Scandal*, and, finally, *Snow-White and the Seven Dwarfs*, 'for the first time on a French screen.'

Indeed, as across the whole of occupied Europe, American popular culture proved remarkably resilient and this was particularly true in the area of popular music. This was particularly true of the vogue for jazz, although not all interpretations of the term 'jazz' were as precise or sophisticated as the reviews in *Les Cahiers du Sud* under the rubric 'La Musique Hot', written by Georges Petit in the 1930s, followed by Charles Delaunay's column 'Disques Hot' in 1939 and 1940, before his departure for the United States. The Marseille press, along with Vichy and the impresarios, was deeply confused about the conflict between ideological rigour and popular taste, and was resigned to the victory of the latter. *Le Sémaphore*, for example, reminded its readers in March 1941 that it had published an article two years earlier, entitled 'Les étrangers chez nous' ('Foreigners in our midst'), warning against the alleged infiltration of 'foreigners' in all aspects of French life, including the artistic. Unsurprisingly, therefore, it was enthusiastic about a performance the previous month by La Troupe des Compagnons de France at the Opéra, whose aim was to revive old French songs, 'which are so rich in spirit, verve and picturesque poetry', accompanied by 'dances borrowed from provincial folklore.'[68] Similarly, it welcomed a new cultural experiment by the Légion Française des Combattants: 'la Rénovation du théâtre par la Révolution Nationale', involving the creation of a music hall 'à la Française', as opposed to the 'American style', which had dominated in the interwar years, with a repertoire chosen, like that of the Compagnons, 'exclusively from French folklore.' For 'the review is an essentially French genre. Let us remain faithful to it. In contact with half-breeds, in recent years it had taken on the taste of exotic drugs. No laughter, no songs: instead, languorous and voluptuous spectacles...'[69] Despite this cry for a return to popular cultural purity, however, concessions were still made to the unquenchable taste for American culture: in the music-hall listings for 14 March, there is an announcement for the French music-hall performance *A la Française!* at the Pathé-Palace, 'with the Band of the 43e Régiment d'Infanterie Alpine', accompanied by 'the new jazz-band of the Légionnaires.'[70]

This ambiguity runs through the Marseille press of the Occupation period. *Midi-Libre*, in an article on music by Claude Gay in September 1942, claims strenuously that 'even in music—through the nationality of the composer and the vast poem which he is evoking—the "land does not lie".'[71] Yet that same edition advertises a performance at the Odéon by 'Django Reinhardt et son orchestre, dans un festival de jazz swing', promoting both a gypsy jazz guitarist and the vogue for the swing-band style of jazz which continued throughout most of the Occupation, in spite of official disapproval. The famous band-leader of the 1930s, Ray Ventura, the epitome of interwar irreverence, best-known for the madcap style of his band the 'Collégiens' and for his song of 1934, 'Tout va très bien, Madame la Marquise', played at the Variétés in May 1941.[72] Meanwhile, the same number of Le Sémaphore which celebrated the Légion review 'A la Française!' and its revival of traditional French music, also advertised its predecessor at the Pathé-Palace, 'Jo Bouillon et son orchestre', attempting to bridge the decadence of American 'swing' and Vichy sports policy: Jo Bouillon, 'who has, amongst the musicians in his swing quintet made popular by the radio, authentic cycling champions like the excellent saxophonist and clarinettist Roland Craene',[73] was the star attraction of a 'Grande journée cycliste de la zone non-occupée, organisée par le Swing-Club de France', on a bill which included Reinhardt and 'Raymond Mill's [sic] et ses boys.' In December 1941, the Embassy cabaret included in its programme the 'inimitable orchestre Tomas et ses merry-boys',[74] a name which, as an early post-Liberation number of the Resistance magazine V reminded its readers, was banned by the Vichy authorities for its American connotations.[75]

As the programmes of both the Marseille music halls and the national radio indicate, the popular taste for American-style music was unassailable, as the Parisian authorities found in their ongoing confrontation with the 'Zazous', and a curious coexistence pertained throughout most of the Occupation, with official pronouncements emanating from Vichy in favour of French cultural traditions being largely ignored by the public and the impresarios. National radio was happy to broadcast French swing bands, like Jo Bouillon, and 'Musique tzigane', and the music halls followed suit. In the same way that the Third Reich found it impossible to eradicate the taste for jazz and finally capitulated by organising its own official jazz-band,[76] Vichy essentially gave up the battle.

There is no better indicator of the continuity of popular culture from the interwar years through the Occupation to the Liberation, fought out, incidentally, on the heights of Notre-Dame de la Garde and in the surrounding countryside primarily by North African troops, than the persistence of jazz swing bands and the return of the much-missed American cinema. The ban on American cinema from December 1942 to June 1944 proved to be merely a hiccough in a long infatuation with Marseille, and *Le Provençal* celebrated the re-opening of the cinemas in early September 1944 with an article entitled 'Bonjour, Mickey!'[77] and two days earlier had carried advertisements for *Le Retour de Zorro*, at the Rialto, and the 'Grand film américain', *La 8e Femme de Barbe-Bleue*, at the cinema of La Plaine.[78] Nor was the music hall slow off the mark, often with official patronage: the FFI sponsored a 'Grand Gala de Music-Hall' at the Pathé-Palace on 22 September, followed in October by the opportunistically-titled 'Merci De Gaulle!' at the Odéon[79] and the review 'Hello Marseille', which opened in December.[80] At the same time, the great music-hall stars returned to Marseille: Fernandel at a gala organised by the SFIO, and Piaf and Montand at the Variétés-Casino in a benefit for the 'Centres d'Entr'aide de la Maison du Prisonnier.'[81]

It was no coincidence that this rapid return of pre-war popular entertainment should include jazz. Marseille, which had been one of the centres, with Paris, of serious jazz music in the interwar years, became an essential venue for American jazz performers after 1945. On 20 October, *Le Provençal* announced a 'Grande Nuit du Jazz' at the Pathé, including a film starring Charles Boyer, *Par la Porte d'Or*, the tenor Otto Fassel, the Red Army Choir, a 'défilé de mannequins' ('fashion show') and, 'for the first time in Marseille, a "jam-session"', with 'Tomas et ses Merry Boys' finally able to use their title again, and 'les meilleurs swingters [sic] français et alliés présents à Marseille' ('the best French and Allied swingsters present in Marseille').[82] The next month, incidentally, *V* magazine felt it necessary to dispel the confusion reigning in Marseille on the meaning of 'jam session' by explaining it as a term introduced by Guy Rinaldo, 'Président du Swing-Club de France' at the jazz club Le Doyen de Paris.[83] In November 1944, *V* reviewed a 'Grand Nuit du Jazz et de la Couture' at the Pathé-Palace, animated once more by 'Tomas et ses Merry Boys' and with allegedly black American musicians, including G. Porumb on clarinet, V-M. Butter on Bass and J. Porubsky on accordion: 'For the first time in Marseille we heard jazz: real jazz, pure jazz.' On 6 January 1945, *V* ran a long feature on 'Harlem, capitale noire: paradis du jeu et du jazz. Enfer de la danse',[84] and also carried an approving article about a

Marseille lawyer who had left his profession and gone to Paris to start a jazz-band: 'Du Barreau de Marseille au Casino de Paris: Léo Valdi en plein jazz'.[85]

Yet, alongside the apparent popular cultural continuity, the Liberation constituted a considerable break with the past and, whilst many of the themes and preoccupations in depictions of the city remained recurrent, they took place in a post-war context which was very different.

PART THREE

8

LE DOCKER NOIR

IMMIGRATION, ARCHITECTURE AND HOUSING

In 1933 Assadour Keussayan opened a photographic studio in Marseille, which moved to the Rue Bernard du Bois, near the Porte d'Aix, in 1954, and became a landmark of Marseille cultural life in the last half of the twentieth century. Keussayan was an Armenian who arrived in Marseille at the age of eight in the 1920s, subsequent to the genocide, a member of a substantial community who integrated into the fabric of the city along with the Italians, Corsicans and Greeks. His 'Studio Rex' specialised in two things: portraits of fellow members of the immigrant community, especially those from West Africa and the Maghreb; and, since it was located close to government social security and immigration offices, identity photographs. With this dual function, providing records and mementoes for families back home as well as documents for the French authorities, the Studio Rex fulfilled the same function in visual form for the immigrant communities as did the public writer, portrayed in Minna Siff's novel *Massalia Blues*, of 2013, and its role is honoured by a reconstruction of the original premises in the Musée de l'Immigration at the Porte de Vincennes in Paris, in what was the centrepiece of the 1931 Exposition Coloniale.

Alongside the often flawed process of reconstruction after the Occupation and Liberation, and intimately connected with it, immigration is the defining factor in Marseille's post-war history and a major contributor to the persistent mythology of the 'Wicked City'. In the post-war era, however, is becomes compounded by a heightened and not-so-casual racism, instanced by the joke made by a French televison presenter in the late 1980s: 'What is the first Arab city crossed in the Paris-Dakar Race?—Marseille.'[1] The city, as we have seen, became largely defined by the successive waves of immigration which had built up a cohesive and, for the most part, harmonious community. After 1945, however, as in France as a whole, immigration changed both in size and in nature, with Marseille called upon to house and integrate a growing North African and West African population for which it was neither equipped nor prepared. The impact of immigration from the 1940s to the 1980s was accentuated by the extensive war-damage on top of an already inadequate urban fabric, failures of urban planning policy at both municipal and national levels, and, crucially, international economic and political developments, in which decolonisation, geopolitics and transport technology all played a role outweighing local and even regional initiatives and contributed to what is commonly seen as a period of dramatic decline in the city's fortunes.

This decline, together with wider social, political and cultural factors at play in the city at the time, can be charted through the image of four boats, three of them sailing from the colonies to Marseille, and one which was built inland from the Plage du Prado. The first three appear in fictional works focusing, in their different ways, on experiences of arrival and immigration in Marseille: Ousmane Sembène's *Le Docker noir*, of 1973, J.M.G Le Clézio's *Désert*, of 1980, and, more obliquely, Jean Lartéguy's *Les Centurions*, of 1960. At the same time, Le Corbusier's ground-breaking Unité d'Habitation, with its connotations of a vast beached ocean liner, built in 1956 on the Avenue Michelet, poses the dominant question of housing—from the inner-city hovels descended from those of the interwar years and which ostensibly led to the destruction of the Vieux-Port, to the *bidonvilles* (shanty towns) on the city's outskirts which were bulldozed to make way for the controversial high-rise and high-density *cités* (housing estates) to the north and the east, which often drew their legitimacy from Le Corbusier's experiment.

Ousmane Sembène, 'Le Docker Noir'

Ousmane Sembène's novel documents the tragic career of a Senegalese writer, Diaw Falla, who travels from his native Senegal to Marseille in the hope of seeing his novel, *Le Dernier voyage du négrier 'Sirius'* ('The Last Voyage of the Slave Ship "Sirius"') published in Paris, only to see the writer to whom he entrusts it, Ginette Tontisane, release it under her own name. In a violent confrontation in Paris, he kills her and is brought to trial, with the court proceedings and newspaper reports, as in Camus' *L'Etranger*, strangely at odds with the reality of the events themselves and the communities from which he comes in Senegal and Marseille.

Aside from the theme of cultural appropriation, Sembène's novel provides an important record of the port in the early 1950s and the Black community in the centre of Marseille. *Le Docker noir* is set in 'le petit Harlem marseillais',[2] in the triangle of streets between the Gare Saint-Charles and the Cours Belsunce formed by the Rue des Petites-Maries, the Rue des Dominicaines and the Rue des Baignoires, and close to the Porte d'Aix where Keussayan set up his Studio Rex. Whereas the Parisian press portrays this district as 'the black quarter, a milieu inhabited by pimps, thieves and pickpockets' (p. 26), this 'southern French Africa' (p. 78) is in fact a lively and sophisticated community with an extraordinary variety of different peoples: Saracolés, Soussous, Toucouleurs, Mandiagues, Dahomeyans, Martiniquais, Moors, and Ouolofs, the 'Black Corsicans', known for their violent changes of mood, and to which Diaw Falla belongs (pp. 78–9). Moreover, not only has this community grown from a dozen or so at the beginning of the century (p. 73), especially during the interwar years when it inhabited the Vieux-Port, as described by McKay, it also rendered distinguished service to the Free French navy during the Second World War: these West Africans were mostly trained sailors, 'with at least two round-the-world voyages under their belts' (p. 78). An old man recalls that he came to France in 1901, served the French during two world wars, and yet has no right to retirement, unemployment or social security benefits (pp. 104–5). A younger man joined the navy in 1940 and fought at the mouth of the River Ogooué before joining the Free French in London and serving on a corvette, but is now French in name only, with none of the civil rights. Far from engaging in crime, this community is concerned uniquely with its social and political struggle—which is why it has dispatched Diaw to Paris to intercede with the region's *députés*.

In *Le Docker noir* the working conditions of the dock workers, especially the Black dockers, are familiar from Londres' and McKay's accounts of the 1920s; little has happened to change them in the intervening twenty-five years, despite the war and the Occupation. The Place de la Joliette is still the same: 'a human torrent; the dock workers arrived by tram, by bus, or on foot on the esplanade lined on one side with bistros and on the other by the goods station' (p. 127). On this mass the inhuman work has taken its toll:

> Their skin was marked by the bites of the sun, tarnished by the bad weather which had lined their faces, their hair eaten away by the insects from the cereals. After years of this labour, a man had become a rag, eaten away from within, with the outer casing only an envelope. Living in this hell every year the docker had taken a huge leap towards his demise. There were countless accidents. Mechanisation had outstripped their physical abilities; only a quarter of them worked, supporting the rhythm of the machines, providing the output of the unemployed workers. It was a competition between bones and steel.
>
> The machines were better looked after than the dockers. (pp. 128–9)

Not only is this work inhuman in itself, it is also subject to the vagaries of the seasons and the climate—winter, for example, is cruel, but it is when the fresh vegetables arrive from Algeria, ensuring full employment for the dockers (p. 133)—and employment in the docks, as in most Western countries in the 1950s, is on a daily basis, arbitrary and dependent on the whims of the recruitment agents, who pitilessly weed out troublemakers.

It is hardly surprising that these conditions should have led to considerable industrial unrest, exacerbated by divisions, often deliberately engineered, within the workforce, between the long-serving dockers and the new arrivals. This was hardly a new phenomenon and it had been the cause of conflict between older generations and recently arrived Italians during the Belle Epoque, as well as between those same Italians, now established dock-workers, and, as we have seen in Chapter 4, West Africans in the 1920s. In Sembène's account of the early 1950s, the 'anciens' had 'gone on strike: men who knew their trade and had unanimously voted to down tools to protect their rights' (p. 127), only to be defeated by the recruitment of ununionized unemployed (p. 128).[3] In one incident, Diaw is unusual in using his eloquence and militancy to support a strike, an act for which he is excluded by his agency, but is reminded by his friend Pipo of the distance he has to travel, in his writing as well as in his militancy:

> Do you remember the strike?
>
> The old-timers were struggling against the infernal work rhythms... the cost of living, the war in Indochina... because of us, their struggle came to nothing. They didn't succeed... The schismatics try to divide us, but the only union representative you'll see here is the CGT one. (p. 149)

The struggle of the black dockers, and, indeed, of the entire Marseille West African community, is thus to be seen in the wider context of the labour conflict in the port, still dominated by the French Communist Party and its powerful union the CGT, which had in fact secured a national agreement for dockers in 1947,[4] and remained implacably opposed to the Indochina War, operating a stringent boycott of war material and military medical supplies[5]—all of which compounded the national, and international, perception of Marseille as a revolutionary, and multi-ethnic, city opposed in some way to the national cause.

The revolutionary period following the Liberation, which was accompanied by the workers' appropriation of major companies like the Aciéries du Nord ('Northern Steelworks') at La Capelette[6] and did much to cement the reputation of Marseille as a 'red' city, was effectively over by 1946, although, as Sembène's novel reminds us, the struggle continued into at least the next decade. With hindsight, however, it was dwarfed in importance by a process far beyond the control of the port authority and the union, or even of the municipality, which had already begun to undermine the foundations of the port itself. For Emile Thémime, the end of the *illusion révolutionnaire* was accompanied by the collapse of the intimately-connected *illusion économique* and *illusion coloniale*, whilst Alèssi Dell'Umbria labels the process more starkly: 'le bateau coule' ('the ship goes down').

This collapse was all the more dramatic for the fact that its initial stages were to all intents and purposes invisible to all but the most professional observers. The port was all-but destroyed at the end of the Occupation: destruction of the transporter bridge, however symbolic, was nothing compared to the loss of two hundred boats, which had been sunk in the docks, many of which belonged to Marseille shipping companies—Fraissinet, for example, lost five of its fleet of fourteen— and these, together with wrecks loaded with cement and rocks, blocked the port for months,[7] with considerable effects on employment. The problem was that, superficially, the port seemed to revert to its pre-war level of activity: from only 6,000 tonnes of non-military freight shipped in January 1945, by 1946 import figures, at 5,300,000 tonnes, had nearly regained the 1929 level, and in 1950, with 7,300,000 tonnes of imports and 3,000,000 tonnes of exports, the peak of 1938 had been overtaken. By 1954, imports had risen to 11,600,000 tonnes and exports to 6,200,000, and in 1956, the overall tonnage passing through Marseille amounted to 20,000,000,[8] in spite of the temporary closure of the Suez Canal. Encouraging as these figures might have seemed, they masked several disquieting trends which within a generation saw the near-collapse of the port and a severe downturn in the city's economy.

In the first place, much of this tonnage passing through Marseille was related to military equipment connected with the wars in Indochina and, after 1954, in Algeria. Another large portion (sixty per cent, exclusive of oil, in 1951)[9] was tied to the colonial trade, which was vulnerable, not merely to the process of decolonisation which began with the loss of Indochina in 1954, but to changes in international industrial practice, in which, for example, suppliers of nut-oil products either sourced their material from non-colonial markets or chose to process them in situ rather than refining them in Marseille. In any case, the Treaty of Rome in 1956 would progressively threaten national protectionist arrangements with existing and former colonies and change the competitive dynamics of the European market. Finally, these buoyant shipping figures were largely accounted for by the massive rise in oil imports—in 1975, oil amounted to 80 million tonnes of traffic, accounting for ninety per cent of imports and sixty-eight per cent of re-exports[10] (from 2 million tonnes in 1946 to 8 million in 1952).[11] This would accentuate the vulnerability of Marseille to international developments. Technological advances in ship-design enabled the creation of much larger vessels, made worse by the temporary closures of the Suez Canal in 1956 and, definitively, in 1967, which necessitated the much longer journey to Europe from the Persian Gulf around the Cape of Good Hope. The problem was that this increasing tonnage and the increasingly larger vessels which conveyed it were beyond the resources of the existing port, and, in the same way that, in the mid-nineteenth century, La Joliette was constructed to deal with the inadequacies of the Vieux-Port, so Marseille a century later was obliged to create a new oil port to the West at Lavéra, near Martigues. Even this was insufficient for new generations of supertankers, however, and in the 1960s the Gaullist central government and the Defferre municipality undertook the development of a vast petro-chemical complex and oil port at Fos, on the Etang de Berre, which would be the driving force of a new regional agglomeration, the 'Grand Delta' rivalling Rotterdam.[12] Indeed, the 'Grand Delta' project harked back, like plans in the 1920s for a 'Mediterranean Crossroads' to the Saint-Simonian vision of a Northern Mediterranean arc, from Barcelona to Genoa, bisected at Marseille by a north-south axis extending up the Rhône corridor to Northern Europe. Yet, as Alèssi Dell'Umbria persuasively argues, the Fos scheme was not merely highly detrimental to Marseille urban and regional planning in the period from 1960 to 1980, it proved highly vulnerable to shifts in the centre of gravity of the European economy, which privileged the North Sea ports, especially Rotterdam, as the ports of transit to the Northern industrial centres of the European Community. The same process was also largely true for container traffic, leaving Marseille as 'a port of transit purely serving the French commercial space', whereas its Mediterranean rivals, Trieste and Genoa, like the Northern ports, 'had been able to impose themselves as international ports of transit'.[13]

The collapse in Marseille's importance as an international freight port was accompanied by the dwindling of its passenger traffic. The era of the great liners vanished across the world in the 1960s, accelerated by the rise of air travel (the Marseille airport, renamed Marseille-Provence, at Marignane, was a rare post-war commercial success) and the loss of empire, leaving as the only vestiges of Marseille's huge network of international sea-routes the ferry services to Corsica, Tunisia and Algeria,[14] although it began to re-invent itself as a cruise-port in the first years of the new millennium. At the same time, much of Marseille's traditional industry vanished with the port activity, beginning with the industries associated with the port, like ship repairs, and spilling over into other areas of heavy engineering, and, as we have seen, extending to the collapse of the companies associated with vegetable oil, mainly soap manufacture. In other words, *Le Docker noir* constitutes an unconscious swan-song for a city whose industrial and social fabric was invisibly unravelling. Diaw and his girlfriend Catherine take a bus to the Canebière:

> the heart of the city, more populous than Babel. There you met people from everywhere, from the ebony-skinned Negro to the Greenlander, via the Siberian Moujik. From the Chinese with cat-like eyes to the Incas, from the albino whites to the half-castes. The most contradictory social layers seemed to have decided to meet here. From the bourgeois to the worker in his China-blue trousers. From the pimps with their triple-soled shoes, from the *demi-mondaines*, from the lottery ticket sellers to the *Sidi* with his carpets, from light-hearted young women to puritan *grandes dames*. From black cassocks, to children and gypsies who were begging. This dense and compact population walked in all directions without bumping into each other.... This street is the central vein of Marseille and the stranger who arrives here for the first time can only be amazed at the carefreeness of the Southerners. Marseille, seen at this time on a Sunday, could only consolidate the universal reputation of Marius and his famous sidekick Olive... (p. 125)

This is a fascinating description of the diversity and inclusiveness of the city, which persists in spite of the racism, the brutality of the dock labour and the fate which ultimately befalls Diaw, in which the buoyancy of *Banjo* is reinforced by the optimism of Pagnol's trilogy and Tourneur's *Justin de Marseille*, and incarnated in the appeal across the French Empire of the resourceful comic duo Marius and Olive.[15] It is an image which was still valid, just, in the 1950s, although severely under pressure by the novel's publication in 1973 and increasingly questionable in later decades.

J.M.G. Le Clézio, 'Désert'

Le Docker noir begins with Diaw's mother watching a ship following the coastline of Senegal as it heads for Marseille in the early 1950s, a reminder of the human cost of France's exploitation of its colonial workforce in the *Métropole*. In Le Clézio's *Désert*, published in 1980, the heroine Lalla sails to the port from Morocco as a Red Cross refugee in the autumn of 1955,[16] at the beginning of an extended episode of a complex novel which juxtaposes the epic chronicle of the retreat of the southern Saharan Muslim tribes, led by the Sheikh Ma el Aïnine, from the encroaching French imperial armies, culminating in their defeat at Agadir in 1912, with the experience of the Sheikh's female descendent in a Moroccan coastal *bidonville* and, later, Marseille thirty-five years on. The city in which the teenage Lalla arrives is not the legendary port recounted by her friend the fisherman and storyteller Naman and which she re-tells to him as he lies dying:

> She spoke to him of the great city of Marseille in France, of the port with its immense quays where are moored boats from all over the world, freighters as large as citadels, with very high forecastles and masts as wide as trees, liners so white, with thousands of portholes, and which had strange names and mysterious flags, the names of cities. Odessa, Riga, Bergen, Limassol... (p. 197)

Instead of this legendary city, the 'white city which Naman the fisherman spoke of' (a reflection of the North African white cities so dear to the Marseillais, Casablanca and, especially, 'Alger la Blanche'), with its

> ...palaces and church towers, there were only endless quaysides the colour of stone and cement, quaysides which opened out on to other quaysides. The boat laden with passengers slid slowly through the black water of the docks... (p. 261)

Lalla's brief sojourn in Marseille provides Le Clézio with the opportunity for an exceptionally vivid imagined reconstruction of the city in the mid-1950s. It radiates out from her base in Le Panier, first at her aunt's apartment and later in the Hôtel Sainte-Blanche, where she finds work as a cleaner, to an extraordinarily extensive exploration by day and night from La Joliette to the Plage du Prado and from the Gare Saint-Charles to the Vieux-Port—all supported by a detailed accumulation of street names. In her odyssey through the 'strange country' of Marseille (p. 267), Lalla's ability to investigate without being observed is guaranteed by her purchase of a brown overcoat (p. 268), which almost envelopes her and from which she refuses to be separated, even when she later briefly becomes a wealthy photographic model: a latter-day Haroun al-Rashid inspecting her kingdom. The most striking aspect of Marseille which she encounters is the life of the dispossessed: the poor migrant workers who live in the Hôtel Sainte-Blanche and, above all, the myriad beggars who crowd the streets:

> There are lots of beggars. At first, when she had just arrived, Lalla was very surprised. Now she has become used to them. But she does not forget to see them, unlike most of the people in the city, who just make a little side-step to avoid walking over them, or who do even step over them when they are in a hurry. (p. 275)

One of these beggars is the young gypsy Radicz with whom she develops a special affinity and who, having graduated to pickpocketing and car theft, is killed when being pursued by the police near the Plage du Prado, an event which becomes commonplace in accounts of the city at the end of the century. At the same time, when walking through Le Panier, Lalla is struck, like visitors to the city in the 1920s, by the proliferation of refuse on the streets:

> As she walks along the narrow grooves of the streets, the Rue du Refuge, the Rue des Moulins, the Rue des Belles-Ecuelles, the Rue de Montbrion, Lalla sees all the rubbish as if it has been thrown up by the sea: rusty tin cans, old pieces of paper, pieces of bone, rotting oranges, broken bottles, rubber bands, dead birds with their wings torn off, crushed cockroaches, dust, powder, all rotting. They are the marks of solitude, of abandonment, as if men had already fled this city, that they had been left prey to sickness, death and forget. As if there were only a few men left in this world, the wretched folk who continued to live in these crumbling houses, in these apartments already like tombs, whilst emptiness penetrated through the gaping windows, the cold of the night which constricted the chest and veiled the eyes of the old and the children. (pp. 306–7)

This vision goes beyond the moral, technocratic and political outrage of depictions of the old quarter in the interwar years, with the implicit equation of human and physical detritus which led to its destruction in 1943. With the authorial perspective of 1980, it looks at the bleakness of a dystopian post-colonial future and the ghost-town which the inner city of Marseille threatened to become—a vision which turns hallucinatory and terrifying when Lalla visits the outcasts in their streets at night (pp. 309–10).

For a vision it undoubtedly is, and Lalla is depicted as a genuine seer (not for nothing is she accompanied by the spirit of 'Es Ser', 'the Secret' [p. 118]), with supernatural powers: 'her gaze... carries the burning strength of the desert. Its light is ardent above her black hair.... Its light is ardent in her amber-coloured eyes, on her skin, on her prominent cheek-bones, on her lips' (p. 332). As such, she can literally 'charm' the head waiter of the port's most exclusive restaurant into serving her and Radicz with whatever they order (p. 336) and captivates a photographer who is dining there to such an extent that he launches her on a national career as a fashion model, under the name 'Hawa', by which her image becomes ubiquitous and powerful—a long way from the more prosaic ambitions of the Studio Rex.

The novel is constructed on a circular principle. Just as the nomadic tribes travel in circles in order to congregate at Ma el Aïnine's city and return south after their defeat at Agadir in 1912, so Lalla returns from Marseille to Morocco to give birth to her daughter under a fig tree on the same beach near the *bidonville* where she was brought up:

> Hawa, daughter of Hawa... And she waits, patiently, for someone to come from the shanty-town of planks and tar-paper, a young boy fishing for crabs, an old woman looking for driftwood or a little girl who simply likes wandering in the dunes to see the sea-birds. (p. 423)

In one important respect, however, the cycle is made complete. We know that the novel takes place in the winter of 1955/6 because Lalla's favourite song, *Méditerranée*, sung by Tino Rossi, was the current hit. Lalla's daughter is thus born in February 1956, the date of Moroccan independence. This may be construed as retribution for the violent colonisation of the country and the entire southern and western Sahara at the beginning of the twentieth century. However, Le Clézio is careful to warn that, although the military operations like the massacre of Oued Tadla of 18 June 1910 were ostensibly under the command of French army officers like General Moinier (p. 373), the real initiative came from a consortium of European banks, led by the Banque de Paris et des Pays-Bas, which had sealed the Treaty of Algeciras effectively ending the Arab uprising and isolating the remaining rebels (pp. 377–80). From the perspective of 1980, Le Clézio suggests that neither Moroccan independence, nor the subsequent efforts of Marseille to reinvent itself after colonisation will be any more independent of the power of international finance than the initial process of empire itself. In the short term, however, the French withdrawal from Morocco, followed by a similar process in Tunisia, marks a crucial break in Marseille's relationship, not just with the Maghreb, but with the Mediterranean as a whole, seriously weakening its role as the *Porte de l'Afrique du Nord* and as the capital of a tightly-knit community along the southern coast of the Mediterranean, of which Algiers was the jewel. In other words, the cosy image fostered by Tino Rossi's *Méditerranée* was about to be fractured for good.

In fact, in the period when the Marseille episode of *Désert* takes place, immigration from the Maghreb was not yet a serious issue. Thémime notes the presence of Algerian migrant workers who had come to the city under the 1946 agreement under freedom of circulation, but who, by 1954, numbered no more than 15,000 in the Bouches-du-Rhône department, most of whom remained in Marseille or neighbouring towns, and who gravitated to the traditional immigrant districts in the city centre around the Cours Belsunce and the Porte d'Aix,[17] in addition to some overflow lodging in the Le Grand Arénas camp. Initially, the agreements on Tunisian and Moroccan independence had little repercussion on Marseille itself, apart from the return of a relatively small and easily assimilable number of administrators and colonialists.[18] As we shall see, however, the situation worsened in 1956 with rising tensions between France and the new republics of Tunisia and Morocco, prompting 'a massive wave of repatriations', mostly white, swollen by refugees from Egypt after the nationalisation of the Suez Canal, which left Marseille receiving 'tens of thousands of people, mostly French, whom they had to look after, at least temporarily',[19] in addition to a rising number of Tunisian or Moroccan immigrants seeking work in France under entry schemes established by the independence treaties. In other words, the snapshot captured of Marseille through Lalla's eyes in the winter of 1955–6 is that of the calm before the crisis.

The essential feature of mass post-war immigration in France is well-known: the supplies of labour drawn on after the First World War from Spain, Italy and Greece had unexpectedly dried up, so that the labour requirements for reconstruction after the Liberation were met by immigration from France's colonies in West Africa and the Maghreb which, against all expectation, became long-term. By far the most significant groups in this process were the immigrants from Algeria, both indigenous Algerians and the Pieds-Noirs white residents. As we have seen, there were unusually close ties between Marseille and Algiers, going back beyond the conquest of 1830 to the days of trade with the Barbary Coast, and the special administrative status of Algeria theoretically rendered freedom of movement easier than from other territories. Thus, after 1946, 'the necessities of reconstruction brought towards the *Métropole*... a large number of Algerian workers, who henceforth disembarked at Marseille "freely and without checks"'.[20] This effectively uncontrolled immigration of Algerian workers often accompanied by their families[21] was to become one of the major contributors to Marseille's post-war housing crisis and its subsequent social problems in the last years of the twentieth century, as inner-city slums and *bidonvilles* were replaced by use of the camps, like the Grand Arénas, and, from the end of the 1950s onwards, by the first public housing developments. Moreover, the Algerian immigrants' position was further weakened by the Algerian War. Not only were they cut off from their families after 1956 by restrictions on movement, they were also subject to political propaganda, especially from the FLN, which had a powerful clandestine organisation on the docks, collected compulsory subscriptions, and staged terrorist attacks, like the bombings in the oil refineries at Mourepiane and on the Etang de Berre, which increased both surveillance and repression on the part of the authorities.[22] The situation changed again with Algerian independence in 1962 and the expanded quota of migrant labourers allowed into France, resulting in an unforeseen rise in the need for housing and public services in all French cities, but affecting Marseille particularly, contributing to the crisis of the *cités* in the following decades.

Jean Lartéguy, 'Les Centurions' and the Pieds-Noirs

After the arrival of Diaw's boat from Senegal in the early 1950s and a year before Lalla's crossing from Morocco in 1955, the third of the ships to arrive in Marseille is the most sinister and has travelled the furthest. On 13 November 1954, the Chargeurs Réunis liner, the *Edouard Branly*, arrives from Saigon, via Singapore, Colombo, Djibouti, Port-Said and Algiers: a roll-call of imperial ports already or soon to be rendered redundant by the processes of decolonisation and technological change. Amongst the *Edouard Branly*'s passengers is a group of French officers, ex-prisoners of war of the Vietminh captured at Dien Bien Phû, who have learned from their victors the techniques of modern ideological warfare and are committed to applying them in the next battle for the Empire. The liner's final call, in Algiers, is on 11 November 1954, the date of the beginning of the Algerian War. Their first view of Marseille is similar to Lalla's: 'under a grey sky, the coastline appeared black. Seabirds passed above the boat with shrill cries.'[23] Nor is their welcome any warmer—'a derisory military band and a detachment of soldiers clumsily presenting arms' (p. 167)— because the country is not particularly pleased to see them. As Lartéguy, who had been a war correspondent, records:

> In 1950, in Orange, a train of wounded from the Far East had been stopped by a Communist who had abused and struck the men on their stretchers. A Parisian hospital asking for blood for transfusions specified that this blood would not be used on wounded soldiers from Indochina. In Marseille, where they could now see Notre-Dame de la Garde, they had refused to unload the coffins of the dead. (p. 167)

In particular, these returning prisoners of war:

> had been abandoned, like those mercenaries suddenly made redundant and massacred by the Carthaginians in order not to pay their wages. Cut off from their country, they had recreated an artificial homeland in the friendship of the Vietnamese... With a certain horror they feared knowing that they had become closer to the Vietminh whom they hated... than to these people waiting for them on the quayside... They had all caught a subtle illness, the 'yellow fever'. They had brought it back to France and these were sick men who disembarked on the quayside in Marseille... (p. 167)

This return of the soldiers of Dien Bien Phû is significant because it announces the beginning of a process which will become apparent in the 1980s and which will be highlighted by Izzo in *Total Khéops*—the threat to civil society of the heirs of these Centurions and Praetorians, similarly alienated from the country to which they return after a new generation of neo-colonial wars and who will make common cause with the Front National.

The Algerian War, which Lartéguy's paratroopers join, had a major impact upon the subsequent development and structure of Marseille for various reasons. Not only, after the Suez debacle and Moroccan and Tunisian independence, was it a key moment in the process of French decolonisation, it also shattered the city's privileged relationship with Algiers, that other *ville blanche*, its Maghrebi 'Other'. The loss of its twin city, rupturing a millennium of rivalry and over a century of close contact, has a traumatic effect, reflected concretely, not so much by the incremental increase in Algerian, Tunisian and Moroccan immigration, as by the wave of panic which struck the Algerian Pieds-Noirs community in June 1962.

Marseille had not been dramatically affected by the estimated 250,000 *rapatriés* from Egypt, Tunisia and Morocco who had come to France since 1956, most of whom were composed of French officials and private employees, Italians from Tunisia, and Moroccan and Tunisian Jews, mainly because by no means all of them passed through the port or stayed there, and also because the process took place over six years.[24] In contrast, the flight of the Pieds-Noirs took place in the three months following the Evian Agreements of 19 March 1962, culminating in the mass exodus of June after the OAS terror campaign and FLN reprisals. In this period, nearly 200,000 Pieds-Noirs refugees arrived in Marseille, which then had a population of less than 800,000: tens of thousands arrived by air at Marignane, whilst in one single day, 25 June, seven boats arrived bringing 9,000 refugees—one of them, the *Kairouan*, with a capacity of 1,172 passengers, arrived loaded with 2,600.[25]

Still in the grip of its own post-war housing crisis, Marseille was simply unable to respond, either practically or emotionally. The religious aid agencies, as during the Occupation, responded as best they could, but there were simply no rooms available and the city was obliged to lodge the refugees in hostels like the Hôtel Bompard, familiar to those in transit during the Occupation, or makeshift camps like the Cité de la Rouguière, an unfinished block of HLM flats (housing schemes subsidised by the government).[26] As Thémime records, a lot

of these refugees eventually moved on, though most remained in the
Midi: in 1964, it was estimated that there were 120,000 refugees from
Algeria in the Bouches-du-Rhône department, of which 96,000 were
resident in Marseille.[27] Apart from the crisis of housing and public
services which confronted the refugees, on this occasion, Marseille's
reputation as a *ville d'accueil* was called into question, and the travellers
from the port's 'sister city' were by no means made to feel universally
welcome. The mayor, Gaston Defferre, infamously suggested that they
should 'leave Marseille quickly' and 're-adapt somewhere else', whilst
the Communist *La Marseillaise* was overtly hostile.[28] Even though many
of the Pieds-Noirs were rapidly able to re-establish themselves in work
and contribute to the local economy (although often outside of
Marseille, in towns like Vitrolles), their resentment at their poor welcome persisted, often compounded by an inept housing policy which
segregated them in ghettos in housing estates like La Cravache or Saint-
Thys, where they cultivated a devotion to a 'lost Algeria'[29] still visible
today on numerous websites.

It is unlikely that they were completely won over by the inauguration in 1971 of the Mémorial des Rapatriés d'Algérie, which takes the
form of a nine metre high propeller blade on the Corniche by the
sculptor César Baldaccini, born and brought up in the Italian quarter
of the Belle-de-Mai, a student at the Ecole des Beaux-Arts, and more
commonly known simply as César, who had made and given his name
to French cinema's equivalent of the Oscars. Designed to be visible far
out to sea in the direction of Algiers and with the inscription, 'La Ville
de Marseille aux rapatriés d'Afrique du Nord et d'Outre-Mer… Notre
ville est la vôtre' ('the City of Marseille to the Repatriated of North
Africa and Overseas… Our city is yours'—a sentiment some of the
dedicatees would have had difficulty in recognising) it was intended as
a monument to the loss experienced by the city itself, and by both the
ethnically French Algerians known as the Pieds-Noirs, who 'returned'
to France, and the Harkis, Algerian soldiers who fought for the French
and who, if they managed to escape punishment in newly independent
Algeria, were taken to internment camps before being settled in housing developments like Les Tilleuls in Marseille, where they were kept
under observation and effectively isolated from the French community.[30] As it is, the monument is not particularly visible from the sea,

being overshadowed by the rising hillside of Roucas-Blanc. Its lacklus-tre location gives it a similarity of spirit to the Mémorial de l'Armée de l'Orient half a kilometre north along the Corniche, commemorat-ing another lost and forgotten army, one which had fought in the Middle East and the Balkans during the First World War.

Le Corbusier: the Unité d'Habitation

In this story of post-war immigration and repatriation, there is an addi-tional ocean liner in the narrative of Marseille alongside those in the novels of Sembène, Le Clézio and Lartéguy, although this one is on dry land. As William Firebrace reminds us, one of Le Corbusier's sketches for his revolutionary Unité d'Habitation housing complex on the Boulevard Michelet, inaugurated in 1952, was that of an ocean liner, moored in what was then open countryside to the south of the city.[31] Le Corbusier had been keen to be involved in the reconstruction of Marseille, as he had been to redevelop Algiers in a series of plans from 1932–1942,[32] but he was excluded from the Vieux-Port renovation as a result of his overtures to Vichy during the Occupation.[33] He was given the housing project which was to become the Unité as a consola-tion prize by the Minister of Reconstruction and Urbanism in the Provisional Government, his close associate Raoul Dautry.[34] With its internal streets, shops, bar and restaurant, a hotel, school and leisure space on the roof, the building constituted a self-contained living unit, but it was not, at least initially, well received. Its modernist design, with the structure mounted on pilotis, was too extreme for the local population, who called it 'la Maison du Fada' ('the loony's house') and distrusted it as a Northern import, foisted on the city by central gov-ernment and out of keeping with the urban Mediterranean land-scape—a view supported to some extent by the fact that it was repli-cated in Nantes, Firminy near Saint-Etienne, Briey in North-Eastern France and Berlin, although William Firebrace argues that now it can be seen as having 'become Mediterranean or even… classically Greek.'[35] What it did not do, however, with its modest 337 apartments, was respond to Marseille's massive housing and reconstruction crisis of the post-war years, which overshadowed residents, migrants and rapatriés alike. On the contrary, it helped to develop the south of the city centre as 'an area for luxury blocks and gated communities', like the Oscar Niemeyer-inspired La Brasilia, Les Jardins de Thalassa, and other complexes built in the 1970s and later,[36] and, if it influenced mass housing at all, it did so, as Alèssi Dell'Umbria points out, negatively, by appearing to sanction all manner of high-rise, high-density 'ensembles', which, with no accompanying facilities or transport links, came to typify the city's housing in the 1970s and 1980s.

In the context of the post-war reconstruction of Marseille, debates concerning the aesthetics of the Unité d'Habitation were overshadowed by two vastly more pressing interconnected concerns: the rebuilding of the Vieux-Port district and the need for the rapid provision of low-cost housing in the face of widespread homelessness. With the changing fortunes of the port and the local industrial base, these two issues became subsumed into the wider planning strategy for the greater Marseille area. The destruction of the area to the north of the Vieux-Port had already provoked conspiracy theories amongst those who spotted that, for all the public health and safety concerns about the decaying buildings and the assumption that their entire population were criminals or refugees, there was the potential for shrewd financial calculation about the value of the prime real estate which lay beneath the slums.[37] Nor were these theories laid to rest by the actual project which took shape. Directly under the supervision of the ministers in Paris—Dautry, followed by François Billoux and Eugène Claudius-Petit—the project was controlled by architects from Paris, especially Auguste Perret, who was responsible for the re-building of Le Havre, and who supported the plans for the buildings fronting the quayside drawn up by his protégé Fernand Pouillon, who was also working on the rebuilding of the La Tourette district in the Quartier Saint-Jean.[38] Pouillon used stone from the Pont du Gard to construct shops and restaurants on the ground floor, with 'arcades, loggias and tiles roofs',[39] with René Egger, André Devin, Yvan Bentz, Dunoyer de Segonzac and Gaston Castel designing the rest of the site, which covered the whole north bank of the Lacydon up to and around the Hôtel-Dieu hospital and sparing only the enclave of Le Panier on the north-western summit of the hill. As Alèssi Dell'Umbria concludes, 'after the Wehrmacht, the Parisian technocrats finished mutilating a site which the Marseillais had taken to for 2,600 years.'[40] The real problem, however, was that it irreversibly altered the social composition of the district, reducing a pre-war population density of 2,000 inhabitants per hectare to 750. This meant that, with the exception of the fishing community of Saint-Jean:

> Only a small number of the previous inhabitants returned... in any case, they hardly had the means to pay for lodging... The previous tenants found themselves in effect excluded by the rents in these new buildings; a number of small house-owners were evicted, pure and simple.[41]

The rebuilding of the Vieux-Port district had as its, probably intended, consequence the gentrification of the area—as, indeed, was the case in Perret's reconstruction of Le Havre—and the 'social cleansing' which, by forcing the working-class population out to the periphery, altered the demography of the city and the dynamics of the centre: the beginning of that process which would see it transformed into an urban desert after business hours,[42] its popular heart ripped out. The Canebière became an uneasy frontier in a buffer zone between the affluent south and the working-class north, whilst the Alcazar music hall, that centre of popular obstreperousness and conviviality, closed in 1966. At the same time, the progressive gentrification of the inner city exacerbated rather than attempted to solve Marseille's most pressing problem after the war: homelessness. It is important to emphasise at this stage, however, that these problems were by no means restricted to post-war Marseille and were not even an exclusively French phenomenon: most French cities, especially those which had suffered extensive war-damage, like Rouen, Nantes or Le Havre, found themselves in a similar predicament, which they shared with many of their European neighbours, just as, indeed, they experimented with similar solutions, both successful and flawed, especially in the domain of high-rise housing. What makes the case of Marseille unusual, however, is the fact that its redevelopment took place against the background of a radically changing social and demographic composition and a decline in its traditional role as an imperial port and Mediterranean capital.

Essentially, the problem stemmed from two causes: the chronic under-investment in housing in the city in the interwar years, leaving much of the city centre north of the Canebière with high-density housing of which much was effectively slum-dwelling. These were the inner-city makeshift encampments in courtyards, like the Peysonnel site in the 3rd Arrondissement, east of Arenc,[43] or the overcrowded *hôtels garnis*[44] featured by Sembène and Le Clézio. To this was added the effects of inner-city immigration following the destruction of the Vieux-Port, together with the unanticipated surges of migrant labour and the permanent settlement of rapatriés. The effect of these flows of immigration, on top of natural growth, was to push the city's population from 770,000 in 1962 to 890,000 in 1968, peaking at 914,000 in 1975, before falling back to just below 800,000 in 1990.[45] The housing crisis was at its most acute in the early post-war years, when, as late as 1951, there were still 36,000 families in need of shelter. As Minayo Nasiali records, this led to mass squatting and the organisation of homeless movements from 1946 onwards.[46]

The city's response to the crisis was in two stages: the use of existing transit and prison camps dating back to the 1930s, principally Grand Arénas in the south and Grande Bastide in the north, followed by the building of public housing projects on a massive scale. As we have already seen, the camp of Grand Arénas, in the quarter of La Cayolle, near the Les Baumettes prison, and also, incidentally, at the end of the Boulevard Michelet on which Le Corbusier's Unité d'Habitation was being built, had been established in the First World War for colonial soldiers, before serving as a concentration camp for Jews and Resistance members during the Occupation. In the early post-war period it served as a transit camp for Jews en route to Palestine and as a residential camp for Vietnamese immigrants.[47] Subsequently, the camp and those like it were used to house immigrant and migrant workers from North Africa, although the overflow was still obliged to resort to the bidonvilles in Saint-Barthélemy and L'Estaque to the north of the centre.[48] Eventually, in the mid-1950s, the municipal government led by Defferre managed to come to terms with the crisis, albeit by making choices which subsequently proved detrimental to both the urban fabric of the city and its social cohesion. As Thémime summarises:

> It was essential to build and build quickly… The building programme presented by the city in 1955 corresponded to this prime need. It prioritised the 'absorption of the bidonvilles' by the construction of housing estates, whose proliferation would within a few years transform the

appearance of the agglomeration at the same time as its living conditions. Open spaces were used, which had once been the preserve of
gardens and commons. Blocks of flats were built, a high-rise habitat,
which was a surprising novelty for Marseille, the city of low buildings.
But everything was done in a hurry and, very often, the result was
mediocre...[49]

Even as early as 1976, a disillusioned Defferre had misgivings about
the policy and its effects.[50] In fact, there were already at the heart of
the Marseille housing project inbuilt inequalities not necessarily
restricted to Marseille, but accentuated by its particular conditions.
The transition under Eugène Claudius-Petit as Minister of Housing and
Reconstruction from the HBM (*Habitation à Bon Marché*, 'Low Price
Housing') to the HLM (*Habitation à Loyer Modéré*, 'Modest Rent
Housing') programme effectively opened up the provision of cheap
public housing for the poorest in society to both the most needy and
also lower middle-class tenants.[51] This both put renewed pressure on
the allocation of housing for the needy, and introduced an element of
clientelism, with influence being wielded by both the Communist
Party and the Defferre administration.[52] At the same time, the inhabitants of the camps and bidonvilles were often invidiously classed by the
authorities as 'asocial', which placed additional barriers in their way to
entitlement to public housing, often imposing a transition period to be
spent in sub-standard buildings with little in the way of services before
access was finally granted to fully-equipped accommodation.[53] Finally,
in 1953, Claudius-Petit's successor, Pierre Courant, introduced a new
programme for public housing, the *Logement million* ('One Million
Accommodation' named after its cost, one million francs, and not a
numerical target for people to be housed), which, in exchange for
speed of construction, reduced the specifications for space and quality.
As Nasiali records, between 1954 and 1960 over 4,000 of these *million*
flats were constructed in Marseille,[54] though only a fraction of the
80,000 dwellings built between 1952 and 1964.[55] The combined public
housing construction project in this period took the form of 'clusters
of buildings... known as a *grand ensemble*',[56] and it was the *grands ensembles*, immense high-rise blocks, often themselves clustered into *cités*,
relegated, as in other French cities, to the periphery, which came to
typify Marseille in the last quarter of the twentieth century. In effect,

in their efforts to extricate themselves from a dire housing crisis, the authorities, both national and municipal, merely plunged themselves into a longer-term planning and social disaster.

In one sense, this disaster was the result of a combination of too little planning and too much. Alèssi Dell'Umbria, a passionate advocate of the organic growth of the medieval-style city, nostalgically recalls the Meyer-Heine Plan of 1949, which proposed a solution to the abnormally long distances travelled by the Marseillais from their homes to their work-places (the bitter strike of 1947 was triggered by an increase in tram-tickets), by rejecting the traditional radiocentric concept of the city (the core, incidentally, of Le Corbusier's *cité radieuse*) and basing the city's expansion on the already-existing villages constituting Marseille's outlying quarters, thereby creating *unités de voisinage* (neighbourhood units) with industrial and manufacturing capacity, and therefore 'secondary centres unifying industrial and residential zones, with services.'[57] This plan, which was never implemented, had the virtue of not merely providing an antidote to the classic tension between urban centre and periphery, but of taking account of one of the most unusual features of Marseille as a civic entity, the immense size of the territory covered by the municipal authority, which makes it the largest city in size in France. Without a rational land-use plan, this considerable terrain, much of it in the 1960s and 1970s open country or semi-rural, fell victim to either the development of highly-concentrated public housing, chosen because it was simply vacant and easily acquirable, or to speculative private residential building on the sites of former bastides, which in turn forced up land values and pushed public housing even further to the periphery, mainly to the north, close to the docks, but also to the east, in, for example, Saint-Marcel, home of the Coder railway engineering works. By 1975, land prices had risen so steeply that the public housing projects came to an end.[58]

As Dell'Umbria suggests, this quintessentially North American urban model, with the city centre reduced to a downtown business district which closed after work, and the population living in distant housing districts of greater or lesser attractiveness, served by suburban hypermarkets, was predicated upon universal access to the automobile, which, with the decline in Marseille's prosperity after the mid-1970s

and the rise in unemployment, became all but impossible for the populations stranded in the outlying cités[59] where they were barely served
by public transport, including the later metro and tram. The inevitable
result, of course, was a reinforcement of the social divisions which had
already existed on geographical lines since the nineteenth century, with
the workers congregated near the docks to the north of the Vieux-Port
and the middle classes to the south. As Thémime concludes: 'the concentration of rental HLMs in certain carefully-targeted arrondissements inevitably contributed to the reinforcement of divisions in the
city', with a 'geography of poverty which essentially concerned the
arrondissements situated in the north',[60] constituting ghettos in all but
name through what was effectively a process of social segregation.[61]
The collapse, or, at any rate, radical scaling-down, of the Fos project in
the 1970s did nothing to ameliorate and much to exacerbate these
social and economic divisions.

The Alcazar and 'Les Cahiers du Sud'

By the 1980s Marseille found itself at one of the lowest points of its
modern history. Its port-trade was reduced to ferry traffic with Corsica
and North Africa; its heavy industry had closed, as had its traditional
plants for the processing of imported oil and flour; most of its viable
high-technology engineering and production had shifted outside
the city to neighbouring towns like Vitrolles or Aix, further reducing
the municipality's revenue. The dream of a new California faded with
the collapse of the Fos project in the 1970s, although the pursuit of
Marseille as a regional, even Mediterranean, capital proved remarkably
resilient. In the short term, however, the dominant image of Marseille
in the national and international imagination was the no less persistent
one of the 'wicked city', beset by rising unemployment, crime and
mass immigration—although, in truth, the immigrant population, even
at its height, never amounted to more than 8.5% of the total.[62]

This dramatic decline in the fortunes of Marseille was symbolised
by the collapse in the same year, 1966, of its two most famous cultural
icons, the Alcazar music hall and Les Cahiers du Sud. The disappearance
of the Alcazar was part of what Pierre Echinard calls 'the extinction of
the great theatres' in the city centre, especially on the major thorough-

fares like the Canebière and the extension of the Allées de Meilhan, including the conversion of the Variétés into a cinema and the temporary closure of the Gymnase, and accompanied by the loss of the traditional *grands cafés*.[63] In one sense, this was part of a national, indeed international, trend of urban development in the post-war era, which, with the movement of a substantial population to the periphery, severely challenged the traditional role of the city centre as a viable commercial, social and cultural hub. At the same time, the great music halls had always been commercially fragile and highly vulnerable to changes in fashion, often undergoing periods of closure or change of use: the Moulin-Rouge in Paris, for example, became a cinema in the 1920s, an example followed in Marseille by the Palais de Cristal and the Alcazar in the 1930s. Nor were the city centre cinemas immune from the process of erosion of 'the traditional places of urban sociability'[64] and they too either disappeared altogether from their traditional location on the Canebière and the Rue Saint-Ferréol or were forced to introduce multiple screens. Once again, the decline in the great city centre cinemas of the interwar years was by no means restricted to Marseille and was a generalised Western phenomenon of the last quarter of the twentieth century, which saw a massive temporary reduction in film audiences in favour of television and video. In the case of Marseille, however, the loss of the Alcazar was particularly poignant symbolically, signalling not merely the end of a particularly local form of popular entertainment which had existed since the mid-nineteenth century, but also the disappearance of a disparate, often rumbustious local audience, in which different social groups—dockers from Le Panier, workers from the Belle-de-Mai, white-collar workers and bourgeois, to say nothing of travellers and seamen in transit—came together in an expression of social cohesion.

If the closure of the Alcazar was the result of a generalised shift in popular taste in entertainment, as well as the radical demographic change which had affected the city since the destruction of the Vieux-Port, the disappearance of *Les Cahiers du Sud* was directly related to the changing post-war international role of Marseille. In practical terms, the rapid decline in long-distance sea travel through the loss of France's colonies and the competition from the airlines led, as we have seen, to the closure of Marseille's great steamship companies, those very companies which, adroitly manipulated by Jean Ballard, had helpèd to sub-sidise the review through advertising and sizeable subscriptions for multiple copies available in their lounges. The progressive removal of this income stream after the war was enough in itself to place *Les Cahiers du Sud* in financial jeopardy, which even the reduction in the frequency of publication was not enough to remedy. More serious, however, was the fact that, with the loss, or at the very least, consider-able reduction of France's presence along the southern and eastern shores of the Mediterranean, a large part of the purpose of *Les Cahiers du Sud* had been removed, just as Marseille's world had progressively shrunk. This is not to deny the journal's consistent pan-Mediterranean cultural interest throughout its career, as evidenced by its special num-bers on Occitanie, Greece and, latterly, Israel, quite independent of any direct French interest. At the same time, however, in the 1930s it drew much of its inspiration and, indeed, readership, from France's mandates, colonies and departments to Marseille's south and east, from Lebanon and Syria in the Levant to Tunisia, Algeria and Morocco in North Africa. The independence of Lebanon in 1943, Syria in 1944, followed by Tunisia and Morocco in 1956 and Algeria in 1962, accom-panied by the nationalisation of the Suez Canal in 1956, did not just severely damage *Les Cahiers'* network of readers, contributors and cor-respondents across half the Mediterranean coastline—including the privileged relationship with Algiers, its university and intellectual groupings like those around Max-Pol Fouchet's review *Fontaine*—it also seriously called into question the notion of the 'Sud' and Marseille's, and France's, relationship to it. Whereas this had been an easy question to answer before the Second World War, when Marseille was not just the Porte de l'Empire, but also the Porte de l'Afrique du Nord and self-styled, but credible, capital of the Mediterranean. By the time of the closure of *Les Cahiers* in 1966, however, the issue was much more complex and the relationship by no means as self-evident. It seemed that Marseille was perhaps losing its way at the end of the Trente Glorieuses, descending into economic difficulty and—at least in the eyes of its cultural production—rampant crime.

9

TOTAL KHÉOPS

MARSEILLE NOIR

In the second half of the twentieth century, and particularly after the Trente Glorieuses ended in the mid-70s, Marseille—which had once enticed and repelled in equal measure as a seething frontier city, its 'invitation to travel' counterbalanced by the frisson of contact with the travellers from outside France—now tended to be associated only with the latter and to be seen, not just as a 'wicked city', but as a bridgehead for external forces of disorder. In this respect, Dell'Umbria's 'sinking ship' of the 1970s gave way to the more sinister 'Total Khéops' of Jean-Claude Izzo, with a new cultural scene emerging in late-twentieth-century Marseille centred on neo-noir literature. The old wickedness of exoticism and personal vice, driven by the proximity of empire, now turned to a more sinister sort of wickedness driven by economic stagnation, with violence and organised crime coming to the fore in Marseille's artistic output.

The French Connection

In her highly perceptive study of Marseille, *A Considerable Town*, M.F.K. Fisher describes a bar on the Vieux-Port and records matter-of-factly that:

213

About four days before we went by, two men had come in and gunned down, in what was generally referred to in the press as 'American style', the barmaid-owner named something like Rita, a good-looking and apparently innocent young man drinking his first or tenth espresso, and two known informers or henchmen in one of the many small gangs that seem to have supplanted any firm organisation of crime in Marseille. The gunsels [gunmen] then left, calmly. I forget whether they were later arrested. Nobody seemed to be much annoyed by anything except the fact that the act was one of petty revenge carried out by amateurs. Where was the old spit and polish in crime? lamented the editorials in everything from *Le Meridional* to *L'Express*. Marseille might be a great centre for the American drug market, but it was sadly lacking in local solidarity, and panache.[1]

What is interesting about Fisher's appraisal, published in book form in 1978, is that it highlights two essential features of Marseille: its reputation since the end of the First World War as the 'Wicked City' par excellence, the crime capital of France, and, indeed, Southern Europe; and the underlying reality of a loss of overall control over its criminal activity, mirroring the city's overall economic collapse: Jean-Claude Izzo's 'Total Khéops'.

Along with a small number of Marseille's *lieux de mémoire*—the Château d'If, Notre-Dame de la Garde, the now-defunct transporter bridge, the Porte de l'Empire at the Gare Saint-Charles, the Vélodrome of Olympique de Marseille and, perhaps, the Unité d'Habitation—film-viewers since 1975 will automatically associate the city with John Frankenheimer's *The French Connection, II* and its long concluding pursuit along the Canebière and the Quai de l'Hôtel de Ville, ending at the mouth of the Vieux-Port under the Fort Saint-Jean. Throughout the film, the experience of Gene Hackman's New York detective 'Popeye' Doyle confirms a prevalent image of Marseille, one which had been common currency for at least the previous fifty years, that of a city which is 'wicked', beset by an all-powerful and ruthless underworld and a police force which veers from the overwhelmed and incompetent to the corrupt, and characterised by its dingy, dilapidated streets, all full of the refuse familiar since Peisson's novel and Germaine Krull's photographs. What is also important, however, is the way in which the film unconsciously charts a turning point in the history of organised crime in Marseille, the high-water mark of the power of the great crime families and their godfathers, which was already beginning to unravel and fragment.

As we have seen, modern crime in Marseille dates from 1846 and the designation of the northern area of the Vieux-Port as a *quartier réservé*—an area already notorious as the battleground between rival gangs of *nervis* romanticised by Joseph Méry. By the beginning of the First World War, criminal activity had, in addition, begun to coalesce into larger groups, mostly of immigrant origin, from Corsica and Southern Italy. These groups founded their trade on prostitution, which had been stimulated by the increase in passenger traffic through the port and by the Exposition Coloniale, and moved their headquarters to the bars around the Opéra. At the same time, the most enterprising amongst them—the prestigious *Voyageurs*—exported their activity to Paris, especially to Montmartre and the Faubourg Montmartre, and commuted regularly between the two capitals of crime.[2]

Londres' reportage of 1927 devotes considerable space to the 'war against crime' in the city, in which the police are no more successful than 'Popeye' Doyle's French collaborators fifty years later, but came slightly too early to detect a new phenomenon which emerges in 1931, namely, the close relationship forged, as in Chicago or Los Angeles, between organised crime and local politicians. In this case, the three key figures are the gangsters Paul Carbone and François Spirito and their political fixer Simon Sabiani. Sabiani, a Corsican and decorated war hero, was elected as a local councillor in 1919 on the Radical list of Siméon Flaissières, before moving to the Communists as a councillor in 1922 and becoming an independent regional councillor in 1925 and *député* in 1928. In 1929, he headed a joint electoral list with Flaissières and the Communist Henri Tissot for the municipal elections. When the weak Tissot was elected mayor, Sabiani became his first *adjoint*, making him the effective ruler of Marseille until he was overthrown in the 1935 and 1936 election campaigns.[3]

Sabiani made common cause with the two dominant figures of the Marseille underworld, his fellow Corsican Carbone and the Southern Italian Spirito, who had established an all-but-invincible empire based on serious crime, protection, prostitution and drugs. They are depicted in Jacques Deray's film of 1970, *Borsalino*, starring Alain Delon and Jean-Paul Belmondo. Thanks to Sabiani, they benefited from municipal corruption and police forbearance, providing in return lucrative kick-backs and muscle in support of Sabiani's municipal and parliamentary election campaigns, which continued after his defeats in 1935 and 1936 and his subsequent membership of Jacques Doriot's Fascist Parti Populaire Français. One crucial ingredient in the success of Carbone and Spirito is its international dimension. Not merely were they, especially Carbone, *Voyageurs* par excellence, but their activities were, literally, worldwide, but centred on the Mediterranean. Their prostitution empire was founded on links between Marseille and the Middle East, especially Egypt, where they established brothels in Cairo and used the sea-link from Marseille to Alexandria to transport women.[4] Subsequently they established brothels in North Africa, especially Tunisia, and used the long-haul shipping-route to Buenos Aires to set up brothels in Argentina: the legendary 'white slave trade' alluded to in Waugh's *Decline and Fall* but which is absent from Londres' inspirational portrayal of the migrants' hotel in Marseille. Internationalisation was also key to the growing drugs trade in the 1930s. The drugs were imported from either Turkey and Iran or from China via Indochina and arrived in Marseille, mainly via Egypt and transported by sailors or returning prostitutes, for processing into opium, cocaine and heroin, depending on changing fashions. Even though the penalties for drug smuggling and distribution in the 1930s were relatively light, and were to remain so until the 1960s, Carbone and Spirito could call upon the good offices of Sabiani's police and customs officials to turn a blind eye. This was important because Marseille, like Le Havre, had become a major transit centre for sending refined drugs to Paris, but also for re-export as part of the growing trade in North America. In this Spirito played a crucial role, negotiating with Vito Genovese, Lucky Luciano's deputy and, like Spirito, from Southern Italy, whilst Carbone travelled to New York to oversee the early days of what would become the 'French Connection'.[5]

Unsurprisingly, this expanding activity brought competition, in particular from Jo Renucci, born in Marseille, who was to become prominent in the 1950s, and the Guérini brothers, Antoine and Barthélémy. These Corsicans, who took over a large part of the Carbone-Spirito prostitution business, were Socialist supporters and came to power and influence with the double defeat of Sabiani's Right in 1935 and 1936 and the election of Henri Tasso as mayor until 1937, when the city was taken into central government administration.[6] The same political demarcations persisted during the Occupation, when Sabiani, Carbone and Spirito actively collaborated with the German authorities. The Liberation saw Sabiani and Spirito forced to flee to exile in Canada and Spain, although Carbone had been killed in December 1943 in a train derailment carried out by the Resistance. This left the Guérinis, who had sided with the Gaullist resistance, as undisputed masters of Marseille, a position reinforced by their subsequent contribution to the Gaullist security organisation, the SAC,[7] headed by the future Interior Minister, the Corsican Charles Pasqua. However, as Jérôme Pierrat reminds us, this apparent hegemony masked a considerable 'disorganisation',[8] especially in the drugs trade, often consisting of small operations concentrated on one gifted chemist. Nor was the supremacy of any one godfather assured: Antoine Guérini was murdered at a petrol station on 23 June 1967 and succeeded by Gaëtan 'Tany' Zampa, who committed suicide in custody in 1984 after being suspected of ordering a series of murders: of the examining magistrate Pierre Michel; Francis Le Belge, suspected of denouncing Zampa and who was shot in a betting shop in Paris in 2000; and Jackie Le Mat, the only survivor of the gang wars of the period 1965–1990. This recognisable and stable criminal landscape, which, in spite of its recurrent internal warfare and vendettas, had persisted since the 1920s, fell apart at the end of the 1980s, with fragmentation into smaller and less predictable gangs and the threats of hostile takeovers from the Mafia and Camorra—reflecting, as we have seen, a similar breakdown in the economic and political infrastructure of the city in the last decades of the twentieth century.

It is unsurprising, therefore, that crime should be a frequent thread in imaginative depictions of Marseille since the Revolution, from Dumas' and Zola's novels, both consciously imitating Sue's *Les Mystères de Paris*, to Peisson's *Hans le marin* and Tourneur's *Justin de Marseille* in the interwar years. Indeed, given the city's reputation nationally and internationally as the French crime capital, an image fostered by the popular daily press and weekly specialist magazines like *Détective*, the remarkable fact is that crime is by no means predominant in the picture of Marseille which emerges from fiction and cinema. This began to change, however, after the Second World War, in two phases: the introduction by Gallimard of its *Série Noire* collection, bringing translations of English and American 'hard-boiled' crime novels to a French market, together with French imitators who often began to surpass their models; and the extraordinary upsurge in Marseille-based crime fiction in the 1980s and 1990s. William Firebrace notes that:

> In the 1990s Marseille reinvented itself as the site for the *polar*, the crime novel. Marseille *polars* had existed for a long while, but little had distinguished them from other French thrillers. In the 1990s, however, they began to take on a particular quality.[9]

Of this new school of Marseille thriller, Firebrace singles out the pioneering Michèle Courbou's *Les Chapacans*; Philippe Carrese's *Trois jours d'engates* of 1994; Izzo's *Total Khéops*, of 1995; and a slew of new writers riding in Izzo's wake, including François Thomazeau, Gilles Del Pappas, Annie Barrière, Ridha Aati, Serge Scotto, Xavier-Marie Bonnot and Franz-Olivier Giesbert, 'some from Marseille, some not, but each with their own style, each assisting in the creation of Marseille as a criminal city.'[10] The transition from the classic Série Noire depiction of Marseille in the post-war years to the stylistically more adventurous and socially more questioning fiction of the 1990s constitutes a sensitive indicator of both the transformation of the city's social and economic fabric and the breakdown of the structure of organised crime which had persisted for over half a century. This transition was highlighted by two novelists, José Giovanni, author of the Série Noire novel *Le Deuxième souffle*, of 1958, subsequently adapted for the cinema by Jean-Pierre Melville in 1966, and the more problematic Jean-Claude Izzo.

'Le Deuxième souffle'

Le Deuxième souffle ('Second Breath') was Giovanni's second novel, coming a year after the success of *Le Trou*, which recounts an escape attempt from La Santé prison in Paris and was filmed by Jacques Becker in 1960. A prisoner himself, Giovanni was encouraged to take up writing by his lawyer Stephen Hecquet, who was also an author, and friend of Roger Nimier and the Hussards. *Le Trou* led to a contract with Gallimard in the classic Série Noire collection, and was followed by a sequence of novels in the late 1950s and the mid-1960s, including

Classe tous risques (1958), *L'Excommunié* (1958), *Histoire de fou* (1959), *Les Aventuriers* (1960), *Le Haut-fer* (1962), *Ho!* (1964) and *Meutre au sommet* (1964), most of which were filmed. He himself became heavily involved in script-writing and moved to film direction in his own right, beginning with *La Loi du survivant*, of 1967, based on an episode of *Les Aventuriers*.

Le Deuxième souffle is typical of Giovanni's crime fiction, heavily influenced by classic Série Noire authors like Albert Simonin, who, in novels like *Touchez pas au grisbi!*, of 1953, filmed (like *Le Trou*), by Jacques Becker, recreates the world of the old-time gangster, bound by the code of honour and integrity, but threatened by a brash new world which no longer respects the old rules. Like their American models, the French Série Noire invented and nurtured an idealised code of honour amongst its gangster heroes, the *loi du Milieu*, founded on traditional Mediterranean values of trust, shame and silence,[11] and implicitly highly critical of the political corruption of the Fourth Republic. In Giovanni's depiction of Marseille in *Le Deuxième souffle*, the stylised image of the gangster becomes a powerful and positive element, a mirror-image of the bluff but decent community around Pagnol's Bar de la Marine.

The novel opens with the escape from the high-security prison of Castres, in South-West France, of Gustave 'Gu' Minda, now aged fifty and referred to as *le vieux Gu* (old Gu), a legendary criminal of the 1930s, responsible for the robbery of *le train d'or* (gold train)[12] and now serving a life sentence. He makes his way gradually to Paris in order to meet up with his former lover, Manouche, owner of a bar on the Champs-Elysées and widow of a gangster referred to only as 'Paul', and her bodyguard, Gu's faithful accomplice Alban. He arrives just in time to save them both from the attentions of two minor gangsters sent by a rival, the Corsican Jo Ricci. Gu goes into hiding in Montrouge, but his murder of the two young gangsters, following his trademark method of shooting them in a moving car, has aroused the curiosity of Commissaire Blot, an intelligent and sophisticated detective. Blot, younger, urbane, ironic and intelligent, instinctively has more in common with the *truands*, the traditional underworld figures he is pursuing, than he has with his colleagues such as the mediocre and brutal Commissaire Fardiano. The remaining two-thirds of the novel takes place in Marseille, from which Gu is planning to leave for Italy and where he becomes involved in a plot to hold up a gold bullion van, led by Jo Ricci's brother, Venture. The robbery is successful, with Gu and the youngest member of the gang, Antoine Ripa, murdering the two gendarmes escorting the van, and Gu lies low with his share of the takings. The plan unravels afterwards, however, when Gu is spotted watching a pétanque game and is tricked by Blot into making a confession which implicates his confederates, who are then tortured by the corrupt Marseille detective Fardiano. Gu manages to escape, but is now more obsessed with clearing his name than fleeing abroad with Manouche. Accordingly, he kidnaps and murders Fardiano, but not before forcing him to write a confession demonstrating Gu's innocence. He then goes to meet the rest of the gang and, in the ensuing shoot-out, is killed along with the others. The novel ends with Blot dropping Fardiano's confession at the feet of a young journalist, thus posthumously vindicating Gu.

The novel is underpinned by a detailed topographical knowledge of Marseille. At the centre there is the Vieux-Port, on which the Greek Théo, who lives off the Rue de la République, and is to take Gu to Italy, moors his boat. To the south-east there are the bars and clubs frequented and run by the Milieu around the Place de l'Opéra and the Rue de Breteuil, where the lone-wolf gangster Orloff has a safe house and where the dénouement takes place, whilst to the north-west there is the *Evêché* (bishopric), the police headquarters next to the Cathédrale de la Major. Away from the centre, there is the luxurious Boulevard Perrier [sic], on the hillside inland from the Corniche, where Venture Ricci has his house, and Mazargues, where Manouche's cousin Gustin has his cabanon, and where Gu hides out before and after the robbery. Mazargues, in the 1950s still an independent village, with its *terrain de boules* on the Boulevard Michelet where Gu is abducted, and now absorbed into the city as part of the 9th Arrondissement, is nevertheless connected to the city by tramway and is also an easy walk from the Avenue du Prado, the Parc Borély and the Plage du Prado, which Gu visits alone on New Year's Eve. The abduction of Fardiano takes place outside his home on the Avenue Longchamp, and Gu drives him to Trois Lucs, due east, near Saint-Julien, where he is shot. Finally, the brutal robbery itself takes place in the wild, mountainous hinterland on the Route Nationale from Salon-de-Provence to Marseille, and the loot is temporarily hidden in the village of Saint-Chamas on the Etang de Berre, later, incidentally, the scene of considerable local protest against the development of Fos.

Giovanni plays adroitly on two familiar themes of classic Série Noire fiction: the aging gangster trying to come to terms with a world which has changed, and his attempt to pull off one last job which will guarantee his future and validate his past. The very first reference to Gu Minda emphasises his age and his frailty after a long prison sentence. The organiser of the break-out, Bernard, looks back from the top of the prison wall at 'old Gu standing on the edge of the balcony, bending down, getting up again, hesitating' (p. 10), and Gu is barely able to leap to the wall or, later, to climb aboard the slow-moving freight train on which they escape: as he later explains to Alban, 'I'm getting old' (p. 92). This is also a thought which occurs to Pascal Léonetti, the fourth member of the bullion gang, who, whilst he has no doubts about Gu's ability to perform during the hold-up, is more concerned by what he might do afterwards. As he explains to Orloff, 'Gu hasn't kept up with change. He still has the old ideas. That could have consequences' (p. 133). Pascal is proven right: Gu acquits himself well of the murder of the *motard*, but makes the mistake of using the Colt automatic which he has already used for the murder of the two gangsters in Paris, which brings Blot hot on his heels. Similarly, his mistake in repeatedly leaving Justin's house in Mazargues to look at, and eventually join in, the *pétanque* game near the Parc Borély, derives from a sloppiness which he would never have tolerated earlier.

This consciousness of old age and what amounts to an increasingly powerful death wish are indicated by his choice of reading matter: American fiction, including Steinbeck and Hemingway, especially *The Old Man and the Sea*, and Joseph Kessel's *Fortune carrée* (pp. 80, 202), which tells the story of an aging adventurer in the Middle East. He sees himself as essentially how he was at the height of his powers, the hero of the gold train robbery and revelling in luxury and wealth on the Côte d'Azur—he still harks back to the age of the *traction-avant*, when he is living in the era of the Citroën DS. Increasingly, especially after falling victim to Blot's trick, a future life with Manouche and his escape plans become secondary to his obsession with clearing his name amongst his peers and for posterity. His final decision to forcibly replace Orloff in the showdown with Jo Ricci and the other gang members has more the air of a suicide than a serious *règlement de comptes*. It is fitting, therefore, that, at the end of the novel, Manouche appears ready to rebuild her life with Orloff, and that Blot, who ties all the strands together, should lie to her that Gu said nothing before he died, whereas in fact his last gasp was the first syllables of her name.

As a reflection of Marseille crime, *Le Deuxième souffle* is as much anchored in the pre-war era as Pagnol's trilogy and, paradoxically, equally sanitised, in spite of the relatively rare and highly stylised violence. It is important to note that, unlike in Izzo's work, for example, in the conventions of Série Noire fiction, no 'civilians' are actually hurt: the only victims are other gangsters or policemen, whom Gu considers, just before embarking on the robbery, as merely part of the forces trying to put him back behind bars (see: p. 144). Not for nothing does the bleak landscape above Marseille where the robbery takes place 'evoke a Western' (p. 143), an aspect reinforced by Melville's film of 1966.

As Olivier Bohler points out,[13] Melville was originally from northeastern France, but had been involved in the Resistance in Marseille, where he had relatives, and had probably had contacts with the local Milieu. Unlike *Le Cercle Rouge* of 1970, which begins on the Canebière, and *L'Armée des ombres*, with its opening abduction and execution sequence, in which Marseille appears only momentarily, however, *Le Deuxième souffle* is predominantly a Marseillais film, although it retains the Parisian scenes in the first part. Since Giovanni wrote the screenplay and dialogue, the film is a faithful adaptation of the novel, with relatively few divergences or modifications. However, there is a line of dialogue which does not appear in the novel, and which Melville inserts during Gu's and Manouche's first dinner together, during which Gu rules out definitively any fresh start: 'But, Manouche: you've understood nothing. It's over. I gambled and I lost.' Also, in what seem like minor changes, there is no reference to Manouche's first husband Paul, whose name is now transferred to Jo Ricci's brother, the leader of the robbery and who is therefore no longer 'Venture'.

Gu is played by Lino Ventura, a professional wrestler before being cast by Becker as the rising gangster Angelo in *Touchez pas au grisbi*, whilst Blot is created by the veteran boulevard actor Paul Meurisse, later to appear as the head of the Resistance network in *L'Armée des ombres*. Melville is at pains from the outset to establish the film as being more than a typical Série Noire product, as having more general ambitions—like Gu's own reading, which does not include *policiers*, but quasi-metaphysical adventure novels, a taste he shares, incidentally, with Izzo's Fabio Montale. Hence the inclusion at the beginning of the film of a written statement which does not appear in the text of the novel, that this is about a man's 'choice of his own death.' Under Marcel Combes' black and white cinematography, the film becomes a highly stylised end-game in which Gu moves inexorably to his chosen finale and where the principal characters are typified by almost ritual costumes: Blot's tightly-buttoned camel-hair coat and pork-pie hat contrasting with the black overcoats and grey borsalinos of the gangsters. As Philip Mann suggests[14] by unexpectedly including Melville in his study of the dandy, Gu, Paul, Pascal, Antoine, and especially Orloff, like many of Melville's heroes, have an unusual preoccupation with dress and appearance. In their bars and nightclubs, the gangsters are impeccably dressed. Gu is brought an elegant wardrobe for his first dinner with Manouche after his escape; all the members of the gang dress up before and after the robbery, as they do for the confrontations with Orloff and Gu. The same stylisation is present in the Marseille location shots: the bleak, waterlogged coastal area near Les Goudes, where Gu is tricked into a partial confession by Blot, contrasting with the bare plane-trees on the Avenue du Prado where Gu watches his *pétanque* matches, to the wind-torn desert landscape where the robbery takes place. Whereas, as we have seen, Giovanni's novel establishes its realist credentials through a painstaking recreation of a recognisable Marseille topography, Melville's locations are curiously vague and elemental, with little that is specific beyond the Vieux-Port where Théo's boat is moored. The Rue de Breteuil, where Orloff has his apartment in the novel, becomes the fictional Rue de Vinci, somewhere near Saint-Victor. In the climactic scene of the platinum heist (the gold bullion in the novel has become platinum in the film), Melville has retained all the connotations of the Western emphasised in the novel, and the scene itself, shot in real time over fourteen minutes, is compelling in its intensity and suspense. The culmination, in which the four gangsters, now re-clad in their formal overcoats and hats and shot from behind, push the empty bullion van over the cliff into the sea and stand briefly watching as it falls, confers on them a kind of unreal nobility which the real world of Marseille cannot live up to. The film plays upon a stark contrast between the reality of the city itself and its tawdry modern Milieu, and what the old image of it represents, namely almost superhuman fraternity and heroism. As Gu says to Antoine, 'the two *motards*... that was us two, and no-one else', whereas he admits to Paul that, even if he could, he would not stay around in what Paul recognises is 'a filthy hole'. Even for leaders of Marseille's underworld, the city itself can no longer measure up to its legend.

It is in this respect that the film diverges significantly from the novel. Melville's interest, as his written introduction makes clear, lies with the hero's choice of the manner of his self-defining death, a choice which plays out against the backdrop of Marseille, but which has a far broader scope. The novel, in contrast, is much more rooted in the city's criminal activity in the interwar years and the Occupation. This was not immediately apparent and did not really come to light until the 1990s, when details of Giovanni's early career itself were revealed. Like his fellow Série Noire author Albert Simonin, Giovanni's criminal past was not merely tolerated by the literary and cinema world, it was seen, rather, as a guarantee of authenticity. It was only after articles in *Le Journal de Genève* and *Libération* in 1993 and a longer study by Franck Lhomeau in *Temps Noir* ten years later that a more sinister picture began to appear, involving collaboration, extortion, torture and murder. Lhomeau discovered that, in Marseille in 1943, the twenty-year-old Joseph Damiani, later José Giovanni, had been introduced by his father to Simon Sabiani, who helped him join the PPF, with whom he tracked down refugees from the German forced-labour scheme, the STO. In Lyon in August 1944, he joined a known collaborator called 'Orloff', who was executed by firing-squad after the Liberation, in the kidnapping and extortion of two Jewish businessmen, and, in May 1944, with his brother Paul and two associates, he tortured and murdered a Jewish wine-dealer and two brothers in Suresnes, outside Paris. Sentenced to twenty years imprisonment for 'intelligence with the enemy' for his activities in Marseille, he was subsequently condemned to death for his part in the Suresnes murders, later commuted, and to a further ten years for the crime in Lyon, being finally given an amnesty in 1956 by President Coty.[15] What is interesting about this story is that it displaces the focus of *Le Deuxième souffle* backwards from the 1950s to the Occupation and, especially, to the golden years of Marseille gangster-ism in the 1930s. Whereas critics of *L'Armée des ombres* quickly noticed that this Resistance drama more closely resembled a Série Noire narrative, they failed to notice that the opposite could also be true, that, as in Becker's *Touchez pas au grisbi*, the tropes of the Fourth Republic gangster stories could equally be a way of constructing a certain narrative of the Occupation and Resistance. Giovanni's novel *Le Deuxième souffle*, unlike Melville's film, can be read as a covert re-writ-ing of political and criminal activity in Marseille and France as a whole during the interwar years and Occupation.

The novel's memory goes back to the 1930s, an era when Giovanni's uncle, Paul Santolini, alias 'Santos', was a real *truand* (crook, villain, gangster), along with his fellow Corsican, Paul 'Venture' Carbone. At this point, the repeated references to Manouche's former husband 'Paul' become clear, especially when the circumstances of his death are detailed:

> Paul had died in a train accident. He was sharing a sleeping compart-ment with an older friend and had let him have the lower bunk. Following the derailment, Paul's thighs were cut off below the torso by the steel girders of the coach. The man sleeping below got off scot-free. (p. 229)

This is an accurate factual account of how Paul Carbone, the ultimate Voyageur, died when his night train from Marseille to Paris was blown up by the Resistance. In other words, whilst Melville's film remains on a more abstract, tragic, level, Giovanni's novel is much more rooted, albeit often covertly, in the murky history of the Marseille Milieu before and during the Occupation, with Gu Minda's having been an associate of Carbone and Orloff's name being provocative, if covert, allusions to continued crime under the Occupation.

'Total Khéops'

Whilst Giovanni's novel looks backwards towards the heroic interwar period of Marseille banditism, with its legendary exploits and iconic gangsters, Melville's *Le Deuxième souffle* acknowledges, if regretfully, the modernity of the Fourth Republic, which is often depicted in the brands of automobiles employed: Venture Ricci's American-style Simca Versailles, which dates from 1955, Antoine's new Citroën DS, which went into production the same year, and the massive American cars used by Blot's inspectors in their tricking of Gu. There are no traces of the mass post-war immigration and consequent housing crisis described in the previous chapter, and 'civilian' activity is limited to the timeless routine of the *pétanque* players on the Avenue du Prado, whilst the representation of crime is restricted to the Milieu's bars around the Opéra and the elite Italian and Corsican gangsters who plan and carry out the grand operations. Even the various representations of the 'French Connection' follow the same hierarchical pattern, with godfathers and their acolytes supported by an army of foot soldiers, although by the 1970s the network of informants had become, as we have seen, much wider and informal.

By contrast, what constitutes the originality of Jean-Claude Izzo's writing on Marseille is his recognition and dissection of the social catastrophe unfolding in the city parallel to the breakdown of the established criminal organisations, whilst, paradoxically, simultaneously identifying its salutary uniqueness. In this sense, his writing encompasses both the dystopian vision of Peisson's 'wicked city' and the more positive currents deriving from the founding myth of the city itself.

Izzo, who was born in 1945 and died in 2000, owes his reputation to a trilogy of violent crime novels which are reminiscent of James Ellroy's novels on Los Angeles, *Total Khéops* (1995), *Chourmo* (1996) and *Solea* (1998), but is also the author of the non-crime novels *Les Marins perdus*, of 1997 and *Le Soleil des mourants*, of 1999. He was also a poet in the tradition of the interwar *Les Cahiers du Sud*, appreciating especially Gabriel Audisio and Louis Brauquier, and the author of a biography of the nineteenth-century socialist Clovis Hughes. It is this historical dimension to his work which renders his fictional portrait of Marseille so interesting: the novels present a precise and detailed awareness of the topography and history of the city itself, constructed through a rich and complex web of references to its culture and especially, its cultural representations in the nineteenth and twentieth centuries which place it firmly within a pan-Mediterranean context.

The hero of Izzo's *Total Khéops* trilogy is Fabio Montale, a member of an Italian immigrant family, born and brought up in Le Panier, transplanted to the Belle-de-Mai after the *rafles* and destruction of the Vieux-Port in 1943, and now living in his father's old cabanon on the coast at Les Goudes. After an early delinquent career in the company of fellow-immigrants, Ugo, from Naples, and Manu, from Barcelona, Montale gives up crime and joins the colonial army, serving as a sergeant in Djibouti, before becoming a police officer, first in Paris and now in his native Marseille. When *Total Khéops* opens, however, he has been sidelined, as *commissaire* in charge of the new Brigade de Surveillance des Secteurs, responsible for policing the immigrant *cités* to the north, but effectively subordinate to the major departments, especially the Brigade de Répression du Grand Banditisme, headed by Montale's nemesis Commissaire Auch.[16] Indeed, Montale's disaffection from his police colleagues is such that, in the final two volumes of the trilogy, he has resigned and acts independently.

The first, and most original, of the novels, *Total Khéops*, follows two plot-lines which are ultimately connected. The first concerns the deaths of Montale's childhood friends Manu and Ugo, the latter gunned down by the police in Le Panier after he had assassinated a fictitious Marseille godfather, Charles Zucca. The second, apparently unconnected, event is the rape and murder of Montale's girlfriend, Leila, who comes from an Algerian immigrant family and has just completed her Masters degree in Comparative Literature at Aix. The links between the two sets of crimes relate to the breakdown of the traditional criminal hierarchies, creating a vacuum being filled by an alliance between the corrupt police detective Morvan and the white supremacist Wepler, who have both served, like Montale, in the post-colonial army in Africa, and are now activists for the Front National. In Izzo's analysis, the 'total chaos' of the novel's title is not exclusively due to Marseille's uneasy social mixture, but much more to the return of the ghosts of the nation's colonial and post-colonial past.

Yet this dystopian vision of the city is matched by an extraordinarily positive one, which essentially resides in a celebration of pan-Mediterranean culture at all levels. Montale conforms to a certain type of maverick investigator who, in spite of his trade and his rough origins, nevertheless has acquired an impressive cultural baggage. After the first day of his unofficial investigation into the two sets of crimes, he notes: 'I poured myself a glass of Lagavulin, put on a record by Theolonious Monk and went to bed with Conrad's *Within the Tides*' (p. 63). Indeed, it is this texture of cultural references which makes the novel so interesting: not merely does Montale have a rich and diverse musical culture ranging from gastronomy to modern jazz and rhythm and blues to rap, the novel is structured on a network of literary echoes all related to the cultural memory of Marseille. He is a connoisseur of malt whisky and the rosé wines from the Var, but also, like his Sicilian counterpart Montalbano, of traditional Mediterranean cuisine, prepared for him by his cook Honorine.[17] In music, he likes the Marseille rap groups Fabulous Trobadors, Boudoucon, Hypnotik, Black Lions, and especially IAM and Massilia Sound System, who sprang up from the 'Ultras', the Olympique de Marseille supporters from the south side of the stadium, and who sing in 'Maritime Provençal: Marseille French, as they say in Paris' (pp. 95, 106). His local literary frame of reference is, as we have seen, similarly eclectic, leading to a complex strand of references to the *Cahiers du Sud* poets Emile Sicard, Toursky, Gerald Neveu, Audisio and Brauquier (p. 80), Dumas' *Le Comte de Monte-Cristo* and Pagnol's *Marius* trilogy.

Les Marins perdus, of 1997, notes that, whereas 'the Atlantic or the Pacific are long-distance seas, the Mediterranean is a neighbourhood.'[18] Like all neighbourhoods it is always prone to split into violently competing rival clans, but this sense of community is also its immense virtue and Izzo's Mediterranean is a coherent cultural entity, from north to south and from east to west, with its own shared mythology. In *Total Khéops*, Leila's masters dissertation is on the work on the Lebanese poet Salah Stétié, who 'built bridges between East and West and across the Mediterranean. She recalled that in the *Thousand and One Nights*, under the guise of Sinbad the Sailor, appeared some of the episodes from the *Odyssey*' (p. 77).

Montale is also well aware of the link: writing of his childhood with Manu and Ugo, he recalls that 'we spent whole days reading the adventures of Ulysses' (p. 52). At the same time, the reference to Sinbad echoes the nom-de-guerre of Dantès in *Le Comte de Monte-Cristo*, another key element in Izzo's Mediterranean pantheon, which he develops at length in *Les Marins perdus*. Lole, the ambiguous sister-figure and lover to Montale, Ugo and Manu, now lives near the site of

Mercédès' home on the Plage des Catalans, and, as one might expect, the Château d'If dominates the horizon of Izzo's fiction, introduced specifically in *Les Marins perdus* to underscore the theme of betrayal. The sailor Diamantis' first love in Marseille, the Italian Amina, is studying Balzac, but 'Balzac bored her. He was a poseur. She preferred Dumas. *La Reine Margot*, *La San Felice*, *Le Comte de Monte-Cristo*. But Dumas was not on the syllabus…' (p. 221). Diamantis remembers that *Le Comte de Monte-Cristo* was Amina's favourite novel. 'She had taken him to see the island, the cell where Dantès was imprisoned, just as he was preparing to marry the beautiful Mercédès. "It's the great novel about injustice", she had said. "Hatred, contempt, jealousy, cowardice"' (p. 248).

Yet, if the memory of Dantès' betrayal, his loss of the 'belle Mercédès' and the dystopian vision of a world dominated by hatred and cowardice, serve to reinforce the plots of Izzo's Marseille novels—the increasingly violent world of the Montale trilogy and the more controlled and modulated *Marins perdus*—that world is retrieved by the positive qualities of the Mediterranean community, which offers an ultimate welcome. The abiding memory of Dumas' novel in *Les Marins perdus* is neither the injustice nor the intricate revenge, but 'the entry into the port of Marseille of the three-master *Le Pharaon*, coming from Smyrna, Trieste and Naples' (p. 248).

Finally, whilst on one level, it seems incongruous to view Izzo's dystopian fiction in the context of Marcel Pagnol's utopian depiction of the Vieux-Port in the interwar years, the relationship is more subtle. Certainly, as with Dumas, Izzo is well aware of Pagnol's role in fashioning the national and international image of Marseille, and the name of his housekeeper, Honorine, pays tribute to Fanny's mother in the trilogy. Similarly, in *Les Marins perdus*, Diamantis 'had sat down at the terrace of the Bar de la Marine, on the port' (p. 152) and, in *Total Khéops*, Izzo underlines its cultural significance. Montale, going to meet his informant Batisti, records:

> I found Batisti at the Bar de la Marine. It was his canteen. It had become the place where the yacht skippers met up. On the wall, there was still Louis Audibert's picture showing the card game from *Marius*, and the photo of Pagnol and his wife on the port. (p. 153)

Later, as we have seen, when Montale draws a confession out of Batisti, it is on the famous ferry-boat once captained by Pagnol's Escartefigue, 'captain of the ferry-boat which crosses the Vieux-Port twenty-four times a day.'[19]

Underneath the undoubtedly realist 'noir' trappings of *Total Khéops*, there emerges the familiar glimpse of the *ville d'accueil* or *ville d'asile* celebrated in Londres' reportage and extended as an essential component of Mediterranean hospitality to all of Marseille's visitors, wherever they come from:

> That was the history of Marseille. Its eternity. A utopia. The only utopia in the world. A place where anyone, of whatever colour, could get off a boat or a train, his case in his hand, without any money in his pocket, and melt into the wave of other people. A city where, as soon as he put his foot on the ground, this man could say 'Here it is: I'm home'. (p. 287)

This is connected to another characteristic of Marseille, its uncanny ability to resemble every visitor's home-town. As the Algerian Abdou remarks in *Le Soleil des mourants*, as he looks at the sea from the Fort Saint-Jean:

> Marseille, at least from this side of the city, always reminded me of Algiers. It's not that I was homesick—don't think that. Home, that didn't exist. I'd never go back to there. I want to forget Algiers. It's just that I wanted to hold on to a few memories. That's all I've got, a few memories.
>
> I was not the only one to come and resurrect them here. Loads of people wandered around the Fort Saint-Jean, alone or in groups. Lots of Algerians like me, but also Africans, Turks, Comorians, Yugoslavs... A guy who wanted to sell me dope thought that Marseille looked like Dubrovnik. 'It looks like what you want it to look like', I told him...[20]

Not only does this episode reinforce the similarity between Marseille and Algiers which runs through the history of both cities, it also echoes the rag-pickers' community by the Fort Saint-Nicolas in Peisson's *Hans le marin*. Similarly, *Les Marins perdus* ('The Lost Sailors') recounts the story of three sailors abandoned on a bankrupt ship in the port: none of them is French—one is from Lebanon, one is from Greece and one from Turkey—but each of them feels at home. Izzo writes of the Greek second-in-command, Diamantis, 'each time he disembarked in the port, he had the feeling of returning home' (p. 95) ... 'It remained for Diamantis the most mysterious city in the world. The most human' (p. 98). In other words, from the traditional dystopian representation of late twentieth-century Marseille, built upon the notion of a diasporic population at odds with themselves and the city, Izzo constructs his improbable utopia, in which for every departure there is a homecoming, and where there are no strangers. The Arab proprietor of Chez Hassan, one of Montale's favourite bars, 'took pleasure in disconcerting his customers. "Hello, strangers", he said, seeing us come in. Here, everyone was the foreign friend. Whatever the colour of their skin, their hair or their eyes' (p. 288), The novel is a powerful affirmation of an unlikely, but real, assimilation.

In spite of the apparent resemblances between Izzo's Marseille and James Ellroy's Los Angeles in their portrayal of violence and corruption, there is a world of difference between them. In the course of *Total Khéops*, Montale loses his two childhood friends, his girlfriend Leila and his colleague Pérol, all as the result of a complex anti-gangster operation orchestrated by Auch and of the clandestine activities of the Front National. Small wonder, therefore, that Montale concludes from his experience in the crime-ridden suburbs that '[o]ur former colonies were now here. Their capital, Marseille. Here, like there, life did not exist' (p. 315). Yet this is not the end and the novel closes with an extraordinary coda on the founding myth of the city, which Izzo uses again in *Les Marins perdus*. The morning following the carnage of the dénouement, Montale goes out in his boat to see the dawn rise over Marseille:

So Marseille revealed itself. From the sea. As the Phocaean must have seen it one morning, centuries ago. With the same wonderment. The Port of Massilia. I knew of its happy lovers, a Marseille Homer could have said, evoking Gyptis and Protis. The voyager and the princess. The sun came up over the hills... (p. 348)

It is ultimately this generosity of the city, be it a 'capital', 'port' or 'porte' ('gateway'), which triumphs, and which, as we shall see, allows Marseille to weather the storms of racial division and political provocation which beset France in 2005.

This is not to say, however, that Izzo's positive message is unproblematic. In the first place, the following two volumes of the Montale trilogy never quite regain the same intensity and focus as *Total Khéops*. The second volume, *Chourmo*, written in memory of Ibrahim Ali, a member of IAM murdered by Front National activists in February 1995, has, like its predecessor, two plot strands. A fashionable and well-connected architect working on the 'Euroméditerranée' development project is found murdered in his house along with a young Algerian, Guitou. At the same time, a social worker, Serge, who has been a friend of Montale, is shot dead in one of the *cités*. Montale is no longer in the police force, but investigates Serge's murder unofficially and follows a trail which reveals municipal corruption with Italian Mafia connections. The title is Marseille slang derived from *chiourme*, meaning 'galley-slave', characterising the dispossessed in contrast with the rich. The novel ends with Montale killing the Mafia assassins on the Corniche and returning home to find the architect's widow and son together with Guitou's girlfriend all having taken refuge in his cabanon and sleeping in his bed: an ending more reminiscent of Daniel Pennac's Belleville novels than of James Ellroy. The final volume, *Solea*, from the title of a Miles Davis piece, develops the Mafia theme, with Babette, Montale's journalist friend, on the run from an Italian gang and all his friends and loved ones being threatened. The novel ends in a shoot-out on the Iles Frioules in which all the characters are killed, but not before Montale himself has alienated his friends', and the reader's, sympathy by a quasi-suicidal obsession with revenge. As the trilogy advances, the law of diminishing returns plays out as the violence, already gratuitous in *Total Khéops* in the pointless death of Pérol, takes over with none of the compensatory optimism. Indeed, this optimism is itself open to question and not necessarily durable. William Firebrace recalls talking with the owner of a bookshop specialising in detective fiction in Marseille who is dismissive of the Montale trilogy: 'Izzo? Well, he's very readable but a bit passé, all that stuff about a romantic detective living in his *cabanon*. No one reads Izzo much anymore, except foreigners, of course...'.[21] Romanticism and thrillers are hardly strangers, however—witness Chandler's Philip Marlowe—but it is certainly true that the lurch from dystopia to the fraternity of Chez Hassan can sometimes stretch credulity.

Moreover, whilst Izzo's apocalyptic vision of a power vacuum at the heart of Marseille criminal activity, brutally filled by an all-encroaching Italian Mafia and the rise of the Front National, has a certain aesthetic appeal, it is not necessarily entirely historically accurate. The journalist and crime novelist François Thomazeau, for example, whose *Marseille, une biographie* is one of the best books on the city, and who often betrays some irritation at Izzo's exaggerated status as a historian, offers a more prosaic explanation for the decline of the Marseille gang-bosses. Chatting with the inspector who is investigating the assault on him by members of a drug gang, he reflects on the 'mania in this city to constantly hark back to a golden age... To my knowledge, organised crime has always scoured the city and acted as an accelerator for the integration of successive waves of immigrants...'[22] This argument only half-convinces the inspector, who counters that:

> In the past, the gangster was out in the open. What he aspired to was respectability, with beautiful flashy houses, nightclubs, money and the women of the Côte d'Azur. The Guérinis controlled the Opéra and the Quai Rive-Neuve, Zampa was installed on the city hall side. But they all did their business in the city centre, which is where the party-goers furnished themselves with drugs. For us it was much easier because the cops frequented the same clubs as the gangsters. Later, Francis le Belge and the Corsicans moved out to Aix and the Cours Mirabeau.... In fact, drugs trafficking followed trade in general. The small shopkeepers in the centre shut down, replaced by supermarkets on the outskirts. And the kids who used to work as security guards at Grand Littoral or the hypermarkets in Plan-de-Campagne are now doing the same thing, but on their estates, for the drug lords.[23]

In this respect, the relationship between crime writing and film-making about Marseille and the social and political reality is more indirect and more pragmatic than it often appears. The elite gangsters who make up the cast of the Série Noire, with their formal language, stylised costumes and rigorous code of honour, constitute a throwback to a perceived Golden Age, in which the buccaneering gangsterism of the interwar years becomes confused with a black and white interpretation of Collaboration and Resistance, and an implicit denunciation of the petty politics and corruption of the post-war Fourth Republic. They are also, as we have seen, however, reflections at both national and local levels of the malaise of a traditional society coming to terms with post-war urban modernity. Similarly, Izzo's *Khéops*, like Le Clézio's *Désert*, is as much a product of global trends in urban development, with migration to the suburbs from the dying city centres as their ultimate corollary, as it is of the more dramatic official corruption, the erosion of the traditional crime families or the ripples emanating from a succession of French colonial and post-colonial interventions. As Alèssi Dell'Umbria emphasises, the descent of the city into a state of 'total dereliction', accompanied by a net fall in the population between 1975 and 1990 of 161,000, taking it to 800,000,[24] was due to highly questionable economic and urban planning decisions at the municipal, regional and national level, which may indeed have involved a measure of corruption, but were far removed from the apocalyptic power struggles in the world of organised crime which constitute the aesthetic dynamic of Izzo's fiction.

It is tempting to see the successors to Izzo and the Marseille *polar* in the early twenty-first century as a third stage in this intricate relationship, with the city now further reduced from dereliction to the role of back-drop. Luc Besson's *Taxi* franchise, for example, is an exercise in screwball comedy which is located in Marseille merely for its criminal associations and which could, to all intents and purposes, be set in any Westernised city: the bank-robbers in the first film, released in 1998, are not even Marseillais, but German; *Taxi 2* is set mainly in Paris, and the endlessly-replicable story-line is eminently adaptable to settings in the United States and India.

More seriously, it was perhaps inevitable, given its drug-related plot, that, in 2016, the fourth series of the long-running French television crime drama *Braquo* should devote several of its episodes to Commissaire Eddy Caplan and his team's visit to Marseille on the track of a Turkish drug gang. The Marseille sequence is, in many ways, strikingly similar to Frankenheimer's *French Connection 2* and Caplan is no more welcome than Doyle, especially when he inadvertently disrupts a long-term surveillance operation set up by his opposite number in the city's police. The emphasis is on the outsider, rather than the city itself, although the series does descend into local, if anachronistic, detail by showing the murder, by his trusted aide, of an aging Marseille godfather in his bastide, and by recycling a now familiar example of the smugglers' ability to fool the police by setting up a decoy container in the port. It is also interesting that the long-running connection between Marseille and Egypt is signalled by an episode entitled *Pharaons*, with echoes of the name of Dantès' ship. Even so, this is a Paris-based drama and the team return to the capital for the bloody dénouement, leaving Marseille marginalised, in what may be seen to encapsulate the city's future in the twenty-first century.

AFTERWORD

After completing his last chapter, 'Total Khéops', dominated by the work of Jean-Claude Izzo, Nicholas Hewitt felt that his book had found a satisfactory ending point. He did not believe there could be a conclusion or even an epilogue. The objective had not been a conventional cultural history of Marseille, or in his words, 'still less a political or social one.' He chose rather to provide a series of 'snapshots' of the city's modern cultural history, albeit in a chronological sequence. He took a broad view: the cultural history of a city, he believed, is an ongoing process that by its very nature could be neither comprehensive nor conclusive. If he had an overarching objective, it was to determine how and why the cultural features captured in the 'snapshots' continued to be sustained long after their origins had faded into the past, especially those of the Good City and Wicked City. This has happened even as the city has changed dramatically, first with the growth of its port and then its subsequent decline.

That Marseille, for most of its history, has been France's largest port, and by the mid-twentieth century also one of the largest French cities in terms of population, has lent the city great regional and national significance. The tension between the port and the capital city in terms of national power and resources was always easily resolved in favour of the capital. Yet Marseille's history, its position as leader amongst Mediterranean ports, the special regional history of its hinterland, always gave it a strong individual identity. Its unique cultural resonances, reflecting and contradicting the narratives of

235

French history, have made it a fascinating and important subject in the history of the nation.

This afterword has been added because of the death of Nicholas Hewitt on 1 March 2019. His love of Marseille was both deep and life-long and writing this book sustained him in his last illness. He first visited and fell in love with the city in his youth, returning many times in the intervening years. Just last year, the last conference he organised, in his capacity as editor of *French Cultural Studies*, was in Marseille and about Marseille. He completed the full revisions of his text just three weeks before he died. As his wife and myself an urban historian, I have had the privilege of preparing the manuscript for publication. I have been able to do so only with the help of experts in the field, some at that last conference workshop, and of many friends who have given generously of their time. I would like to name particularly Mike Kelly, Keith Reader (who read the entire manuscript), Judith Still, Diana Knight (who has both read the manuscript and been a huge support in collecting images), and Nora Lafi who guided me to key French sources for many images. Finally, Nick Alfrey, Jenny Swann, Elizabeth Boa and Meesha Nehru have all given help and advice. I am also very grateful to Lara Weisweiller-Wu, the publishing editor, who has worked with me on text and images and been totally supportive.

Helen Meller

NOTES

INTRODUCTION

1. See: Richard Cobb, 'Marseille', in *Paris and Elsewhere* (New York: New York Review Books, 2002), pp. 246–90.
2. See, for example, François Thomazeau, who, in *Marseille, une Biographie* (Paris: Stock, 2013), gives an account of the discovery of the Cosquer Grotto off the coast of Marseille which revealed details of a sophisticated Gaulish civilisation prior to the Phocean arrival (pp. 57–60).
3. See: Emile Thémime, ed., *Migrances*, five volumes (Aix-en-Provence: Edisud, 1989).
4. The term was used as the sub-title of the Franco-American film version of Peisson's *Hans le marin* in 1946, but the concept of Marseille as inherently evil was common currency by the end of the 1920s. Even the partially wet-behind-the-ears poet Laurie Lee, barely one year out of his remote Gloucestershire village of Slad, was aware of the relative straightforwardness of a Spanish port like Algeciras compared with the malevolence emanating from its Northern Mediterranean neighbour.
5. See: Marcel Roncayolo, *L'Imaginaire de Marseille. Port, Ville, Pôle* (Marseille: Chambre de Commerce et d'Industrie de Marseille, 1990).
6. See: M.F.K. Fisher, *A Considerable Town* (New York: Alfred Knopf, 1978).
7. Jean-Louis Fabiani and Sophie Bias, 'Marseille, A City beyond Distinction', in Tania Woloshyn and Nicholas Hewitt, eds., *L'Invention du Midi: The Rise of the South of France in the National and International Imagination*, *Nottingham French Studies*, 50, 1, 2011, pp. 83–94.
8. See: Louis Chevalier, *Classes laborieuses, classes dangereuses à Paris pendant la première mitié du dix-neuvième siècle* (Paris: Plon, 1958).
9. See the 2017 MuCEM exhibition *Vies d' Ordures, de l'économie des déchets*, ed. Denis Chevalier and Yann-Philippe Tastevin (Paris: Artlys, 2017).

10. See: Philippe Pujol, *La Fabrique du monstre* (Arles: Les Arènes, 2016), p. 198.
11. See: Peraldi et al, *Sociologie de Marseille*, p. 114.
12. Dylan Thomas famously commented on the presence of 'professional Irishmen' on the professional lecture-circuit in the United States in the 1950s. See: Dylan Thomas, 'A Visit to America', *Quite Early One Morning* (New York: New Directions, 1954), p. 147.
13. See: Pujol, p. 264.
14. Robert L. Cioffi, 'A Palm Tree, a Colour and a Mythical Bird. *In Search of the Phoenicians*, by Josephine Quinn', *London Review of Books*, 3 January 2019, p. 15.
15. Pujol, p. 265.

1. *LE COMTE DE MONTE-CRISTO*: THE VIEUX-PORT AND THE HINTERLAND

1. See: Eric Baratay, *Biographies animales* (Paris: Seuil, 2017).
2. Herbert Adams Gibbons, *Ports of France* (London: Jonathan Cape, 1927), p. 294.
3. Pierre Guiral, 'Marseille de 1814 à 1870', in Edouard Baratier, ed., *Histoire de Marseille* (Toulouse: Privat, 1973), p. 319.
4. See: Michel Vovelle, 'Marseille et Napoléon', in ibid., p. 303.
5. See: Pierre Guiral, 'Marseille de 1814 à 1870', in ibid., p. 311.
6. See: Michel Vovelle, 'La Révolution', in ibid., p. 276.
7. See: Emile Thémime, *Histoire de Marseille de la Révolution à nos jours* (Paris: Perrin, 1999), p. 18.
8. Ibid., p. 19.
9. See: ibid., p. 18.
10. Vovelle, p. 201.
11. See: Joseph Méry, *Marseille et les Marseillais* (Marseille: Editions de la Grande Fontaine, 1860).
12. Eleanor Elsner, *Romantic France. The Enchanted Land of Provence* (London: Herbert Jenkins, 1926), pp. 254–5.
13. David Bellos, in his study of Victor Hugo's *Les Misérables*, plausibly suggests that Dantès' imprisonment and plans for revenge begins in the same year, 1815, as Jean Valjean's career and that the two works 'bookend' each other. See: David Bellos, *The Novel of the Century. The Extraordinary Adventure of 'Les Misérables'* (London: Particular Books, 2017), p. 168.
14. See: Graham Robb, *The Discovery of France* (London: Picador, 2007), p. 282.
15. Claude Camous, *Alexandre Dumas à Marseille. Du Château d'If au Gai Paris* (Aubagne: Editions Autres Temps, 2014), p. 62.

16. Ibid., p. 63.
17. The novel is set in the outskirts of Marseille, but was in fact entirely written in Trouville, before Dumas had even visited the South. See: ibid., p. 75.
18. See: ibid., pp. 57–8.
19. Emile Thémime pays tribute to Méry in his *Histoire de Marseille* as 'one of the most valuable chroniclers of Marseille. As Director of the Bibliothèque Municipale, he welcomed into the city all the great contemporary writers'. See: Thémime, p. 18.
20. See: ibid., p. 58.
21. Ibid., p. 62.
22. Robin Buss, 'Preface' Alexandre Dumas, *The Count of Monte Cristo* (Harmondsworth: Penguin, 1996), p.xii.
23. Alexandre Dumas, *The Count of Monte Cristo* (Ware: Wordsworth Editions, 1997), p. 5.
24. A specialist study by Anna Valère-Bernard, *Le Costume de Marseille. Guide pratique* (Marseille: Editions du Roudelet Felibren dou Pichoun-Bousquet, 1954), essentially corroborates and amplifies Dumas' description of Provençal dress.
25. See: Cammous, pp. 57–8.
26. See: Thémime, pp. 27, 30.
27. See: Castans, p. 181.
28. See: ibid., p. 450.
29. Ibid., p. 454.
30. The fort is referred to in the film as the Fort Saint-Nicolas and Pascal Ory even confuses it with the Château d'If, but its position and architecture is undoubtedly that of the Fort Saint-Jean.
31. For details regarding the funding of *La Marseillaise*, see: Ory, pp. 450–1.
32. See: ibid., p. 457.
33. Ibid., p. 456.
34. Thémime, p. 28.
35. Quoted in ibid., p. 34.
36. Quoted in ibid., p. 37.
37. See: ibid., p. 43.
38. Letter of 19 February 1867, quoted in Henri Mitterand, 'Notice', Emile Zola, *Les Mystères de Marseille*, *Oeuvres Complètes*, I, ed. Henri Mitterand (Paris: Cercle du Livre Précieux, 1966), p. 507.
39. See: Robert Abirached, 'Introduction', *Les Mystères de Marseille*, p. 223.
40. See: ibid., p. 222.
41. Emile Zola, *Les Mystères de Marseille*, *Œuvres Complètes*, 1 (Paris: Cercle du Livre Précieux, 1966), p. 229.

42. See: David Crackanthorpe, *Marseille* (Oxford: Signal Books, coll. 'Innercities Cultural Guides', 2012), p. 52.
43. Jean-Claude Izzo, *Total Khéops* (Paris: Gallimard, coll. Folio Policier, 1995), pp. 270–1.
44. François Thomazeau, *Marseille, une biographie* (Paris: Stock, 2013), p. 34.
45. See: Abirached, p. 222.
46. Pierre Guiral, 'De 1814 à 1870', p. 336.
47. See: ibid., pp. 336–7.
48. See: Mitterand, 'Notice', p. 507.
49. See: Guiral, p. 336.
50. See: ibid., p. 337.
51. Ibid., p. 338.
52. Ibid., p. 338. Interestingly, the Italians repaid this gesture of French solidarity in 1870, when Garibaldi landed at Marseille offering his help in the Franco-Prussian War, during which he served as a general in Alsace.

2. *TARTARIN DE TARASCON*: LA JOLIETTE, ALGERIA AND THE 'MEDITERRANEAN SYSTEM'

1. Alphonse Daudet, *Aventures prodigieuses de Tartarin de Tarascon* (Paris: E. Dentu, 1882), p. 87.
2. Raymond Bernard's film of the novel, released in 1934, with a script by Pagnol and starring Raimu and Charpin, omits the Marseille scenes altogether and moves directly to the steamship.
3. The *Zouave* was built in 1856/7 for the Société Arnaud, Touache Frères et Compagnie, founded in 1850 and renamed as the Compagnie de Navigation Mixte, one of Marseille's most famous shipping companies, in 1858. See: Bernard Bernadac, *Histoire de la Compagnie de Navigation Mixte et des relations maritimes France-Afrique du Nord de 1850 à 1969* (Marseille: Payan, 1985).
4. See: François Thomazeau, *Marseille, une Biographie* (Paris: Stock, 2013).
5. Thémime, pp. 73–4.
6. See: Guiral, 'Marseille de 1814 à 1870', in *Histoire de Marseille*, p. 332.
7. See: Thémime, pp. 83–4.
8. See: ibid., pp. 84–5.
9. See: Guiral, pp. 346–7.
10. See: Willam H. Sewell, Jr., *Structure and Mobility. The Men and Women of Marseille, 1820–1870* (Cambridge: Cambridge University Press, 1985), p. 24.
11. See: Sewell, *Structure and Mobility*, p. 22.
12. See: Thémime, p. 86.

13. See: Guiral, p. 345.
14. See: Thémime, p. 87.
15. See: ibid., pp. 85–6.
16. See: ibid., p. 88.
17. See: ibid., p. 89.
18. See: Guiral, p. 332.
19. See: Thémime, p. 81.
20. Ibid., p. 81.
21. See: Jenny Uglow, *Mr Lear. A Life of Art and Nonsense* (London: Faber and Faber, 2017), p. 274.
22. See: Thémime, p. 80.
23. See: Thémime, pp. 80–1.
24. See: Thémime, pp. 90–5.
25. See: Marcel Roncayolo, *Les Grammaires d'une ville. Essai sur la genèse des structures urbaines de Marseille* (Paris: Editions de l'Ecole des Hautes Etudes en Sciences Sociales, 1996), pp. 140.
26. See: ibid., pp. 94–7.
27. See: ibid., p. 95.
28. See: Sewell, p. 5.
29. See: Marcel Roncayolo, *Les Grammaires d'une ville*, pp. 115, 126.
30. Guiral, p. 344.
31. Quoted in ibid., p. 345.
32. Samuel S. Cox, *Search for Winter Sunbeams in the Riviera, Corsica, Algiers and Spain* (London: Sampson Low, Son, and Marston: 1869), p. 118.
33. Ibid., p. 119.
34. Ibid., p. 120.
35. See: Kamel Kateb, *Européens, 'Indigènes' et Juifs en Algérie (1830–1962). Représentations et réalités des populations* (Paris: Editions de l'Institut National d'Etudes Démographiques, 2001).
36. The total population of the country was nearly 3 million, made up of 122,000 French, nearly 95,000 Southern European, 2.6 million Muslims and 34,000 Jews. See: Kamel Kateb, 'Le Bilan démographique de la conquête de l'Algérie (1830–1880)', in Abderrahmane Bouchène, Jean-Pierre Peyroulou, Ouanassa Siari Tengour, Sylvie Thénault, eds., *Histoire de l'Algérie à la période coloniale (1830–1962)* (Paris: La Découverte; Algiers: Editions Barzakh, 2012), p. 83.
37. Robert Aldrich, *Greater France. A History of French Overseas Expansion* (Basingstoke: Macmillan, 1996), p. 25.
38. Ibid., p. 25.
39. Ibid., p. 26.
40. See, for example, Jennifer E. Sessions, *By Sword and Plough. France and the Conquest of Algeria* (Ithaca, NY and London: Cornell University Press, 2011), p. 317.

41. See: Jan Laymeyer, "Algeria Historical Demographic Data of the Whole Country", *Population Statistics*, 11 October 2003.

42. See: Kamel Kateb, 'Le Bilan démographique de la conquête de l'Algérie (1830–1880)', p. 83.

43. See: Aldrich, p. 28.

44. See: Thémime, p. 76.

45. Quoted in Pamela Pilbeam, *Saint-Simonians in Nineteenth-Century France. From Free Love to Algeria* (Basingstoke: Palgrave Macmillan, 2014), p. 106.

46. See: ibid., p. 110.

47. See, for example, Sheila Crane, *Mediterranean Crossroads. Marseille and Modern Architecture* (Minneapolis and London: University of Minnesota Press, 2011).

48. See: Louis M. Greenberg, *Sisters of Liberty. Marseille, Lyon, Paris and the Reaction to a Centralised State, 1868–1971* (Cambridge, Mass.: Harvard University Press, 1971), p. 170. However, this was not enough to get him elected as a candidate for Marseille in the 1869 legislative elections, in spite of them coinciding with the opening of the Canal and his programme promising traditionally popular Marseille policies like decentralisation and the protection of local rights.

49. Quoted in Thémime, pp. 76–7.

50. Quoted in ibid., p. 77.

51. See: Pilbeam, p. 129.

52. See: ibid., pp. 178–181.

53. See: Joseph Méry, *Marseille et les Marseillais* (Marseille: Editions de la Grande Fontaine, 1860), pp. 68–9.

54. See: Olivier Bourra, *Marseille ou la mauvaise réputation* (Paris: Arléa, 2001), pp. 43–4.

55. Conrad's novel was written at the end of his life, in 1922, but evokes his late adolescence as an apprentice seaman in Marseille in the 1870s, when the city was a centre for Spanish Carlist revolutionary activity.

56. See: Victor Combarnous, *L'Histoire du Grand-Théâtre de Marseille, 31 octobre 1787–13 novembre 1919. Notes et souvenirs* (Marseille: 1927; Marseille: Laffitte Reprints, 1980), pp. 41–120.

57. See: ibid., p. 42.

58. Ibid., p. 42.

59. See: Lucien Gaillard, *Victor Gelu. Poète du peuple marseillais* (Marseille: Editions Jeanne Laffitte, 1985), p. 12.

60. Emile Ripert, *La Renaissance Provençale (1880–1860)* (Paris: Champion, 1917), p. 290.

61. See: Victor Gelu, *Marseille au XIXe siècle* (Paris: Plon, 1971), pp. 129–30.

62. Gaillard, pp. 15–16.
63. Ibid., p. 16.
64. See: Gelu, p. 165.
65. See: Ripert, p. 223.
66. Ibid., pp. 223–4.
67. See: ibid., p. 225.
68. Ibid., p. 229.
69. Quoted in Gaillard, p. 19.
70. Quoted in ibid., p. 19.
71. Quoted in Ripert, p. 295.
72. Ibid., p. 297.
73. See: Pierre Guiral, 'Gelu et Marseille', in Victor Gelu, *Marseille au XIXe siècle*, p. 16.
74. Ripert, pp. 301–2.
75. Ibid., p. 294.
76. Ibid., p. 313.
77. Quoted in ibid., p. 93.
78. See: Gelu, *Marseille au XIXe siècle*, pp. 338–9.
79. Ibid., p. 49.
80. See: ibid., pp. 139–40.
81. See: Louis Chevalier, *Montmartre du plaisir et du crime* (Paris: Laffont, 1980).
82. See: ibid., pp. 41–2.
83. Ibid., p. 247.
84. Ibid., p. 335–7.
85. Méry, p. 234.

3. *MA PETITE TONKINOISE*: THE EXPOSITION COLONIALE AND THE BELLE EPOQUE

1. 'Don't cry if I'm leaving you, little Ana, little Ana, little Annamite/ you gave me your youth/Your love and caresses/You were my little wife/My Tonkiki, my Tonkiki, my Tonkinoise/In my heart I will keep always/The memory of our love!' Interestingly, the song had a second life during the First World War, when the Montmartre cabaret singer Théodore Botrel adapted the lyrics for his chauvinist and militarist 'Ma Mitraillause', a love-song of a soldier to his machine gun.
2. Inscription on the plaque on the Quai des Belges at the end of the Vieux-Port, quoted in the fronticepiece to M.F.K. Fisher, *A Considerable Town* (New York: Alfred A. Knopf, 1978).
3. See: Françoise-Albane Beudon, *David Dellepiane. Peintre. Affichiste. Illustrateur* (Marseille: Editions Parenthèses, 1999). According to Beudon, it was the poster for the twenty-fifth centennial which launched

Dellepiane's career, and the project was commissioned so late that Dellepiane recruited the staff of the Hôtel-Dieu to act as models for the Gauls (p. 8).

4. See: Philippe Joutard (ed.), *Histoire de Marseille en treize événements* (Marseille: Jeanne Laffitte, 1988), p. 4.

5. See: Emile Thémime, 'Des Rêves d'aventure à la nostalgique du passé. Marseille de 1875 à 1932', in Beudon, *David Dellepiane*, p. 19.

6. See: Florian Sanchez (ed.), *L'Histoire de l'Olympique de Marseille* (Paris: Hugo et Compagnie, 2015), p. 18.

7. Thémime, *Histoire de Marseille*, p. 186.

8. See: ibid., p. 187.

9. See: Eliane Richard, 'La première exposition colonial française', in Joutard, ed., *Histoire de Marseille en treize événements*, p. 183.

10. Thémime, *Histoire de Marseille*, p. 187.

11. See: ibid., p. 185.

12. See: ibid., p. 182.

13. Ibid., p. 181.

14. See: ibid., p. 181.

15. See: ibid., p. 182.

16. Ibid., pp. 182–3.

17. Quoted in ibid., p. 183.

18. Quoted in Richard, p. 194.

19. See: ibid., p. 194.

20. Quoted in Thémime, *Histoire de Marseille*, pp. 189–90.

21. Ibid., p. 190.

22. See: Richard, pp. 189, 193.

23. See: ibid., pp. 189–90.

24. See: ibid., p. 184.

25. See: ibid., p. 194.

26. Ibid., p. 190.

27. See: ibid., p. 185.

28. Thémime, p. 188.

29. Richard, p. 186.

30. See: Thémime, p. 188.

31. See: Richard, p. 188.

32. See: ibid., p. 186.

33. See: ibid., p. 187.

34. See: Thémime, p. 191. The year in question is 1890.

35. Jean-Roger Soubiran, 'Foyer marseillais. L'Ecole de Marseille, 1875–1900', in Françoise Beck, ed., *Peintres de la couleur en Provence, 1875–1920* (Marseille, Paris: Office Régional de la Culture Provence-Alpes-Côte d'Azur, Réunion des Musées Nationaux, 1995), p. 114.

36. Ibid., p. 115.
37. Ibid., p. 115.
38. See: Sophie Biass-Fabiani, 'Le Fauvisme provençal: un mouvement introuvable?', in Beck, ed., p. 181.
39. Quoted in ibid., p. 181.
40. See: Soubiran, p. 114.
41. Ibid., p. 115.
42. See: Biass-Fabiani, p. 181.
43. Ibid., p. 181.
44. Ibid., p. 182.
45. Quoted in ibid., p. 182.
46. See: ibid., p. 182.
47. Ibid., p. 183.
48. Quoted in ibid., p. 183.
49. Quoted in ibid., p. 183.
50. Soubiran, p. 117.
51. See: Marielle Latour, The Painters of Marseille, trans. Alfred and Betty Rozelaar-Green (Marseille: Jeanne Laffitte, 1990), p. 13.
52. Ibid., p. 17.
53. Denis Coutagne, 'Paul Cézanne. Aix-en-Provence, 1839–1906', in Beck, ed., p. 326.
54. Latour, p. 24.
55. Ibid., pp. 26–7.
56. Biass-Fabiani, p. 174.
57. See: Hilary Spurling, The Unknown Matisse. A Life of Henri Matisse, I (London: Hamish Hamilton, 1998), chapters 10 and 11.
58. See: Biass-Fabiani, p. 178.
59. Quoted in ibid., p. 181.
60. See: Latour, pp. 62–8. Dufy, in his Usine à L'Estaque, of 1908, is engaged in a similar Cubist experiment.
61. Ibid., p. 62.
62. See: Biass-Fabiani, p. 175.
63. Ibid., p. 176.
64. See: Latour, pp. 38–41.
65. See: Biass-Fabiani, p. 178.
66. Ibid., p. 179.
67. Edmond Rostand, 'Le Vol de la Marseillaise' (Revue des Deux Mondes, 37, 1917).
68. See: Robert Parienté, 'André Suarès, entre mer et terre' (La Pensée du Midi, 1, 2000/1), pp. 84–9.
69. André Suarès, Marsiho (Marseille: Jeanne Lafitte, 2012), p. 13.
70. See: ibid., pp. 9–10.

71. Ibid., p. 187.
72. Edmond Jaloux, *Le Pouvoir des choses* (Geneva: Editions du Milieu du Monde, 1943), p. 110.
73. Ibid., p. 34.
74. See: ibid., p. 240.
75. Ibid., p. 123.
76. Ibid., p. 123.
77. See: A. Mattalia, 'L'Opéra de Marseille en 1900: histoire d'une passion fin de siècle', *Revue Marseille*, p. 43; E. Spiteri, 'La Performance de l'Opéra à Marseille', *Revue Marseille*, 149, 1987, pp. 29–33.
78. See: J. Bazal, *Marseille entre les deux guerres, 1919–1939* (Grenoble: Les 4 Seigneurs, 1977), pp. 69–71.
79. For a more comprehensive account of Marseille entertainment in the Belle Epoque, see: Jean Bazal, *Marseille sur scène. Artistes marseillais d'hier et d'aujourd'hui* (Grenoble: Editions des 4 Seigneurs, 1978), Chapter 1: 'Salles de spectacle'.
80. See: 'Le Casino de la Plage', *Revue Marseille*, 1986, pp. 79–85.
81. Baratier, *Histoire de Marseille*, p. 413.
82. See: *L'Histoire de l'Olympique de Marseille*, p. 18.
83. See: P. Echinard, 'Les Premières cabarets montmartrois à Marseille', *Revue Marseille*, 145, 1986, pp. 76–8.
84. From the name of another popular Montmartre cabaret.
85. See: Echinard, p. 78.

4. *THE WICKED CITY*: THE PORT IN THE INTERWAR YEARS

1. Basil Woon, *From Deauville to Monte Carlo: a Guide to the Gay World of France* (London: Horace Liveright, 1929), quoted in Stuart Jeffries, 'In Praise of Dirty, Sexy Cities: the Urban World According to Walter Benjamin', *The Guardian*, 21 September 2015.
2. Evelyn Waugh, *Decline and Fall* (London: Chapman and Hall, 1928. Quotes from the Penguin edition, Harmondsworth, 2017), p. 202.
3. Ibid., p. 203.
4. See, for example, Olivier Boura, *Marseille ou la mauvaise réputation* (Paris: Arléa, 2001).
5. Jérôme Pierrat, *Une Histoire du Milieu. Grand banditisme et haute pègre en France de 1850 à nos jours* (Paris: Denoël, 2003), p. 54.
6. Contrary to some assertions, however, it is unlikely that Mac Orlan's *Quartier Réservé* is based on Marseille, a city he did not know particularly well, unlike, say, Hamburg, Rouen or Palermo, and whose topography does not correspond to the description in the story. It is more likely that *Quartier Réservé* constitutes an amalgam of Southern ports,

which enables Mac Orlan to develop his major theme, explored further in his concept of the 'fantastique social', of the quasi-magical power of the modern phenomena of wireless waves and gramophone recordings.

7. See: Eliane Richard, 'La Première Exposition Coloniale Française', in Philippe Joutard (ed.), *Histoire de Marseille en treize événements* (Marseille: Jeanne Laffitte, 1988), p. 184.

8. See: A. Olivesi, 'Contrastes sociaux et luttes politiques sous la Troisième République', in Baratier, ed., *Histoire de Marseille*, p. 412.

9. In fact, the ill-informed comments of Senator Gervais, who was mayor of the Parisian suburb of Issy-les-Moulineaux, had serious consequences and led to at least two court-martials of innocent infantrymen. The resulting scandal caused the cheese-manufacturer Fromages Gervais to distance itself by publicly disowning any connection with the Senator.

10. See, for example: Denis Chevalier and Yann-Philippe Tastevin, *Vies d'ordures. L'Economie des déchets* (Marseille, Paris: MUCEM, Artlys, 2017).

11. See: Emile Thémime, *Histoire de Marseille*, p. 221.

12. See: ibid., p. 220. There were in fact two services, the 'Peninsular Express', which went via Paris to Brindisi, where it connected for the boat for India, and the 'Bombay Express', inaugurated in 1891, which travelled from Calais to Marseille in a time of 22 hours and 23 minutes, with ten postal wagons, a restaurant car, two first-class carriages and two goods wagons.

13. See: ibid., p. 225; A. Olivesi, 'Contrastes sociaux et luttes politiques sous la IIIe République', in Baratier, ed., *Histoire de Marseille*, p. 390.

14. Richard Cobb, *Paris and Elsewhere. Selected Writings* (New York: NYRB Books, 2002), pp. 263–4.

15. Ibid., p. 265.

16. See: Thémime, *Histoire de Marseille*, p. 235.

17. See: Olivesi, p. 385.

18. Ibid., p. 386.

19. See: Thémime, p. 220.

20. See: Olivesi, p. 387.

21. See: ibid., p. 387.

22. See: Thémime, p. 221.

23. Ibid., pp. 221, 230.

24. See: Olivesi, p. 387.

25. Quoted in Thémime, p. 231.

26. See: Olivesi, p. 387.

27. Thémime, p. 229.
28. See: Michel Samson, 'Pourquoi Marseille n'a pas explosé', *Le Monde*, 15 December 2006, pp. 20–1.
29. See: Olivesi, pp. 387–8; Thémime, p. 234.
30. See: Thémime, pp. 232–4.
31. See: Olivesi, p. 391.
32. See: ibid., p. 387.
33. Ibid., p. 387.
34. Albert Londres, *Marseille, Porte du Sud* (Monaco: Le Serpent à Plumes, 1927), p. 20.
35. See: Pierrat, *Une Histoire du Milieu*, pp. 124–7.
36. See: Louis Chevalier, *Montmartre du Plaisir et du crime* (Paris: Robert Laffont, 1980).
37. See: Pierrat, *Une Histoire du Milieu*, Ch. 4 'Marseille, de faux airs de Chicago'. For an excellent, and historically accurate, reconstruction of the complex links between crime, politics and municipal corruption in Marseille in the 1930s, see: François Thomazeau, *Marseille confidential* (Paris: Plon, coll. 'Sang Neuf', 2018).
38. Ibid., pp. 24–5.
39. Herbert Adams Gibbons, *Ports of France* (London: Jonathan Cape, 1927), p. 290.
40. Ibid., p. 291.
41. Emile Thémime, *Histoire de Marseille*, p. 239.
42. Albert Londres, pp. 16–7.
43. See: Caryl Phillips, 'Claude McKay and *Banjo*: an Introduction', in Claude McKay, *Banjo* (London: Serpent's Tail, 2008), pp.x-xv.
44. Claude McKay, *Banjo*, p. 116.
45. See: ibid., p. 207. Maran's novel *Batouala* had won the Prix Goncourt in 1921.
46. Edouard Peisson, *Hans le marin* (Paris: Grasset, coll. Les Cahiers Rouges, 1929), p. 120.
47. Ibid., p. 123.
48. André Donzel, 'Marseille: Conjurer le stigmata de la ville sale', in Denis Chevalier and Yann-Philippe Tastevin, *Vies d'ordures*, p. 124.
49. See: ibid., p. 125.

5. *MARIUS*: MARCEL PAGNOL AND THE 'GOOD CITY'

1. See: François Thomazeau, *Marseille, une biographie*, p. 305.
2. See: ibid., p. 305.
3. See, for example, Jean Epstein's film *Marius et Olive à Paris*, of 1935.
4. See: Raymond Castans, *Marcel Pagnol, biographie* (Paris: J.C. Lattès, 1987), pp. 15,18.

5. See: ibid., p. 20.
6. See: ibid., p. 28.
7. See: ibid., p. 36.
8. Ibid., p. 37.
9. Ibid., p. 37.
10. Ibid., p. 33.
11. Ibid., p. 48.
12. See: ibid., pp. 78–9. Jean Marius Richard became a close friend of Pagnol's, and under the name of Carlo Rim became a well-known Parisian cartoonist and film writer; he produced the script for *Justin de Marseille*.
13. See: ibid., pp. 78–9. As Castans notes, Sylvain's interest in Pagnol was motivated by his wish to enrol Marius Richard's support for an open air theatre, the Théâtre Sylvain, which still exists.
14. See: ibid., p. 72. Interestingly, Albert Londres was himself from Lyon and came to Paris at the same time as Béraud and Dullin. Pagnol became close friends with Achard, along with Steve Passeur and Henri Jeanson.
15. Pagnol disliked the film intensely and made his own version in 1936. There was also a Hollywood version in 1933, with John Barrymore and Myrna Loy, and, in 1961, an English adaptation by Peter Sellers.
16. See: Castans, p. 133.
17. See: ibid., p. 113.
18. Ibid., p. 114.
19. See: ibid., p. 113.
20. See: ibid., p. 244. The revival was the idea of the popular singer, Alibert, Vincent Scotto's son-in-law, whose hits included *Cane... Cane... Canebière*, from the operetta *Un de la Canebière* and *Les Gangsters du Château d'If*, from the operetta of the same name, and who was now in charge of the Théâtre des Variétés in Paris.
21. See: ibid., p. 144.
22. The article appeared in *Le Journal* on 17 May 1930. See: Castans, p. 146.
23. See: ibid., p. 145.
24. See: ibid., p. 147.
25. In fact, as part of an inter-studio agreement, *Marius* was actually shot at the Joinville studios.
26. See: Castans, pp. 154–5. At the box-office, the film easily beat the then most popular French sound film, Jean Choux's *Jean de la Lune*, based on a comedy by Pagnol's friend Marcel Achard and with French stage actors Madeleine Renaud, Michel Simon and René Lefèvre.
27. See: Castans, pp. 159–60.

28. For a complete discussion of Scotto's career, see: Jean Bazal, *Marseille sur scène*, Ch.VIII, 'Vincent Scotto, le compositeur aux 4000 chansons'.
29. Georges Sadoul, *Histoire du cinéma français*, I *1890–1962* (Paris: Club des Editeurs, 1962), p. 217.
30. Ibid., p. 64.
31. Colin Crisp, *The Classic French Cinema, 1930–1960* (Bloomington and Indianapolis: Indiana University Press; London: I.B. Tauris, 1997), pp. 280–1.
32. See: Castans, pp. 167–9.
33. See: ibid., p. 166.
34. See: ibid., pp. 178–9; 182–3.
35. See: ibid., p. 222.
36. See: ibid., p. 209.
37. See: ibid., pp. 238–9.
38. Sadoul, p. 84.

6. *LES CAHIERS DU SUD*: MARSEILLE MODERN

1. Walter Benjamin, 'Marseille', in *Reflections. Essays, Aphorisms, Autobiographical Writings* (New York: Schocken Books, 2007), p. 131.
2. Walter Benjamin, 'Hashish in Marseille', in *Reflections*, p. 137.
3. Sheila Crane, *Mediterranean Crossroads*, (Minneapolis: University of Minesota Press, 2011).
4. Germaine Krull, *Marseille* (Marseille: Editions Jeanne Lafitte, 1976, frontispiece).
5. Ibid., pp. 22–3.
6. Ibid., pp. 86–7.
7. Quoted by Raymond Jean, 'Traversée des Cahiers', in Michèle Coulet, 'Jean Ballard, les *Cahiers du Sud* et Marseille: une exposition', in Michèle Coulet, ed., *Jean Ballard et les Cahiers du Sud* (Marseille: Ville de Marseille, 1993), p. 36.
8. Michèle Coulet, 'Jean Ballard, les *Cahiers du Sud* et Marseille: une exposition', p. 48.
9. Paul Chaulot, 'Adieu aux *Cahiers du Sud*', *Esprit*, 358 (3), 1967, p. 560.
10. The history of *Les Cahiers du Sud* has been well-documented since the opening of the Fonds Jean Ballard at the Bibliothèque Municipale de Marseille, notably by Alain Paire and Michèle Coulet.
11. Alain Paire, *Chronique des 'Cahiers du Sud'*, (Paris: IMEC, 1993), p. 61.
12. Michèle Coulet, 'Jean Ballard, les *Cahiers du Sud* et Marseille: une exposition', p. 49.
13. Paul Chaulot, 'Adieu aux *Cahiers du Sud*', p. 560.
14. Ibid., p. 62.

15. Michèle Coulet, 'Jean Ballard, les *Cahiers du Sud* et Marseille: une exposition', p. 62.
16. Ibid., p. 62.
17. Alain Paire, *Chronique des 'Cahiers du Sud'*, p. 35.
18. Michèle Coulet, 'Jean Ballard, les *Cahiers du Sud* et Marseille: une exposition', p. 51.
19. Ibid., p. 51.
20. Ibid., p. 75.
21. Ibid., p. 50.
22. Ibid., p. 50.
23. Alain Paire, '*Les Cahiers du Sud* et *Le Grand Jeu*', *La Revue des revues*, 14, 1992, p. 26.
24. Ibid., p. 27, Michèle Coulet, 'Jean Ballard, les *Cahiers du Sud* et Marseille', p. 68.
25. Alain Paire, '*Les Cahiers du Sud* et *Le Grand Jeu*', p. 27.
26. Michèle Coulet, 'Jean Ballard, les *Cahiers du Sud* et Marseille', p. 66.
27. See: ibid., p. 47.
28. Alain Paire, René Piniès, 'Joë Bousquet et Jean Ballard. Vingt ans de correspondance', *La Revue des revues*, 16, 1993, pp. 15–16.
29. Michèle Coulet, 'Jean Ballard, les *Cahiers du Sud* et Marseille', p. 70.
30. Jean Michel Guiraud, *La Vie intellectuelle et artistique à Marseille à l'époque de Vichy et sous l'Occupation 1940–1944*, (Marseille: CRDP, 1987), p. 40.
31. Paul Chaulot, 'Adieux aux *Cahiers du Sud*', p. 560.
32. Michèle Coulet, 'Jean Ballard, les *Cahiers du Sud* et Marseille', p. 72.
33. See: Gabriel Audisio, *Jeunesse de la Méditerranée* (Paris: Gallimard, 1933).
34. See: Gabriel Audisio, *Louis Brauquier* (Paris: Seghers, coll. 'Poètes d'aujourd'hui', 1966).
35. For a detailed discussion of Camus' role in this Mediterranean culture, see: Neil Foxlee, *Albert Camus' 'The New Mediterranean Culture': A Text and its Contexts*, (Oxford: Peter Lang, 2010).
36. Gabriel Audisio, 'Vers une synthèse méditerranéenne', *Les Cahiers du Sud*, March, 1936.
37. Michèle Coulet, 'Jean Ballard, les *Cahiers du Sud* et Marseille', p. 70.
38. See: Sheila Crane, *Mediterranean Crossroads*, p.
39. See: ibid., p. 18.
40. Alèssi Dell'Umbria, *Histoire universelle de Marseille*, p. 472.
41. See: ibid., pp. 32–8.
42. Ibid., p. 35.
43. Ibid., p. 35.
44. Ibid., p. 38.
45. Quoted in Dell'Umbria, p. 473.

46. Quoted in ibid., p. 473.
47. The Greber Plan, like its successors, entered Marseille mythology, perhaps not without reason, as connected to corruption and property speculation at the highest levels. Most recently, it serves as the basis for the plot of François Thomazeau's *Marseille confidential*, of 2018.
48. Jean Ballard, 'Marseille, Porte de'Empire', *Les Cahiers du Sud*, January, 1939 (unpaginated).
49. See: Crane, p. 69.
50. See: ibid., p. 76.
51. Herbert Adams Gibbons, *Ports of France* (London: Janathan Cape, 1927), p. 304.
52. See: Crane, pp. 86–7.
53. Ibid., p. 95.
54. See Crane, p. 86.
55. See: *Cooks Continental Timetable*, August 1939, pp. 391–2. The times are for the Compagnie de Navigation Mixte (formerly Tartarin's Compagnie Touache) for Algiers and Tunis and the Paquet Line for Casablanca.
56. See: Alèssi Dell'Umbria.
57. See: ibid., p. 82. Marseille-Provence Airport has already replaced the port and maritime transport as the privileged, sometimes only, means of communication with Marseille's Mediterranean neighbours.

7. *TRANSIT*: OCCUPATION, DESTRUCTION AND LIBERATION

1. Edmonde Charles-Roux, *Elle, Adrienne* (Paris: Tallandier, coll. 'Le Cercle du Livre', 1971), p. 63.
2. See: Emile Thémime, *Histoire de Marseille*, p. 271.
3. See: ibid., p. 273.
4. See: A. Olivesi, 'Marseille Contemporaine', in Baratier, (ed.), *Histoire de Marseille*, pp. 125–6.
5. See: Thémime, pp. 278, 280–1.
6. Ibid., p. 272.
7. Ibid., p. 272.
8. See: ibid., p. 272; Donna F. Ryan, *The Holocaust and the Jews of Marseille: The Enforcement of Anti-Semitic Policies in Vichy France* (Urbana/Champain: Ill., University of Illinois Press, 1996), p. 88.
9. Up until 1941, flights from the Marseille airport at Marignane still operated to the French North African territories. In 1944, Warner Brothers released a film, again directed by Curtiz and starring most of the cast of *Casablanca*, *Passage to Marseille*, in which a freighter bound for Marseille from New Caledonia with a cargo of nickel ore picks up

a canoe carrying escaped French convicts from Cayenne. Unlike the Vichy-ite engine-room crew and the Pétainist officer Duval, played by Sydney Greenstreet, the convicts support the captain's decision to divert the ship from Marseille, where the ore will fall into the hands of the Germans, to Britain, where they enrol in the French Air Force.

10. *Transit* was also adapted for cinema by René Allio; the film version, released in France in 1990, was very closely based on Seghers' text.

11. Anna Seghers, *Transit*, trans. Margot Bettauer Dembo (New York: New York Review Books, 2013), p. 23.

12. Ibid., p. 35.

13. Ibid., p. 35.

14. Ibid., p. 41.

15. Peter Demetz, 'Introduction', in Walter Benjamin, *Reflections*, p.xvii.

16. Ibid., pp.xviii-xix. For a fuller account, see: Momme Brodersen, *Walter Benjamin. A Biography* (London, New York: Verso, 1996), pp. 250–62.

17. Thémime, p. 277.

18. See: ibid., p. 276.

19. Quoted in ibid., p. 277.

20. Seghers, p. 64. The HICEM was the Jewish emigration company, which kept operating in Marseille until November 1942. The HIAS (Hebrew Immigrant Aid Society) was an American aid organisation.

21. Quoted in John K. Roth and Elisabeth Maxwell, *Remembering for the Future: The Holocaust in an Age of Genocide* (London: Palgrave, 2001), p. 347.

22. See: Mary Jane Gold, *Crossroads Marseille* (New York: Doubleday, 1980), *Varian Fry et les candidats à l'exil. Marseille 1940–1941* (Arles: Actes Sud, 1999).

23. Thémime, p. 279.

24. For a full account of the Villa Air-Bel, see: Rosemary Sullivan, *Villa Air-Bel: World War II, Escape and a House in Marseille* (New York: HarperCollins, 2006).

25. On Tzara, see: Henri Béhar, *Tristan Tzara* (Paris: Oxus, 2005), p. 168.

26. Thémime, p. 272.

27. See: Renée Dray-Bensoussan, 'Quelques aspects particuliers de l'aryanisation des entreprises à Marseille', in Hervé Joly, ed., *L'Economie de la zone non-occupée, 1940–1942* (Paris: Editions du CTHS, 2007).

28. See: ibid., pp. 279–80.

29. See: ibid., p. 280.

30. Anne Spartiello, 'La Destruction des Vieux Quartiers', in Philippe Joutard, ed., *Histoire de Marseille en treize événements* (Marseille: Editions Jeanne Laffitte, 1988), p. 203.

31. See: ibid., p. 204.

32. See: ibid., p. 205.
33. See: ibid., pp. 205–6.
34. See: ibid., p. 211; Thémime, p. 282.
35. Quoted in Spartiello, p. 203.
36. See: ibid., p. 201.
37. See: Thémime, p. 286.
38. See: ibid., p. 284.
39. See: Marceline Block, ed., *World Film Locations: Marseilles* (Bristol: Intellect, 2013), pp. 30–1.
40. See: Jean Michel Guiraud, *La vie intellectuelle et artistique à Marseille à l'époque de Vichy et sous l'Occupation* (Marseille: Editions Jeanne Laffitte, 1998).
41. Charles-Roux, p. 398.
42. Ibid., p. 403.
43. Ibid., p. 404.
44. Ibid., p. 405.
45. Jean-Claude Izzo, *Solea* (Paris: Folio Policier, 1998), p. 102.
46. Quoted in Spartiello, p. 211.
47. Helen Meller, *European Cities, 1890–1930s* (Chichester, New York, Weinheim, Brisbane, Singapore, Toronto: Wiley, 2001), p. 181.
48. Quoted in Spartiello, p. 212.
49. See: Olivesi, p. 426.
50. Spartiello, p. 214.
51. Quoted in Jean Michel Guiraud, *La Vie intellectuelle et artistique à Marseille â l'époque de Vichy et sous l'Occupation, 1940–1944* (Marseille: Jeanne Laffitte, 1998), p. 183.
52. 'La Réalisation de *Médor* se poursuit', *Le Sémaphore*, 21 March 1941, 41.
53. See: ibid., p. 231.
54. See: ibid., pp. 216–7.
55. Louis Ducreux, interviewed 2 March 1942, quoted in ibid., p. 216.
56. See: ibid., pp. 211–3.
57. See: ibid., p. 218.
58. See: ibid., p. 219.
59. See: ibid., pp. 222–3.
60. See: ibid., pp. 229–30.
61. See: ibid., p. 239.
62. See: ibid., p. 241.
63. See: ibid., pp. 242–3.
64. See: ibid., p. 245.
65. See: *L'Histoire de l'Olympique de Marseille*, p. 36.
66. For a detailed study of Sabiani, see: Paul Jankowski, *Communism and*

Collaboration: Simon Sabiani and Politics in Marseille, 1919–1944 (New Haven: Yale University Press, 1989).

67. 'La Prochaine saison du Théâtre du Gymnase', *Midi-Libre*, 10 October 1942, p. 11.
68. 'La Troupe des Compagnons de France a obtenu un grand succès à l'Opéra', *Le Sémaphore*, 22 February 1941.
69. 'Tournée officielle de la Légion Française des Combattants', *Le Sémaphore*, 5 March 1941.
70. 'Les Programmes', *Le Sémaphore*, 14 March 1941.
71. Claude Gay, 'Musiques', *Midi-Libre*, 17 September 1942.
72. See: 'Les Spectacles de Marseille', *Le Mot d'Ordre*, 31 May 1941, p. 4.
73. *Le Mot d'Ordre*, 2 June 1941, p. 4.
74. *Le Mot d'Ordre*, 9 December 1941, p. 4.
75. *V. Magazine illustré du MLN*, 4 November 1945, p. 5.
76. See: Michael H. Kater, *Different Drummers. Jazz in the Culture of Nazi Germany* (New York: Oxford University Press, 1992).
77. *Le Provençal*, 7 September 1944.
78. *Le Provençal*, 5 September 1944, p. 2.
79. *Le Provençal*, 22 September 1944, p. 2; 20 October 1944, p. 2.
80. *V*, 30 December 1944, p. 14.
81. *Le Provençal*, 29 October 1944, p. 2.
82. *Le Provençal*, 21 October 1944, p. 2.
83. *V*, 4 November 1944, p. 5.
84. *V*, 6 January 1945, pp. 8–9.
85. Ibid., p. 9.

8. *LE DOCKER NOIR*: IMMIGRATION, ARCHITECTURE AND HOUSING

1. Alèssi Dell'Umbria, *Histoire universelle de Marseille. De l'an mil à l'an deux mille* (Marseille: Agone, 2006), p. 11.
2. Ousmane Sembène, *Le Docker noir* (Paris: Présence Africaine, 1973), p. 77.
3. This is the subject of Paul Carpita's film *Le Rendez-vous des quais*, released in 1955 but immediately banned and not screened until 1990.
4. See: Emile Thémime, *Histoire de Marseille*, p. 299.
5. See: ibid., p. 327. A graphic representation of this anti-war militancy can be seen in Boris Taslitzky's 1951 painting *Riposte*, depicting a violent confrontation between workers and police on the dockside at Port-de-Bouc, to the west of Marseille.
6. See: ibid., pp. 300–2.
7. See: ibid., pp. 295–6.

8. See: ibid., pp. 313–4.
9. See: ibid., p. 316.
10. Alèssi Dell'Umbria, p. 523.
11. See: Thémime, *Histoire*, p. 317.
12. See: Alèssi Dell'Umbria, p. 537.
13. Ibid., p. 524.
14. See: ibid., p. 525.
15. Marius and Olive were the two heroes of a series of comic sketches and embodied the popular image of the Marseillais. They figured, for example, in Jean Epstein's film of 1935, *Marius et Olive à Paris*.
16. J.M.G Le Clézio, *Désert* (Paris: Gallimard, 1980), p. 259.
17. See: Thémime, *Histoire*, pp. 330–1.
18. See: ibid., p. 331.
19. Ibid., p. 332.
20. Thémime, *Histoire*, p. 329.
21. See: ibid., p. 334.
22. See: ibid., p. 333. It is important to recall that in the early years of the Fourth Republic, Marseille already had the reputation as a base for clandestine political activity on the part of its population in transit. The Indochinese, predominantly Vietnamese, population, made up of colonial troops or workers and dating from the beginning of the Second World War, numbered some 25,000 at the Liberation, spread across the South, but mainly concentrated in the Marseille area. Housed in camps, especially the Viet-Nâm Camp to the south of the city, this community was highly politicised and close to the PCF and CGT, giving a warm welcome to Ho Chi Minh on his visit to Marseille in June 1946. With the beginning of the Indochina War in November 1946, this often fractious small community, supported by the PCF, was considered by the authorities as made up 'of potential enemies in what was now an open conflict'. Similarly, after 1946, the Jewish population, mainly from Eastern Europe or North Africa and clandestinely in transit to Palestine, under the auspices of the Haganah, whose headquarters was in the Rue des Convalescents, was kept under surveillance by the authorities.
23. Jean Lartéguy, *Les Centurions* (Paris: Presses de la Cité, 1960), p. 167.
24. See: Thémime, *Histoire*, p. 337.
25. See: ibid., p. 338.
26. See: ibid., p. 339.
27. See: ibid., p. 340.
28. See: ibid., p. 341.
29. See: ibid., p. 342.
30. See: Thémime, *Histoire*, pp. 341–2.

31. See: William Firebrace, *Marseille Mix* (London: Architectural Association, 2010), p. 230. The Unité d'Habitation, incidentally, is often referred to wrongly as the *cité radieuse* (radiant city), which was Le Corbusier's name for his concept of the modern planned metropolis, radiating out from its centre.
32. See: Sheila Crane, pp. 87–8.
33. See: Firebrace, p. 230.
34. See: ibid., p. 230.
35. Firebrace, p. 231.
36. Ibid., pp. 232–3.
37. Municipal corruption and speculation on the Plan Greber in the 1930s are at the basis of François Thomazeau's *Marseille Confidential*.
38. See: Dell'Umbria, pp. 500–1.
39. Ibid., p. 501.
40. Ibid., p. 501.
41. Ibid., p. 500.
42. A phenomenon spotted by Jean-Claude Izzo in *Total Khéops*.
43. See: Minayo Nasiali, *Native to the Republic. Empire, Social Citizenship and Everyday Life in Marseille since 1945* (Ithaca, NY: Cornell University Press, 2016), pp. 62–76.
44. See: Thémime, *Histoire*, p. 367.
45. See: ibid., p. 364.
46. See: Nasiali, Chapter 1.
47. See: Emile Thémime and Nathalie Deguigné, *Le Camp du Grand Arénas: Marseille, 1944–1966* (Paris: Autrement, 2001). A first-hand account is provided by François Thomazeau in his conversations with the Vietnamese Marseillais Tao (see: Thomazeau, pp. 150–3).
48. See: Thémime, *Histoire*, p. 376.
49. Ibid., p. 368.
50. See: ibid., p. 368.
51. See: Nasiali, p. 45.
52. See: Nasiali, pp. 50–3; Dell'Umbria, p. 561,
53. See: Nasiali, p. 38.
54. See: ibid., p. 46.
55. See: Thémime, *Histoire*, p. 369.
56. Nasiali, p. 46.
57. Dell'Umbria, p. 503.
58. See: ibid., p. 549.
59. See: ibid., pp. 506–7.
60. Thémime, *Histoire*, p. 371.
61. See: ibid., p. 372.
62. See: ibid., p. 366.

63. Pierre Echinard, 'L'Espace du spectacle à Marseille, deux siècles d'évolution', *Méditerranée*, 2,3, 1991, p. 41.
64. Ibid., p. 41.

9. *TOTAL KHÉOPS*: MARSEILLE NOIR

1. M.F.K. Fisher, p. 47.
2. See: Pierrat, *Histoire du Milieu*, pp. 54–7.
3. See: ibid, pp. 119–20.
4. See: ibid., p. 121.
5. See: ibid., p. 126.
6. See: ibid., pp. 132–6.
7. See: ibid., p. 311.
8. See: ibid., p. 308.
9. Firebrace, *Marseille Mix*, p. 172.
10. Ibid., pp. 173–4.
11. See, for example, J.G. Peristiany, *Honor and Shame: The Values of Mediterranean Society* (Chicago: University of Chicago Press, 1966).
12. José Giovanni, *Le Deuxième souffle* (Paris: Gallimard, coll. 'Série Noire', 1958), p. 33.
13. See: Olivier Bohler, 'The Underworld is in his Hands', in Marceline Block (ed.), *World Film Locations: Marseilles* (Bristol: Intellect, 2013), p. 49.
14. See: Philip Mann, *The Dandy at Dusk. Taste and Melancholy in the Twentieth Century* (London: Head of Zeus, 2017).
15. See: Franck Lhomeau, 'Joseph Damiani, alias José Giovanni', *Temps Noir. La Revue des Littératures Policières*, 16 September 2013.
16. See: Jean-Claude Izzo, *Total Khéops* (Paris: Gallimard, 1995), pp. 61–3.
17. As Firebrace observes, Montale's love of cuisine is a characteristic of the *polar méditerranéen*, shared by Manuel Vázquez Montalbán's Pepe Carvalho or Andrea Camilleri's Salvo Montalbano (see: Firebrace, p. 174).
18. Jean-Claude Izzo, *Les Marins perdus* (Paris: Flammarion, 1997), p. 136.
19. Pagnol, *Marius*, p. 7.
20. Jean-Claude Izzo, *Le Soleil des mourants* (Paris: Flammarion, 1999), p. 194.
21. Firebrace, p. 175.
22. Thomazeau, *Marseille, une biographie*, pp. 279–80.
23. Ibid., p. 280.
24. Dell'Umbria, p. 555.

INDEX

A propos de Nice, 142
Aati, Ridha, 218
Abdelkader ibn Muhieddine, 48
Abetz, Otto, 177
Abirached, Robert, 30
Abraham, Marcel, 149
Académie de Marseille, 82
Académie Française, 85
Académie Méditerranéenne, 153
Achard, Marcel, 121, 132, 249 n.14, 26
Aciéries du Nord, 191
Action Française, 67, 68, 108, 151, 179
Adamov, Arthur, 170
Adams Gibbons, Herbert, 15, 103, 158
Affaire des Fiches (1900–1904), 86
Agadir Crisis (1911), 195, 197
L'Aiglon, (Rostand), 82
Aiguier, Auguste, 74
Aix-en-Provence, 43, 76, 85, 119, 121, 164, 179, 209, 227
Alabama, 107
Alcazar music hall, 4, 9, 46, 87, 180, 205, 209–10
Aldrich, Robert, 49
Alès, 43
Alexander I, King of Yugoslavia, 3, 4

Alexandria, Egypt, 15, 43, 216
Algeciras conference (1906), 197
Algeria, 5, 38–9, 46–52, 71, 230
  Cahiers du Sud in, 152, 211
  French invasion (1830), 10, 36, 38, 48, 56, 66
  Economic and Tourist Board, 152
  emigration to, 49
  emigration from, 66, 70, 97, 98, 103, 199, 201–3
  Évian Accords (1962), 201
  ferry services to, 194
  Front de libération nationale (FLN), 118, 199, 201
  Harkis, 202
  independence (1962), 211
  iron ore, 42
  Jewish emigration, 45, 201
  Organisation Armée Secrète (OAS), 201
  in paintings, 73, 74, 80
  Pieds-Noirs, 199, 201–2
  population, 48, 49, 241 n.36
  vegetables from, 190
  War of Independence (1954–62), 192, 199, 200, 201
  World War II (1939–45), 162, 163, 165

Algiers, 8, 37, 46–8, 52, 112, 158, 174, 198
  Audisio and, 152–3
  Cahiers du Sud in, 152, 211
  Le Corbusier and, 155, 157, 203
  Opera House, 152
  'Parisian meridian' and, 158
  port, 41
Alhambra music hall, 87
Ali Pasha, 22
Ali, Ibrahim, 231–2
Allée de Meilhan, 17, 87, 140, 210
Allée de Noailles, 17
Allées de Meilhan, 20
Allégret, Marc, 129, 130
Allio, René, 253 n.10
Amable Chanot, Jean-Baptiste, 71
Amants terribles, Les, 177
Amiens, 75
Amsterdam, 69, 144, 158
anarchism, 66, 143
Angèle, 24, 132, 133
Angkor Wat, 71, 106
Annam, 1, 65
Anouilh, Jean, 177
Antibes FC, 179
Antilles, 71
Antoine, André, 121
Antwerp, 69
apaches, 53, 61
aqueduct, 35
Arabian Nights, 23, 39, 112, 228
Arc de Triomphe, Porte d'Aix, 61
architecture, 154–6
Arenc, 41, 85, 108, 140, 206
Arendt, Hannah, 167
Argenteuil, 78
Argentina, 42, 104, 163, 216
Ariège, 121
Arles, 27, 43, 58, 60, 61
Armée de l'Orient, 95
L'Armée des ombres, 173, 222, 223, 225

Armenians, 2, 98, 100, 102, 187
Arnoux, Léopold, 29
Arrow of Gold, The (Conrad), 23, 53, 54, 86, 242 n.55
Arsenal des Galères, 73
Art Nouveau, 72
Artaud, Antoine, 150
Asie, 42
al-Asnam, 49
Asnières, 32
Aspects du Génie d'Israël, 153
Assouad, Albert, 132
Ateliers Nationaux, 33
Athénée, 54, 57, 58
Aubagne, 56, 118
Aubanel, Teodor, 60
Aubert, Augustin, 56
Audisio, Gabriel, 84, 152–3, 226, 228
Audisio, Victor, 152
Aumont, Jean-Pierre, 111
Auquier, Philippe, 75
Australia, 104, 152
Auteuil, 78
Auteuil, Daniel, 134
Auteurs Associés, Les, 132
Auvers-sur-Oise, 77
Avant-port de L'Estaque (Monticelli), 79
Aventuriers, Les (Giovanni), 219
Avenue Cantini, 133
Avenue de Noailles, 6, 96
Avenue des Chartreux, 119, 164
Avenue du Prado, 17, 54, 86, 132, 220
Avenue Longchamp, 220
Avenue Michelet, 188
Avierinos, Fernand, 120
Avignon, 27, 43, 60, 61
Axelrod, Towla, 143
Aygalades, 31, 37–8
Aznar, Emmanuel, 179

INDEX

Baigneuses, Les (Grésy), 74
Baldaccini, César, 52, 202
Ballard, Jean, 76, 119, 145–51,
  153, 155–7, 168, 175, 176, 211
Ballets Russes, 179
de Balzac, Honoré, 86, 229
Banana Bottom (McKay), 107
Banjo (McKay), 100, 104, 107–11,
  139, 189, 194
Banque de Paris et des Pays-Bas,
  197
Bar d'Escale, Le (Brauquier), 152
Bar de la Marine, 123, 126, 219
Barbary Coast, 2, 47, 199
Barbizon School, 38, 74
Barcelona, 8, 45, 50, 193, 227
Bardec, Auguste, 105
Barras, Paul, 28
Barraud, Pierre, 172
Barrière, Annie, 218
Barrymore, John, 249 n.15
Barthou, Louis, 3
Bassin de la Pinède, 69
Bassin National, 69
Bastia, 163
bastides, 17, 31, 47, 52, 57, 85,
  119, 140, 169, 206, 208, 234
Battle of Dien Bien Phû (1954),
  200
Battle of Valmy (1792), 26
Batum, 158
Baudelaire, Charles Pierre, 126, 140
Bauen in Frankreich. Bauen in Eisen.
  Bauen in Eisenbeton, 142
Bauhaus, 143
Baumettes Prison, 155
Baumettes, Les, 206
Baur, Harry, 88, 122, 124, 177
Baux, Les, 84
Bay of Naples, 1
Beaucaire, 43
Beaudouin, Eugène, 157, 175

de Beaumarchais, Pierre-Augustin
  Caron, 125
Beaumont, 99
Becker, Jacques, 218, 219, 222, 225
beggars, 142, 194, 196
Béguin, Albert, 154
Beirut, 104
Le Belge, Francis, 217, 233
Bell, Marie, 177
Belle Epoque (1871–1914), 9, 67,
  75, 80, 134, 190
  art in, 11, 37, 56, 73–81
  cabaret in, 61, 66, 87, 88–9, 148
  literature in, 7, 38–40, 46–7,
    48, 61, 81–6
Belle-de-Mai, 45, 86, 99, 104, 172,
  202, 210, 227
Bellos, David, 238 n.13
Belmondo, Jean-Paul, 215
Ben Barek, Larbi, 118
Ben Bella, Ahmed, 118
Bénédicte, Daniel, 169
Benjamin, Walter, 7, 10, 138–41,
  154, 167–8
Bennett, James Gordon, 103
Bentz, Yvan, 204
de Béranger, Pierre-Jean, 58, 59
Béraud, Henri, 121, 249 n.14
Bérengier, Henri, 77
Bergen, 195
Berlin, 203
Berlin. Symphony of a City, 142
Bernard, Raymond, 240 n.2
Bernhardt, Sarah, 82
Berri, Claude, 134
Berry, Duchesse de, *see* Marie-
  Caroline de Bourbon-Sicile
Bertin, Gabriel, 154
Bertin, Horace, 88
Bertin, Pierre, 177
Berval, Antonin, 124
Besson, Luc, 234

INDEX

Bias, Sophie, 6
Biass-Fabiani, Sophie, 81
Bibémus, 79
Bibliothèque Municipale de
  Marseille, 250 n.10
bidonvilles, 188, 195, 197, 199, 206
Billancourt, 129
Billoux, François, 204
Bizerte, 158
Black Lions, 228
Black Sea, 29, 96, 112, 158
Blaue Reiter group, 81
Bofa, Gus, 137
Bogart, Humphrey, 180
Bohème, La, 120
Bohler, Olivier, 222
Boîte à Musique, 89
Bokanowski, Galerie, 137
Bombay Express, 43, 96, 247 n.12
Bône, 49, 52
Bonnard, Pierre, 77
Bonne Mère, 38, 84, 130, 139
Bonnot, Xavier-Marie, 218
Bonsoir, 121
Bordeaux, 75, 86, 157
Bords du Bosphore à Bebeck, Les
  (Brest), 73
Borsalino, 215
Botrel, Théodore, 243 n.1
Bouches-du-Rhône, 88, 198, 202
Boudoucon, 228
Bouillon, Jo, 182
Boulevard Chave, 119
Boulevard de la Madeleine, 166–7
Boulevard de la Major, 108
Boulevard de Longchamp, 140
Boulevard Michelet, 7, 118, 179,
  203, 220
Bourbon Restoration (1814–1830),
  16, 26, 27, 42, 55, 58
Bourde, Yves, 120
Bourgade, La, 56

Bourra, Olivier, 53
Bourse, 32, 97, 156
Bousquet, Joë, 149, 151–2, 153, 179
Bousquet, René, 172
Boyer, Charles, 183
Braque, Georges, 75, 77, 78, 79,
  80, 81, 85
Braquo, 234
Brasilia, La, 204
Brasillach, Robert, 154
Braudel, Fernand, 22
Brauquier, Louis, 84, 152, 226, 228
Brazil, 42, 104, 105, 112, 163
Brébant theatre, 164
Brémond, Henri, 178
Brent, Georges, 180
Brest, Fabius, 73
Breton, André, 139, 167, 170
Bricks, Les, 139
Briey, 203
Brindisi, 96, 247 n.12
Brittany, 84
Broadway Melody, 127
Brun, Arno-Charles, 132
Buenos Aires, 42, 163, 216
Buss, Robin, 19–20

cabanons, 17, 52, 57, 58, 108, 140,
  220, 227, 232
Cabaret de Trèfle, 89
Cabaret des Truands, 89
Cabaret Music-hall, 180
Cabaret Poupon, Le, 89
cabarets, 61, 66, 87, 88–9, 148
Café de la Bourse, 89
Café de l'Europe, 58
Café de l'Univers, 89
Café de la Souris, 89
Café des Cours Belsunce, 140
Café Martino, 89
Café Maure à Alger, café des platanes
  (Brest), 73

Café Méridan, 89
Café Vertoux, 165
café-concerts, 66, 87, 88
Cahiers de la Quinzaine, Les, 147
Cahiers du Sud, Les, 11, 22, 61, 76,
    84, 93, 120, 137, 138, 145–57,
    209–11
  closure of (1966), 209–11
  on detritus, 115
  English literature in, 154
  Fascism, opposition to, 154, 168
  Fonds Jean Ballard, 250 n.10
  Fortunio, establishment as
    (1914), 120, 146, 149
  Greek culture in, 153, 211
  humanism, 76, 151, 153–4, 168
  Islam in, 153
  Izzo, influence on, 226, 228
  jazz in, 181
  Jewish culture in, 153, 211
  Occitanie, 61, 76, 138, 151,
    152, 153, 211
  numéros spéciaux, 149, 154
  pan-Mediterraneanism, 50, 75,
    138, 147–8, 151–4, 168, 179
  refugees, aiding of, 149, 154,
    168–9, 170
  Sud concept, 147–8, 151
  Surrealism, sponsorship of,
    150–52, 170
  urban planning in, 154–7, 175
caïds, 101, 174
Caillols, Les, 85
Caisse d'Epargne, 77
calanques, 16, 155
Calder, Alexander, 137
Calmann-Lévy, 177
Cambodia, 71
Camille, Georgette, 150, 154
Camilleri, Andrea, 258 n.17
Camoin, Charles, 78, 79, 80, 81
Camorra, 217

Camous, Claude, 19
Camp des Milles, 170
Camp Mirabeau, 99
Camp Oddo, 99
Camp Victor Hugo, 99
Camus, Albert, 153, 189
canal, 33, 44
Candide, 85
Canebière, 2, 3, 17, 51, 53–4, 100,
    210
  Alexander I assassination (1934),
    3, 4
  Benjamin on, 140
  cabarets on, 89
  Daudet on, 39
  Dumas on, 20, 53
  in *French Connection II* (1975
    film), 214
  Hôtel du Louvre, 53
  Krull on, 143
  luxury hotels, 96, 97
  Maison Dorée café, 53
  Méry on, 52–3, 86
  Moholy-Nagy on, 142
  Nouvelle Galeries fire (1938),
    3, 4
  renovation, postwar, 205
  Revolution (1848), 33
  Seghers on, 165
  Sembène on, 194
  twenty-fifth centenary celebra-
    tions (1899), 67
  Théâtre du Gymnase, 54, 55,
    57, 87, 120, 177, 210
  Zola on, 32, 33
Cannes, 152
Cannes, AS, 179
Capelette, La, 191
Capitole, 120
Capri, Agnès, 180
Caracas, 166
Caravansérail à Trébizonde, Un
    (Brest), 73

Carbone, Paul, 3, 102, 173, 215–17, 225
Carcassonne, 151
Cardiff, 112
caricatures, 52–3, 126
Carlist Wars (1833–76), 23, 33, 242 n.55
Carmes, Les, 155
Carné, Marcel, 87
Carrera, Augustin, 76
Carrese, Philippe, 10, 218
Carry, 62
Carteaux, Jean Baptiste François, 28
cartoon, 7, 118, 137
Casablanca, 37, 158, 163, 164–5, 252 n.55
Casablanca (1942 film), 164, 252 n.9
Casals, Pablo, 179
Casino de la Plage, 88
Cassis, 80, 155
Cassou, Jean, 149
Castans, Raymond, 120, 249 n.13
Castel, Gaston, 148, 155, 156, 157, 204
de Castellane-Majastre, Henri-César, 24
Castellane, 61
Catalans, 2, 20–21, 67, 98, 103
Catalonia, 22, 98
Cathédrale de la Major, 40, 54, 108, 140, 141, 220
Catholicism, 56
Catulle (Pagnol), 122
Cauvet, Gilles-Paul, 76
Cayolle, La, 206
Cellony, Joseph André, 72
Celts, 84
censorship, 177
Centre Culturel Méditerranéen, 178

Centre Intellectuel Méditerranéen, 178
Centre Universitaire Méditerranéen, 152
Centurions, Les (Lartéguy), 188, 199–201
Cercle Artistique, 75, 76
Cercle Rouge, Le, 222
César (Pagnol), 123–6, 128
1936 film, 129, 130–31
César cinema, 133
Cévennes, 43
Cézanne, Paul, 7, 66, 74, 75, 77–80
Chabaud, Auguste, 77, 79, 81
Chagall, Marc, 137
Chaîne de l'Etoile, 38
Chamber of Commerce, 67, 68, 149
Champs-Elysées, 54, 102
Chansons Provençales (Gelu), 56, 58–9
Chant de l'Armée du Rhin, 24, 25
Chantecler (Rostand), 83
Chantiers, 151
Chapacans, Les (Courbou), 218
Chaplin, Charles, 126, 132
Char, René, 170
Chargeurs Réunis, 163
Charles X, King of France, 15, 48, 50
Charles-Roux, Edmonde, 7, 161, 164, 173–4
Charles-Roux, Jules, 61, 68, 70, 72, 75–6, 82, 94
Charpin, Fernand, 125, 129, 240 n.2
Chat Noir, 88–9
Chat Rieur, Le, 89
Château Borély, 84
Château d'If, 1, 18, 19, 26, 123, 214, 229

INDEX

Château de la Buzine, 133
Château de ma mère, Le (Pagnol), 119
  1990 film, 134
Château de Saint-Cloud, 15
Château Fallet, 85
Châtelet cinema, 133
Châtelet-Théâtre, 88, 120
Chatou, 79
Chaulot, Paul, 146, 147, 151
Chevalier, Louis, 9
Chevalier, Michel, 50, 51
Chicago, 102, 215
Chienne, La, 132
chiffonnier, *see* rag pickers
China, 96, 100, 112, 152
cholera, 18, 34–5, 44
Chopin, René, 172
Chourmo (Izzo) 226, 231–2
Choux, Jean, 249 n.26
Christiné, Henri, 65
Cid, Le, 154
cinemas, 88, 127, 133, 180, 183,
  210
  see also film
Cinématographe Indo-Chinois, 71
Cioffi, Robert, 11
Ciotat, La, 2, 80
Cité de la Rouguière, 201
cité radieuse, 208, 257 n.31
cités, 5, 9, 188, 199, 207, 209, 227,
  232
Classe tous risques (Giovanni), 219
classes laborieuses, 9
classical music, 178–9
Claudel, Paul, 83
Claudius-Petit, Eugène, 204, 207
Le Clézio, Jean-Marie Gustave, 7,
  10, 106, 188, 195–8, 206, 233
coal, 43–4, 104
Cobb, Richard, 1, 97
cocaine, 216
Cochin-China, 1

Coder railway engineering works,
  208
Cohen, Albert, 120
Colisée-Plage, 180
Collégiens, 182
Collioure, 77, 80
Colombo, 200
colonies, *see* French Empire
Combarnous, Victor, 55
Combes, Émile, 86
Comédie Française, 121
Comédie Phocéenne, La, 178
Commune (1871), 28, 59, 66
Communist Party, 3, 173, 191,
  200, 202, 207, 215, 256 n.22
Comoedia, 121
Compagnie de la Lune Rousse, 89
Compagnie de Navigation Mixte,
  42, 240 n.3, 252 n.55
Compagnie des Docks et
  Entrepôts, 41, 69–70
Compagnie des Quatre-Vents, 178
Compagnie Fraissinet, 6, 42, 192
Compagnie Nationale
  Transatlantique, 42, 111
Compagnie Paquet, 5, 42, 111,
  149, 163, 252 n.55
Compiègne, 170, 171, 172
Comte de Monte-Cristo, Le (Dumas),
  9, 18–24, 53, 61, 217
  Canebière in, 20, 53
  Les Catalans in, 20–21, 67
  Grand-Cours in, 86
  Izzo and, 228, 229
  Mediterranean identity, 18–24,
    29, 35–6
  Pharaon, Le, 18, 20, 22, 23, 29,
    32, 40, 46, 229, 234
  Provençal culture in, 21–2
  Revolution in, 26–7
  Vieux-Port in, 18–24, 35–6, 40
Concert des Courses, 89

INDEX

Confédération Générale du Travail (CGT), 3, 191, 256 n.22
Confrérie de la Tasse, 57
Confrérie du Dahlia Bleu, 89
Congrès International de l'Architecture Moderne (CIAM), 155
Congrès International pour la Défense de la Culture contre le Fascisme, 154
Congress of Berlin (1884–5), 69
Conrad, Joseph, 7, 23, 53, 54, 86, 228, 242 n.55
Conseil Administratif, 178
Conseil Général, 67
Considerable Town, A (Fisher), 213
Constantine, 49
Constantinople, 42, 74
Convention, *see* National Convention
Corbusier, Le (Charles-Édouard Jeanneret), 7, 50, 115, 155, 156, 158, 188, 203, 206, 208, 257 n.31
Corinth, 106
Corniche, 52, 71, 173, 202–3, 220, 232
Corot, Jean-Baptiste-Camille, 74
corruption, 3, 4, 10, 94, 114, 216, 219, 231–4, 248 n.37, 257 n.37
Corsica, 5, 22, 163, 193
Corsicans, 2, 16, 45, 98, 99, 102, 103, 109, 187, 215, 216
Corti, José, 150
Côte d'Azur, 2
Coty, Jules Gustave René, 225
Coudenhove-Kalergi, Richard, 158
Coulet, Michèle, 150, 250 n.10
Courant, Pierre, 207
Courbou, Michèle, 218
Cours Belsunce, 17, 24, 54, 96, 99
  Alcazar music hall, 4, 9, 46, 87

Benjamin on, 140
Cobb on, 97
Dumas on, 20
Seghers on, 165
Sembène on, 189
Suarès on, 84
Zola on, 32
Cours Bonaparte, 32, 62
Cours d'Estienned'Orves, 148
Cours du Vieux-Port, 148
Cours Julien, 17, 56, 149
Cours Lieutaud, 17, 86, 119
Cours Pierre-Puget, 32, 140
Cours Saint-Louis, 112
Cox, Samuel, 47–8
Craene, Roland, 182
Crane, Sheila, 142, 156, 157
Crau, 2, 43
Cravache, La, 202
Crevel, René, 150
Criée, La, 148
crime, 3, 4, 8, 9, 10, 11, 93–4, 101–2, 118, 213–34
  Second Empire period (1852–70), 53, 61, 101, 215
  Inter-War period (1918–39), 93–4, 101–2, 118, 139, 142, 215–17, 224, 225, 233
  Vichy period (1940–44), 173, 175, 217, 222, 223, 224–5
  Post-War period (1945–), 189, 211, 213–14, 218–34
Crisp, Colin, 131–2
Cuba, 19, 167
Cubism, 77, 79, 80, 137
Curtiz, Michael, 164, 252 n.9
Cyrano de Bergerac (Rostand), 82, 88, 120, 122
Cyrunez de Blaigerac, 88
Czóbel, Béla, 79

Dabit, Eugène, 112

Dahomey (c. 1600–1904), 68
Dakar, 112, 158, 163
Damascus, 104
danseuses cambogiennes, 71
Dark Victory, 180
Daudet, Alphonse, 7, 38–40, 46–7,
    48, 61, 110, 126, 127, 179
Daudet, Léon, 108
Daumal, René, 148, 150
Dautry, Raoul, 203, 204
Davenport, Miriam, 169
Davis, Bette, 180
Davis, Miles, 232
Decline and Fall (Waugh), 93–4, 96,
    100, 108
Defferre, Gaston, 193, 202, 206,
    207
Del Pappas, Gilles, 218
Delacroix, Ferdinand Victor
    Eugène, 73
Delaunay, Charles, 181
Dell'Umbria, Alèssi, 191, 193,
    204, 208, 213, 234
Dellepiane, David, 67, 70, 72, 243
    n.3
Delon, Alain, 215
Demazis, Orane, 124
Demetz, Peter, 167
Denis, Maurice, 77
départements, 17
Derain, André, 77, 79, 80, 81
Deray, Jacques, 215
Description de l'Égypte, 50
désenclavement, 5
Désert (Le Clézio), 10, 106, 188,
    195–8, 206, 233
Détective, 3, 102, 217
detritus, 3, 10, 95, 172, 174, 196
    Benjamin on, 139
    Le Clézio on, 196
    Krull on, 142, 214
    Londres on, 104, 156

McKay on, 108
Moholy-Nagy on, 142
Peisson, 113–15, 214
    Seghers on, 166
Vieux-Port destruction (1943)
    and, 172, 174, 196
Deuxième souffle, Le (Giovanni),
    218–25, 226
Devin, André, 204
Diaghilev, Sergei, 179
Diamant et la vengeance, Le
    (Pauchet), 19
Dickson, Gloria, 180
Dien Bien Phû, battle of (1954),
    200
Digne, 121
Direct au Coeur, Un (Pagnol), 122
'dirty city', 143, 174
Djibouti, 200, 227
Docker noir, Le (Sembène), 104,
    106, 188, 189–91, 194, 206
dockers, *see portefaix*
Don Carlos, 52
Donzel, André, 114
Doriot, Jacques, 216
Dos Passos, John, 114
Dranem, Armand, 120
Drôle de guerre (1939–40), 162,
    163
drug trade, 101, 102, 214, 215,
    216, 217, 233, 234
Dubrovnik, 16, 28
Duchamp, Marcel, 170
Ducreux, Louis, 178
duel social, 33, 35
Dufy, Raoul, 79
Dullac, Paul, 125
Dullin, Charles, 121, 249 n.14
Dumas, Alexandre
    Le Comte de Monte-Cristo, see
        Comte de Monte-Cristo, Le
    Monsieur Coumbes, 19

Reine Margot, La, 229
San Felice, La, 229
Duport, Claire, 11
Durance river, 33, 35, 44
Durio, Paco, 81

Echelles du Levant, 28, 29
Echinard, Pierre, 209
Ecole de Dessin de Marseille, 56
Ecole de Marseille, 11, 37, 56,
    73–81
Ecole des Beaux Arts, 55, 73, 75,
    81, 178, 202
Ecole des Chartreux, 119
Ecole des Ponts et Chaussées, 44
Ecole Normale Supérieure, 83, 121
Ecole Polytechnique, 44, 49
Egger, René, 204
Eglise Saint-Victor, 32
Egypt, 8, 15, 23, 29, 42, 43, 50,
    198, 216, 234
Eiffel Tower, 143
Elba, 22, 23
Eldorado cinema, 88
Eliot, Thomas Stearns, 154
Elle, Adrienne (Charles-Roux), 161,
    164, 173–4
Ellroy, James, 226, 231
Eluard, Paul, 150
Emergency Rescue Committee,
    169, 173, 176, 179
Endoume, 121
Enfantin, Barthelémy-Prosper, 50
Enfants du Paradis, Les (Carné), 87
Engalière, Marius, 73–4
Enlightenment, 154
Epstein, Jean, 256 n.15
Ernst, Max, 170
Espérandieu, Henri-Jacques, 38
Espervisa, 170
Esprit, 146, 147
L'Estaque, 1, 5, 7, 41, 66, 75,
    77–81, 85, 137, 206

L'Estaque (Cézanne), 80
L'Estaque (Renoir), 78
Esther, 177
Et l'au-delà de Suez (Brauquier), 152
Etang de Berre, 5, 193, 199, 221
L'Etranger (Camus), 189
Eugénie Grandet (Balzac), 86
Eugénie, Empress consort of the
    French, 51
'EurAfrica', 158
Europe, 145
European Community, 193
Évian Accords (1962), 201
'exception marseillaise', 6
L'Excommunié (Giovanni), 219
Exode (1940), 133, 161, 163–70
Expositions Coloniale
    1906 7, 54, 61, 65–6, 68–73,
        75–6, 85, 86, 87, 95, 138,
        215
    1922 97, 138
    1931 187
L'Express, 214
Expressionism, 81

Fabiani, Jean-Louis, 6
Fabulous Trobadors, 228
Fairbanks, Douglas, 132
Fanny (Pagnol), 124–6, 128, 129
    1932 film, 129, 130, 131
Fantasio, 135
Fascism, 153, 154, 216, 224
fashion shows, 183
Fassel, Otto, 183
Faubourg Montmartre, 102, 215
Faulkner, William, 154
Faure, Elie, 76
Faust, 177
Fauvism, 7, 75, 77, 79–81, 89, 137
Favorite, La, 55
Federalist revolts (1793), 3, 16,
    27–8

Félibrige, 22, 27, 59, 60, 67, 68,
  72, 85, 151, 179
Femme du boulanger, La, 132
'Fenian e grouman', 58
Ferdinand, Roger, 132
Fernandel (Fernand Joseph Désiré
  Contandin), 7, 11, 53, 119, 177,
  180, 183
ferries, *see* ships
Feu, Le, 76, 77, 85, 148, 152
Feuillère, Edwige, 122
Feuillière, Pierre, 178
FFI (Forces françaises de
  l'Intérieur), 183
Figueroa, Luis, 44
film, 127–35, 141–3
  Inter-War period (1918–39), 18,
    24–6, 27, 29, 114, 117, 122,
    127–35, 141–3
  Vichy period (1940–44), 127,
    133, 180, 183
  Post-War period (1945–), 214,
    215, 218–19, 220–24, 234
Films Marcel Pagnol, Les, 129
Fiquet, Hortense, 78
Firebrace, William, 203, 218, 232
Firminy, 203
First World War (1914–18), *see*
  World War I
Fisher, Mary Frances Kennedy, 4,
  213
fishing, 16, 26, 41, 73, 78, 100,
  131, 143, 195, 205
Flaissières, Siméon, 67, 87, 95, 98,
  102, 215
Flamant, Geroges, 177
flights, 8, 11, 252 n.57
Fluchère, Henri, 154, 178
Foire de Marseille, 71
Fonds Jean Ballard, 250 n.10
Fontaine, 211
Fontaine de Vaucluse, 19

Fools for Scandal, 180
football, 4, 7, 68, 88, 118, 179,
  214, 228
Football Club de Marseille, 88
Foran, John Nicholas 'Dick', 180
Fort Notre-Dame, 27
Fort Saint-Jean, 27, 38, 39, 41,
  141, 214, 230
Fort Saint-Nicolas, 27, 38, 39–40,
  141, 230
Fortune carrée (Kessel), 221
Fortunio, 120, 146–7, 149, 152
Fos Port, 5, 193, 209, 221
Fouchet, Max-Pol, 153, 211
founding myth, 20–21, 67
Fournier, Marguerite, 178
Fragonard, Jean-Honoré, 72
Fragson, Harry, 120
Franco-Prussian War (1870–71),
  73, 240 n.52
Frankenheimer, John, 9, 214, 234
Frankfurter Zeitung, 140
Free French forces, 189
free music school, 54
Freeman, Judi, 79
Fregonese, Hugo, 171
Fréjus, 171, 172
French Connection II, 9, 214, 215, 234
French Empire, 1, 3–4, 8, 65–6,
  68–73, 187–203, 211
  Algeria (1830–1962), *see under*
    Algeria
  Antilles (1635–), 71
  Dahomey (1892–1958), 68
  Egyptian Campaign (1798–
    1801), 8, 23, 50
  Expositions Coloniale, *see*
    Expositions Coloniale
  Indian colonies (1673–1954), 71
  Indochina (1887–1954), *see*
    under Indochina
  Madagascar (1885–1958), 69, 71

Martinique (1635–), 167
Morocco (1912–56), *see under*
    Morocco
Réunion (1642–), 71
Senegal (1659–1960), 1, 42,
    106, 112, 158, 163, 188, 189,
    194, 199
Somaliland (1883–1967), 200,
    227
Syria and Lebanon Mandate
    (1923–43), 211
Tunisia (1881–1956), *see under*
    Tunisia
West Africa (1895–1958), 71,
    96, 98, 158, 163, 189
French Revolution, *see* Revolution
French urban riots (2005), 99
Fréron, Louis-Marie Stanislas, 28
Fresnay, Pierre, 124, 125, 129, 130
Friesz, Achille-Émile Othon, 77,
    79, 80, 81
From Deauville to Monte Carlo
    (Woon), 93
Front de libération nationale
    (FLN), 118, 199, 201
Front National, 9, 201, 227, 231,
    232
Front Populaire, 18, 24, 26, 134,
    149, 168
Fry, Varian, 169, 173, 176, 179
FTP-MOI (Francs-tireurs et parti-
    sans—main-d'œuvre immigrée),
    173
Fuller, Loïe, 71
fun-fair rides, 71

Gaillard, André, 149, 150, 151–2
Gaillard, Lucien, 57
Gallimard, 102, 218
gambling, 88
Gant rouge, Le (Rostand), 82
Gardanne, 43

Garde Nationale, 33
Gare d'Arenc, 171
Gare Saint-Charles, 1, 43, 45, 96,
    195, 214
    Ballard on, 148
    Camp Victor Hugo, 99
    Castel on, 148
    Le Clézio on, 195
    Cobb on, 1, 97
    Exposition Coloniale (1906)
        and, 71
    Hôtel Splendide, 169
    McKay on, 108
    Sembène on, 189
Garibaldi, Giuseppe, 23, 240 n.52
Gasnier, Louis, 122, 129
Gasquet, Joachim, 76
Gaston Mouren, 178
Gauguin, Eugène Henri Paul, 81
Gaul, 2, 67
de Gaulle, Charles, 173, 183, 193,
    217
Gaumont, 133
Gay, Claude, 181
Gelu, Noël, 56
Gelu, Victor, 7, 11, 22, 33, 52,
    56–63, 68, 82, 126, 168, 178
*Génie d'Oc et l'Homme Méditerranéen,
    Le*, 153, 179
Genoa, 8, 21, 22, 28, 32, 69, 83,
    96, 193
Genovese, Vito, 216
George-Philipar, 100
Germany, 43, 69, 81, 96, 138–45,
    154
    Nazi period (1933–45), *see* Nazi
        Germany
    Romanticism, 138, 154
Gervais, Auguste, 95, 103, 247 n.9
Gestapo, 167
Ghardaïa, 158
Gide, André, 83, 176

Giedion, Siegfried, 142
Giesbert, Franz-Olivier, 218
Giono, Jean, 118, 132, 133, 134
Giovanni, José, 218–25
giraffes, 15–16, 18, 50
Girieud, Pierre, 79, 81
Gleizes, Albert, 153
Gloire de mon père, La (Pagnol), 119
1990 film, 134
von Goethe, Johann Wolfgang, 26
Gold, Mary Jane, 169
Golden Age, 40–46
'Good City', 10
Goudes, Les, 227
Grand Arénas camp, Le, 198, 199, 206
Grand Casino, 120
Grand Delta, 193
Grand Entrepôt, 41, 44
Grand Jeu, Le, 150
Grand Littoral, 233
Grand Lupanar, 84
Grand Palais, 71, 72
Grand Théâtre, 54–5, 57, 87, 177
Grand Trunk Mail service, 43, 96, 247 n.12
Grand-Cours, 86
Grand-Rue, 84
Grande Bastide, 206
Gravey, Fernand, 180
Great Depression (1929–39), 96, 127, 149
Greber, Jacques, 155–6, 174, 252 n.47, 257 n.37
Greece
Ancient, 16, 23–4, 67, 153, 228
emigration, 2, 42, 45, 98, 103, 105, 187, 199
Suarès and, 84
War of Independence (1821–9), 15, 22
Grenier, Jean, 153

Grésy, Prosper, 74
Griffith, David Wark, 132
Grosz, George, 137
Guédiguian, Robert, 9
Guenin, Joachim, 56
Guérini, Antoine and Barthélémy, 173, 216, 217, 233
Guggenheim, Peggy, 170
Guigou, Paul Camille, 72, 74
Guiral, Pierre, 16, 33, 34, 45, 54
Guiraud, Jean Michel, 176
Gyptis, 20–21, 67

Haas, Monique, 179
Hackman, Gene, 214
Haganah, 256 n.22
Hamburg, 45, 69, 94, 144
Hamlet (Shakespeare), 121
Hans le marin (Peisson), 9, 10, 100, 104, 111–14, 139, 217, 230, 237 n.4
Harkis, 202
Harlem Renaissance, 107, 111
Harun al-Rashid, Abbasid Caliph, 196
'Hashish in Marseille' (Benjamin), 140–41
hat stealing, 94, 139
Haussmann, Georges-Eugène, 54
Haut-fer, Le (Giovanni), 219
Havana, Cuba, 19
Le Havre, 42, 79, 94, 95, 162, 204, 205, 216
HBM (Habitation à Bon Marché), 207
Heart of the North, 180
Hebrew Immigrant Aid Society (HIAS), 169, 253 n.20
Heckel, Edouard, 68, 72
Hecquet, Stephen, 218
Heller, Gerhard, 177
Hemingway, Ernest, 221

INDEX

heroin, 216
Herriot, Edouard, 149
HICEM, 169, 253 n.20
hinterland, 17, 18, 22, 29, 31, 57,
  58, 61, 118, 134, 235
  in painting, 74, 75
hip-hop music, 11, 61, 228, 231–2
Hirschman, Albert, 169
Histoire de fou (Giovanni), 219
Hitler, Adolf, 172
HLM (Habitation à Loyer Modéré),
  201, 207, 209
Ho! (Giovanni), 219
Ho Chi Minh, 256 n.22
Hollywood, 132
Holocaust (1941–5), 170, 171–2,
  206, 224, 253 n.20
Home to Harlem (McKay), 107
Honegger, Arthur, 179
Hôtel Astoria, 173
Hôtel des Bains, 78
Hôtel Bompard, 164, 201
Hôtel-Dieu, 112, 204
Hôtel des Emigrants, 104, 105
Hôtel du Louvre, 53
Hôtel Mistral, 78
Hôtel d'Orient (Algiers), 47
Hôtel de la Providence, 167
Hôtel Rome et Saint-Pierre, 173
Hôtel Sainte-Blanche, 196
Hôtel Splendide, 169, 173
Hôtel Terminus, 164
Hôtel de Ville, 10, 127, 130, 143,
  155, 156, 172
hôtels garnis, 206
hotels, 96, 97
housing estates, *see cités*, 5
Hughes, Clovis, 226
Hughes, Langston, 111
Hugo, Victor, 34, 238 n.13
8e Femme de Barbe-Bleue, La, 183
humanism, 76, 145, 151, 153–4,
  156, 168

Hundred Days (1815), 26, 29, 61
Hussards, 218
Huveaune, 86
Hypnotik, 228
Hytier, Jean, 153

IAM, 11, 228, 231–2
'Idle and Greedy', 58
'If I were a Turk' (Gelu), 60
Iles Frioules, 1
'imaginaire de Marseille', 3, 6, 71
immigration, 2, 4, 6, 8, 9, 10, 11,
  28, 40, 45, 97–100, 102–11,
  187–203
  Algerians, 66, 70, 97, 98, 103,
    199, 201–3
  Arabs, 45, 97, 103, 104, 109,
    188
  Armenians, 2, 98, 100, 102, 187
  Belgians, 104
  Catalans, 2, 20–21, 67, 98, 103
  Chinese, 194
  Corsicans, 2, 16, 45, 98, 99,
    102, 103, 109, 187, 215
  Greeks, 2, 45, 98, 103, 105,
    187, 199
  Indochina, 256 n.22
  Italians, 2, 16, 21, 45, 66, 98,
    99, 102–4, 109, 172, 173,
    187, 190, 199, 215
  Jews, 2, 45, 83, 201
  Lebanese, 45, 104
  Maltese, 109
  Mesopotamian Christians, 104
  Moroccans, 97, 195–8, 199, 201
  Pieds-Noirs, 199, 201–3
  Poles, 104
  rapatriés, 52, 201–3, 206
  Serbs, 104
  Spaniards, 2, 45, 56, 98, 100,
    103, 104, 105, 109, 173, 199
  Syrians, 45, 104

INDEX

Tunisians, 97, 103, 198, 201
West Africans, 98, 100, 109–11,
  187, 188, 189, 190, 199
Impasse des Peupliers, 132
Impressionism, 75, 78, 79
Impressions of Marseille's Old Harbour
  (Moholy-Nagy), 139, 141–3,
  155
India, 42, 43, 71, 96
Indian Trunk Mail service, 43, 96,
  247 n.12
Indochina (1887–1954), 1, 42,
  65–6, 69, 96, 99, 112, 163, 192,
  200
  Anti-French War (1946–54),
    191, 200, 256 n.22
  drug trade in, 216
  emigration, 256 n.22
Industrial Revolution, 44
Influenza epidemic (1918–20), 83
Institut Colonial, 68
Institut d'Urbanisme, 155
Inter-War period (1918–39), 6, 7,
  8, 22, 93–115
  crime, 93–4, 101–2, 139, 142,
    215–17, 224, 225, 233
  film, 18, 24–6, 27, 29, 114,
    117, 122, 127–35, 141–3
  immigration, 97–100, 102–11
  pan-Mediterraneanism, 50
  red-light district, 84, 94, 100
  theatre, 9, 32, 106, 117–27
Intérieur du port de Marseille
  (Vernet), 73
'L'Internationale', 113
Iran, 216
iron ore, 42
Islam, 153
Israel, 211
Istanbul, 157
Italian language, 21
Italy, 21–2

bombing of Marseille (1940),
  162, 170, 171, 176
emigration, 16, 21, 45, 66, 98,
  99, 102–4, 109, 172, 173,
  187, 190, 199, 215
Fascist period (1922–43), 153,
  162, 170
Franco-Prussian War (1870–71),
  240 n.52
in paintings, 74
Suarès and, 84
unification (1815–1871), 23, 34
World War I (1914–18), 98
World War II (1939–45), 162,
  170, 171, 176
Izzo, Jean-Claude, 22, 61, 111,
  134, 213, 214, 218, 225–34
on Arabian culture, 23–4, 153,
  228
Cahiers du Sud, influence of, 226,
  228
Chourmo, 226, 231–2
and civilian casualties, 222
on colonialism, 106, 227
on Greek culture, 23–4, 153, 228
Marins perdus, Les, 226, 228, 229,
  230, 231
Solea, 9, 174, 226
Soleil des mourants, Le, 226, 230
Total Khéops, 23–4, 31, 172, 200,
  213, 214, 218, 223, 225–34

Jaccottet, Philippe, 150
Jacobins, 27
Jaloux, Edmond, 66, 76, 82, 85–6
Jaloux, Les, 178
jam sessions, 183
Jamaica, 107
Japan, 112, 163
Jardins de Thalassa, Les, 204
Jasmin, Jacques, 60
Jazz (Pagnol), 122, 177

jazz music, 8, 108, 138, 140, 141, 180–84, 228
Jean de Florette (Pagnol), 134, 135
Jean de la Lune, 249 n.26
Jeanson, Henri, 249 n.14
Jésus et la Samaritaine (Loubon), 73
Jeunesse de la Méditerranée, 152, 153
Jewish people, 2, 45, 83, 153, 164, 169–73, 177, 179, 201, 224
   Holocaust (1941–5), 170, 171–2, 206, 224, 253 n.20
   Palestine, migration to, 206, 256 n.22
Jofroi, 132
Joinville, 128
La Joliette, 32, 38, 40–41, 43, 54, 97, 193
   Le Clézio on, 195
   Cobb on, 97
   Krull on, 143
   Londres, 103
   McKay on, 108
   Sembène on, 190
Jongegeans, Georges, 179
Journal, Le, 127
Journal de Genève, Le, 224
Journal des Débats, 18
Jouvet, Louis, 122
Julien, Marc-Antoine, 28
July Monarchy (1830–48), 16, 27, 29, 33, 35, 40, 49, 54
Justice, James Robertson, 171
Justin de Marseille, 117, 194, 217, 249 n.12
Kabylie, 98, 103
Kairouan, 201
Kansas State University, 107
Kessel, Joseph, 173, 221
Keussayan, Assadour, 6, 187, 189
Kochno, Boris, 179
Korda, Alexander, 128, 130
Kosma, Joseph, 179

Kra, Simon, 150
Krull, Germaine, 10, 84, 138, 142, 143–5, 156, 214

Lacydon, 16, 67, 127, 175, 204
de Lamartine, Alphonse, 57
Lambert, Albert, 121
Landry, Géard, 177
langue d'oc, see Occitan
langue d'oïl, 2
Lartéguy, Jean, 188, 199–201
Latour, Marielle, 77, 78, 79
Lausanne, 85
Lausanne Treaty (1923), 98
Lavéra, 193
Lazaret, 41
Lear, Edward, 43
Lebanon, 98, 104
Lebasque, Henri, 77
Lee, Laurie, 237 n.4
Lefèvre, René, 249 n.26
Légion Française des Combattants, 181, 182
Lekain, Esther, 120
Lemoine, Marcel, 172
de Lesseps, Ferdinand, 1, 49, 50–51, 106, 242 n.48
Levant, 28, 29, 42, 45, 69, 98, 105, 211
Lévi-Strauss, Claude, 167
Lhomeau, Franck, 224
Liberalism, 154
Liberation (1944), 10, 146, 149, 162, 163, 182, 183–4
Libération, 224
Liberator, The (McKay), 107
Librairie Laffitte, 54
libretti, 52
Liguria, 98
Lille, 75, 122
Limassol, 195
Lisbon, 163, 164, 165, 167

INDEX

Liste Otto (1940), 177
literature
  July Monarchy period (1830–
    48), 9, 18–24, 53, 61
  Second Empire period (1852–
    70), 7, 9, 17–19, 22, 29–36,
    37–8, 50, 52–63, 68, 69
  Belle Epoch period (1870–
    1914), 7, 38–40, 46–7, 48,
    61, 81–6
  Inter-War period (1914–39), 7,
    9, 11, 32, 53, 57, 82, 100–
    115, 117–27, 138–41
  Post-War period (1945–), 10,
    23–4, 31, 104, 106, 172, 188,
    189–201, 213, 214, 218–34
littérature prolétarienne movement,
  112
Liverpool, 41
Livre des Morts Tibétain, Le
  (Daumal), 148
Logement million, 207
Loi du survivant, La, 219
Lombard, Alfred, 75, 76–7, 81
Lombard, Carole, 180
London, 41, 43, 53, 69, 82, 144,
  158
Londres, Albert, 7, 39, 84, 96,
  100–7, 110, 112, 138, 139, 144,
  167
  on crime, 101, 215
  on detritus, 103–4, 156
  on dock workers, 104, 109, 190
  on Exposition Coloniale (1906),
    97
  on immigration, 98, 102–7,
    167, 216, 230
  on *invitation au voyage*, 4, 106,
    126
  on Planier lighthouse, 107, 113,
    130
  realism, 127, 145

and 'white man's burden', 106
and *ville d'accueil*, 230
Los Angeles, 215, 226, 231
Loubon, Emile, 37–8, 56, 62, 73,
  74
Louis XV, King of France, 73
Louis XVI, King of France, 25, 26,
  27
Louis, Prince Napoléon, 19
Louis Philippe I, King of the
  French, 33
Loy, Myrna, 249 n.15
Luce, Maximilien, 77
Luciano, Charles 'Lucky', 216
Lugné-Poe (Aurélien-Marie
  Lugné), 121
luxury hotels, 96, 97
Lyautey, Marshall, 157
Lycée Condorcet, 121, 122, 147
Lycée Impérial, 56
Lycée de Marseille, 56, 82, 83,
  119, 121, 146, 152
Lycée Thiers, 56, 82
Lyon, 2, 11, 43, 56, 101, 121, 149,
  177, 224–5

Ma el Aïnine, 195, 197
Ma Petite Tonkinoise (Scotto), 7,
  65–6, 129, 243 n.1
Mac Orlan, Pierre, 94, 246 n.6
Madagascar, 69, 71
Madrid, 22
Maeterlinck, Maurice, 83, 84
Mafia, 217, 232
de Magallon, Xavier, 76
Maillol, Aristide, 77
Mainz, 137
Mairie, 73, 123
Maison Dorée café, 53
Maisons à L'Estaque (Cézanne), 79,
  80
Malraux, André, 145, 176

INDEX

Malta, 109

Man with a Movie Camera, 114, 142

Manguin, Henri, 79

Mann, Philip, 223

Mann, Thomas, 169

Manon des Sources, 134

Maran, René, 108

Marcel, Gabriel, 148

Marchand, Léopold, 129

Marchands de gloire, Les (Pagnol), 122

Mare Nostrum', 153

Marie-Antoinette, Queen consort of France, 25, 26

Marie-Caroline de Bourbon-Sicile, Duchesse de Berry, 62

Marignane, 11, 193, 201

Marins perdus, Les (Izzo), 226, 228, 229, 230, 231

Marius trilogy (Pagnol), 106, 119, 120, 123–7, 134, 194, 222
    film adaptations, 123, 124, 128–31, 134
    Izzo and, 228, 229–30
    stereotypes and, 9, 125, 126
    Vieux-Port in, 32, 119, 123, 124, 125, 131, 229–30

Marius (1931 film), 128–9, 130

Marius et Olive, 7, 118, 194, 256 n.15

Marius et Olive à Paris, 256 n.15

Marked Woman, 180

Marquet, Albert, 77, 79, 81

Marsalés, Pierre-Paul 'Polin', 120

Marseillaise, La (1938 film), 18, 24–6, 27, 29, 133

'Marseillaise, La' 3, 18, 24–9

'Marseille' (Benjamin), 139–40

Marseille (Krull), 84, 143–5

Marseille (newsletter), 175

Marseille, porte du Sud (Londres), 100, 101–7, 167

Marseille, une biographie (Thomazeau), 232–3

Marseille au XIXe siècle (Gelu), 56, 61

Marseille Battalion, 18, 24–7

Marseille Confidential (Thomazeau), 257 n.37

Marseille et les Marseillais (Méry), 19, 52, 69

Marseille et les peintres (Latour), 77, 78, 79

Marseille Fair, 71

Marseille Métropole (Castel) 157

Marseille Vieux-Port (Moholy-Nagy), 139, 141–3, 155

Marseille-Provence Airport, 8, 11, 252 n.57

Marseille, Marius, 178

Marsiho (Suarès), 84–5, 143, 144

Martigues, 74, 80, 193

Martin du Gard, Roger, 176

Martin, Paul, 75

Martinique, 167

Martinů, Bohuslav Jan, 179

Mas de la Santo Estello, 72

Mascotte, La, 180

Massalia Blues (Siff), 187

Massilia Sound System, 11, 61, 228

Massilia!, 120

Masson, André, 170

Le Mat, Jackie Le, 217

Matisse, Henri, 79, 80

Maurel et Prom, 70

Mauriac, François Charles, 86, 149

Maurras, Charles-Marie-Photius, 68, 151, 179

de Max, Édouard, 121

Mayol, Félix, 120

Mayor de Montricher, Franz, 44

Mazargues, 220, 221

McKay, Claude, 100, 104, 107–11, 112, 113, 189, 194

medical schools, 54, 68
'Mediterranean system', 50–51
Méditerranée mer de surprises
    (Morand), 158–9
'Méditerranée' (Rossi), 197, 198
Médor, 177
Mehemet-Ali, Wāli of Egypt, 15, 50
Melville, Jean-Pierre, 173, 218,
    222–4, 225, 226
Mémorial de la 'Marseillaise', 24
Mémorial des Rapatriés d'Algérie,
    52, 202–3
Menton, 152
Méridional caricature, 53, 126
Meridional, Le, 214
Merle Blanc, Le, 89
Méry, Joseph, 7, 19, 50, 52–6,
    62–3, 69, 82, 139, 140
    on Barcelona, 50
    on Canebière, 52–3, 86
    caricature, use of, 52–3, 126
    on Château Fallet, 85
    on *nervis*, 53, 215
    on theatres, 54–5
    Thémime on, 239 n.19
    on *ville-campagne*, 17, 52
Mesopotamian Christians, 104
Messager de Provence, Le, 29
Messageries Maritimes, 6, 42, 152
Métal (Krull), 143
Meunier, Mario, 76
Meurisse, Paul, 223
Meutre au sommet (Giovanni), 219
Mexico, 165, 166–7
Meyer-Heine Plan (1949), 208
Michel, Peraldi, 11
Michel, Pierre, 217
Midi-Libre, 180, 181
Midsummer Night's Dream, A
    (Shakespeare), 179, 180
Mihalovici, Marcel, 179
Milieu, 3, 102, 173, 175, 215–26,
    233

Mill, Raymond, 182
Miller, Henry, 154
Milles, Les, 164
Millet, Jean-François, 74
Ministère de l'Education Nationale
    et des Beaux-Arts, 149
Mirès, Jules, 44, 45
Misérables, Les (Hugo) 34, 238 n.13
Mistinguett (Jeanne Florentine
    Bourgeois), 180
Mistral, Frédéric, 59, 60, 72, 75
Modern cinema, 88
Modernism, 89, 115, 135, 137–45,
    150, 155, 156, 158
Moholy-Nagy, Lazslo, 10, 138,
    141–3, 155, 156
Moinier, Charles Émile, 197
Moïse, 55
el-Mokrani, Mohamed, 48
Molière (Jean-Baptiste Poquelin),
    125
Monaco, 153
Monet, Claude, 77, 78
Monk, Theolonious, 228
Monsieur Coumbes (Dumas), 19
Mont Saint-Michel, 19
Montand, Yves, 183
Monte Carlo, 122
Monte Cristo cigars, 19
Montero, Germaine, 179
Montevideo, 42, 163
Montez, Maria, 111
Monticelli, Adolphe, 72, 74, 78–9,
    140
Montmartre, 74, 81
    cabaret, 88–9, 243 n.1
    crime, 102, 215
Montredon, 178
Morand, Paul, 108, 158–9
Moreau, Gustave, 81
Morocco, 97, 106, 195–8, 199,
    201

INDEX

Agadir Crisis (1911), 195, 197
Algeciras conference (1906), 197
Cahiers du Sud in, 211
emigration, 97, 195–8, 199, 201
football players, 118
independence (1956), 197, 201, 211
Prost in, 157
protectorate established (1912), 69
ships to, 42, 113, 163
World War II (1939–45), 163, 164, 167
Moscow, 107
Moulin Rouge, 87, 210
Mounet-Sully, Jean, 121
Mouren, Gaston, 120
Mourepiane, 199
MuCEM, 7, 114
Murcia, 98
Murray's Handbook for Travellers in France, 20
Musardises, Les (Rostand), 82
Musée d'Histoire Naturelle, 44
Musée de l'Immigration, 187
Musée des Beaux-Arts, 44
music
classical, 178–9
jazz, 8, 108, 138, 140, 141, 180–84, 228
hip-hop, 11, 61, 228, 231–2
music halls, 4, 7, 9, 11, 53, 66, 87, 180
music school, 54
Musique Légère, 178
de Musset-Pathay, Alfred Louis Charles, 120
Musset, 177
Mussolini, Benito, 153
Mystères de Marseille, Les (Zola), 9, 18, 19, 22, 29–35, 37–8, 61, 217

Mystères de Paris, Le (Sue), 19, 29, 217

Nadar (Gaspard-Félix Tournachon), 6
Nantes, 203, 205
Naples, 2, 28, 98, 138, 227, 229
Napoleon I, Emperor of the French, 10, 16, 18, 29
Arabic chair, founding of (1807), 29
exile on Elba (1814–15), 22, 26
Egyptian Campaign (1798–1801), 8, 23, 50
Hundred Days (1815), 26, 29, 61
Napoleon III, Emperor of the French, 51
Nasiali, Minayo, 206, 207
Nathan, 177
National Convention (1792–5), 3, 10, 103
National Radio, 177, 178
National Workshops, 33
Nazi Germany (1933–45), 154, 161, 162
bombing of Marseille (1940), 162, 170, 171, 176
Holocaust (1941–5), 170, 171–2, 206, 224, 253 n.20
refugees from, 4, 154, 161, 162, 163–70
theatre, policies on, 177
transporter bridge, destruction of (1944), 157, 162, 171, 192
United States, declaration of war against (1941), 180
Vieux-Port, destruction of (1943), 10, 115, 157, 162, 166, 170, 171, 172–6
see also Occupation period; Vichy France

Neapolitans, 2, 98, 227
Neige fondue à l'Estaque, La
  (Cézanne), 78
Neiges de Kilimandjaro, Les, 9
Nelli, René, 153
Neo-Romanticism, 83
Nerthe Tunnel, 1, 2, 43
nervis, 53, 61, 101, 215
Neue Schweitzer Rundschau, 139
Neveu, Gerald, 228
New Caledonia, 252 n.9
New York City, 104, 107
New York Herald, 103
Nice, 101, 133, 142, 152, 176, 177
Nice, OGC, 179
Niemeyer, Oscar, 204
Niger river, 158
Nîmes, 81
Nimier, Roger, 218
Nivoix, Paul, 121, 122
Norma, 55
Northern Steelworks, 191
Noth, Ernst Erich, 154
Notre-Dame de la Garde, 1, 7, 35,
  38, 143, 182, 200, 215
Nouvelle Galeries departmental
  store, 3, 4
Nouvelle Revue Française, 83, 145,
  147, 150, 151, 154
Nouvelles Littéraires, Les, 85

Oberg, Karl, 172, 173
Occitan, 2, 8, 11, 56, 58–61, 76
Occupation period (1942–4), 7,
  83, 157, 162
  Cahiers du Sud in, 146, 149, 154,
    175
  censorship in, 177
  cinema in, 127, 133, 180, 183
  crime in, 173, 175, 217
  deportations of Jews (1943),
    170, 171–2, 224

music in, 181–2
Quartier Réservé, destruction of
  (1943), 10, 115, 166, 173–4
Resistance, 162, 170, 173, 174,
  183, 206, 217, 222, 223, 225
theatre in, 177
transporter bridge, destruction
  of (1944), 157, 162, 171, 192
urban renewal in, 143
US bombing (1944), 162, 170,
  171, 176
Vieux-Port, destruction of
  (1943), 10, 115, 157, 162,
  166, 170–76, 192, 196, 227
Odéon, 120, 181
Odessa, 157, 195
Odyssey (Homer), 228
oil, 192, 199
Old Man and the Sea, The
  (Hemingway), 221
Old Town, 3
Olivesi, Antoine, 100
Olympique de Marseille, 4, 7, 68,
  88, 118, 179, 214, 228
On purge bébé, 132
100 x Paris (Krull), 143
Opéra, 120, 152, 155, 177, 181,
  215, 226, 233
opera, 8, 48, 54–5, 66, 87
opium, 101, 102, 216
Oran, 49, 52, 112, 158, 163
orange boxes, 105
Ordures, 114
Organisation Armée Secrète
  (OAS), 201
organised crime, 3, 4, 9, 101–2,
  173, 175, 213–26
Orientalism, 50, 73, 114
Orléansville, 49
Ory, Pascal, 25
Ottoman Empire (1299–1922),
  15, 22, 23, 29, 42, 73, 96, 98

Oued Tadla massacre (1910), 197
Ouistiti, 89

P & O, 43, 96
PAEE (Plan directeur
  d'Aménagement, d'Extension et
  d'Embellissement), 155–6, 174
Pagnol, Joseph, 119
Pagnol, Marcel, 7, 11, 24–5, 53,
  57, 65, 82, 117–35
  film, 127–35, 249 n.15
  Fortunio, 120, 146–7
  Izzo and, 228, 229
  Marius trilogy, see under *Marius*
    trilogy
  on Vieux-Port, 11, 32, 119, 123,
    124, 125, 131, 229–30
Painters of Marseille, The (Latour),
  77, 78, 79
painting, 7, 11, 37–8, 54, 56–8,
  66, 72–81
  Ecole de Marseille, 11, 37, 56,
    73–81
Paire, Alain, 250 n.10
Palais de Cristal, 87, 120, 210
Palais de Justice, 20, 173
Palais Longchamp, 54, 100, 119
Palestine, 73, 206, 256 n.22
Pamiers, 121
pan-Mediterraneanism, 50, 75,
  138, 147–8, 151–4, 168, 179,
  226, 228
Panama Canal, 50, 106
Panier, Le, 1, 16, 41, 45, 86, 145,
  148, 210
  Benjamin on, 140
  Le Clézio on, 195, 196
  Corsican community, 16
  Greber on, 155
  Italian community, 16, 98, 99,
    173, 229
  Izzo on, 172, 229

Krull on, 144
Peisson on, 112
renovation, postwar, 204
Resistance in, 173
paniers, 105
Pankhurst, Sylvia, 107
Par la Porte d'Or, 183
Paramount, 128–9, 132
Parc Borély, 71, 87, 88, 220
Parc Chanot, 71
parcs populaire, 71
Paris, 8, 10–11, 18, 19, 37, 43
  apaches, 53, 61
  Ateliers Nationaux, 33
  Canebière joke, 53
  Chat Noir, 88–9
  crime in, 53, 61, 102, 215
  départements, 17
  Ecole Normale Supérieure, 121
  Exposition Universelle (1900),
    68, 71
  Fauvism in, 79, 81
  Institut d'Urbanisme, 155
  Lycée Condorcet, 121, 122, 147
  Moulin Rouge, 87, 210
  Musée de l'Immigration, 187
  Occupation period (1940–44),
    174, 176–7
  100 x Paris (Krull), 143
  railway connections to, 1–7, 35,
    43, 51, 96, 158, 247 n.12
  Revolution (1789–99), 18, 24–9
  Revolution (1848), 34
  Théâtre des Arts, 122
  Théâtre des Variétés, 122
  Zarafa, arrival of (1827), 15
Paris-Lyon-Méditerranée
  Company, 43
'Parisian meridian', 158
Paroisse Saint-Victor, 123
Parti communiste français (PCF),
  see Communist Party

Parti Populaire Français (PPF), 216, 224
Passage de Lorette, 140
Passage to Marseille, 252 n.9
Passeur, Stève, 132, 249 n.14
Pastré, Lily, 178–9, 180
Pathé, 128
Pathé-Palace cinema, 178, 181, 183
Pauchet, Jacques, 19
Paulhan, Jean, 83, 147
Pavillon de Provence, 72
Pearl Harbour attack (1941), 163, 180
Péguy, Charles, 147
Peisson, Edouard, 9, 10, 100, 104, 111–14, 139, 214, 217, 230, 237 n.4
Peninsular Express, 247 n.12
Pépé-le-Moko, 174
Péreire, Émile and Isaac, 42, 49
Peret, Benjamin, 150
Péret, Pierre, 170
Permanence de la Grèce, 153
Perret, Auguste, 204, 205
peseur-juré, 73, 119, 148–9
Pétain, Philippe, 175
pétanque, 131, 220, 221, 223, 226
Petiot, Marcel, 171
Petit Provençal, Le, 121
Petit, Georges, 181
Petit, Jean-Armand, 179
Petite Sicile, La, 99
Petite Tonkinoise, La, 7, 65–6, 129, 243 n.1
Petronius, 84
Peysonnel, 206
Philippe Pujol, 11
Philippeville, 163
Phocaea, 2, 67, 106, 147
Phoenicians, 11
Piaf, Edith, 180, 183
Pianosa, 22, 23

Pickford, Mary, 132
Pie qui Chante, La, 89
Piedmont, 2, 98
Pieds-Noirs, 199, 201–2
Pierrat, Jérôme, 217
piracy, 46, 47
Piraeus, 103
Place aux Huiles, 123
Place aux Oeufs, 32
Place Beauveau, 54
Place Castellane, 71, 133
Place Général de Gaulle, 32
Place Jean-Jaurès, 119
Place de la Joliette, 103, 190
Place de l'Opéra, 220
Place Royale, 32
Plage des Catalans, 20, 229
Plage du Prado, 54, 86, 87, 188, 195, 220, 223, 226
plague, 16, 98
Plaine Saint-Michel, 51, 119, 120, 132, 183
Plan Beaudoin (1943), 157, 175
Plan-de-Campagne, 233
Planier Lighthouse, 107, 113, 130
plastic arts, 54, 55
PLM (Paris à Lyon et à la Méditerranée) railway, 158
Poëte, Marcel, 156
poetry, 11, 19, 22, 33, 57, 152
polars, 11, 218–34
Polin (Pierre-Paul Marsalés), 120
Pomme, La, 169
Pont du Gard, 204
Pont-Aven, 77, 84
population, 1, 16, 35, 40, 45
  Restoration period (1814–1830), 16, 45
  July Monarchy period (1830–48), 16, 35, 40
  Second Republic period (1848–1852), 35, 40

Second Empire period (1852–70), 16, 66

Third Republic period (1870–1940), 45, 70, 98, 100

Post-War period (1945–), 1, 201, 205, 206, 209, 234

Port-Said, 200

Porte d'Aix, 6, 56, 57, 141, 187, 198

Porte de l'Empire, 2, 66, 96, 123, 211, 214

Porte de Vincennes, 187

portefaix, 16, 30, 39, 41, 55, 73, 104, 107–8, 189–91

Portugal, 163, 164, 165, 167

Post-Impressionism, 137

Pouillon, Fernand, 204

Poulaille, Henri, 112

Pouvoir des choses, *Le* (Jaloux), 85–6

Powys, Theodore Francis, 154

Prague, 166

pre-fabricated moles, 41

Présentines prison, 164

Prim, Suzy, 177

Princesse Lointaine, *La* (Rostand), 82, 83

Prost, Henri, 157

prostitution, 102, 215, 216
    Charles-Roux on, 174
    in Egypt, 216
    McKay on, 109, 111
    Moholy-Nagy on, 142
    Pagnol on, 127
    Peisson on, 113, 114
    Sembène on, 194
    Verteuil on, 55
    Vichy period (1940–44), 173
    Waugh on, 94
    Zola on, 30
    see also Quartier Réservé

Protis, 20–21, 67

Provençal, 2, 11, 56, 58–61

Provençal, *Le*, 183

Provence, 2, 3, 8, 17–18, 21–2

Puget, Pierre, 20, 54, 72

Pupu, 89

Puy, Jean, 77, 79, 81

Quai des Belges, 20, 54, 73, 140, 142, 243 n.2

Quai du Canal, 148, 168

Quai d'Orléans, 20

Quai de l'Hôtel de Ville, 127, 143, 156, 214

Quai du Port, 16, 73

Quai de Rive Neuve, 32, 73, 117, 123, 127, 142, 233

Quartier de l'Arsenal, 148

Quartier Bourse, 32, 97, 156

Quartier Breteuil, 62

Quartier de la Plaine, 51, 119, 120

Quartier des Princes, 62

Quartier Réservé, 10, 41, 100, 215
    Benjamin on, 139
    Crane on, 156
    destruction of (1943), 10, 115, 166, 173–4
    Mac Orlan on, 94, 246 n.6
    McKay on, 108–11
    Pagnol on, 127
    Peisson on, 112
    in *Seven Thunders*, 171
    Suarès on, 84
    Waugh on, 93–4, 100
    Zola on, 32

Quartier Saint-Jean, 16, 52, 62, 67, 172, 204, 205

Quartier Saint-Just, 31

Quartiers Nord, 5, 9

Quint, Léon-Pierre, 150, 154

Race Nègre, *La*, 108

racism, 98, 118, 188, 153, 194

Radical Party, 3, 215

INDEX

radio, 177
Radiodiffusion Nationale, 177, 178
rag pickers, 10, 106, 112, 113, 230
Ragusa, 16, 28
railways, 1–5, 10, 35, 43–4, 69, 96, 158, 247 n.12
Raimu (Jules Auguste Muraire), 7, 11, 53, 124, 125, 129, 240 n.2
Rains, Claude, 180
Razzia par les Chasseurs d'Afrique (Loubon), 73
Red Army Choir, 183
'red city', 191
Red Cross, 195
Red Sea, 100
red-light district, *see* Quartier Réservé
Réda, Jacques, 150
Reeperbahn, 94
refugees, 4, 154, 161, 162, 163–70
Regain, 132, 133–4
Régent cinema, 88
Reine Margot, La (Dumas), 229
Reinhardt, Django, 181, 182
Renaissance provençale, Une (Lombard), 75
Renaud, Madeleine, 177, 249 n.26
Renoir, Jean, 18, 24–6, 27, 129, 133
Renoir, Pierre, 122
Renoir, Pierre-Auguste, 77, 78
Renucci, Jo, 216
Resistance, 162, 168, 170, 173, 174, 183, 206, 217, 222, 223, 225
Restaurant Basso, 140
Restoration (1814–1830), 16, 26, 27, 42, 55, 58
Retour aux myths grecs, 153
Retour de Zorro, Le, 183
Réunion, 71
Revolution and Revolutionary Wars (1789–1802), 3, 8, 16, 18, 24–9
  Battle of Valmy (1792), 26

British intervention (1793), 29
  Federalist revolts (1793), 3, 16, 27–8
  Insurrection (1792), 18, 24–7
  Marseillaise, La (1938 film) 24–6, 27, 29
  National Convention (1792–5), 3, 10, 103
  Terror (1793–4), 28
  Ville Sans Nom law (1794), 3, 28, 95
Revolution (1848), 18, 23, 29, 30, 32–4
Revue de l'Ecran, La, 180
Revue des Deux Mondes, 83
Revue Européenne, La, 150
Revue Méditerranéenne, La, 85, 86
Rheims, 150
Rhineland, 69
Rhône river, 40, 43, 51, 163, 193
Rialto cinema, 183
Ribemont-Dessaignes, Georges, 150
Ribot, Georges, 155
Richard, Eliane, 71
Richard, Jean Marius, 121, 249 n.12
Richard, Marius, 121, 249 n.13
Richebé, Roger, 129, 131, 132
Richepin, Jean, 59
Rictus, Jehan, 59
Rideau Gris, Le, 178
Riga, 195
Rimbaud, Jean Nicolas Arthur, 126
Rinaldo, Guy, 183
Rio de Janeiro, 42, 105, 112, 163
riots (2005), 99
Ripert, Emile, 57, 58, 59, 120, 168, 178
Ripert, Henri, 161
Riposte (Taslitzky), 255 n.5
Rivière, Jacques, 83

283

Robb, Graham, 19
Robert, Yves, 134
de Rodellec du Porzic, Marie, 172
Rodin, François Auguste René, 76, 77
Romanesques, Les (Rostand), 82
Romanticism, 138, 154
Rome, 22
Roncayolo, Marcel, 3, 44
Rond-Point du Prado, 71, 132
Roosevelt, Eleanor, 169
Roquefavour Aqueduct, 44
Roquevaire, 57
Rosenberg, Alfred, 174
Rossi, Tino, 117, 197, 198
Rostand, Edmond, 7, 66, 82–3, 88, 120, 122
Roth, Joseph, 97
Rothschild family, 43
Rotterdam, 193
Rouault, Georges, 77, 79
Roucas Blanc, 52, 83, 84
Rouen, 94, 162, 165, 205
Rouffe, Alida, 125
Rouget de Lisle, Claude Joseph, 24, 25, 83
Rougon-Macquart, Les (Zola), 30, 32
Roumanille, Joseph, 60
Roussel, Theodore, 77
Roussin, André, 178
Route de L'Estaque, La (Cézanne), 80
Route Nationale, 221
Roux, Marius, 29
rubbish, *see* detritus
Rue Bouterie, La (Seyssaud), 81
Rue d'Aix, 50
Rue des Baignoires, 189
Rue des Belles-Ecuelles, 196
Rue de la Bouterie, 94, 108, 127, 139, 140
Rue de Breteuil, 45, 220, 223
Rue des Capucines, 141

Rue de la Caisserie, 94
Rue des Chapeliers, 97
Rue des Charettes, 94
Rue des Convalescents, 256 n.22
Rue Dastre, 32
Rue des Dominicaines, 189
Rue Emile Pollak, 173
Rue Fauchier, 104
Rue des Feuillots, 53
Rue Fongate, 86
Rue des Gallions, 94
Rue du Grand-Cours, 20
Rue Haxo, 89
Rue Jean-Mermoz, 132
Rue de Lancerie, 94
Rue de la Loge, 94
Rue de Lyon, 140
Rue des Minimes, 119
Rue de Montbrion, 196
Rue des Moulins, 196
Rue Neuve, 141
Rue Nicolas, 77
Rue de Noailles, 20
Rue Paradis, 50, 89, 140
Rue des Petite Maries, 96
Rue des Petites-Maries, 189
Rue Pisançon, 89
Rue de la Providence, 165
Rue du Radeau, 94
Rue du Refuge, 196
Rue de la République, 54, 108, 165, 220
Rue de la Reynarde, 94, 108, 127
Rue de Rome, 17, 54
Rue Saint-Ferréol, 210
Rue du Tapis-Vert, 51
Rue Terrusse, 119
Rue Thubaneau, 24, 27, 83
Ruhr, 19
Russian Empire (1721–1917), 96, 98, 99
Ruttmann, Walter, 142

'S'eri Tur' (Gelu), 60
Sabiani, Simon, 102, 114, 155, 173, 180, 215–17, 224
SAC (Service d'Action Civique), 217
Sadoul, Georges, 129–30, 133
Sagittaire, Le, 150
Saigon, 200
Saint-Antoine, 99, 140
Saint-Barnabé, 31, 85
Saint-Barthélemy, 206
Saint-Chamas, 221
Saint-Cloud, 32
Saint-Etienne, 203
Saint-Etienne, AS, 179
Saint-Gothard Tunnel, 69
Saint-Jérôme, 99
Saint-Joseph, 31
Saint-Julien, 99, 220
Saint-Lazare, 140
Saint-Louis, 163
Saint-Loup, 99, 119
Saint-Marcel, 31, 208
Saint-Maurice, 128
Saint-Menet, 86
Saint-Simonians, 49–51, 148, 158, 193
Saint-Thys, 202
Saint-Victor, 61, 223
de Sainte de Maréville, Louis, 179
Sainte-Victoire, 79, 84
Salle Mazenod, 178
Salon de l'Araignée, 137
Salons d'Automne, 80, 81
Salons de Provence, 76–7, 221
Salons des Indépendants, 81
Samaritaine, La (Rostand), 82
Samson, Michel, 11, 99
San Felice, La (Dumas), 229
Santolini, Paul, 225
Saroyan, William, 154
Schéma de la Ville de Marseille, 155

Schutzstaffel (SS), 171, 172, 175
Schwartz, Lucien, 179
Scotto, Serge, 218
Scotto, Vincent, 7, 65, 117, 129, 132
Second Empire (1852–70), 16, 40, 41, 49, 55
Second World War (1939–45), see World War II
Secrétain, Roger, 148
Seghers, Anna, 165–70, 253 n.10
de Segonzac, Dunoyer, 204
Seine river, 78
Seine-Saint-Denis, 11
Sellers, Peter, 249 n.15
Sémaphore, Le, 163, 181, 182
Sembène, Ousmane, 7, 104, 106, 188, 189–91, 194, 206
Senegal, 1, 42, 106, 112, 158, 163, 189, 194, 199
Senghor, Léopold Sédar, 108
Septèmes, 140
Serbs, 104
Serge, Victor, 167, 169, 170
Série Noire, 218–25
Sète, 2, 163
Seven Thunders, 171
Seyssaud, René, 72, 79, 80–81
SFIO (Section française de l'Internationale ouvrière), 183
Shanghai, 152
Sheridan, Ann, 180
shipping, 5–6, 42–3, 162–3, 191–4
   Second Empire period (1852–70), 42–3
   Belle Epoch period (1870–1914), 69
   Inter-War period (1918–39), 149
   Vichy period (1940–44), 162–3, 176
   Post-War period (1945–), 5–6, 191–4, 209
Sicard, Emile, 76, 85, 228

INDEX

Siff, Minna, 187
Signac, Paul, 77, 78
Signoret, Simone, 119
silk weavers' rebellion (1831), 56
Simon, Michel, 249 n.26
Simonin, Albert, 219, 224
Sinbad the Sailor, 23–4, 39, 228
Singapore, 200
Sirdey, Théodore, 89
Sitte, Camillo, 156
slavery, 17
smallpox, 98
Smyrna, 22, 23, 29, 229
Snow-White and the Seven Dwarfs, 180
socialism, 59, 66, 67, 95, 216, 226
Société Arnaud, Touache Frères et Compagnie, 240 n.3
Société de Géographie de Marseille, 68
Société des Films Marcel Pagnol, 132
Société des Frères Endormis, 58
Société des Purs, 58
Société Générale des Transports Maritimes, 42, 163
Société Patriotique des Amis de la Constitution, 24
Sociologie de Marseille (Peraldi, Duport and Samson), 11
Solea (Izzo), 9, 174, 226
Soleil des mourants, Le (Izzo), 226, 230
Sörgel, Herman, 158
Soubiran, Jean-Roger, 73
South America, 42, 45, 94, 104, 105
Soviet Union (1922–91), 107
Spain
  Carlist Wars (1833–76), 23, 33, 242 n.55
  Civil War (1936–9), 98, 167, 168
  emigration, 2, 45, 56, 98, 100, 103, 104, 105, 109, 173, 199
  French invasion (1823), 22
  in paintings, 74
  World War II (1939–45), 165, 167
Spanish Influenza epidemic (1918–20), 83
Spartiello, Anne, 176
spectacle perpétuel, 71
Spender, Stephen, 148
Spirito, François, 102, 173, 215–17
Sporting Club de Marseille, 88
steamships, 16, 40, 42, 44
steel, 5, 44–5, 84, 191
Steinbeck, John, 221
Stétié, Salah, 228
STO (Service du travail obligatoire), 224
Strasbourg, 158
Studio Rex, 6, 187, 189, 197
Studios Marcel Pagnol, 132
Suarès, André, 66, 82, 83–5, 143, 144
Sue, Eugène, 19, 29, 217
Suez Canal
  crisis (1956), 192, 193, 198, 201, 211
  opening (1869), 1, 42, 43, 50, 51, 66, 69, 106
sugar, 45, 70
Suresnes, 224
Surrealism, 138, 150–52, 170
Swiss Guards, 25
Sydney, 152
Sylvain, Eugène, 121
Symbolism, 135
Syndicat de la Presse Marseillaise, 67
Syria, 98, 104, 161

Tabaris, 89

Talabot, Paulin, 41, 42, 43, 44, 49, 51, 69, 70
Tales of the Arabian Nights, 23, 39, 112, 228
Tangiers, 158
Tarascon, 121
Tartarin de Tarascon (Daudet), 38–40, 46–7, 48, 61, 110, 127, 240 n.2
Taslitzky, Boris, 255 n.5
Tasso, Henri, 161, 217
Taverne de l'Epoque, 89
Taverne de la Cigogne, 89
Taxi franchise, 234
Temps Noir, 224
Terror (1793–4), 28
TGV (Train à Grande Vitesse), 4–5, 10
theatre, 7, 8, 48, 54–5, 57, 66, 87, 177, 209–10
Pagnol, 9, 32, 106, 117–27
Théâtre Chave, 119, 120
Théâtre de l'Alhambra, 122
Théâtre des Arts, 122
Théâtre de la Colonne, 57
Théâtre Français, 57
Théâtre du Gymnase, 54, 55, 57, 87, 120, 177, 210
Théâtre Impériale d'Alger, 48
Théâtre de la Madeleine, 122
Théâtre du Marais, 178
Théâtre de Paris, 122
Théâtre de la Porte Saint-Martin, 82
Théâtre de la Renaissance, 82
Théâtre Sylvain, 121, 178, 249 n.13
Théâtre du Temps, 178
Théâtre des Variétés
Marseille, 88, 122, 182, 210
Paris, 122
Thémime, Emile
on canal, 44

on colliers, 109
on Cours Julien and Lieutaud, 17
on Flaissières, 67
on housing, 206–7, 209
on *illusion révolutionnaire*, 191
on immigration, 97, 98, 99, 106, 198, 201–2
on Méry, 239 n.19
on Revolution (1789–99), 27
on Suez Canal, 69
on *ville piège*, 170
Thérèse Raquin (Zola), 29
They Made Me a Criminal, 180
Third Republic (1870–1940), 42, 66, 78, 127
Thomazeau, François, 31, 118, 218, 232–3, 252 n.47, 257 n.37
Thousand and One Nights, 23, 39, 112, 228
Tientsin Treaty (1885), 69
Tilleuls, Les, 202
Tissot, Henri, 215
tobacco, 19, 45–6
Toller, Ernst, 154
Tomas et ses Merry Boys, 183
Toni, 24, 25, 133
Tonkin, 1
Tonton, ou Joseph veut rester pur (Pagnol), 122
Topaze (Pagnol), 122, 129, 135, 249 n.15
Torrents, Stanislas, 72
Total Khéops (Izzo), 23–4, 31, 172, 200, 213, 214, 218, 223, 225–34
Touchez pas au grisbi! (Simonin), 219, 222, 225
Toulon, 2, 48, 56
Toulouse, 157
Tourette, La, 204
Touring Club de France, 157

INDEX

tourism, 155
Tourneur, Maurice, 117, 194, 217
Toursky, Alexandre, 228
trade unions, 66, 70
trains, *see* railways
tramways, 87
Trans-Saharan railway, 158
Transit (Seghers), 165–9, 253 n.10
transporter bridge, 7, 107, 112,
    130, 142–3, 156, 157, 171, 172,
    192
Travail, Famille, Patrie, 178
Treaty of Algeciras (1906), 197
Treaty of Lausanne (1923), 98
Treaty of Rome (1956), 192
Treaty of Tientsin (1885), 69
Treille, La, 119, 131, 132, 133,
    134
Trenet, Charles, 180
Trente Glorieuses, 134, 211, 213
Trianon cinema, 88
Trieste, 69, 96, 193, 229
Trocadéro, 71
Trois jours d'engates (Carrese), 10,
    218
Trois Lucs, 220
Troù, Le (Giovanni), 218, 219
Troubadours, 60, 83
Troupe des Compagnons de
    France, La, 181
Tunis, 112, 152, 158
Tunisia
    Cahiers du Sud in, 152, 211
    Dumas on, 23
    emigration, 97, 103, 198, 201
    Expositions Coloniale, 71, 97
    independence (1956), 198, 201,
        211
    Italians in, 66
    Peisson on, 112
    prostitution in, 216
    protectorate established (1881),
        69

ships to, 5, 158, 162, 193
Turkey, 2, 98, 187, 216, 234
    see also Ottoman Empire
Turks, 39, 60, 73
Tuskeegee Institute, 107
twenty-fifth centenary celebrations
    (1899), 7, 67
twin cities, 8, 37, 48, 52, 201
typhus, 98
Tzara, Tristan, 170

Ultras, 228
Ulysse ou l'intelligence (Audisio), 153
Union Coloniale, 68
unions, 66, 70
Unité d'Habitation, 7, 155, 188,
    203, 206, 214, 257 n.31
United Artists, 132
United Kingdom
    coal industry, 44, 112
    French Revolutionary Wars
        (1793–1800), 29
    Indian colonies (1612–1947),
        43, 96
    Irish, caricatures of, 53
    P & O, 43, 96
    ports, 41, 69
    World War I (1914–18), 95
    World War II (1939–45), 162
United States, 95, 107, 112
    film in, 132, 180
    music in, 181, 182
    World War II (1939–45), 162,
        163, 169, 170, 171, 176, 180
Université d'Alger, 48
université populaire, 57
Urbain, Ismail, 51
Uruguay, 42, 163
USA (Dos Passos), 114

V, 183
Valabrègue, Antony, 29

Valence, 2
Valencia, 98, 163
Valéry, Paul, 83, 152
Vallon de la Fausse-Monnaie, 121
Vallotton, Félix, 77
de Valmalète, Cécile, 178
Valtat, Louis, 79
Van Dongen, Cornelis Theodorus
  Maria 'Kees', 77, 79, 137
Van Gogh, Vincent, 74, 75
Van Loo, Jean-Baptiste, 72
Var region, 171
Variétés-Casino, 120, 183
Vattier, Robert, 125
Vázquez Montalbán, Manuel, 258
  n.17
Vélodrome stadium, 4, 9, 118, 214
Venezuela, 166
Venice, 28, 74
Ventura, Lino, 223
Ventura, Ray, 182
Verdi, Giuseppe, 52
Verdilhan, Louis Mathieu, 81
Vernet, Joseph, 73
Verteuil, Armand, 55
Vertov, Dziga, 114, 142
Viaduc (Cézanne), 80
Viaduc à L'Estaque (Cézanne), 80
Vichy France (1940–44), 7, 83,
  127, 143, 154, 162, 168–83
  anti-Jewish laws (1940), 170
  Cahiers du Sud in, 146, 149, 154,
    168–9, 170, 179
  cinema in, 127, 133, 180, 183
  Conseil Administratif, 178
  Le Corbusier and, 203
  crime in, 173, 175, 217, 222,
    223, 224–5
  deportations of Jews (1943),
    170, 171–2, 224
  Emergency Rescue Committee
    in, 169, 173, 176, 179

'Marseille Meridian' and, 158
music in, 178–9, 180–82
music halls in, 180
Occitan culture in, 179
Resistance, 162, 168, 170, 173,
  174, 183, 206, 217, 222, 223,
  225
theatre in, 177–8
transporter bridge, destruction
  of (1944), 157, 162, 171, 192
Vieux-Port, destruction of
  (1943), 10, 115, 157, 162,
  166, 170–76, 192, 196, 227
urban renewal in, 143
Victorine Studios, 133
Vie de Haroun el Rachid, La
  (Audisio), 153
Viet-Nâm Camp, 256 n.22
Vietnam, 206
Vieux-Port, 1, 5, 7, 10, 11, 15–18,
  31, 40, 100
  bastilles, 27
  Benjamin on, 140
  Le Clézio on, 195
  Le Corbusier and, 203
  Crane on, 156, 157
  detritus in, 3, 10, 108, 113–14,
    139, 142, 174
  Dumas on, 18–24, 35
  in Fanny (1932 film), 130
  Fisher on, 213–14
  in French Connection II (1975
    film), 214
  Giovanni on, 220, 223
  Greber on, 155–6, 252 n.47,
    257 n.37
  Krull on, 143
  in Marius (1931 film), 130
  McKay on, 108–11
  Moholy-Nagy on, 139, 141–3
  Pagnol on, 11, 32, 119, 123,
    124, 125, 131, 229–30

in paintings, 78, 81
red-light district, *see* Quartier Réservé
renovation, postwar, 203, 204–5
Seghers on, 165
Suarès on, 84
transporter bridge, 7, 107, 112, 130, 142–3, 156, 157, 171, 172, 192
twenty-fifth centenary celebrations (1899), 67
Vichy destruction of (1943), 10, 115, 157, 162, 166, 170–76, 192, 196, 227
Waugh on, 94
Zarafa, arrival of (1826), 15–16, 18
Zola on, 32
Vieux-Port et Notre-Dame de la Garde, Le (Seyssaud), 81
Vigo, Jean, 142
Villa Air-Bel, 169
ville bourgeoise, 18
ville carrefour, 4
ville d'accueil, 4, 9, 20, 106, 164, 168–9, 170, 230
ville d'asile, 4, 230
ville piège, 170
ville populaire, 18
Ville Sans Nom, 3, 28, 95
ville-campagne, 17
Ville-Nouvelle, 17
Villeneuve-Tourettes, Marquis de, 27
Villiers, François, 111
Vitrac, Roger, 150
Vitrolles, 202, 209
de Vlaminck, Maurice, 79, 80
Vol de la Marseillaise, Le (Rostand), 83
Volterra, Simonne and Léon, 122
Vovelle, Michel, 17

Voyage du Condottière (Suarès), 84
Vrai visage de la Dame aux Camélias, Le, 177
Vue de Marseille prise des Aygalades un jour de marché, Une (Loubon), 37–8
Vue de Nazareth (Loubon), 73

Wagner, Richard, 83, 84
Wahran, *see* Oran
Wall Street crash (1929), 127
Warner Brothers, 164, 252 n.9
Washington, Booker Taliaferro, 107
waste, *see* rubbish
water flume, 71
water supply, 33, 35, 40, 44, 46, 52
Waugh, Evelyn, 93–4, 96, 100, 108
weights and measures inspectors, 73, 119, 148–9
Weil, Berthe, 81
Weil, Simone, 168
West Indies, 29, 42
white man's burden, 106
White Russians, 98
white slave trade, 43, 102, 216
White Terror (1815–30), 61, 66
'wicked city', 3, 6, 9, 10, 28, 93, 118, 215, 237 n.4
immigration and, 188
McKay and, 131
Moholy-Nagy and, 143
Pagnol and, 131, 134
Peisson and, 131, 226
Tourneur and, 117
Vieux-Port destruction (1943) and, 172, 174
Wicked City (1949 film), 111
William Tell, 55
Within the Tides (Conrad), 228
Woon, Basil, 93
Workers' Dreadnought, 107
World War I (1914–18), 3, 6, 8,

28, 70, 73, 86, 88, 95, 138, 243 n.1
World War II (1939–45), 7, 8, 10, 83, 127, 143, 154, 161–84
bombings of Marseille (1940, 1944), 162, 170, 171, 176
Free French forces, 189
Holocaust (1941–5), 170, 171–2, 206, 224, 253 n.20
liberation (1944), 10, 146, 149, 162, 163, 182, 183–4
refugees, 4, 154, 161, 162, 163–70, 176
Resistance, 162, 168, 170, 173, 174, 183, 206, 217, 222, 223, 225
transporter bridge, destruction of (1944), 157, 162, 171, 192

Zampa, Gaëtan 'Tany', 217, 233
Zarafa, 15–16, 18, 50
Zay, Jean, 149
Ziem, Félix, 72, 74
Zola, Émile, 9, 18, 19, 22, 29–35, 37–8, 57, 217
Zone Libre (1940–42), 133, 162, 176, 177
Zouave, 40, 42, 46, 240 n.3